Canada's War in the Air

by

LESLIE ROBERTS

PER ARDUA AD ASTRA

ALVAH M. BEATTY

Publications Limited
1111 Beaver Hall Hill
MONTREAL
1943

LESLIE ROBERTS

THE chapters which follow constitute an attempt to tell the glamorous story of the biggest job ever done in Canada—the creation, organization and bringing into production of that far-flung force of men and machines which constitute the British Commonwealth Air Training Plan, and the battle squadrons which are its result. With it is coupled a bird's eye-view of Canada's Miracle Industry and its people—the men and women who have made this young nation the greatest aircraft producer, per capita, of the democratic world.

The purpose of this book, then, is to lift one great part of Canada's war job out of the patchwork of disconnected things and to present it as a unified whole. In one man's opinion what has been done in the air and in our air-industry since September 1939 constitutes the greatest single achievement of the Canadian people since our provinces came together in the Confederation that is Canada. But let us make no mistake about the nature of that achievement. It is the achievement, first, of the young men who, in their tens of thousands, have offered themselves, their lives if need be, to the cause of humanity . . . the lads who are raining down bombs on the heart of Germany, the fledglings who, as this is written, are trying their wings over the fields of the Prairies, Ontario, Quebec and the Maritimes, the men who service the aircraft on a hundred fields, the men who make and assemble the ships the fledglings fly, the men who built the airports, the men who directed all these. It is the achievement of Canadian Industry and Canadian Labour, without either of whom the Plan would be a hollow shell. It is an achievement on which we can look with pride, provided we do not rest on our oars as we look back, but use our knowledge of achievement as the turbine to thrust us forward to even greater action.

There will be no pretence of perfection in what you read. No edifice of the size of the British Commonwealth Air Plan could have been rushed to completion within the space of months without mistakes being made. No plane-producing industry, such as Canada's, could have mushroomed into being without blunders occurring. Mistakes there have been in plenty, blunders, blind spots and bottlenecks. These are the things against which the critics have railed. In some of their criticisms they have been, on surface, completely justified. But when the mistakes are placed in proper perspective to the achievement itself, the fair-minded reader will discover that what matters is what is to be found on the credit side of the ledger, not the occasional entry which must be made in red ink. Judged by such standards the Canadian Air effort ranks as the greatest single national enterprise in our history.

It might easily have been otherwise. We were slow to start. Not merely Canadians but the men who came to Canada from Britain and other countries of the Commonwealth did not, in the beginning, foresee the dire peril which still faces all freemen. The feeling was abroad in the beginning that we had plenty of time, that our vast resources, our productive power, must in the end lead to Germany's defeat. Not until Dunkirk did any nation of the Commonwealth, including Britain itself, recognize and accept the full impact of the Hitler threat. What happened then, when we discovered ourselves virtually without equipment, with not much but a series of half-completed schools and an aircraft industry geared to British production on our hands, with young men besieging the recruiting offices only to be told to come back some other day, is one of the miracles without which the Air Plan could never have been. What happened in the factories, on the assembly lines, wherever men heard the call to redoubled effort, is one of the heroic tales of a people at war. If this book succeeds in conveying to the reader that sense of increasing tempo, the power of that determined drive, its publication will have been justified.

What follows, then, is a bird's-eye view of what Canada and its partner-nations have done, the story of men of infinite resource who have never for a moment accepted the thesis of It-can't-be-done. It is the story of the lads who have gone out to fight, of their younger brothers soon to follow. It is the story of a time in which the impossible has been done every day. It is the story of a nation which, despite its hyper-modesty, its tendency to self-belittlement and self-criticism, has reason to be proud, but which must never let pride slacken its pace until the final victory is won.

The writer is proud that he is a Canadian, proud of the lads who follow the winged heels of the Bishops, the Barkers, the Collishaws, all that gallant band who were the heroes of the world's first war in the skies, proud of the men who in factory, field, and office have made it all possible. If some of that pride in young Canada, in this land and its people may be communicated to the reader in the pages which follow, the job will not have been in vain.

Leslie Roberts

MONTREAL, 17th March, 1942.

VII ✳

Canada's War in the Air

by

LESLIE ROBERTS

BOOK ONE

PER

ARDUA

AD

ASTRA

PER ARDUA AD ASTRA

TABLE OF CONTENTS

MAJOR THE HONOURABLE CHARLES GAVAN POWER, M.C., M.P.

Born in Sillery, Quebec, of Irish extraction. In the first World War, "Chubby" Power fought in France with the Third Battalion, then with Montreal's Fighting Fourteenth. Winning the Military Cross, he was twice seriously wounded. Member for Quebec South since 1917. Appointed Minister of Pensions and National Health, October 23rd, 1935; Postmaster General, September 19th, 1939. Appointed Minister of the newly created Department of National Defence for Air, May 23rd, 1940, and in addition was appointed Associate Minister of National Defence, July 12th, 1940, which two portfolios he still holds.

INTRODUCTION BY:
MAJOR THE HONOURABLE CHARLES G. POWER, M.C., M.P.
MINISTER OF NATIONAL DEFENCE FOR AIR

Canada's War in the Air, is the story of a notable Canadian achievement, in which Britain and the sister nations of the Commonwealth have played correspondingly important parts. I might even go further and say that the story of the creation and development of the British Commonwealth Air Training Plan is perhaps the finest example of whole-hearted cooperation between partner-nations in a common cause in our history as an association of free peoples.

When Leslie Roberts first discussed with me his proposal to write a work of current history, so suitably titled, I hesitated to give him what he engagingly calls a Green Light. Is the time opportune, I asked myself? Will its readers think that those who have been closely associated with the Air Training Plan and the development of the Royal Canadian Air Force, have embarked on a work of special pleading, trying to tell the world that we have done a good job? Then there was the thought that perhaps history should never be written until the job is finished. Mr. Roberts, who has been as close to the Air Plan as any Canadian writer and who was a member of the late, beloved Norman Rogers' personal staff during the months of organisation, soon converted me to his way of thinking.

As to the question *Is the time opportune?* his answer was extremely simple. "There is a tremendous story waiting to be told," he said. "This is the Canadian people's war and the Air Plan is our greatest single contribution to it, a long-term task which has as its object the mastery of the air over Europe. People are waiting to be told about it, not patchwork-fashion, but as a connected piece which will enable them to see the broad panorama."

The third question *Should anyone attempt to write a history until the job is done?* ties in closely with the first point. Mr. Roberts has written history before, tales of things not far behind. "You'd be amazed," he told me, "how much gets lost, and how quickly. Statistics and records may live. The figures may all be in the files. But unless you can get the human side of the story down on paper while it is glowingly alive, the great splashes of colour will get away from you." I couldn't argue with that. The human things can be lost very quickly in a filing system.

I gave Roberts his Green Light. I am glad I did. I think what has emerged is a clean-cut, frankly told story of something of which every Canadian should be proud. I repeat, it is not the achievement of the Staff of the Air Force, not that of any group of officials, except as they have been the instruments of the Canadian people. It is the achievement of Canadian youth, the achievement of the boys who are flying over there and of those who are following in their footsteps. The story of how it was made possible is something which ought to be set down while the fire is hot.

Canada's War In The Air has been written and published, then, as a private venture on the part of its author and his associates, chief of whom has been Mr. A. M. Beatty, of Montreal, with whom Mr. Roberts is associated in the magazine publishing field. It is not in any sense of the term a Government job. Nobody has subsidized the author or publishers. It has been done under the driving power of Roberts' own enthusiasm for a story he wanted to tell, that nobody could have stopped him telling, unless the facts could be hidden away in a vault, or we could have locked our doors to him. Somehow he has managed to convey in words the things we all feel about these gallant youngsters who are fighting for us. Somehow he senses the importance of the manner in which Industry and Labour alike have given the best that is in them to make it all possible. In short, Roberts has cut through the externals of red tape and everything which obscures the basic things and has gone straight to the heart of his story.

I hope everyone who reads *Canada's War In The Air* will get from it the thrill that has been mine. It seems to me that this is what would be described in a college course as Required Reading for anyone who wants to know what Canada has done and is doing in taking on again the gallant role she played in that other War In The Air a quarter-century ago. As such it has my hearty endorsation.

Charles G. Power

OTTAWA, 15th January, 1942.

Acknowledgments

The list of friendly helpers in the work of research and compilation of Canada's War In The Air is almost without end. The cooperation and counsel of Canada's Air Minister, Hon. C. G. Power, M.C., have been given without stint. The Air Secretary, Wing Commander Jimmie Sharpe, has been a constant smoother of rough spots in the road. The same must be said for Isobel Gough, Major Power's Private Secretary, and of every member of the Minister's staff. The writer's long-time friend, Joe Clark, Director of Information, Canadian Armed Forces, has always been available for counsel. Without the help of his former assistant, Wallie Ward, presently a Flight Lieutenant and valued Intelligence Officer, this book would have taken a lifetime to compile . . . a sweeping remark, but no overstatement.

As to that part of the book which deals with the industrial aspects of Canada's War In The Air, the ever ready and friendly aid of Ralph P. Bell, O.B.E., Director General of Aircraft Production, is gratefully acknowledged. Warm thanks go to his Secretary, Miss D. P. Munro, as they do to Fred Smye, Director of the Aircraft Production Programme, and various members of The Production Control Unit of The Aircraft Branch, Department of Munitions and Supply. To Rielle Thomson, Director General of Publicity, Department of Munitions and Supply, and to his aides, Gordon Garbutt and Fred Field, a journeyman's thanks for blessings received, as to W. H. van Alan, Director of Publicity for the Department of Transport. The writer wishes to thank another friend of many years' standing, J. A. Wilson, M.E.I.C., Canada's Director of Civil Aviation, for permission to quote his illuminating Report on aerodrome construction.

Beyond the realm of Government, acknowledgments go to Richard Thruelsen, Associate Editor of *Saturday Evening Post,* now on leave from his desk to serve his country overseas, for copyright release of the author's article *Convoys Don't Advertise,* excerpts from which appear in the body of this book. To numerous friends in the offices of the MacLean Publishing Company, to A. D. Dunton, Editor of the Montreal *Standard* (now on loan to the Wartime Information Board), George Rogers and Marjorie Leslie of Toronto *Star Weekly,* to publicity advisers of corporations too numerous to mention, to professional and amateur photographers by the dozen, to Hyacinthe Lambert of the Canadian Flying Clubs Association, to public relations officials of Trans-Canada Air Lines and Canadian Pacific Air Lines, to men and women whose name is legion . . . many thanks.

The list would not be complete if it failed to express appreciation again to the onetime pilot and outstanding typographer who is responsible for whatever artistic merit the original edition of this book possessed. John Loggie's contribution was immeasurable. The artistry of his fingers lives on in this, the third and enlarged edition of Canada's War In The Air.

Canada's War in the Air

by LESLIE ROBERTS

THE WAR DRUMS ROLL:

TURN back the clock hands to 1918. A war has ended. Canada's sons in their tens of thousands are making their way home from the battlefields of Europe, from Egypt, from Mesopotamia, from Palestine and from the seven seas. Behind them they leave row on orderly row of wooden crosses, at Vimy, along the Somme, across the scarred face of the Ypres Salient, the Glorious Dead with whom a materialistic world soon will break faith.

Infantry battalions marched through the streets of their home cities to disband and disperse their man power to the factories and farms of the nation. People cheered. The pipes skirled. Drums rolled. Arms were piled, as countless thousands of young men, escaped from inferno, celebrated the homing, vowed aloud "Never again!" Canada was enjoying its last fling . . . its Victory fling . . . as the boys came marching home.

Meanwhile there were quieter homecomings. From ships and pullmans young men in uniform, wings on their breasts, wings underlaid on hundreds, if not thousands, of tunics with the ribbon-strips which bespeak dauntless courage, slipped quietly away to join their families and take up the tasks of humdrum living again. No bands played them through the streets. No crowds thronged the sidewalk's edge to cheer them into barracks from the last parade. In twos and threes and fives and tens they slipped quietly into town; unhonoured, no, but unsung. The lads of the old Royal Flying Corps and Royal Naval Air Service, joined in mid-war as the R.A.F., had come home from the wars.

. . .

To see in perspective the effort put forward by Canada and our sister nations in the vast British Commonwealth Air Training Plan, in this second World War in a quarter-century and the world's second War In The Air, it is urgent, first, to look back to those other days and, from them, down the corridor of the intervening years.

When Young Canada marched away to war in 1914, Canadians knew virtually nothing of flight. Here and there such intrepid spirits as J. A. D. McCurdy had taken to wings, but these were the pioneer adventurers. Ninety-nine Canadians out of a hundred had never seen an aircraft in flight. The call was for soldiers, for infantrymen, gunners, truck-drivers, horsemen . . . but who had ever dreamed of battles fought in the clouds, bar the occa-

sional hyper-imaginative writer seeking to read the fantastic crystal of the future?

Across the Atlantic what few trained pilots and such aircraft as could be found were being impressed into service. Bravely they wallowed through the skies of Belgium and France, armed (so Gladstone Murray, now General Manager of Canadian Broadcasting Corporation and one of the early British Observers, attests) with rifles, if at all, the Pilots thinking of themselves, hopefully, as eyes of the armies, but not as potential fighters in the skies. Nevertheless, man's inventive genius was at work and from the factories of Britain came forth such behemoths as the RE8, the BE2C and its sister, 2E. Pilots began to take off from rough aerodromes in France armed with machine guns, some synchronized to fire between whirling propeller blades, others from swivel mounts in the observers' seats. The first War In The Air had begun.

. . .

As the years wore endlessly on, machines and armaments moved speedily forward. Older-typed aircraft, lumbering *camions* of the air, became artillery target-spotters (and easy marks, sitting birds, for enemy marauders riding high in Albatross or Fokker). Came the Pup, the Camel, the SE5, speedsters of the rapidly developed battle of the clouds. Came such fighting craft as the Bristol, the DH4 and DH9, huge Handley-Page bombers to drop their loads behind German lines, while Germany's Gothas rained down death on France and Britain. As the planes came, so came the Canadians. Here was something new. Here was lightning speed. Here was warfare made to measure for a gay d'Artagnan, as opposed to the mud and misery of a land-war fought in trenches thigh-deep in muck. They came in droves, these Canadians. They came out from regiments of the line in France, from gunpits dug in beside the cobblestone roads of Flanders. They came from the schools and universities of North America, from training fields in Texas. This was young Canada's kind of war. This new species of fighting had speed, individualism, romance about it.

Mostly they went into battle half-trained, bright wings sewn to their breasts almost before they could loop, do an Immelman turn, or pull out of a spin. Many of them died in battle before they knew the answers in instincts which must flash lightning signals to fingers and toes. But others lived, to share with departed

5 ✹

Whence winged north the lumbering freighters which provided communication for new citi[es] in the Wilderness.

comrades the glory of the fighting-man's new art, the art of flight which was to revolutionize warfare itself.

So came home Bishop, Barker, Collishaw, all that gallant band who fought through the first War In The Air and lived, men who were the cream of the air fighters, men with the crimson ribbon of the Victoria Cross, with their D.S.O.s, their M.C.s, their D.F.C.s and Allied decorations gleaming on their breasts. Here they came, the grown-up schoolboys of 1914 and 1915, numbering amongst them some of the greatest pilots the world will ever know. Here, then, was Canada, with thousands of skilled airmen homing to its shores . . . and nothing for them to fly.

. . .

All Canada is air-minded today. But in the halcyon, victory-celebrating months of 1919 the nation's attitude to all matters connected with aviation was to keep-one-foot-on-the-ground. It was in mid-1919 that this writer learned the viewpoint first hand. Parliament was in session. A youngster just home from the wars had repaired to Ottawa's Press Gallery to turn an honest shilling. To him came three compatriots, just out of the R.A.F., who wanted to keep flying. Between them they had a little money, the price of a couple of half-disabled Jennies. Would a newspaper man have any idea what could be done about it? Did he know any Minister who would listen to reason? Would there be any chance to talk the Government into a mail contract to operate over a triangular shuttle, Montreal, Ottawa, Toronto? The reporter, who was this operative, said he'd try, and went to see the late A. K. MacLean, then pinch-hit Minister in the waning war-years Government. This is what MacLean had to say:

"Tell your young friends to keep their money and get them-selves jobs. Canadian fliers have done remarkable work on the other side. But aviation is a war business. There'll never be a place for it in a world of peace."

So the trio of ex-aviators went and found jobs. Such was the status of aviation in Canada when the Bishops and the Barkers came home from that other war.

. . .

The years rolled along. Some of the old Jennies, picked up for a song, were tied together with bits of haywire and flown around the fairs, wherever young adventurers who couldn't get flying out of their thoughts and their blood, could turn a five dollar bill. North of the tracks the first post-war mining booms ex-ploded like bombs. A couple of the Jennies began to make round-trips between Haileybury and Rouyn. Ontario's Govern-ment took up forestry patrol. The United States began to develop commercial aircraft. Jack Hammell borrowed a couple of forestry machines and freighted the first loads of mining-camp supplies into Red Lake. So a new flying era opened. Canada began to hammer together the nucleus of an Air Force, but a force de-signed more for the purposes of peace than for those of war. Everyone knew no more wars, involving civilized peoples, would be fought in our time, if ever. The War to end War had just been fought and won!

Meanwhile we were creating something new under the northern sun on our own account, were developing a use for aircraft in which Canada was to lead the world, the use of heavier-than-air machines for the intrinsic purposes of our peaceful commerce. Other nations, more populous, might open passenger lines to compete with and take business away from the railroads. But Canada was using aircraft to replace the dogteam and the kicker-canoe in the country back-of-beyond, where the new mines were being brought in. Soon Canadian freight-planes were winging north from jumping-off towns across the wide map . . . Saint Felicien, Oskelaneo, Amos, Rouyn, Sioux Lookout, Hudson, these and many another were the place-names whence winged north the lumbering freighters which provided communication

for new cities in the wilderness, bringing to outposts as much as a thousand miles north of the nearest railway, supplies of fresh food, canned goods, machinery, all the things which go into the making of mines and the comfort of those who work them. Fort McMurray, three hundred miles north of Edmonton, jump-off point into the vast Northwest Territories, became the world's greatest air-freight terminal, into whose landing-harbour twenty to thirty air-freighters swooped down in a day when the weather was fair. Canada had found a sensible use for aircraft, the prosecution of its peaceful commerce in the empire north of the tracks.

. . .

In the meantime, what of the Air Force? Slowly, painstakingly, it had been built up during the later 1920s. Actually its pilots and technicians had rendered signal service in the development of our northern operations, particularly in such fields as the mapping of hinterland areas, in photographic service and kindred activities, all looking to the development of unpopulated regions rich in untapped resources. A few semi-obsolete fighting air-craft were in the country. But, basically, the Air Force itself was constructed primarily for the purposes of peace. Then came 1930 and the cry for retrenchment in public expenditure to meet economic depression and the increasing costs of unemployment . . . and, with the retrenchment cry, the scuttling of even the nucleus of a fighting air force. Shooting wars were behind us. We had a war to win on the economic front!

Five years passed, the years of the locust, years during which the few remaining ranking air officers sat behind desks in Ottawa hideouts and, being human, wished aloud that they had listened to the advice of their elders and given the King's uniform a wide berth. By 1935 most Canadians had forgotten the very existence of an Air Force in their country. The man-in-a-uniform was viewed askance, as an unjustifiable charge on the public purse. But the rumours out of Europe began to be disturbing. A man named Hitler had appeared on the scene; was rearming Germany, although nobody, apparently, wanted to stop him. Canadians began to talk about their country's defences. But Europe still seemed a long way off. Maybe we should spend a little, a few millions here and there, but times were still hard and what was happening on the far side of the Atlantic was obviously an out-size game of bluff. And so through the Ruhr to Austria and *anschluss,* to Berchtesgaden, Godesberg and Munich, then on to Prague and the thundering roll of the war drums across Europe, in a free world which still refused to meet power with power.

Finally even Britain's patience fled. Unprepared for war, Cham-berlain none the less gave Poland, threatened over Danzig's status, a guarantee that, if attacked, Britain would come to her aid. The game of bluff continued. Then Hitler marched again. And flaming, all-out war burst once more over the continent where men had refused to see in Ethiopia, or in the clash between Fascist and Republican Spain, the testing ground for a new world cataclysm in which a new technique in aerial combat would be developed, almost at the outset.

Canada was caught unprepared, in which she was by no means alone. Her naval strength was infinitesimal, her land forces a mere nucleus, still largely patterned on the military ideas of 1918. In the air the Dominion could muster a few fighter aircraft, a handful of skilled pilots and other personnel. These were rushed to the coasts to embark at once in seaboard patrols and, as soon as shipping could be organised, convoy duty. Meanwhile the Navy rushed its port protection devices into service, placed submarine nets across harbour-mouths. Army units detrained and moved out to the headlands where long-range guns (but pitifully few of them) pointed their long snouts out to sea. And in Ottawa grim-faced Commoners and Senators moved anxiously

A Special Session of Parliament was called by Rt. Hon. W. L. Mackenzie King at the beginning of September, 1939, and War was declared on Germany by Canada. UPPER: His Excellency the Governor General, Lord Tweedsmuir, reads the Speech from the Throne in the Senate Chamber. LOWER: The Prime Minister addresses the House of Commons.

through the corridors of Parliament, debating the crisis which had come upon us. Already Britain had gone to war. For the second time in a quarter-century the people of a young and peace-loving nation, one of the richest lands on the earth's surface, faced the choice between fighting for Freedom, between facing up to the responsibilities of partnership in the British Commonwealth, and isolating themselves from Europe behind the continental barriers of the Western Hemisphere. What the answer would be was not in doubt for a moment. But this time Canadians would speak for themselves as an independent nation, as a self-determining people.

. . .

The Governor General, the late Lord Tweedsmuir, sounded the keynote in his Speech from the Throne, which read:

"As you are only too well aware, all efforts to maintain the peace of Europe have failed. The United Kingdom, in honouring pledges given as a means of avoiding hostilities, has become engaged in war with Germany.

"You have been summoned at the earliest moment in order that the Government may seek authority for the measures necessary for the defence of Canada and for co-operation in the determined effort which is being made to resist further aggression and to prevent the appeal to force instead of to pacific means in the settlement of international disputes. Already the Militia, the Naval Service and the Air Force have been placed on Active Service and certain other provisions have been made for the defence of our coasts and our internal security under the War Measures Act and other existing authority. Proposals for further effective action by Canada will be laid before you without delay . . .

"The people of Canada are facing the crisis with the same fortitude that today supports the people of the United Kingdom and others of the nations of the British Commonwealth. My Ministers are convinced that Canada is prepared to unite in a national effort to defend to the utmost liberties and institutions which are a common heritage."

. . .

Those who were present at the Special Session of Parliament in September, 1939, will never forget the taut atmosphere which hovered over Parliament Hill during its brief hours. As the House met, the very air in the galleries seemed to tremble in the ominous quality of the moment. What would the Prime Minister say? Would Lapointe speak up for French-Quebec? What about the Isolationists? No doubt there would be opposition to Canada's entry, but would it be important numerically, or merely sporadic? What was happening beyond our borders? What about the *Athenia?* Were we facing another five years, perhaps ten, of ruthless murder on the high seas? Had you heard the rumours about the bombing of London? Could Hitler pierce the Maginot Line? Could we blockade him? Looking back, more than two years later, the scenes enacted then on Parliament Hill are as scenes from another world, the Alice-in-Wonderland world of the '20's and '30s, a world that is gone forever. Tense and strung to the breaking point were the men who sat on either side of Mr. Speaker that day, but little did they know of what lay ahead. Had they known, they would have done exactly as they did.

Clearly and lucidly the Prime Minister stated the case for the Government, told of such action as had been taken in the crisis, of the request which would be made for the support of the House in a declaration of war, of the emergency measures which would be laid before the Members. Stirringly Ernest Lapointe, his voice throbbing with the emotion so deeply embedded in the men and women of his race, pledged French-Canada to the cause. From one outspoken isolationist, Joseph Thorson of Winnipeg, named months later as Canada's Minister of National War Services, came the clear-cut reversal of his stand. From all that great assembly of the representatives of the Canadian people

came only four dissenting voices. In the hour of need men of sharply divided opinion were closing their ranks in the face of a common foe. Unprepared we were, if only because the very thought of war was, and is, abhorrent to the people of this country. Unprepared we were because no Government could have faced the Canadian people in the pre-war days, even up to the hour of Munich, with a policy of full-out rearmament, with all the hundreds of millions of dollars involved in such a program, and have been returned with so much as a corporal's guard at its Leader's beck. Thus war came again to the Canadian people, while the memory of the last great march-out remained undimmed in the minds of men only reaching the middle years.

We were not alone in our lack of preparation but, whereas our Allies were at least ready in part, Canada was virtually unarmed. For protection she relied on Britain's navy and, continentally, on the friendship and pledges of a great neighbour-people. It was from this position, then, that Canadians faced another war, determined to fight through to the end at the side of all those who would stand against tyranny. To meet the exigencies of aerial warfare, or even of training for aerial war, Canada was virtually *sans* equipment. But on the credit side of the ledger several imponderables were to be taken into account.

First of these must be set down as the known flair of Canadian youth for aerial combat, clearly established in the world's first War In The Air.

Second was the manner in which Canadians had innovated in the realm of commercial flight during the years between wars, clear evidence that the flair remained.

Third was the existence of a great national airway, boasting a series of major fields spread across the width of the continent, an asset soon to prove invaluable, as this tale shall tell.

Fourth was the natural adaptability of the Canadian terrain itself to conditions of flight, with particular stress on its quality as a training area, due to its great unpopulated regions and huge flatlands.

But greater than all these was the indomitable determination of a free people to play again a high role in the battle to maintain our western civilization and its free institutions.

Such was Canada's status when, at midnight on Saturday, September 9th, 1939, its Government requested His Majesty to inform Germany that a state of war existed between the People of Canada and the Third Reich.

. . .

The state of war became effective without a vote. True, two members attempted to introduce an amendment to the war motion, "expressing regret" for Canada's participation, but lacked support of the five members necessary to procure a division of the House. During the debate two other voices had been raised against war, one that of the conscientiously pacifist J. S. Woodsworth, then leader of the Co-operative Commonwealth Federation group, the members of which did not support their leader. Prime Minister King himself had clearly stated at the outset that the question of War or Isolation was for Parliament, not the Government (although the Government had clearly stated its own policy) to decide. Thus the motion actually passed without a vote and Canada went to war, the ensuing proclamation stating that:

"Now therefore we do hereby declare and proclaim that a state of war with the German Reich exists and has existed in our Dominion of Canada as from the 10th day of September, 1939."

We have come through many vicissitudes since that dark day, and the end is not yet. But we have come far.

FOUNDERS OF BRITISH COMMONWEALTH AIR TRAINING PLAN:

J. R. Smyth, United Kingdom; F. R. Howard, United Kingdom; C. V. Kellway, Australia; Air Commodore E. W. Stedman, Canada; Group Captain A. Gray, United Kingdom; Lt.-Col. K. S. MacLachlan, D/M. National Defence, Canada; Group Captain J. M. Robb, United Kingdom; A. D. P. Heeney, Prin. Sec. to Prime Minister, Canada; Group Captain L. N. Hollinghurst, United Kingdom; R. E. Elford, Australia; W. L. Middlemass, New Zealand; J. B. Abraham, United Kingdom; Dr. O. D. Skelton, Under Secretary of State for External Affairs, Canada; T. A. Barrow, Air Secretary, New Zealand; Sir Gerald Campbell, High Commissioner for the United Kingdom; Hon. I. Mackenzie, Minister of Pensions and National Health, Canada; Wing Commander George Jones, Asst. Chief of Air Staff, Australia; Hon. C. D. Howe, Minister of Transport, Canada; Dr. W. C. Clark, Deputy Minister of Finance, Canada; Air Vice Marshal G. M. Croil, Chief of Air Staff, Canada; Air Chief Marshal Sir R. Brooke-Popham, United Kingdom; Col. the Hon. J. L. Ralston, Minister of Finance, Canada; Group Captain H. W. L. Saunders, Chief of Air Staff, New Zealand; Hon. Senator R. Dandurand, Canada; The Lord Riverdale, United Kingdom; Rt. Hon. W. L. Mackenzie King, Prime Minister of Canada; Hon. J. V. Fairbairn, Minister of Air, Australia; Rt. Hon. E. Lapointe, Minister of Justice, Canada; Capt. H. H. Balfour, Under Secretary for Air, United Kingdom; Hon. N. M. Rogers, Minister of National Defence, Canada; Air Marshal Sir C. Courtney, United Kingdom.

MEMBERS OF AIR COUNCIL AND AIR OFFICERS COMMANDING THE COMMAND AREAS OF THE ROYAL CANADIAN AIR FORCE

BACK ROW, *left to right*, Air Commodore A. A. L. Cuffe, A.O.C., E.A.C., Halifax, former Air Member for Air Staff; Air Commodore A. B. Shearer, A.O.C., No. 2 Training Command Headquarters, Winnipeg, Manitoba; Air Commodore G. V. Walsh, M.B.E., Air Attaché Canadian Legation, Washington, D.C. formerly A.O.C., No. 3 Training Command Headquarters, Montreal; Air Vice-Marshal N. R. Anderson, Air Member for Air Staff formerly Air Officer Commanding, Eastern Air Command, Halifax; Air Commodore G. E. Brookes, O.B.E., Air Officer Commanding, No. 1 Training Command Headquarters, Toronto; Group Captain C. M. McEwen, (M.C., D.F.C.), R.C.A.F. Group Headquarters, St. Johns, Newfoundland, formerly Air Commodore and Air Officer Commanding No. 3 Training Command, Montreal; Air Commodore S. G. Tackaberry, special advisor of Supply, Canadian Legation, Washington, D.C., formerly Air Member for Supply; Air Vice-Marshal G. O. Johnson, Deputy Chief of the Air Staff; Air Vice-Marshal H. Edwards, Air Officer Commanding in Chief, R.C.A.F. Overseas, formerly Air Member for Personnel; Air Vice-Marshal Robert Leckie, D.S.O., D.S.C., D.F.C., Air Member for Training. FRONT ROW, *left to right*, Air Commodore A. E. Godfrey, M.C., A.F.C., V.D., Deputy Inspector General, formerly Air Officer Commanding, Western Air Command; Air Commodore A. T. N. Cowley, Air Officer Commanding, No. 4 Training Command, Calgary, Alberta; Air Vice-Marshal E. W. Stedman, O.B.E., Air Member for Aeronautical Engineering; Air Vice-Marshal G. M. Croil, A.F.C., Inspector-General; Mr. S. L. deCarteret, Deputy Minister; Major the Honourable C. G. Power, M.C., Minister of National Defence for Air; Air Marshal L. S. Breadner, D.S.C., Chief of the Air Staff; Air Commodore W. R. Kenny, D.F.C., now retired but formerly Air Attaché to Washington. Other members not in the picture are Mr. Terence Sheard, Air Member for Supply, Air Commodore L. F. Stevenson, Air Officer Commanding, Western Air Command, Victoria, B.C., and Air Commodore J. L. E. A. deNiverville, Air Officer Commanding, No. 3 Training Command, Montreal.

THE BIRTH OF THE AIR PLAN:

As Parliament went home and the Proclamation of War was issued, no mention was heard in the country of the role Canada was soon to play in the skies. Rather the cry was for the raising of infantry divisions, for in the minds of Canadians (and particularly of those who had fought in the armies of 1914-18) we stood committed to a campaign which obviously would be a replica of the fighting we had known from Ypres to Mons. Hence, said Public Opinion, Canada must raise at once huge land forces and despatch them overseas to whatever places where trenches might be dug.

Such talk as was heard during the early weeks of September, supported by the news stories which came from the Press Gallery, had to do mainly with plans for the recruiting of troops, the provision of supplies, our hopes of receiving huge war orders from Britain, the possible northward movement of new American factories banned from selling us goods in the United States by virtue of our belligerency, talk of ship-space shortages . . . scarcely a mention of Air. Even though stories cabled from Britain accentuated the need for Navy and Air expansion, Canada, in mid-September was still thinking and talking only in terms of land armies of the First World War pattern. In fine, the Canadian people, including most of their political leaders, had no vestige of idea of the nature of the war machine they had chosen to face and fight. Thus when the Honourable Norman Rogers, transferred from the Department of Labour to the Ministry of National Defence, in the Cabinet shuffle of September 19th (Which also moved Major Power from Pensions to the Postmaster Generalship, transferred Hon. Ian Mackenzie from Defence to Pensions and brought Hon. Norman McLarty into the Government as Minister of Labour) announced, on September 29th, that two divisions were being recruited, one for service overseas, the other to act as a reserve at home, the public clamoured "Not enough!", but still made no inquiries as to what we proposed to do at sea and in the air.

It was not until October 10th, in fact, that any talk was heard of proposals to engage in large-scale Air Training on Canadian soil. True, the Cabinet had pondered the question long and late and the basic plan had been in preparation for some days before any information reached the public. That is not the point. The point is that the thought apparently had not been born in the minds of the Canadian people that they had embarked upon a war which lacked any basis for comparison with other wars they had known. The over-running of Poland and the part played by the *luftwaffe* in the crushing of Warsaw made little, if any, impression. We of the west were firmly entrenched behind the Maginot Line and in our island fortress across the Channel, where the Navy would keep us safe from major alarms. Our job, as Canadians saw it then, would be to rush troops over to take their places in the Line in France, from which point of vantage, with the help of naval blockade, we should win again in a war of attrition, backed by the vast resources of the Commonwealth transported to Britain over open sea lanes. That was our mentality in September, 1939, and it is as well that it should be noted in the record.

Two years later our Air Plan pilots were in action in Europe, our Navy playing a prominent part in the crucial Battle of the Atlantic. Our Army, on the other hand, still languished in Britain and had seen little action other than the bomb raids it had shared with the civil population.

Not until October 10th did the word Air appear prominently in the nation's press. But when it reached the headlines it did so in a manner to galvanize public attention, for what was announced was the genesis of what is known today as the British Commonwealth Air Training Plan. It seemed, in our pre-Dunkirk state of mind, to be a veritable behemoth. So it seemed, too, to its sponsors in Britain, in Australia, New Zealand and Canada. Yet it was picayune in comparison with the Plan as we know it today. It called, in the words of Britain's Air Minister, Sir Kingsley Wood, for the training in Canada of 25,000 men per annum for the duration of the war to "achieve overwhelming air strength." Announcing "acceptance in principle" of the idea by Britain, Canada and the down-under Dominions (South Africa elected to train its airmen at home), Wood told Britain's Commons that "Canada will be used as an advanced training centre for pilots and airmen of all parts of the British Empire," who would send to the Dominion graduates from elementary schools for advanced training. Simultaneously, Sir Kingsley spoke of speeding up aircraft production in Canada, his words implying that this *desideratum* could be achieved overnight, a circumstance which, since it did not and could not happen after such fashion, soon brought the wrath of the Government's critics down on its head. We had not yet learned that huge industries cannot be created by a political speech.

Later the same day Prime Minister Mackenzie King made official announcement of the scheme from Ottawa in a statement which marked the inception of the plan. Said the Prime Minister:

"The Governments of the United Kingdom, Australia, New Zealand and Canada have recently reached agreement upon a development of great importance which they believe is destined to make a most effective contribution to the successful prosecution of the war.

"His Majesty's Government in the United Kingdom put forward in September for the consideration of His Majesty's Governments in Canada, the Commonwealth of Australia and New Zealand, an outline of arrangements for the rapid expansion of air training on a co-operative basis. The arrangements provide a training organization for pilots, observers and air gunners required first for the enlargement and then for the maintenance on an enlarged basis of the Air Forces of the respective countries, this to be combined with an expanded production of aircraft.

"The Governments of Canada, Australia and New Zealand have signified their agreement in principle to these arrangements.

"It has thus been ensured that the many facilities and the great natural advantages for the training of the pilots and the other personnel and the production of aircraft which these countries offer in areas comparatively free from any risk of enemy interference will be utilized to the fullest extent and to the best advantage.

"Training schools will be established and maintained in each of these countries. The more comprehensive and technical facilities required for the advanced training apart from those available and to be made available in the United Kingdom will, in the main, be concentrated in Canada.

"Personnel from elementary schools in Australia and New Zealand as well as a substantial proportion of young men passing out of similar establishments in the United Kingdom will proceed to Canada to receive with similar personnel from schools here the advanced training which will fit them all for service in the Line.

"The young men so trained will join either the Air Force squadrons maintained by their respective Governments in the theatre of operations or the United Kingdom Royal Air Force units, while those who get their final training in Canada will go back to join the Royal Air Force squadrons in the field.

Imperial Airways Flying Boats Blaze the Atlantic Trail—CALEDONIA *piloted by Captain A. S. Wilcockson, O.B.E., reaches the St. Lawrence from Britain, July 7th, 1937.*

"The undertaking is one of great magnitude. Its development would result in a great and rapid increase in the number of training schools, already large, and achieve an increasing output of first line pilots, observers and air gunners which, combined with the output of the United Kingdom, would ensure the greatly increased requirements in trained personnel being fully met. The aim, in short, is to achieve by co-operative effort, air forces of overwhelming strength.

"A mission from the United Kingdom, headed by Lord Riverdale—who will be aided by a specially selected technical staff—is already on its way to Canada to meet here corresponding missions from Australia and New Zealand. These missions will discuss with the Canadian authorities all further steps that are to be taken for the rapid execution of the Plan, including provision of necessary aircraft, instructors, ground personnel and aerodromes.

"It will be seen that the scheme involves a concentration of air training largely in Canada. The Government of the United Kingdom has indicated its opinion that, with the facilities that Canada possesses, this co-operative effort may prove to be of the most essential and decisive character. The Canadian Government concurs in this view and has accordingly decided to participate in the plan."

This, then, was the original concept. How different from the Air Plan that we knew two years later! But here was a beginning. At last we were on the move. The newspapers editorialised of "hundreds of millions" to be spent and of the benefits and boons to accrue for ever to Canadian civil aviation. As the Riverdale Mission arrived in Ottawa on October 15th, writers were urging the immediate formation of a Canadian Air Ministry. So began Canada's War In The Air.

For emphasis' sake it should be said again that the lack of air-mindedness was that of the public, rather than of the airmen or the Government. The proposal which resulted in creation of the British Commonwealth Air Training Plan came from Britain on September 26th, that is to say, in the fourth week of hostilities, and was accepted by Canada two days later. Meanwhile the stage was being set in Ottawa for the long weeks of parley.

*   *   *

During this period the eyes of Canada were directed towards the Province of Quebec and political war on the home front, rather than to the distant places where the shooting war began to take form and shape. Before the war was a month old, Maurice Duplessis, "Nationalist" Prime Minister of the Province which abuts on the lower Saint Lawrence, the Gulf and the open sea (and which, therefore, must always be regarded as one of Canada's most highly vulnerable areas) had dissolved his Legislature and called a General Election on a battle-cry perilously bordering on anti-war. Actually Duplessis, in calling for dissolution and an appeal to the electorate, based his referendum on the alleged infringement of provincial rights by the Federal Government, through the medium of its numerous war measures. In his first speech, setting the keynote of the campaign, the Prime Minister had declared to an audience in his home constituency, Trois Rivières, that if participation in war should mean the loss, or partial loss, of provincial autonomy, he stood against participation. The issue was promptly joined by Hon. Adelard Godbout, as Leader of the provincial Liberals, to whose side rallied Rt. Hon. Ernest Lapointe, Minister of Justice, Hon. C. G. Power, then Postmaster General, and other Federal Ministers from Quebec, with the declaration that, should Duplessis triumph, they, and other Quebec political leaders, would accept the verdict as a vote of no-confidence and retire at once from the Federal Government. Private members from Quebec resigned their seats to contest provincial ridings. The issue was translated squarely into that of War versus Isolationism. Duplessis

made several attempts to explain, even almost to reverse, his original position, but without success. And on October 25th, Quebec's French-speaking electorate snowed the Nationalist Government under an avalanche of ballots which placed Godbout and his followers in power, occupying ninety percent of the seats in the Legislature. It was to this vivid political phenomenon, then, that Canadian eyes were turned in the early weeks of Armageddon, rather than towards the more prosaic functions of military organisation and preparation.

*   *   *

Meanwhile the Air Missions were gathering in the Canadian capital. Lord Riverdale, as head of the United Kingdom delegation, was accompanied by Air Marshal Sir Robert Brooke-Popham, later Commander-in-Chief of Allied forces in the Orient, with Headquarters at Singapore. They were joined, a few days later, by Captain H. H. Balfour, Britain's Parliamentary Under-Secretary of State for Air. The Australian delegation, headed by the Honourable J. V. Fairbairn, named Minister for Air in his homeland during the course of the deliberations, and since killed in an air accident near Canberra, did not reach Ottawa until November 1st. Two days later the New Zealanders arrived in the Canadian capital, led by Group Captain Saunders, Chief of the Air Staff for New Zealand. Meanwhile the preliminaries were in hand on Parliament Hill.

Canada was represented by the Prime Minister (Rt. Hon. W. L. Mackenzie King) and the Ministers of Defence (Hon. Norman McL. Rogers), Finance (Col. the Hon. J. L. Ralston), Transport (Hon. C. D. Howe), and Pensions (Hon. Ian Mackenzie), assisted by numerous high officials of these Departments and others from the Department of External Affairs. The Prime Minister himself presided over the more important sessions and initialled the final agreement in Canada's behalf. As delegates met across the council table in Ottawa, the experts visited various sections of the Dominion and inspected sites and proposed sites for schools and airfields. What reached the public, therefore, when the Agreement was made public on December 17th by the Prime Minister of Canada, was not a Plan in process of formation, but a *fait accompli*. At the time of its inception the Plan was acclaimed throughout the Commonwealth as a long-term operation designed to give the Allies ultimate command of the skies, perhaps even to be the deciding factor of the war itself. Since then, however, expansion and the constant broadening of its functions have made of it the greatest concept in Canadian history and, as you shall see, one which already has proved itself of inestimable value in the fight for Freedom.

It must not be assumed, however, that the Plan came together in one piece without presenting problems to be unravelled. International delegations, even though they may be representatives of partner-nations, are not without guile. Thus, during the weeks of negotiation, Ottawa was a capital of rumours, of undercurrents and grapevines, as each delegation sought to assure itself that the interests of its own country were not overlooked. The pretence is always put forward, of course, that all such proceedings take place in an atmosphere of complete harmony, culminating in a love feast and general agreement. Agreement there was between the nations of the Commonwealth when the Plan was finally accepted by all the participants. But as it meandered towards finality all the conditions common to international discussion were present. What held the delegates together was the urgency of war itself, the knowledge that they *must* bring forth an agreement acceptable to all, or suffer the wrath of their own people, anxious for action, not quibbling debate. Thus the Prime Minister was able to stand before the microphone on Sunday evening, December 17th, on his sixty-fifth birthday, and inform the Canadian people of the signing of the Agreement.

CALEDONIA *welcomed to Canada by* Hon. C. D. Howe (*top left*) *and* President S. J. Hungerford *of Canadian National Railways* (*top right*); Philip Johnson (*centre left*), *later General Manager of Trans-Canada Air Lines chats with* Captain A. S. Wilcockson, O.B.E., Captain G. J. Powell *and his officers of* CAMBRIA, *which reached the St. Lawrence in August 1937. Lower photos show* CAMBRIA.

The Prime Minister's address, as an historic document, is quoted virtually verbatim:

"I am pleased to be able to announce that agreement has now been reached by the Governments of the United Kingdom, Canada, Australia and New Zealand on a co-operative air training plan, to be known as the British Commonwealth Air Training Plan. The agreement was signed last night very shortly after midnight in my office on Parliament Hill. It is based on a proposal made to the Governments of Canada, Australia and New Zealand, on September 26, by the Government of the United Kingdom.

"In addition to a rapid and extensive increase in the air training program of each of the three Dominions, the plan visualizes joint training in Canada, in the more advanced stages, of pupils from Canada, Australia, New Zealand and the United Kingdom.

"The undertaking is one of great magnitude.

"It will establish Canada as one of the greatest air training centres in the world. Its development will result in a rapid increase in the number of air training schools in this country, and will achieve a steadily increasing output of highly trained pilots, observers and air gunners.

"The plan will enable the four countries to meet the greatly increasing requirements of trained personnel for their respective Air Forces, and for such service as the combined Forces may be called upon to perform in the theatres of war. The aim, in short, is to achieve, by co-operative effort, Air Forces whose co-ordinated strength will be overwhelming.

"The Canadian Government accepted the United Kingdom proposal in principle on September 28, that is two days after it was received. The proposal was also accepted in principle, without delay, by the Governments of Australia and New Zealand.

"No time was lost in making arrangements for carrying on the negotiations. Much detailed consideration obviously was necessary to ensure a co-operative scheme which would be completely co-ordinated with the development of the Air Forces of the different parts of the British Commonwealth engaged in the joint endeavor, and to determine its financial, administrative and other aspects.

"In working out the plan, the existing air training programs of all four countries engaged in the discussions, were fully taken into account. As already mentioned, the plan provides for a continuance of training in the United Kingdom, for an enlargement of the training programs of Canada, Australia and New Zealand, and for a joint training program in Canada. As the United Kingdom proposal contemplated joint training to be carried on in Canada, it was appropriate and, in fact, essential that the details of the program should be worked out at Ottawa.

"The broad problem was to decide on the speediest and most effective means of training the maximum number of pilots and airmen to meet the exigencies of war. In working out the agreement, Canada, Australia and New Zealand had, necessarily, to keep in mind local defence considerations, such as the training, equipment and service of the pilots and other air personnel required to keep up their own air defences.

"To reach the main objective, namely, the rapid training of the greatest number of pilots and airmen, the facilities in these countries, in excess of local needs, are to be used to train Australians and New Zealanders for service overseas with the Royal Air Force. The existing training facilities in the United Kingdom will continue to be used by the Royal Air Force.

"Under the agreement, as it relates to joint training in Canada, the program of training of personnel for the Royal Canadian Air Force, already enlarged since the outbreak of war, will be vastly increased. The Canadian training program will be merged with the program of joint training in Canada. In this way, co-ordinated air training will proceed simultaneously in all four countries.

"The joint air training program provides for the training of many thousands of pilots in Canada each year, about three-fifths as many air observers, and a slightly larger number of air gunners than pilots. The pilots, of course, are those who actually operate the planes. The observers handle the reconnaissance cameras and the bomb sights, and as well, do the navigating. The gunners use the machine guns in action, and also act as wireless operators.

"The facilities in Canada will be used, in varying degrees, by all four parties to the agreement. Practically all air recruits in the United Kingdom will be trained at home. In Australia and New Zealand, all air recruits will receive their initial and elementary flying training at home.

"Most of the Australian pupils and some of the New Zealand pupils will also receive advanced training in their own countries. Under the agreement, however, about one-fifth of the pupils to receive advanced training in Canada will come from the other two Dominions. Some pupils will be received from the United Kingdom, Newfoundland and elsewhere. The great majority of the pupils will, however, be Canadians.

"The first stage of training in this country will be initial training, which is a ground course to prepare recruits for flying and for Air Force life in general. This will be given in three large schools. At the end of four weeks' initial training, a selection will be made of those to be pilots, observers or gunners, and they will then go to the appropriate schools.

"Pilots will go to one of the elementary flying schools, where they will learn to get the feel of a plane, and to fly light machines. After some eight weeks, they will graduate to the service flying schools.

"It is at this stage that the Australian and New Zealand pilots, who will receive their initial and elementary training in their own countries, will come to Canada to continue their training. In the service flying schools, of which there will be 16 in Canada, pilots will spend about 14 weeks learning intermediate and advanced flying, including night and instrument flying. They will receive instruction in bombing and fighting as well.

"The air observers, including those from abroad, will spend about 12 weeks at the air observers' schools. There will be 10 of these schools at which pupils will be taught navigation, reconnaissance and photography.

"They go on from air observers schools to bombing and gunnery schools for a course in the theory and practice of bombing and gunnery. The course will take about six weeks. There will be 10 bombing and gunnery schools. Finally, in order to learn more advanced navigation, the observers will spend about four weeks in one of two air navigation schools.

"The air gunners, who also serve as wireless operators, after their initial training either in Canada or abroad, will take a 16 weeks' course in the wireless training schools. There will be four wireless training schools. In them, air gunners will be taught not only the essential principles of radio work, but also operating practices in the air. They will then proceed to the bombing and gunnery schools for four weeks, to learn that phase of work before proceeding overseas.

"Schools will also be needed, at the outset, for training instructors and administrative staffs. And before the training program is brought to full capacity, ground crews and maintenance staffs will be required in large numbers to man the various schools and establishments. Repair and equipment depots, headquarters and commands, recruiting centres and records offices will also be required.

"In addition to the 58 schools for the training of pilots, observers and air gunners, and schools needed, at the outset, for training instructors and administrative staffs, several much larger

Canada's Transcontinental Airway inaugurated, July 21, 1937. Hon. C. D. Howe, th[e] Minister of Transport flew the route with the inaugural flight. (Top left) Phillip Johnso[n] General Manager of T.C.A. and President S. J. Hungerford of Canadian Nation[al] Railways. Other photos show Hon. C. D. Howe and notables at various stages of t[he] transcontinental tour.

schools will also be required to train the personnel for ground crews and maintenance staffs. The total number of schools required, in Canada, for the joint training program will be 67.

"Nearly 40,000 officers and men will be required to man all the various schools, depots and other parts of the organization when it is in full operation. This will include about 2,700 officers and about 6,000 civilians. The remaining 30,000 will be members of the Air Force other than officers. These numbers do not include the pupils undergoing training, who will also be numbered in thousands. Many of the airmen required for training the pupils will be mechanics and other skilled artisans, who constitute ground crews and maintenance staffs.

"For the program of joint training full use will immediately be made of the existing facilities of the Royal Canadian Air Force, as well as of facilities generously made available by Trans-Canada Airways. However, to put the extensive program into full operation, a great deal of construction and production will be necessary.

"Throughout the country, about a score of existing air fields will have to be enlarged, and some 60 odd new air fields constructed. The schools will be established in different parts of Canada. Large supplies of equipment and stores of various kinds, will be required to furnish the schools, and also the equipment and repair depots. The construction and other industries of Canada may be relied upon to meet effectively the demands which this program will involve.

"Great quantities of aircraft and their parts will, of course, be required. The United Kingdom, as her part of the costs of the undertaking, has agreed to supply most of the aircraft including engines and spares. Apart from the aircraft supplied by the United Kingdom, the light aircraft for elementary training and a portion of the other aircraft will be made in Canada.

"The aircraft to be made in Canada will be included with the other costs of the joint training program, which are to be divided between Canada, Australia and New Zealand in proportion to the use to be made of the various facilities by the pupils of the three countries. This means that, excluding the cost of the aircraft provided by the United Kingdom, Canada will bear the cost of the initial and elementary training in Canada, and about four-fifths of the remaining costs of the program.

"The duration of the agreement is until March 31, 1943, in other words, a little over 3 years. This period of time may, however, be extended or terminated by mutual agreement.

"While any estimate of costs made at this time is subject to a wide margin of error, the total cost for the entire program in Canada, for the period agreed upon, will approximate $600,000,000. Canada's share will be around $350,000,000.

"Up to the beginning of next September, the expenditure on the joint training program will amount to about $90,000,000. Of this $90,000,000, Canada's share will be about $48,000,000.

"This amount will be in addition to the $315,000,000 which the Minister of Finance estimated would be the cost, in the first year of the war, of the military program already undertaken before the air training plan was proposed. In other words, in this first year of war, Canada will be spending on her military effort alone about $1,000,000 a day.

"Under the terms of the agreement, the joint air training program which is to be carried out in Canada, is to be administered by the Government of Canada. The organization and executive command of the training schools is entrusted to the Royal Canadian Air Force. For the general supervision of the joint air training program, a supervisory board will be established in Canada. The board will supervise the financial administration of the program. It will also, from time to time, inspect the progress being made in the setting up of the organization, and carrying out the training.

"The supervisory board will be under the chairmanship of the Minister of National Defence. It will also include the Minister of Finance, the Minister of Transport, representatives of the Governments of the United Kingdom, Australia and New Zealand, the Deputy Minister for Air of the Department of National Defence, and the Chief of the Air Staff. Contact with the Government will be maintained by the board through its chairman, and with the Royal Canadian Air Force through the Chief of the Air Staff.

"The representatives on the board of the Governments of the United Kingdom, Australia and New Zealand, are to report to their own Governments regarding the progress of the joint training program.

"They will also have authority to visit, at any time, any stations or units, and to make criticisms or suggestions to the board. It is expected that they will assist in keeping the Royal Canadian Air Force advised as to new developments in training technique which may come to their notice.

"All four Governments will co-operate in the provision of staff and teaching personnel. The staff officers and instructors from the United Kingdom, Australia and New Zealand will, during their period of service in Canada, hold temporary appointments in the Royal Canadian Air Force. This further co-operative arrangement should go far to assure the successful working of the joint air training program.

"It is desirable, at this point, to clear up a misconception which has become current through frequent repetition, but which is wholly without foundation.

"It has been asserted that the air training plan would have been in existence before this had the present Government not declined to meet an earlier request of the United Kingdom Government for the training of British pilots in Canada. Within the past week or two, it has, for example, been said: 'Had we agreed to the British proposal of two years ago for the establishment of air training facilities in Canada, today Canada would be, in reality, the air training centre of the Empire.'

"More recently it has been said that 'so far as the Empire air training scheme is concerned this was proposed by the British nearly two years ago but apparently discouraged by the King Government until after the outbreak of war.'

"I assume that what is referred to are certain informal, exploratory conversations concerning facilities for the training of British pilots in Canada which took place, not two years ago, but in May and June of last year. The facts were clearly set forth in a statement I subsequently made to Parliament.

"The conversations did not relate to a joint air training plan. Their purpose was to ascertain whether it would be agreeable to the Canadian Government to have United Kingdom schools for the advanced training of pilots of the Royal Air Force established in Canada, under the authority and direction of the Air Ministry of the United Kingdom.

"It was represented that it was becoming increasingly difficult to secure in the British Isles the open spaces needed for long distance flying and gunnery practice. What was contemplated was a British training establishment in Canada, organized and controlled by the Air Ministry of the United Kingdom, in no way responsible to the Canadian Government, but responsible solely to the Government of the United Kingdom.

"When the matter was broached, speaking on behalf of the Government, I immediately said I was sure the Canadian people would gladly have pilots of the Royal Air Force come to Canada for advanced training and would be prepared to provide the necessary facilities, but that I believed they would feel that the necessary establishments should, under terms to be agreed upon, be organized and controlled by the Royal Canadian Air Force, and that the responsibility for their administration should be

From Coast to Coast with Trans-Canada Air Lines—Montreal and Winnipeg are sho[w]... left and right centre.

that of the Government of Canada, rather than that of the Government of the United Kingdom. I added that I felt such a basis was indispensable to friendly and effective co-operation between the two air forces as well as between the two governments.

"Long ago, the constitutional principle was accepted that military establishments in Canadian territory should be owned, maintained and controlled by the Government of Canada, responsible to the Canadian people. That principle has been acted upon ever since. British naval stations and British army garrisons have been withdrawn.

"Canada, herself, has assumed responsibility for all defence establishments in Canadian territory. It was felt by our Government that a reversal of the principle underlying this historical process was something which the Canadian people would not wish to entertain.

"The attitude of the Canadian Government, in this matter, was, however, far from being a negative one. Our desire to co-operate in the most effective manner was made abundantly clear in the following statement which I made in Parliament with respect to Canada's position. 'We, ourselves,' I said, 'are prepared to have our own establishments here and to give in those establishments facilities to British pilots to come and train here, but they must come and train in establishments which are under the control of the Government of Canada and for which the Minister of National Defence will be able to answer in this Parliament with respect to everything concerning them.'

"This declaration of Canadian policy was cordially welcomed by the Government of the United Kingdom. On July 7th, 1938, in answer to a question in the British House of Commons as to whether his attention had been drawn to this statement by the Prime Minister of Canada, Sir Kingsley Wood, the Secretary of State for Air, replied: 'Yes sir. An offer in this sense has been communicated to His Majesty's Government in the United Kingdom, by the Canadian Prime Minister, through the Canadian High Commissioner. A reply has been sent expressing warm appreciation of the offer, and arrangements are being made in accordance with the suggestion of the Canadian Prime Minister for an officer to be sent immediately to Canada to explore, in co-operation with the Canadian Government, the possibility of working out a scheme for training facilities in Canada.'

"A few weeks later, an officer of the Royal Air Force was sent by the British Government to conduct the exploratory investigations referred to. During the stay in Canada of this expert from the Air Ministry, a careful survey was made of requirements and facilities available for joint advanced training of pilots for the Air Forces of the United Kingdom and of Canada. The survey was made in collaboration with officials of the Department of National Defence and senior officers of the Royal Canadian Air Force.

"At the ensuing session, on the recommendation of the Minister of National Defence, our Parliament appropriated the sum of $6,000,000 for the joint training of pilots. This grant was over and above the already greatly increased appropriations for air defence.

"In presenting the estimates to Parliament the Minister said: 'It is possible to say now that agreement has been reached on a scheme whereby pilots from the United Kingdom will come to Canada to be given intermediate and advanced stages of training under the auspices of the Canadian Department of National Defence'. I should like to emphasize the fact that the scheme was one for joint training. In answer to a question, the Minister added that the duration of the scheme would be three years.

"Here we have the real beginning of the present plan for joint training in Canada of pilots from the United Kingdom, Canada, Australia and New Zealand, which, under the pressure of war, has assumed the proportions of which the world is now aware.

"The government has not awaited the conclusion of the present agreement to begin work on the development of the additional air training facilities which the plan contemplates. Considerable progress has already been made. The Royal Canadian Air Force schools at Trenton and Camp Borden have been converted into schools for the training of instructors. For some weeks past they have been in use for that purpose.

"The air training facilities which were being developed on a less extensive scale before the war, are being brought rapidly to completion. Of about 125 air fields already developed in Canada, 42 are up to the standard set by Trans-Canada Airways. Many of these will be used for the joint training program.

"Under arrangements made with the provincial governments, the highways staffs of all the provinces have been used for surveying additional airdrome sites. Full advantage has been taken of the favorable weather, and most of the sites have already been surveyed. The War Supply Board has anticipated the requirements of the program and has organized production to meet them.

"The enormous variety of equipment required for the program is being listed in detail, so that orders may be promptly placed. To prevent delays in obtaining supplies, required from outside Canada, protective orders have already been placed. Now that the agreement is in force the War Supply Board will immediately begin to let the necessary contracts. Plans for the schools have already been prepared, and no time will be lost in their construction.

"The new program is of such magnitude, that some little time must necessarily elapse, while schools are being built, equipment obtained, and the training of additional instructors completed, before student pilots, observers and air gunners can be accepted for their training, and before the first pilots and observers, trained under the scheme, will be sufficiently skilled to proceed to the theatres of war.

"In the meantime the United Kingdom Government, appreciating the desire of the Canadian people to be represented as soon as possible by an air force unit on active service in Europe, has arranged for the immediate formation of a Squadron to be commanded by a Squadron Leader of the Royal Canadian Air Force. All the Pilots in the Squadron will be Canadian. The Canadian commander and Pilots will be selected from Canadians at present serving with the Royal Air Force.

"The formation of this Squadron has been made possible by the practical co-operation, in the training of air personnel, in recent years between the Royal Canadian Air Force and the Royal Air Force. This co-operation has resulted in the presence in the Royal Air Force of a considerable number of Canadians, some of whom, as you are aware, have already achieved distinction in the present war.

"Perhaps I should mention here that, under the Commonwealth Air Training Plan, provision has been made, after their training is completed, for the identification, in the field, of the pupils with their respective Dominions, either by the method of organizing Dominion units and formations, or in some other way.

"In embarking upon the vast co-operative enterprise, envisaged by the Commonwealth Air Training Plan, the Government had naturally to give the most careful consideration to the plan in its relation to Canada's military effort as a whole.

"This aspect was, of course, very fully discussed with the Government of the United Kingdom. It is obviously all-important that our effort should be co-ordinated with the effort of our allies in a single strategic plan for carrying on the War. When the Plan, in its broad outlines, was proposed by the Government of the United Kingdom, it was stated that the immense influence which the development and realization of such a great project might have upon the whole course of the war, might even prove decisive.

From Coast to Coast with Trans-Canada Air Lines—Vancouver, end of the sky-trail, lower right.

"On October 10th, at the time of announcing agreement by the several governments on the principle of the proposal, I stated that 'The Government of the United Kingdom has indicated its opinion that with the facilities which Canada possesses this co-operative effort may prove to be of the most essential and decisive character.'

"The United Kingdom Government has informed us that, considering present and future requirements, it feels that participation in the air training scheme would provide for more effective assistance towards ultimate victory than any other form of military co-operation which Canada can give. At the same time the United Kingdom Government wishes it to be clearly understood that it would welcome no less heartily the presence of Canadian land forces in the theatre of war at the earliest possible moment.

"You will recall that, on September 19, the Government announced that a division was being organized for service overseas, and, as you are aware, no time is being lost in our endeavor to meet the wish of the United Kingdom for the early dispatch of an expeditionary force.

"I have spoken of the magnitude of the joint air training plan, of what it is likely to mean in numbers of men to be trained, and in additional financial outlay upon Canada's war effort. It is well, however, to remember that, in the vast expansion of air power which Canada has undertaken, in collaboration with her partners in the British Commonwealth, something wholly different, and much more vital than numbers or material wealth, is involved.

"It is the lives of our young men which are being pledged. Like our soldiers and our sailors, the pilots and airmen who are to be trained in thousands, are going forth to battle to risk their lives in conflict with forces more sinister than any the world has known.

"Tonight, I am speaking particularly of those belonging to the Royal Canadian Air Force. The young men, equally with others of maturer years with whom they will be associated, are, I am convinced, fully aware of the appalling nature of the situation facing the world today, and of what it will demand by way of sacrifice ere peace is again restored.

"It is not in a spirit of adventure that they are pressing forward in such numbers. Rather are they enlisting in the spirit of the Crusaders of old, prepared, if need be, to give their lives for what, to them and to us, is holy and sacred—the birthright of liberty and happiness in a free land. This fortitude and devotion must be guarded and protected by every power we possess.

"In making provision for this vast undertaking, the Government has done so knowing that nothing can be left to haste or to chance. The intricate machine must be perfect. In every phase of their work, the men must be trained by the highest skill, and under the best conditions it is possible for the country to provide. In no other arm of the defence services is a man obliged to rely more completely upon his own initiative, his own knowledge, and his own judgment.

"It is the possession of these qualities in such large measure which has given to Canadians the reputation as airmen they already enjoy. Those who enlist in Canada's Air Force may be depended upon to do their part, however perilous it may be. We must do ours to assist them in every possible way by adequate training and proper equipment, and by all the influences for good by which it is possible to surround their lives.

"I need not say to those who may come from other lands to receive their training, how warmly they will be welcomed during their brief stay in our midst. I know something of the heart of the Canadian people. I am sure, therefore, that our homes will be as open to them as they are to those of our own land, with whom they are already united as brothers, in an heroic effort to serve the world's need at this hour of its greatest peril.

"Let there be no mistake about the significance of the present war. It is a desperate struggle for existence itself. On its outcome will depend the fate not of Canada alone, nor even, it seems to me, of the British Empire, the fall of which would shatter the world, but of humanity itself, in all its higher aspects. To save mankind from such a catastrophe, the airmen of the British Commonwealth, whether setting their course by the North Star or the Southern Cross, are dedicating their lives. To hasten the day when peace may be restored is, I believe, the governing motive of all our forces, whether on sea, or land, or in the air."

A wave of enthusiasm swept the country and the Free World. The feeling spread through Canada that we were really at war. Press and public alike spoke in warmest praise of the Plan, in which regard the leading editorial of the *Montreal Star*, Monday, December 18th, offers a fair example of the public attitude and is reproduced as such. Said the *Star*:—

"Although the main features of the great British Commonwealth air scheme have been made public from time to time, the vast magnitude of the plans could not be realized before as fully as they were last night after the Canadian people had listened to Premier King's birthday address, in which he reviewed the negotiations leading up to the signature just after midnight yesterday of the agreement between Great Britain, Canada, Australia and New Zealand.

"The statistics alone are well-nigh staggering. Of the total estimated cost over the three-year period covered by the agreement, namely, six hundred million dollars, Canada will pay no less than three hundred and fifty million dollars. The twenty existing air fields will be enlarged and sixty new ones constructed; sixty-seven schools will be built; upwards of forty thousand men will be required for staff and maintenance purposes, exclusive of the many thousands of pupils who will be taught to fly. Great Britain will supply most of the aircraft, including engines and spare parts, as her share of the cost. This Dominion, Australia and New Zealand will share in the total cost in proportion to the use made of the scheme by the pupils from these three countries. It is important to bear in mind that not only will Canada provide the bulk of the fliers, but the major part of the work will be carried out in this country under the direction of the Royal Canadian Air Force. Canadians may well take a legitimate pride in this fact. It means that Canada will play an all-important part in the winning of the war,—a part she is eminently well qualified to play, alike on the record of her magnificent air fighters in the past and because of the exceptional qualifications which geography and resources enable her to bring to the task.

"It is only fair that full credit should be given Premier Mackenzie King and his associates for the speedy manner in which they have dealt with this colossal scheme. From the first the Premier and his aides tackled it on a business basis, meeting the practical members of the special commission sent over by Great Britain and the representatives from the Antipodes in well-nigh continuous sessions. But long before the signatures were appended to the actual documents yesterday morning, the ramifications of this stupendous enterprise had been appreciated by our Ministers, and an actual start had been made in several directions; so that now the accord is a legal fact, the scheme does not begin; it continues, and its development will be speeded up to the utmost possible point consistent with efficiency. The result, in Premier King's pregnant phrase, will be 'to achieve by co-operative effort air forces whose co-ordinated strength will be overwhelming'.

"There is another aspect of the whole vast plan which thinking Canadians will appreciate at its real importance. It is this: At

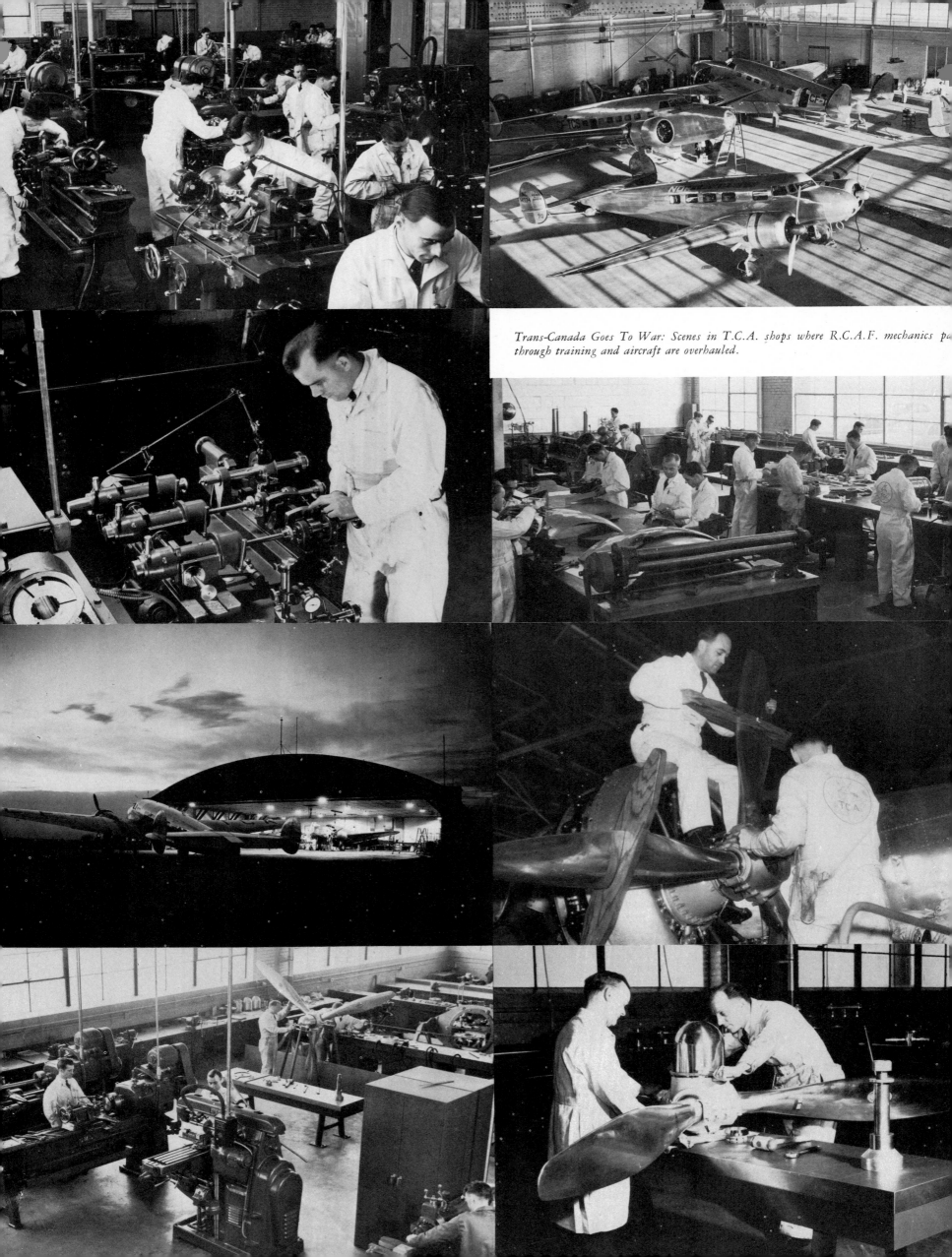

Trans-Canada Goes To War: Scenes in T.C.A. shops where R.C.A.F. mechanics pass through training and aircraft are overhauled.

the end of the war Canada will be equipped probably better than any other nation in the world to utilize her great aerial resources for the purposes of civil aviation in time of peace. What this will mean, it is impossible to visualize with any degree of accuracy; but we do know that this is the era of air travel, that aerial transportation, both of passengers and goods, is bound to develop speedily, once the war is over, and that it is altogether probable the not far distant future will see aerial freight transports as well as passenger traffic on a scale comparable with the once derided dreams of Jules Verne, Rudyard Kipling, and H. G. Wells.

"Canada as a young country has most to gain by being ready to take the lead when the opportune moment arrives. With the vast and efficient equipment we shall possess through the present British Commonwealth scheme, we shall only have ourselves to blame if we are not both prepared and competent to leap into the van and place Canada in a position of undeniable superiority in the air.

"But first we have to win the war, and in this connection Premier King's peroration last night was impressive. There can be no possible misunderstanding either of the magnitude of the task that awaits us or of the determination with which this Dominion has set its hand to the achievement of that task. Animated by the spirit its scope and plans reveal, and by the immovable resolution of the Canadian nation, we cannot fail."

*   *   *

Much has happened since the historic day when the partner nations committed themselves to the great Training Plan. On that December day in 1939 the basic figures revealed were "wellnigh staggering." To most of us the physical scope of the Plan was even more so . . . the enlargement of twenty existing fields and the building of sixty new ones (Was our construction industry equal to the job? we asked each other) . . . Sixty-seven schools . . . forty thousand officers and airmen in the permanent personnel of the Plan, exclusive of the lads we planned to train (Could we raise such a corps, equip it, train it and produce aircrews to meet the promised deadline?). But much more was done. The old-time pilots checked in from the bush. As many as could be spared forsook airline jobs. The Flying Clubs, the Sunday pilots, all the others, leaped to the task. The contractors ripped open the countryside to make new aerodromes in record time. The supplier forced the pace in factory and warehouse. Huge freights rolled over the great transcontinental railroads the Jeremiahs once claimed were bankrupting us. The aircraft supply line bottlenecked, as France fell.

We fixed that. The brief sentence makes it sound very simple. But when you break a bottleneck in aircraft deliveries for a flying scheme as great in its measurements as, say, the Canadian Pacific Railway, the job of fixing is not as simple as the job of writing about it, or as that of rising in the House to criticise the manner in which it is, or isn't, done. Later the way in which the now-famous Anson problem was brought into adjustment will be discussed *in extenso,* but a brief summary at this juncture will enable the reader to judge of the difficulties which were to run

through the whole Plan assembly-scheme and to realise that the miracle of our war-effort is that the Plan has been brought to fruition at all, not that it took so long.

The Anson is an advanced trainer, used primarily in the S.F.T.S. for the final-stage education of the young men who as graduates will fly bombers. Under the original terms of the Plan the Anson was to be the principal aircraft used in such work and it was to come from Britain. As the first thin trickle of machines began to reach these shores, however, France fell and the trickle ceased. So here was a Plan, but a Plan with little in the way of flying equipment, bar the elementary trainers which came from Canadian factories such as De Haviland (Tiger Moth) and Fleet Aircraft (Finch). What were we to do? People unversed in the chores of tailoring aeroplanes viewed the problem as extremely simple of solution. The job, they said, was simply to make the things here. But several thousand bits and pieces require to be put together before an Anson emerges from the assembly line. And what were we going to use for engines? Seeking solution, the Minister flew post haste to Washington, taking with him high officers of his Department. As a stop-gap measure, they secured aircraft in the United States and made arrangements for engines as well.

On their return to Canada the gentlemen went into long hours of conference with engineers, manufacturers and other knowledgeable aircraft men. Could we re-design the Anson to take American engines and make it here? Could we do *this?* Could we do *that?* From out the welter of confusion Federal Aircraft emerged as a Government-owned company to coordinate Anson construction. Throughout the country manufacturers were impressed into service to make individual parts. The frame was redesigned to accept new power plant. New bottlenecks now replaced old. The critics scoffed. Where was this highly-touted Anson programme? What kind of experts were we hiring? Was it not true that we had a Training Programme minus equipment in which to do the job? It was. It was true simply because Hitler had marched through France and Britain stood alone. Meanwhile Canada must re-estimate its whole concept and get into the serious production of advanced trainers. And Canada did. So goes the story of one bottleneck, of which more will be read later.

So somehow the classes were enlisted, equipped and sent aloft. The first Wings Parades were held. Months ahead of schedule the stream of Pilots, Observers and Air Gunners began to flow overseas from flying fields not even included in our plans when the great original concept was laid down. We moved into mass production of training aircraft as other doors of supply were closed. Elsewhere we turned out fighters and bombers for front line duty. We opened our doors to the R.A.F., provided schools and aerodromes to relieve Britain's overcrowded countryside. We provided the western terminals whence the great bombers flew the ocean in constantly increasing numbers during the months of urgent need. It is well that Canadians should remember all this as they assess their country's record in the skies. The job has been well and truly done. And the end is not yet.

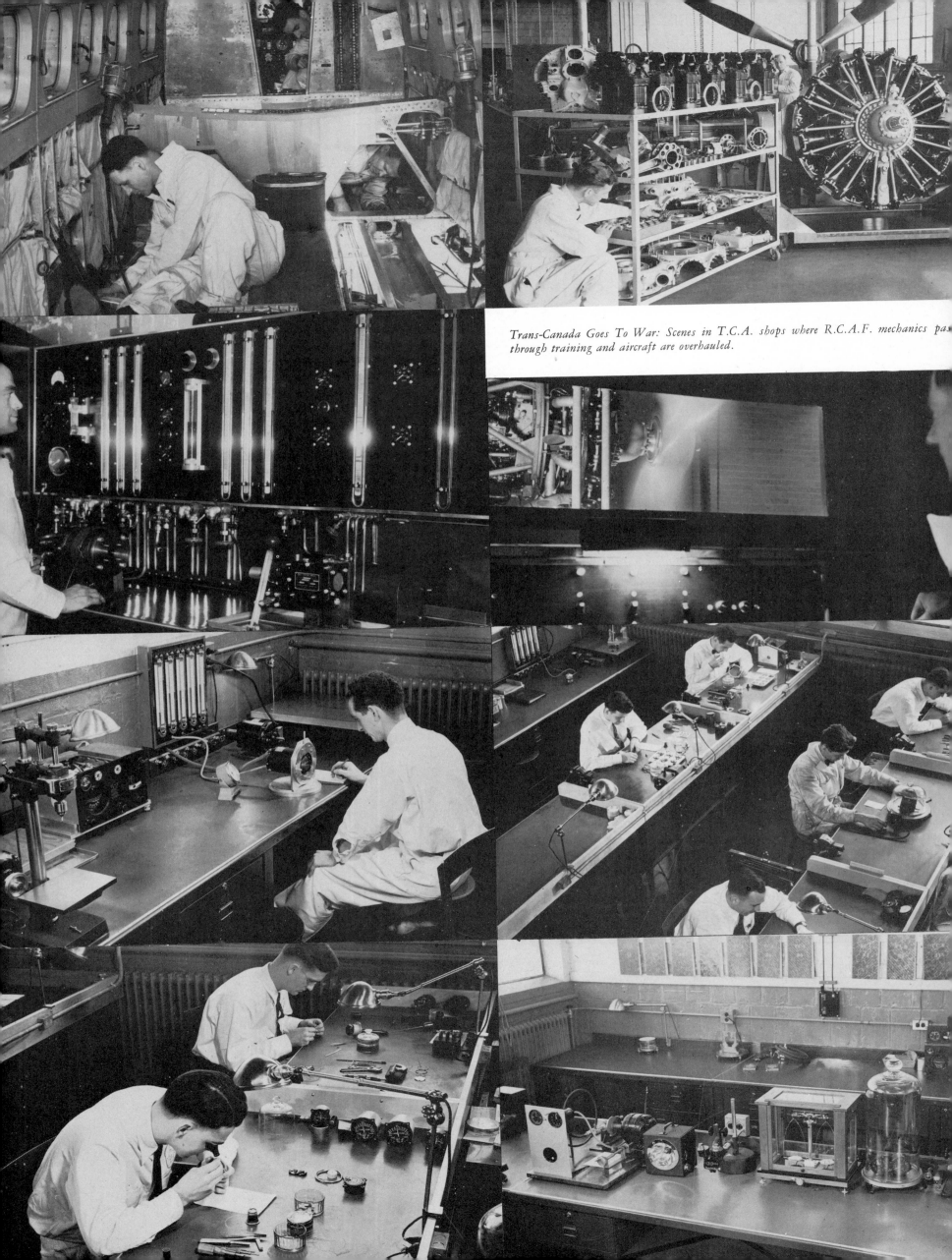

Trans-Canada Goes To War: Scenes in T.C.A. shops where R.C.A.F. mechanics pass through training and aircraft are overhauled.

THE ORGANISATION PERIOD, 1939-40

ALTHOUGH final agreement between the high contracting parties was not completed until December, the scale and scope of the British Commonwealth Air Training Plan were established in principle at the beginning of October. Early-stage work began at once.

The original concept provided for sixty-four flying training stations, of which twenty would be opened during 1940, beginning in the month of June, thirty-six in 1941 and the remainder during the early months of 1942. To these must be added two relief aerodromes to each Service Flying Training School, which were to be sixteen in number, giving a total of ninety-six airfields. That was the first plan.

Events overseas were soon to revolutionize both Plan and schedule, however. Dunkirk and the fall of France, instead of breaking the morale of the British peoples, served only to gear it to new high speeds under the driving power of the urgent necessity of the tragic hour. The crowding of available facilities in the United Kingdom, caused on the one hand by the withdrawal of British forces from the mainland of Europe and, on the other, by the vast expansion of the British war effort under Churchill, Bevin and Beaverbrook, brought about the establishment of new Royal Air Force schools in Canada, under Old Country officers and the jurisdictional control of the R.C.A.F. The end of the second year, therefore, found 124 units functioning directly under the Plan, plus the numerous centres established by the R.A.F. In Canada's War In The Air, today's impossibility is invariably eclipsed by tomorrow's actuality.

Of the flying schools originally planned, twenty-six were to be for Elementary Flying, sixteen for Service Flying (intermediate and advanced training), ten were to be Bombing and Gunnery Schools, ten Air Observers' Schools and two Air Navigation Institutions. But by the end of 1940 the Plan was already months ahead of schedule. Sixteen Elementary Flying Training Schools were in operation. Seven Service Flying Training Schools had been completed and opened. Four Air Observers' and three Bombing and Gunnery stations were in full swing and the first Air Navigation School had received its first pupils. In addition the Central Flying School at Trenton, used primarily for the training of instructors, had been absorbed into the Plan on the first of February.

This was not the sum total of the year's work, however. Before recruits could be accepted in large numbers airports were needed. Before airports could be of use, training aircraft must be bought, begged or borrowed. Before these things could happen a fundamental organisation must be created. Somehow from a total personnel of 4,000 men and 500 officers a permanent cadre of 40,000 must be built up, this without regard to the number of students, in tens of thousands, who would pass through their hands. Thus, in addition to the building of airfields, hangars, barracks and all the other structures which go into the making of war 'dromes, the working basis, fanning out from Headquarters in Ottawa, first had to be hammered together and equipped with its own specialised man-power.

The first year saw the establishment of four Training Command Headquarters in Montreal, Toronto, Regina and Winnipeg and 18 Recruiting Centres within the Commands. Four Manning Depots were opened and a sub-depot was established at Picton, Ontario, to provide for overflow. Two Initial Training Schools, to which the student-flier repairs after being changed from civilian into embryo-airman at the Manning Pool, were set up in Toronto and Regina. The huge Technical Training School at St. Thomas, Ontario, began to grind out air mechanics. A School of Aeronautical Engineering was located in Montreal and an Inspectors' School at Toronto. The new-born Equipment and Accounting Training School went to St. Thomas, the School of Administration, the Air Armament School and the Motor Boat Crewmen's Training School to Trenton, Ontario. Schools for the training of wireless specialists were opened in Montreal and Calgary during the year. Four Equipment Depots (Montreal, Toronto, Winnipeg and Calgary) and three Repair Depots (Trenton, Winnipeg and Calgary) were established, Technical Detachments were put to work at Ottawa, Toronto, Winnipeg and Edmonton. At the end of the first year of operation, the rapidly expanding Plan could boast 32 flying stations (excluding relief aerodromes) and 30 ground establishments (excluding Ottawa Headquarters and the Recruiting Centres throughout the country). How was it done?

The writer can testify to the ceaseless vigil that was kept in Ottawa's Woods and Jackson Buildings during those early months. Primarily it was all made possible by the tireless devotion of the man who, in the beginning, carried on his slender shoulders the burden of the nation's three armed services, Navy, Army and Air Force, the Honourable Norman McLeod Rogers, Minister of National Defence, who was to perish in June, 1940, in a tragic air accident while flying from Ottawa to Toronto to address a service club luncheon. To Norman Rogers belonged the God-given power to inspire men to give ceaselessly of their best. No member of his staff ever gave a moment's thought to hours of work as the days telescoped into each other. Far into the night, lights shone over Ottawa's Elgin Street from the Minister's office, from that of the Acting Deputy Minister for Air, Colonel K. S. Maclachlan, and from those of the secretariat. Across on Bank Street the lights of the Jackson Building testified to the midnight oil burned by Air Vice-Marshal G. M. Croil, Chief of Air Staff (now Inspector General) and all his high ranking officers. In the Department of Transport, engineers pored over maps and plans as the huge scheme took shape. Supply men and contractors settled questions involving the immediate building of new fields.

The Ottawa of late 1939 has often been described as a madhouse by those who visited the Canadian capital, there to wait for days on end for appointments with key officials. Some declared splenetically that the cabinet, the military staffs and the Civil Service were running around in circles, getting nothing done and not knowing "what it's all about." Mainly these were people who came in search of political favours, however, or who sought war contracts which the Government was not yet in a position to give. No nation can move from Total Peace onto the foundations for Total War overnight without serious dislocation of the functions of Government. Yet underneath the surface of what seemed to many to bear all the earmarks of incipient dementia, the War Effort was beginning to take shape. As young men stormed recruiting centres of the Royal Canadian Air Force throughout the nation and went their ways disgruntled because no openings were immediately available for them, the great Air Plan of today was taking form in ministerial and departmental offices as airport builders hastily assembled materials and supply officials combed the market place for aircraft and spares with which to equip Democracy's great university of the air.

Of the flying establishments put into service during the first year only five R.C.A.F. aerodromes had been ready for use at the time of the declaration of war. Six others were under construction. Not even all these in serviceable condition were available for training use, however, as those in coastal areas were immediately requisitioned as bases for service squadrons posted to defence and convoy duty. The permanent pre-war inland stations

The Construction Period: Building a great chain of Aerodromes for the British Commonwealth Air Training Plan.

at Trenton and Camp Borden, Ontario, were absorbed immediately into the Plan, however, as were other facilities, fashioned by the far-sighted men who had created the Dominion's great coast-to-coast Trans-Canada Air Lines, without detriment to the flow of transcontinental air travel, sharply increased by the demands of a people at war.

The months of autumn and winter, 1939-40, then, were devoted to acquisition of land and construction of aerodromes, to the recruiting and training of the men who were to become the permanent personnel of the Plan and to obtaining essential equipment for large-scale training, once the wheels should begin to roll. To the pre-war flying clubs, through the medium of charters granted to them as Flying Training Schools, and to commercial operators, by similar device, went a great part of the duty of elementary pilot and observer training. The nation, in short, was taking advantage of every capable organisation of experience within its borders. Thus the first eight Elementary schools, opened in June and July, 1940, at Malton, Fort William and London, Ontario, at Windsor Mills, Quebec, Lethbridge, Alberta, Prince Albert, Saskatchewan, Windsor, Ontario and Vancouver, B.C., were operated in each instance by groups of ardent and patriotic men who came from the civilian flying world of pre-war days. The fortnight from October 14th to 28th saw six further elementary establishments in operation at St. Catharines, Ontario and Mount Hope, adjacent to the city of Hamilton, at Cap de la Madeleine, near Three Rivers, Quebec, at Goderich and St. Eugene, Ontario and at Portage la Prairie, Manitoba. The two remaining schools required to fill out the elementary flight structure opened before the year's end (on November 11th) at Regina and Edmonton.

By the end of 1940 seven Service Flying Training Schools had been opened. The term signifies nothing of the task involved. First came the surveying of sites innumerable during the autumn of 1939 and the selection of the most favourable. Then came the job of grading and levelling, often even of stumping the fields-in-the-making, the building of hangars, barracks and all the adjunctive buildings which go into the making of a great aerodrome, the whole topped with the laying of runways.

The first Service Flying Training School (Number One) required no such construction work, as it was allocated to the existing field at Camp Borden, north of Toronto. It began to function, for the training of instructors, on November 1st, 1939. Number Two followed on August 5th, 1940, at Uplands, Ottawa, on the field adjacent to the city originally built as the capital's commercial airport, primarily for the use of the Trans-Canada line. Number Three Service Flying Training School opened at Calgary on October 28th, and No. Five at Brantford, Ontario, on Armistice Day. Numbers Six and Seven, at Dunnville, Ontario and MacLeod, Alberta, received their first classes on November 25th, and Number Eight, at Moncton, New Brunswick, on the 29th.

Meanwhile four Observers' Schools, under civilian direction, had been put into commission at Malton (Toronto), Edmonton, Regina and London, on May 27th, August 5th, September 16th and November 25th. Numbers 1, 2 and 4 Bombing and Gunnery Schools were opened on August 19th, September 28th and November 25th, at Jarvis, Ontario, Mossbank, Saskatchewan and Fingal, Ontario. Number One Air Navigation School was in operation on the 1st of February on the great air field at Trenton, whence it was subsequently moved to Rivers, Manitoba, on completion of the field on the prairies. Thus 31 flying establishments directly under the Plan were in operation at the end of 1940, in addition to the Central Flying School at Trenton, primarily for the training of instructors and other aspects of advanced flying. The great Plan was on the way to maximum production. As to the manner in which the physical structure of the Plan was put together, the report of J. A. Wilson, M.E.I.C., Director of

Civil Aviation, Department of Transport, Ottawa, is highly clarifying. The Report, covering the first year, states in part:

"While the discussions leading to an Inter-Governmental Agreement were proceeding, organizations were being created to supervise and execute the Training Plan. A Supervisory Committee was formed consisting of three members of the Canadian Cabinet, the Minister of Defence for Air, the Minister of Munitions and Supply, and the Minister of Finance; the High Commissioners for the United Kingdom, and Australia; the Chief of Air Staff, R.C.A.F.; the Air Member for Training, R.C.A.F.; Senior Officers for the Royal, the Royal Canadian, the Royal Australian and the Royal New Zealand Air Forces, and a representative of the Treasury.

"Under this committee the responsibility for the administration of the Training Plan was placed in charge of the Air Member for Training of the Canadian Air Council, Air Commodore G.O. Johnston, M.C. A committee was formed in his organization to deal with aerodrome construction. The committee consists of the Chief of Air Staff, Air Vice-Marshal L. S. Breadner, D.S.C., Chairman, and the following members: Mr. J. S. Duncan, Deputy Minister for Air; Air Commodore G. O. Johnston, M.C., Air Member for Air Organization and Training; Air Commodore R. Leckie, D.S.O., D.S.C., D.F.C., Director of Training; Group Captain F. W. Long, Director of Air Organization; and an R.C.A.F. Officer as Secretary.

"With this committee the officers of the Civil Aviation Division have worked in the closest liaison. The Superintendent, Airways, Department of Transport, Mr. A. D. McLean, and Air Inspectors and Engineers of the Civil Aviation Division attend its meetings and furnish the committee with full information on all matters under consideration. The committee indicates to the Department of Transport desirable locations for the various types of schools. Following preliminary investigation reports, a field party, consisting of an Inspector and an Engineer of the Department of Transport and an Air Force Officer, decides in the field on the sites upon which detailed surveys should be made. When detailed surveys are received by the Department of Transport engineering plans and estimates for the development of the site are prepared and submitted to the Director of Air Services and the Deputy Minister of Transport for approval. If approved, these are passed to the Deputy Minister of National Defence for Air in a letter giving these estimates in detail. This estimate is then considered by the Aerodrome Development Committee, the merits of the site compared with others, and a final decision is reached as to whether it should be developed. The committee then recommends to the Minister of Defence for Air that funds be made available from the appropriations for the Air Training Plan for the development of the site. If this is given, a Financial Encumbrance making available to the Department of Transport the sum necessary for the development is prepared allocating funds for the purpose.

* * *

"The Superintendent, Airways, of the Civil Aviation Division, is in charge of the detailed execution of all work for the plan undertaken by the Department of Transport. He has wide experience in aviation, having been a pilot in the last war, and made the original aerodrome selections in the Prairie Provinces in 1929 and 1930 for the Trans-Canada System and has since then been responsible for the airport planning and construction on the Trans-Canada Airway and elsewhere in the Dominion.

"The selection of the airport sites and their survey was the responsibility of the District Airway Inspectors, Messrs. W. S. Lawson, Western District, British Columbia and Alberta; J. R. Robertson, Central Saskatchewan and Manitoba; S. S. Foley, Ontario; S. Graham and E. Hickson, Quebec and the Maritime Provinces. In the Fall of 1939 every member of the staff who

The Construction Period: Building a great chain of Aerodromes for the British Common
wealth Air Training Plan. (Top right) In the beginning at Pendleton, Ontario. (Lowe
right) The same scene a few weeks later.

could be spared was put on this work so that ground surveys might be started as quickly as possible. Their job was to select the sites; supervise the detailed surveys and see that all pertinent information was placed on the survey plans; assist as necessary the Canadian National Railways' Land Agents in obtaining options; and consult with the Civil Engineering Staff in regard to the efficient construction of the airport from the airman's point of view.

"The formation of a suitable Engineering Organization to carry out the construction work was simplified because the Department already had an engineering staff which had been busy on the building of the Trans-Canada Airway for the past eight years and had, therefore, a wide experience in this new phase of engineering which could only be obtained through practical experience.

They were familiar with the conditions and problems to be faced in the different districts of the Dominion. This organization, however, was comparatively small and it was necessary to enlarge it greatly. The size of the programme and the speed with which it must necessarily be carried out made it desirable to divide the work between two organizations at Headquarters so as to reduce the burden on the key engineers of the organization.

"The existing Airway Engineering Staff were fully familiar with the then existing airports as they had built them. It was accordingly decided that they should be made responsible for the improvement of the aerodromes which might be used for the Plan and all work connected with them, and that the new temporary Airway Engineering Organization should be formed to deal with all new aerodromes. This new organization was given the services of certain of the experienced key men from the permanent staff to assist them.

"The idea underlying this division of engineering work was that so far as circumstances permitted, the continuity of work on the Trans-Canada System should not be interfered with by this large, new programme which had suddenly been imposed on the Division and that when the Air Training Plan work was over the temporary staff could be released and our permanent organization would continue their normal duties. In addition, it should be remembered that, though the Trans-Canada Airway had been in successful operation for two years, much work was still required every year to bring it up and maintain it to the required standard.

"Mr. G. L. McGee, Chief Airway Engineer, and most of his staff were, therefore, put in charge of this phase of the work, while a parallel organization was formed to design and build the new airports. This new organization was placed in charge of Mr. F. C. Jewett who had just finished the construction of the Newfoundland airport, one of the largest in the world. Mr. A. B. Holand, who was formerly Assistant Chief Engineer in the Airways Section, and had wide experience in airport work, was detailed to assist Mr. Jewett in the new organization.

"This form of organization, though adopted with some misgivings at the time, seemed to be the best way of getting the work done in time, and it has worked admirably. This division of responsibility only applied to Headquarters, as in the field the work all comes under the District Airway Engineers, most of whom had had long experience in such work under the Department. These were Messrs. F. Proctor, British Columbia; A. L. Somerville, Alberta; T. Chillcott, Saskatchewan; E. F. Cooke, Manitoba; G. W. Smith, Southern Ontario and A. B. Flintoff, Eastern Ontario; O. L. Colborne, Quebec; and A. S. Donald the Maritime Provinces. All work in each Province was controlled from the District Offices and Resident Engineers were appointed on each project to supervise the work.

"An Electrical Engineering section was already in existence in the Civil Aviation Branch to deal with problems arising out of lighting, power and communication services.

"Engineers with specialized knowledge and training were added to the Headquarters staff to deal with paving specifications and inspection, water supply, and the production of turf surfaces on the aerodromes.

* * *

"A rough and ready classification of airports in Canada on October 1st, 1940, showed:—

(1) Airports of developed dimensions of 3000 feet or more. 37

(2) Airport sites known to be capable of development to 3000 feet or more and of which surveys had been made. 5

(3) Airports then in use under 3000 feet. 46

(The total number of airports and airport sites still undeveloped, but about which information was on record, was 153).

"In the first two classes were the airports of the Trans-Canada System and those in preparation for its extension. This had been built for civil transportation but when the crisis came its construction was seen to be doubly justified. No project of more importance to National Defence had been undertaken since the World War. Good airports at 100 mile intervals, with emergency landing fields at closer spacing in unsettled and difficult country, hangar accommodation, weather and communication services, and radio aids to air navigation and lighting, were in being from Coast to Coast, which allowed the free movement of aircraft and gave the R.C.A.F. fine modern airports for the rapid expansion of their service.

"The Trans-Canada airports had been built as transport airports, that is, they were not all-way turf fields as preferred by the Air Force, but built on the landing strip principle by which a system of two or more landing strips 500 feet wide by 3000 feet or more long are laid out on the field in the form of a "△", "+" or "T" shape and the rest of the field cleared and rough graded only. This was the most economical development and fully met transport requirements. Since the sites had been carefully selected and planned for future development, to adapt these airports to Air Force use for Elementary and Air Observers' Schools was comparatively simple, calling for the fine grading and seeding of the other portions of the transport aerodromes not previously finished and by adding taxi strips to give access to R.C.A.F. hangars as necessary. Experience has shown that if an aerodrome is required for use at all seasons of the year, hard surface runways were necessary to give sufficient bearing during the Spring and Fall seasons. Such runways had been built at all major airports on the airway system.

"Certain sections of the Trans-Canada Airway and its connections were not suitable for training purposes because of inaccessibility, climate, proximity to the international boundary, or the nature of the surrounding country. This applies particularly to Northern Ontario and the Rocky Mountains. Nova Scotia was considered out of bounds too, as far as training was concerned, as it was the scene of intensive Active Service operations. Many fine aerodromes could, therefore, not be considered, but the Department of Transport was able to offer for the use of the Training Plan, as soon as buildings to accommodate the training schools could be built, twenty-four airports which required, in most cases, comparatively little work to adapt them for training purposes. As some of the larger airports could accommodate both an Elementary and an Air Observers' School, these twenty-four airports could accommodate 14 Elementary, 1 Air Navigation, 6 Air Observers, 2 Bombing and Gunnery schools, besides the main aerodromes for 12 Service Flying Training

The Construction Period: Building a great chain of Aerodromes for the British Commonwealth Air Training Plan.

Schools and Relief aerodromes for 2 more. The existence of these ready-made airports made possible the acceleration of the Training Plan. Twice as many Elementary Flying Training Schools and Service Flying Training Schools will be open before the end of 1940 as had originally been contemplated.

* * *

"As shown in the preceding paragraph, existing airports could take care of about one-half of the original programme. New sites must, therefore, be found for the remainder. Time pressed. October (1939) was already half gone and the advent of snow would increase the difficulty of making reliable surveys. Field parties were, therefore, organized as quickly as possible in the three Prairie Provinces, Southern Ontario and Quebec, and the Maritime Provinces, to find all the new sites required before the Winter set in. These parties consisted of an Airway Inspector, an Airway Engineer, both experienced in the location and construction of aerodromes, and an R.C.A.F. Officer.

"The selection of aerodrome sites even in the Prairie Provinces and in good agricultural land is not an easy task. Good drainage is the first essential. All approaches to the aerodromes must be clear of obstructions. The ordinary amenities of civilization are very necessary near these schools. They must, therefore, be easy of access by road or rail to some nearby centre of population. Ample water supply, proximity to a reliable power supply and to good road building material are also essentials.

"The Air Force organization for the Training Plan provided for four separate Training Commands, two in Western Canada and two in Eastern Canada. It was desirable that the whole programme should be divided between these four Commands as equally as circumstances permitted. On other grounds it was desirable that the activities of the Training Plan should be as widespread as the physical character and climate of the Dominion permitted.

"In the Prairie Provinces the climate and terrain were particularly suitable for a Plan of this kind. Western Canada could have accommodated the whole programme, if this had been necessary. The uncertainty of water supply and difficulty of growing good turf were handicaps as well as its distance from the main centres of population and industry. The endeavour has been to secure, to all parts of the country, the benefits arising from the large expenditures involved in building aerodromes for the Training Plan. Every effort has been made as well, in the location of the new aerodromes, to ensure that they will be of some use in the post war period and will serve the peace time needs of our growing civil air transportation system.

"The plan of operation of the survey parties was to study in the office the topographical maps available of each district and mark on them the locations where a level area of approximately one square mile could be obtained. A reconnaissance was then made from the air of such areas, noting particularly the approaches to the site, its accessibility by road and rail, and indications of drainage so as to avoid swampy and low lying areas. After this reconnaissance an examination on foot was made of the apparently suitable sites and preliminary investigation reports of these were prepared. These survey reports were then forwarded to Ottawa by Air Mail for discussion with the Air Training Command. The most favourable were then approved for detailed ground surveys. A reconnaissance was made of approximately 2000 sites, survey reports were filed of over 200 and topographical surveys were made of about 150 sites. It is safe to say we know the location of practically every suitable aerodrome site in the districts covered.

"It was essential, if real progress was to be made during the Summer construction season of 1940, that detailed engineering surveys of the sites required during 1940 and 1941 should be available in the Ottawa offices by the end of 1939. This would enable construction plans and specifications to be drawn up for

the work during the Winter months so as to permit of tenders being called for early in the Spring so that work might start just as soon as the frost was out of the ground. If this could be done, the full working season of 1940 would be taken advantage of.

"All sites required during that year and two-thirds of 1941 must be completed in the Fall of 1940 as Winter conditions do not permit of aerodrome construction in this country.

* * *

"The problem of putting fifty or sixty survey parties to work at short notice was solved with the assistance of the Provincial Highway Departments who were then laying off their highway survey parties for the winter. The wholehearted co-operation of these services and the open nature of the Fall season of 1939 made possible the completion of 80% of the surveys before the snow fell. This saved at least six months in the execution of the programme and gave the Airway Engineering Service of the Civil Aviation Division the four winter months to prepare their plans and specifications. The contour plans of the aerodrome sites furnished by the Provincial Highway Engineering Departments were certainly a credit to these services.

"The work was done with great speed but in spite of this, the most accurate details were given of our requirements. All winter long, as the survey plans were received, work went on in laying out the aerodromes to take the best advantage of the natural features of the site. Plans and specifications for the grading, drainage, hard surfacing and lighting were then put in hand. At the same time, full information was made available to the R.C.A.F. so that their buildings might be planned to fit in with the general development.

"The Elementary Schools call for an all-way turf surface as only light aircraft are used and, with the exception of a week or two in the spring when the frost is coming out of the ground, experience shows that in most districts no expensive hard surfaces were necessary. The Air Observers, Bombing and Gunnery, Air Navigation, and Service Flying Training Schools required hard surfaces as their aircraft are all heavier types and the continuous operation required could not be guaranteed at all seasons of the year without pavements. These were usually laid out in a triangular form to provide for 3000 foot runways, sea level basis, in six directions of wind.

"The interior triangle bounded by the runways is fine graded and seeded to grass, as well as a 250 foot strip on the outside of the pavements. At the Service Flying Training Schools it was necessary to provide for the landing of five aircraft abreast. The landing strips were, therefore, at least 1000 feet wide with two hard surfaced and three grass runways. Under the worst conditions, the two hard surfaced runways provide for two simultaneous aircraft movements, or provide for one-way traffic with a return strip for taxiing on the ground.

* * *

"The adequate zoning of the aerodromes presented another problem. Power was taken under the Defence Air Regulations to pass regulations preventing the building of obstructions on property adjacent to an aerodrome used for National Defence purposes at a ratio of 50 : 1, that is, 1 foot vertical for every 50 feet horizontal from the end of each landing strip for a flightway width 600 feet wider than the landing strip of 500 feet-1000 feet, and one in 20 at other points on the perimeter. Wherever possible ample land was taken to provide for the extension of the landing strips to 5000 feet should this be found necessary.

"The zoning of the aerodromes must not only prevent the building of obstructions on its boundaries but must also provide that buildings on the aerodrome do not interfere with the free use of the landing areas by aircraft. Buildings were, as far as possible, concentrated in one area, preferably convenient to the

Building One of The World's Greatest Aerodromes, ''Somewhere in Canada'', 1940.

landing strip in the direction of the prevailing wind to reduce the amount of taxiing to the minimum and to good entrance roads. Hangars were set back on a zoned line parallel to this strip with provision for a 150 feet taxi strip and a 200 feet apron in front of the hangar entrance so that aircraft could stand out for refuelling and running up, and awaiting their turns to use the field without interference with flying operations. Clearing rights on adjacent properties were obtained where necessary and buildings, trees, power lines and other obstructions were removed to the required ratios.

* * *

"The acquisition of land for aerodromes up to date has involved the purchase of approximately 40,000 acres in every Province of the Dominion. To solve this problem the assistance of the Canadian National Railways was sought. They had, under Colonel F. Clarke, Chief Land Surveyor and Property Commissioner, a Dominion-wide organization familiar with this work. As soon as an aerodrome was approved for detailed survey, a description of the property required was given to Colonel Clarke and his local Land Agent was instructed to obtain options on it wherever possible.

"Nearly every aerodrome involved several properties and it was not always possible to obtain options covering the whole area, but every endeavour was made to obtain options on part of it at least, which would govern a fair price for the remainder to some extent. This has involved an immense amount of work. Over 500 separate options were secured for the purchase of property and, in addition, another 235 covering the clearance of obstructions such as trees, barns, windmills, within the zoned area, and the right to construct ditches for drainage purposes where necessary.

"The value of the property purchased or on which options are still outstanding is over two and a quarter million dollars and an additional fifty thousand dollars has been paid for clearances, etc. Leases have been arranged on all the properties required for Air Firing and Bombing Ranges by the C.N.R. Lands Department as well.

"As soon as final approval had been given by the Department of National Defence for the development of any site, these options were taken up, or failing that, an expropriation plan was filed to cover the area required. In no case has the work been delayed through failure to secure the necessary rights to enter properties in time to permit the contractors to start work.

* * *

"The Department of Transport also undertook to provide power, lighting and telephone. Here again we had an experienced organization, under Mr. H. Ainsworth, ready to tackle this phase of the work as it was no different from equipping the Trans-Canada Airway with similar facilities.

"The provision of power is a major item. Certain schools have as much as 1000 horse-power. Most of this energy is required for lighting, with a smaller part for motor load. This load is the equivalent in size to a town of a thousand to fifteen hundred population.

"In the Eastern provinces, including Quebec and Ontario, little difficulty is experienced in meeting the power requirements. These provinces are covered with a power network, so that comparatively short lines only are required. However, for the larger loads, it has been necessary in most cases to reconstruct substations.

"In the Western provinces power is at a premium, particularly where it is generated by steam or Diesel plants. It has necessitated interlinkage of smaller systems to get better diversity and increase quantity. In some instances, stand-by plants are brought into continuous operation. In one case, it has been necessary to add Diesel plants.

"It might be of interest to note that the total demands for all schools will probably be as high as 20,000 kilowatts. This is a good sized load, but due to its being distributed across Canada it has been established without major plant construction.

"It is the responsibility of this Department to negotiate for such power line and distribution system construction as required, to see that incoming lines do not obstruct flightway approaches, and to see that existing lines are removed where necessary. The problem of salvage must be considered, if at some future date the projects are abandoned, contracts must be prepared to allow for construction, and for energy consumed. Provision of power for water supplies and for heating equipment must also be undertaken.

"In lighting the fields for night flying, only the Advanced Training Schools are equipped. In this regard, the Department acts as contractor by preparing plans, ordering materials and organizing field crews to actually install all equipment. In short, the equipment consists of contact lights for each hard-surface runway, a rotating beacon, code beacon, an illuminated wind tee and a ceiling projector for measuring cloud height at night.

"These lighting facilities will be provided, with certain variations, at some fifty-five schools.

"A telephone system is provided at each site, and at the larger schools a regular switchboard is required. Connections have to be made to bombing ranges, which, in most cases, require ten to twenty miles of interconnecting lines. Trunk lines must be established between the school and the urban centre that is close by.

"The establishing of these three services for all schools is well advanced, in spite of periodic advancement of opening dates. It is estimated that these services will amount to more than two and a half million dollars when completed.

"In all this work the Department has had the ready co-operation of Provincial Power Commissions, power companies and municipalities all over the Dominion. A great deal is due to them for their wholehearted assistance.

"In the communication field the help of the Bell Telephone Company has been invaluable. They have not waited our instructions, but have anticipated them in a wonderful way by preparing connections as soon as the sites were selected so that by the time the orders were placed we found the connecting lines available. They have acted in this way not only for their own systems but for Provincial and local telephone services as well. The Department is greatly indebted to Mr. M. B. Hamilton of the Bell Telephone Company for advice and co-operation at all times which has facilitated this phase of the programme.

* * *

"Due to the heavy aircraft traffic it was necessary to construct hard surface runways and taxi strips on all Service Flying Training Schools' main aerodromes and one relief aerodrome to each main, as well as on all Bombing and Gunnery Schools, Air Navigation Schools and Air Observers' Schools.

"As has been seen, the Service Flying Training School's main aerodrome has three double runways, 100 feet wide and 2500 feet long, each at sea level. The Reliefs have three single runways, 100 feet wide and 2500 feet long at sea level, but the layout on the relief aerodrome is designed so as to provide room for three additional runways if required.

"The Bombing and Gunnery Schools, Air Observers' Schools and Air Navigation Schools have three single runways, 150 feet wide and 2500 feet long, at sea level.

* * *

"Competent technical advice has been secured and thorough investigation made to ensure a dependable, clean and adequate water supply for each aerodrome. The gallonage per day varies with the different types of schools, the Elementary calling for

Typical Aerodrome layouts under the Air Training Plan across Canada. Note var
patterns of runways to suit local conditions.

8,000, the Observers 12,000, the Service Flying Training and Air Navigation 40,000, and the Bombing and Gunnery 45,000 gallons.

"Sources of supply have been determined by considerations of safety, health and economy. Thus, provision must be made for the protection of buildings and personnel against fire; the Department of Pensions and National Health has co-operated with Provincial Departments of Health in making chemical and bacteriological analyses; and careful study has been given to comparative costs of available sources, equipment and appurtenances.

"Sources of water supply fall naturally into two groups. In the larger of these are the airports for which an independent supply has been obtained by the development of ground or surface water by means of wells or from lakes or rivers. In the other group are those aerodromes adjacent to towns or cities in which a municipal waterworks system is now adequate or can be made adequate to take care of the requirements of the aerodrome.

* * *

"Many of these municipalities have not waited to be approached in this connection, but have themselves taken the initiative. In addition to submitting proposals to supply water, in some instances at rates less than the actual cost to the municipality, municipal corporations and Public Utilities commissions have placed the facilities of their organizations and the particular knowledge of local problems at the disposal of the government. A willingness to embrace the opportunity to advance such work characterizes the attitude of civic officials and commissioners in every case.

"Among the municipalities which have co-operated in this manner are Brantford and Picton in Ontario; Brandon, Dauphin and Portage la Prairie in Manitoba; Moose Jaw, North Battleford, Saskatoon and Yorkton in Saskatchewan; and Claresholm, McLeod and Medicine Hat in Alberta.

"As may be imagined, many difficult problems have been faced in this phase of the work and it should be remembered that owing to the urgency of the programme it was not always possible to await a final solution of all its many sides before starting construction work. This was specially true in Western Canada but in no case has the opening of any school been delayed through the failure to obtain a satisfactory water supply. In one or two cases, however, construction on an otherwise satisfactory site has had to be abandoned for lack of a good supply of water.

* * *

"On many of the airports a grass turf is to be used exclusively, and even where hard-surfaced runways are provided the turf is most important. In all cases a satisfactory turf has to be obtained in a minimum length of time to make the airports available for immediate use.

* * *

"Contract plans and specifications began to trickle through to the Contracts Branch in February, 1940, and increased rapidly to a steady stream during March and April. Public tenders were called for during these months and tenders were awarded to the lowest bidder whose tender complied with Departmental requirements. Herr Hitler's rapid work in Europe then hastened the tempo of the Training Plan, and, to save the inevitable delay this course entails, restrictions were withdrawn and many contracts have been negotiated direct on an agreed unit price basis with known reliable contractors. The calling of public tenders on the earlier jobs had established a range of fair prices for each class of work in different districts which made a good guide for these negotiations. So many contracts were being let that the services of all reliable contractors experienced in highway work could be used as soon as the plans and specifications were completed and the properties purchased. Later in the

Summer it was necessary to ask Eastern contractors to invade the West as firms there all had their hands full.

"To press the work and finish as many projects as possible before cold weather came in the Fall, the contractors were put on their metal; and it is very gratifying to be able to state that practically without exception they rose to the emergency, keeping their units operating twenty-four hours a day and seven days a week, whenever weather permitted. The main contracts included clearing, stumping, drainage, grading, paving, seeding and fencing. Aerodrome lighting was done by our own field parties whose foremen had made all installations on the Trans-Canada Airway and were more familiar with the work than any contractor's gang could be. Power, telephone and water supply were, in all cases, separate contracts.

"To September 30th, 1940, aerodrome construction contracts had been let as well as a very large number of subsidiary contracts covering miscellaneous necessary works and material not provided for in the main contracts.

"To date the sum made available by the Department of National Defence from the Joint Air Training Plan's appropriation to the Department of Transport is $24,313,810. This sum is based on the estimated total cost of the development of each project based on our construction plans and specifications plus the land value. Main contracts have been let for 94 projects involving approximately $11,577,628. In addition, the Department has purchased direct for use on these projects $1,870,915 worth of bituminous materials for paving; grass seed and fertilizer, $105,678.; lighting equipment, $717,271.; contracts for power line construction and power services let to date, $138,140.; water services, $186,-185. Work done by Departmental forces excepting lighting installations has cost $117,600., and the cost of Departmental engineering inspection and services, $289,802. The total sum encumbered to date is $17,793,000. These contracts involve the moving of some 20,000,000 cubic yards of earth; the laying of some 300 miles of drains from 6 inches to 36 inches in diameter and the paving of 10,000,000 square yards, equivalent to over 800 miles of standard highway 21 feet wide.

"The average cost of aerodromes for the different classes of schools is as follows:—

"Elementary School aerodrome, all-way field, with grass surface, acreage from 200 upwards........ $100,000

"Air Navigation, Gunnery and Bombing and Air Observers' School aerodromes, all-way fields with three hard surfaces 3,000 feet x 150 feet and hard surfaced taxiways 500 acres and upwards....... $350,000

"Service Flying Training School—1 Main field, where all living quarters, hangars, shops, etc., are concentrated, with double triangular hard surfaced runways; 1 Relief field with hard surfaced triangular runways and one all-way turf Relief field—

"TOTAL for all three aerodromes.................. $800,000.

* * *

"In spite of exceptionally wet weather in May and June, which made grading in clay soils very difficult and jeopardized the success of the programme in some districts, work has gone well. The contractors and their staffs have been in most cases fired with patriotic zeal and have worked manfully day and night to meet the emergency.

"In the case of the earliest opening of schools, construction had to be finished while the school was in operation but part at least of the field was ready for use. The staffs of such schools have carried on cheerfully in spite of the inconvenience of having contractors' machinery working on part of the field.

"Progress to date justifies the statement that in no case will the opening of any school by the revised dates required by the R.C.A.F. be held up by the lack of a usable aerodrome. Expansion

The Construction Period: Typical hangars and Airmen's living quarters under construction on an R.C.A.F. aerodrome, Summer 1940 ''Somewhere in Canada''.

of the programme in July modified greatly the sites originally selected for Elementary or Air Observers' Schools and on which grading was already well advanced. Some of these were now modified for use as Service Flying Training Schools and the additional property required for the larger school was acquired. Elsewhere an Air Navigation School was added on an aerodrome which previously had only been proposed as an Elementary School and the necessary modifications were made to the contract specification. In some cases too the size of the Elementary School was doubled so as to avoid having to construct a new aerodrome. Out of a total of 75 schools, 32 will have their aerodromes completed by September 30th, 1940, with a further 33 scheduled for completion for December 31st, 1940. Compared with the original programme of 64 schools for which aerodromes had to be completed by June 30th, 1942, we shall have completed aerodromes for 65 schools in 1940, leaving only 10 to be carried over into 1941. The following table shows the position:—

DATES OF COMPLETION
(Except Seeding in Some Cases)

	By Sept. 30/40	By Dec. 31/40	1941	TOTAL
E.F.T.S......	13	12	1	26
A.N.S........	1	1	1	3
A.O.S.......	7	1	3	11
B. & G.S.....	2	8	1	11
S.F.T.S......	9	11	4	24
	32	33	10	75

* * *

"A cataclysm of the magnitude of the present War affects all civil activities. Aviation has been no exception. Every phase of flying has been gravely affected by the change-over from peace to war. While meeting the Air Force requirements in all respects, the aim of the Department of Transport has been to ensure that when the time comes to return to normal peace conditions, as much as possible of the war effort and expenditure may be adapted to increasing the facilities for civil air transport in the Dominion.

"The aerodrome situation at any rate will be vastly improved. The size of all the main aerodromes on the Trans-Canada Airway and its principal feeder lines has been increased. New hard surfaces have been added and many fine hangars and other buildings have been built on the aerodromes. Some of these no doubt will still be required by the R.C.A.F. when the war is over, but much may be surplus to their requirements and can be made available for the expansion of our civil transport services. In addition, aerodromes have been built to serve many new districts."

* * *

The broad landscape of the Construction and Get-going problem is ably visualised in the Report of Mr. Wilson, one of Canada's ablest Civil Servants. Other problems, arising from human frailty, were not as simple of solution as might appear from the terminology of an official report, however. Troubles did not begin and end with the selection of airfield sites, nor with the construction of hangars, nor with the acquisition of aircraft. Democracy being the strange institution it is, one not guided entirely by pure reason and human unselfishness, the mere announcement that Canada was about to embark upon an ambitious project involving the construction of aerodromes and other training establishments throughout the country, brought upon Ottawa the descent of locusts invariably to be found when public monies are about to be expended in large amounts. It must not be thought, however, that all those who came entertained only the selfish idea of

bringing revenue into their home areas. The people of every section of the nation urgently wanted to feel the closeness to actuality which the opening of training schools in their immediate vicinities would give. Not always could they understand why they must be left out. Some, of course, were not without guile. The construction of an air field, hangars and barracks means the expenditure of vast sums of money. The subsequent billeting of hundreds of young men adjacent to a town means that much of their pay will reach the cash registers of local merchants. The reader knows only too well that the North American concept of such matters is that every available log should be rolled, every atom of influence be brought to bear to prevail upon those in authority to build at, say, Corner Crossing. Hence the weeks during which the skeleton of the Plan was being hammered together on the Hill were also weeks during which delegations from all over the Dominion descended on Ottawa, demanding, pleading, cajoling, running the whole gamut of that strange institution known as "pull" in order to secure the placing of each flying field "where it will do the most good". The writer recalls the story of the mayor of a small Canadian city who publicly announced to his townsmen his impending departure for Ottawa to secure an air establishment. "I shall not come back," he cried, "until I have an Air Force station to bring home with me!" History does not record the gentleman's present whereabouts. For all the writer knows he may still be sitting in a Minister's anteroom, determined to implement his pledge. But one thing is sure. There is no air station in his town. Too many hills abut upon its environs to make the region safe country for the tyro pilot.

So the story ran. Delegations rounded up their local members. Prominent hometown business men indicated to their M.P.'s that they had better persuade "the Minister" to come across, or things might not be so pleasant back home come election time. Members talked to Ministers with tears in their eyes. Ministers looked blandly back across the tops of their desks and declared themselves powerless. The airports, the Initial Training Schools, the E.F.T.S. establishments and the S.F.T.S. fields were going to be put where the engineers said they *should* go, not where any politician wanted them. That was that. Probably for the first time in Canadian history tens of millions of dollars of the public's money were about to be expended without an eye on the ballot box, this despite an impending General Election.

* * *

Meanwhile, as the delegations besieged the anterooms of Cabinet and the offices of private Members, while the engineers and surveyors checked and double checked potential aerodrome sites from coast to coast, and while the construction industry began to gather together its tools for the greatest task it has ever performed, the Plan was taking shape in other directions. Once the air fields were under way, once the training aircraft and other equipment had been found, what were we going to do about personnel with which to tackle the young recruit and make a flying man of him? In this direction the Canadian Government wisely made use of every available experienced human unit on which its hands could be laid. Although the fact is not generally realised by the public, the British Commonwealth Air Training Plan, in the beginning and now, was and is a combination of civilian and Service effort. Canada, in short, marshalled its air-experienced man-power for the task ahead. For example: Almost before the ink on the British Commonwealth Air Training agreement had been dry, the organisation for elementary flying training had been created through the medium of the Flying Clubs, that nation-wide association of "Sunday pilots", many of them veterans of the last war in the air, who had done so much to keep air-mindedness alive in Canada between wars. Representations were made immediately on the outbreak of war by

With Canada's Pre-war "Sunday Pilots"; (upper left) the Cape Breton Club; (u...
right) Hawker Furies of the R.A.F. visit St. Hubert (Montreal); (centre left) Ha...
Flying Club; (centre right) Ottawa Flying Club; (lower left) Border Cities Aero C...
(lower right) Regina Flying Club.

the Flying Clubs, through their national association, that Elementary Flying Training Schools should be established on a civilian basis and the Clubs entrusted with the organisation and operation of these schools, each Club to function in its own locality. Obviously the Clubs possessed invaluable experience in pilot-training, accumulated over a number of years. Moreover they were prepared to undertake the task on a patriotic basis. Thanks to the vision of the Minister of National Defence, the late Norman Rogers, the basis was accepted and, as the Plan took form during 1940, seventeen Clubs were called upon to organise schools.

The idea was not entirely new. As early as 1937 representations had been made by the Association with a view to having the elementary training of R.C.A.F. pilots placed on a civilian basis in which the Clubs could participate. These were revived towards the end of 1938. In February, 1939, the Clubs again approached the Ministers of Transport and National Defence, shortly prior to the announcement of an enlarged pilot-training programme for the R.C.A.F. The Clubs then entered into negotiations with officers of the Royal Canadian Air Force and a form of contract was in process of being hammered together by the end of March. As a result eight selected Flying Clubs were given contracts for pilot-training and began their initial classes on June 5th, 1939. The Plan was immediately extended on the outbreak of war, the Clubs being invited to bring their remaining fourteen units into the programme.

It was while this scheme was in the development stage that announcement of the British Commonwealth Air Training Plan proposal was made by the Prime Minister. Immediately the Flying Clubs put forward to the Minister of National Defence the view they should be permitted to continue to give Elementary training to embryo Service pilots in the expanded scheme. In addition the Executive urged that thirteen full-scale Elementary Flying Training Schools, then being discussed, should be converted into twenty-six half-scale schools, so that every Flying Club in the country should have an opportunity of conducting a school and all the man-power and experience of the Clubs be placed at the nation's disposal. Discussion continued through November and December while the intra-Commonwealth Plan was taking form.

Immediately prior to New Year's Day, 1940, the Clubs were called into final conference by the Minister of National Defence. Meetings with the Minister, Department officials, the Chief of the Air Staff and other high officers of the R.C.A.F., as well as with the heads of the United Kingdom Air Mission, followed. At these the terms of a proposed contract with civil companies, stemming from the Flying Clubs, for the operation of Elementary Flying Training Schools were discussed, as was a cost schedule. The meetings lasted throughout the first week of January and a form of contract was worked out which has been in effect from that day forward.

During the discussions the Clubs' executive urged that the units which were to be called upon to operate schools under the Air Plan should be kept occupied with continuing classes of pupil pilots until the Plan itself should be ready to go into operation, a proposal to which Mr. Rogers agreed, although the idea was at variance with plans in process of formation for the larger task.

After much discussion another knotty problem was settled when the Government concurred in the Clubs' suggestion that the Elementary schools should not be created through competitive bidding, as this might have the effect of destroying the Club movement, based on patriotic impulse rather than on making profits. Original plans called for the establishment of eight Elementary Schools before the end of 1940. Instead sixteen were in operation prior to the year's close, and of these fifteen stemmed directly from Flying Club organisations. As a result of speed-up

orders two schools were opened in less than four weeks from the first call to organise. One school actually opened a year ahead of time. All, excepting the first two, went into operation months ahead of originally anticipated dates. In addition they handled from the beginning substantial increases over the numbers of students originally contemplated.

To say that Canada's patriotic civilian flying men proved equal to their self-imposed task is sheer understatement. As the Chief of Air Staff said at a luncheon of school managers on October 21st, 1940, "We didn't think you could do it. Now we know you can." In one case the entire capital required to finance the company organised by a Club to operate a school was supplied from that Club's own treasury. In other cases it was given, or subscribed with or without interest, by local friends and supporters. At no school organised by a Flying Club does any individual or commercial organisation share in any surplus which may accrue from the service performed. Thus allotment of the Elementary Schools to the Flying Clubs immediately brought to the Government the patriotic services of civil organisations experienced in pilot training and removed from the operation any question of private profit. All proceeds remaining after bills are paid are ploughed back into the coffers of the Clubs themselves, to be held as a financial backlog for the promotion of civil aviation after the war.

Community interest has been greatly encouraged, too, by the attachment of elementary schools to local organisations. In the words of the Annual Report of the Canadian Flying Clubs Association for 1939 "The combination of civil and Service organisation offers opportunities for exercise of local enthusiasm and patriotic service unique in the national war effort." Management is for the most part supplied by business men, generally pilots of the last war, who are anxious to serve and who find in the elementary schools an outlet for their energies. The community also has an opportunity to serve in providing the necessary amount of capital for the companies arising from the Clubs. In some cases this was given outright and in others it was loaned with the stipulation that no interest will be accepted. At one school the County Council looked after the financing and at another, city authorities saw it through. In this manner, then, did patriotic Canadians get behind their own Air Training Plan. Community organisations of all kinds actively supported the schools. In the City of Vancouver, for example, an Air Supremacy Drive was organised which raised more than $100,000 and paid for fourteen out of a total complement of twenty-six aircraft issued to No. 8 E.F.T.S. In St. Catharines, No. 9 E.F.T.S. has the support of a Women's Auxiliary which has financed and furnished, and now maintains, a canteen. Recreation rooms at the school have been furnished by the women of the city. Accommodations are provided for visiting relations of young airmen and the ladies of the town may be said to have taken charge of the school's social life. The Hamilton Gyro Club provided a piano for the recreation centre at No. 10 E.F.T.S. A sportsmen's organisation donated hockey equipment. Throughout the country the Elementary Schools bear witness to the fact that this is a people's war by the manner in which communities everywhere have rallied to the support of this great civilian enterprise.

* * *

By the beginning of 1941 more than half of the Elementary Flying Training Schools of the Commonwealth Air Training Plan had been brought into operation, and all were on a civilian basis. A considerable number remained to be established, including several of double size, and a measure of doubt appeared to exist in some official quarters as to whether the Flying Clubs and those associated with them were capable of carrying through to successful conclusion a task which had, admittedly, been well begun.

With Canada's Pre-war "Sunday Pilots"; (upper left and right) Director of C...
Aviation, J. A. Wilson, during Toledo Cruise in 1938. (Centre left) judges at Web...
Competition, Saskatoon 1938. (Centre right) Webster Competition 1935; (lower left)...
Kingston Club 1938; (lower right) Instructor Ernie Taylor of Hamilton Aero Club with pu...

During the course of the year, however, all of the remaining E.F.T.S. called for under the Plan were established on a civilian basis, and every call for expansion of training over the original schedules was met successfully by the civilian organisations. Assistance was rendered by the Clubs in the organisation of new schools, such as at Oshawa where three groups were brought together to form an operating company, and at Quebec, where existing schools were called upon heavily in order to assist the Quebec E.F.T.S. to organise in a short period of time. The Board of Directors of No. 13 E.F.T.S. at St. Eugene (an offshoot of the Ottawa Flying Club) loaned the services of their manager for the organisation period, and at one time twenty-three of the key men from St. Eugene were at Quebec to ensure the smooth functioning of the new school. So goes the tale of co-operative effort.

An important development during 1941 through the medium of the Flying Clubs Association, was the voluntary reduction by the operating companies of the amount of profit per flying hour under the contract, already mentioned. On account of the increase in hours flown, through increase in the size of the E.F.T.S., the amount of profit being earned was nearly double that originally intended. The offer of the operating companies to reduce the original rate by 50%, dating back to the time when the number of pupils was first increased, was acknowledged and accepted by the Minister of National Defence for Air.

Close contact with the Department has been maintained in the matter of supply and distribution of flying instructors, and in arranging transfers and replacements. Under the original civilian instructor scheme, later changed, as will be noted later, some 350 offers of service were dealt with by the Association, and approximately one-third of these were subsequently accepted for training by the R.C.A.F.

Instructor-training has been one of the primary problems of the British Commonwealth Air Training Plan from its inception. Today, of course, with the Plan itself in full swing, such difficulties tend to disappear. But in the beginning the problem at times seemed insoluble. Instructors for the Service Flying Training Schools were provided from the inception of the schools, of course, by the permanent Royal Canadian Air Force and, later, from the ranks of those who had passed through the schools. In the Elementary Schools, due in part to their civilian formation, a problem of altogether different aspect had to be faced. In the beginning the Clubs provided instructors from their own membership and employed, as well, numbers of commercial pilots. In August, 1940, however, this plan was changed. Men with from 50 to 150 hours of flying in their log books were taken into the R.C.A.F. with the rank of AC2 (Aircraftman, second class) and were sent to the Central Flying School at Trenton, for instructors' courses. On completion of these, successful candidates were given indefinite leave of absence without pay and the companies operating the E.F.T.S. establishments then hired them as instructors. From this new system arises one of the subjects of debate, unavoidable in a combined Civilian-Service operation. The Service thinks well of it. The Civilians do not. Possibly difficulties lie ahead as this is written, late in 1941. But they will be resolved. That is our way.

"The present policy," says a Report of the Flying Clubs Association, "whereby all replacement and future instructor requirements of the E.F.T.S. are to be provided from the graduates of the Empire Air Training Plan and sent to the schools on a civilian basis, appears to present many problems, especially as regards control and adequacy of supply. Unless the individual schools are to be permitted to train their own instructors, a plan which many favour but which appears unlikely of acceptance, then a satisfactory solution remains to be found."
So goes Democracy at war!

At the end of 1941, 10,000 people were employed in staff positions at the Elementary Schools.
In any case, operation of the Elementary Flying Training Schools of the Training Plan by companies formed out of the Flying Clubs has provided final and conclusive evidence of the worth of the Flying Club movement, first established by the Civil Aviation authorities in 1927. The two primary objectives of the Flying Clubs, to develop airports and encourage air mindedness, were achieved several years ago. The third objective, the training of pilots, has reached its climax in the operation of the E.F.T.S. by the Flying Clubs.
"No greater reward," says the Association's Report for 1941, "could have come to those who have supported the Flying Club movement through 15 years, than that they should be granted the responsibility which is now in their hands. No greater service could have been rendered to Canada. Investment of public funds in Flying Club support, never large, has been repaid many times over. The faith and vision of the Civil Aviation officials behind the Flying Clubs, and particularly of Mr. J. A. Wilson, Director of Air Services and formerly Controller of Civil Aviation, has been well rewarded."
The Committee of the House of Commons appointed in March, 1941, to examine into War Expenditures appointed a sub-committee to inquire into, among other matters, contracts with civilian Flying Clubs, associations or companies. In its first report, presented on June 4, the sub-committee stated that the Training Officers of the R.C.A.F. had expressed their complete satisfaction in the training results of the Elementary Flying Training Schools, and went on to say: "The committee recommends that we should continue to take advantage of the services of these civilian flying companies, and that the services rendered by them be extended to their full capacity."
In its second report, presented on November 3, the sub-committee concluded that the Elementary Flying Training Schools are managed with a high degree of efficiency, and stated that good management and a marked degree of *esprit de corps* had reduced the cost of training per pupil 12 percent below the original estimate, high testimony to the unselfish patriotism of those sponsoring the movement, who turned back to the people of Canada the overage in proceeds.

* * *

To summarise the civilian effort in the establishment of Elementary Flying Training Schools under the British Commonwealth Air Training Plan, the following Table reveals the nation-wide nature of this activity. Schools, location and sponsorship are listed in numerical order:—
No. 1—Malton—Malton Flying Training School Ltd., Malton, Ontario.—E. O. Houghton, Managing Director. (A development of the Toronto Club); No. 2—Fort William—Thunder Bay Air Training School Ltd., Fort William, Ont.—H. F. Dougall, President. (An offshoot of the Lakehead Club); No. 3—London—London Elementary Flying Training School Ltd., London, Ontario.—G. S. Durand, Manager. (The background of which is the London Club). No. 4—Windsor Mills—Windsor Mills Flying Training School Ltd., Windsor Mills, Quebec.—J. K. M. Green, Manager. (Developed by the Montreal Light Aeroplane Club); No. 5—High River—High River Flying Training School Ltd., High River, Alta.—D. K. Yorath, Managing Director. (Stemming from the Calgary Aero Club); No. 6—Prince Albert—Northern Saskatchewan Flying Training School Ltd., Prince Albert, Sask.—S. McKercher, General Manager. (Saskatoon Flying Club); No. 7—Windsor—Windsor Flying Training School Ltd., Windsor, Ontario.—A. A. J. Pelzer, Manager (Border Cities Club); No. 8—Vancouver—Vancouver Air Training Co., Ltd., Sea Island Airport, Eburne, B.C.—L. J. Martin, General Manager (Aero Club of B.C.); No. 9—St. Catharines—

With Canada's Pre-war "Sunday Pilots"; (upper left) Calgary Aero Club; (upper r...
Bill Sumner, Test Pilot, Cub Aircraft, Hamilton; (centre left) an Autogiro takes ...
(centre right) a Gypsy Moth, original trainer of the Flying Clubs; (lower left) student ...
off on his first solo, Toronto Flying Club; (lower right) Pre-war fledglings for the R.C. ...

St. Catharines Flying Training School Ltd., St. Catharines, Ontario.—F. S. Pattison, Manager. (St. Catharines Flying Club); No. 10—Hamilton—Hamilton Flying Training School Ltd., Hamilton, Ontario.—G. Moes, Manager. (Hamilton Aero Club); No. 11—Cap de la Madeleine—Quebec Airways (Training) Ltd., Cap de la Madeleine, P.Q.—H. L. Weber, Manager. (Not associated with any Flying Club); No. 12—Goderich—Huron County Flying Training School Ltd., Goderich, Ont.—J. R. Douglas, General Manager. (Kitchener-Waterloo Club); No. 13—St. Eugene—Eastern Ontario Flying School Limited, St. Eugene, Ontario.—Wm. Davidson, Manager. (Ottawa Flying Club); No. 14—Portage la Prairie—Central Manitoba Flying Training School, Portage la Prairie, Manitoba.—C. T. Kaake, Manager. (Winnipeg Flying Club); No. 15—Regina—Regina Elementary Flying School, Limited, Regina, Saskatchewan.— G. C. Rooke, Manager. (Regina Club); No. 16—Edmonton— Edmonton Flying Training School Ltd., Edmonton, Alberta.— D. M. Plunkett, Managing Director. (Edmonton and Northern Alberta Aero Club); No. 17—Stanley—Stanley Flying School, Stanley, Hants County, N.S.—W. H. Stuart, Manager. (Halifax Aero Club); No. 18—Boundary Bay—Boundary Bay Flying Training School Ltd., Ladner, B.C.—L. J. Martin, Managing Director. (Same background as No. 8 E.F.T.S.); No. 19—Virden —Virden Flying Training School Ltd., Virden, Manitoba.— J. R. Morgan, Managing Director. (Moose Jaw and Brandon Clubs in cooperation); No. 20—Oshawa—Ontario County Flying Training School, Oshawa, Ontario.—Charles Robson, Manager. (Kingston and Brant-Norfolk Flying Clubs); No. 21—Chatham —Miramichi Flying Training School Ltd., Chatham, N.B.— J. W. Humphrey, Managing Director. (Moncton, N.B., Club); No. 22—Quebec City—City of Quebec Elementary Flying Training School, Limited.—Ancienne Lorette, P.Q.—Wm. Davidson, Acting Manager. (No club tie-up, organised by private citizens).

*   *   *

Civilian activities under the British Commonwealth Training Plan have by no means been confined to the Elementary Flying Training Schools, however. Under the Plan proper, due to the nature of training involved, Air Observers' Schools have also been operating from the inception of the Plan through private companies formed for the specific task, the operators in many cases stemming from pre-war commercial flying companies engaged primarily in the northern trade with mining camps beyond the railway tracks. Thus No. 1 Air Observers' School at Malton (Toronto) is under the control of Dominion Skyways, Limited, which formed a special Training Company for the job. Canadian Airways (Training) Limited, has No. 2 School at Edmonton. Prairie Flying School, Limited, operates No. 3 Air Observers' School at Regina. No. 4, situated at Crumlin Airport, London, Ontario, is in the hands of Leavens Brothers (Training), Limited and No. 5 at Winnipeg under Winnipeg Air Observers' School, Limited. School No. 6 at Prince Albert is operated by Prince Albert Air Observers' School Limited, No. 7, at Portage la Prairie, Manitoba, by the Portage Air Observer School, Limited, and No. 8 at Quebec by Quebec Airways. Dominion Skyways have a second school, No. 9, at St. Johns, Quebec. No. 10 is at Chatham, N.B., and is operated by Northumberland Air Observer School, Limited.

Many veteran pilots are in service at the Observers' Schools, their primary function being to fly aircraft in which pupils and instructors pursue the practical phases of Observer-training.

Many civilians are also in service at the Bombing and Gunnery stations, where the function of pilots is that of operators of aircraft in which pupils undertake training in special tasks. It is interesting to note that approximately 700 United States pilots were in service at the end of 1941 at the Bombing and Gunnery establishments, and in communications work in various parts of the Dominion. World War pilots below the age of 46 years are accepted at Bombing and Gunnery schools and at the Air Navigation stations.

In reviewing the general scheme of organisation of the Plan, then, it should be noted that, as originally conceived and as at present operated, the great Air Training Scheme is in part civilian and in part Service in its functions. The basic schools (Manning Depots and Initial Training Schools, the functions of which will be discussed in Chapter IV) are Service-operated. Elementary Flying Training Schools are operated by civilian organisations in close association with the pre-war Flying Clubs, Observer Schools function under civilians whose background is primarily commercial aviation. Pre-war pilot-personnel has been impressed into service throughout the country, with the result that in virtually every compartment of the Plan, where the use of civilian flying men is possible, the services of old-time pilots have been utilised, leaving to the Service flier the role of advanced training of the war-flier-to-be.

*   *   *

No round-up of civilian activities in connection with the Air Training Plan and no assessment of Canadian preparedness would be complete without stressing the great part played by the nation's great chain of transcontinental airfields and by the personnel and equipment of its great coast-to-coast airway, Trans-Canada Air Lines. Constructed during the immediate pre-war years, under the driving leadership of Hon. C. D. Howe, then Minister of Transport in the Federal Government and later wartime Minister of Munitions and Supply, the airway was conceived more as a means of bringing the widespread population elements of the thinly settled country into closer communication with each other than with any thought of military benefit. This, at least, was the public's view as it marvelled at the new carrier which could whisk the eastern business man from Montreal to Vancouver in the course of a day. With the coming of war, however, Canadians discovered that they possessed a chain of completely modern military flying fields and equally modern scientific devices to assure safe transportation from point to point across the continent. Thus, as the Plan took form, the first training establishments could be located on the great fields used by the commercial carrier. Hangars, repair shops, many other contributory aids, were at the country's service. Soon 75% of the passengers carried were either Service people or men travelling on business directly associated with the war effort. The occupancy-ratio of Trans-Canada planes quickly became the highest on the American Continent. Mail poundage doubled and redoubled, again because of the war task. Pilots, asked to stay on the job as a national service, gave and still give of their spare time to instruct young men about to enter the Service, or in ferrying military aircraft to fields where they are required for immediate use. The Line's repair shops were placed at the service of the Air Plan. Its instrument shop at Stevenson Field, Winnipeg (operational headquarters of Trans-Canada), was doubled in capacity and soon was working full time in overhauling and repairing aircraft instruments for the R.C.A.F. New buildings have been constructed to speed the job. Trans-Canada service is available to the R.C.A.F. wherever the twain meet. Thus what was conceived as a great peace-time air-line immediately became an integral part of the nation's victory effort, an important line of communication of Canada's War In The Air.

*   *   *

In this chapter, then, the attempt has been made to show the manner in which the Plan itself was brought together and put into operation. A general eye-view of the problems of construction has been given, more specific illustration of which will be found in a later chapter dealing with Canadian industry's great contribution to the fashioning of the Air Plan. The manner in

Mother Fields of the Commonwealth Air Training Plan—Scenes at Central Flying Sch Trenton, Ontario.

which Elementary Schools were founded and put into production has been considered in detail and attention has been paid to various other civilian contributions to the Plan. The problems of development of a purely Canadian aircraft industry, largely devoted to the production of trainers, will be found in the Industrial Section. (Chapter Six).

* * *

Before passing along to the more personal aspects of flier-training, it should be noted that what may be called the Year of Organisation, 1939-40, was largely that of Elementary Training, insofar as the student was concerned. The production of winged pilots, as at Borden and Trenton, was mainly that of instructors. Service Training Schools were opened at Ottawa (August 5th), Saskatoon (September 9th), Calgary (October 28th), Brantford (November 11th), Dunnville, Ontario (November 25th), MacLeod, Alberta (November 25th) and Moncton, New Brunswick (November 29th), but advanced training was only beginning to function as 1940 drew to a close. It will be discussed at length in a later chapter.

Schools opened during 1940 have been listed in an earlier paragraph. As 1940 ended Canada was on the way!

The first intake of aircrew pupils came in the Spring of 1940, when 169 candidates entered No. 1 Initial Training School, at the former Eglington Hunt Club, Toronto, to begin the first tip-to-toe course leading towards winged graduation for service overseas. As the year drew towards its close the Plan was reaching production. On October 28th, the first Pilot class marched on Wings Parade with suitable ceremony at No. 1 S.F.T.S., Camp Borden. On the same date 38 Air Observers received the single-wing emblem of their craft at No. 1 Air Navigation School, Rivers, Manitoba. On November 26th, 26 Wireless-Air Gunners graduated from No. 1 Bombing and Gunnery School at Jarvis and 24 from No. 2 at Mossbank. As 1940 ended, therefore, the great Plan could be said to be reaching the production stage.

Meanwhile the R.C.A.F. had gone into action overseas. In February 1940, No. 110 Army Co-operation Squadron left Canada under command of Squadron-Leader W. D. Van Vliet. No. 112 Squadron followed in May, commanded by Squadron-Leader William Hannah. No. 1 Fighter Squadron under Squadron-Leader E. A. McNab, arrived in the United Kingdom in time to render signal service in the Battle of Britain, taking its own Hurricanes from Canada, but being issued with new aircraft on arrival in the Old Country. Late in the summer of 1940, No. 112 was changed from Army Cooperation to Fighter duties, but did not see action until after the great German blitz. In the main the personnel of these three "token" squadrons was made up from the officer membership of the permanent Royal Canadian Air Force, however, and was not, therefore, a product of the Plan.

* * *

The year brought important changes and one irreplaceable casualty in the realm of administration.

On May 23rd, in order to make lighter the burden resting upon the shoulders of Hon. Norman Rogers who, as Minister of National Defence, had been charged with supervision of the three armed services, Hon. C. G. Power was transferred from the portfolio of Postmaster General to the new Department of National Defence for Air. Thus, for the first time in its history, Canada's flying forces were given their own Ministry, which Major Power continued to administer at the close of war's second year. On July 12th, Mr. Power was also appointed as Associate Minister of National Defence.

Disaster struck on June 10th, when Hon. Norman Rogers who, as Minister of National Defence, had supervised the creation of the Plan, was killed in a flying accident while en route from Ottawa to Toronto. Although the catastrophe has already been mentioned, let it be said again that in Norman Rogers Canada

lost one of its ablest and best beloved sons. Still in early-middle life, a private soldier in the last World War, Mr. Rogers had come to the realm of public affairs from the seats of learning, following a brilliant career as student, culminating in selection to a Rhodes Scholarship at Oxford after World War I. He had served Rt. Hon. William Lyon Mackenzie King as a member of the Prime Minister's secretariat, and was first elected to Parliament in the General Election of 1935, immediately after which he became Minister of Labour. Serving at Labour until shortly after the outbreak of war, he took on the onerous duties of National Defence in the cabinet shuffle of October, 1939, where he remained until his untimely death on June 10th, 1940. As Minister he was indefatigable in his devotion to duty. Throughout the difficult months following the outbreak of war, as Canada moved from what has been described as a standing start into the full swing of the War Effort, the Little Minister was to be found in his office by day and by night. Of frail physique, a sufferer from physical ailments resulting from the last Great War, Norman Rogers gave himself without stint to his new and great role. Those who worked with him . . . Admirals, Generals, Senior Air Officers, civilian members of his personal staff . . . knew him for a great Canadian, a man in whom dwelled great wellsprings of friendship and integrity. Canada has never known a finer son, will never meet greater individual loss than that of the Minister who met his death that June day in the mists of the Lake Ontario shore.

James S. Duncan, Vice-President of the Massey-Harris Company, Limited, of Toronto, served as Acting Deputy Minister of National Defence for Air from April 11th, 1940, to January 31st, 1941. He was replaced as Deputy Minister by S. L. de Carteret, Vice-President of the Canadian International Paper Company, Limited, Montreal, on February 1st, 1941.

* * *

The year 1940 began under strange emotional auspices. Before it was a fortnight old, Prime Minister King, wearying of the assaults of his political critics, dissolved Parliament and sought a vote of confidence from the electorate. For weeks opposing political forces toured the Dominion, the Government staunchly defending its war policies, its critics charging unpreparedness. Certainly the charge held. Canada was not prepared for war. For more than twenty years every effort had been directed towards the ways of peace. Every Government, no matter its shade, had sought the ploughshare, not the sword. No political party which had advanced proposals for all-out armament could have carried a handful of seats in any province. Although a slight increase was made in the arms tempo during the years immediately prior to 1939, it went unheard amid the rumble of cannon wheels in the Old World. Doubtful, indeed, it was if Canadian public opinion could have been carried for war abroad until the nature of the War itself was brought home to the people. Hence when war came it found a nation unprepared. Pacifism changed overnight to a demand for all-out preparation and participation, but the change could not be made in an hour, a day, a week, nor even in a year. Thus, as members of the Administration toiled day and night to move the national machine onto a war footing its critics demanded action. Where was the equipment for our recruits? Where were the training aircraft? With what did we propose to implement our contract with our partner nations, under which we proposed to become the air training centre of the Commonwealth? Where were the spares, the engines, the propellers, the aerodromes? So ran the cry. But the counting of the ballots in March brought a firm commitment from the people in support of the Government of the Day, which was returned to power by an overwhelming majority.

With its re-establishment in power only a few brief weeks behind it, the Government faced the dire news of the Fall of France and the Escape from Dunkirk. Throughout what remained of

Mother Fields of the British Commonwealth Air Training Plan—Training scenes at Camp Borden, Ontario.

the Free World men were lost in the gloom of apparent defeat. What could Britain do now? Could she go on alone? Would she? Would London seek Peace terms to save the British people? Who could have blamed Churchill had he done so? Instead Britain elected to stand or fall alone, to see the fight through to the end, come what might. American Isolationists were saying it would be folly to send more arms and supplies to the beleaguered isle off the coasts of Europe. Better to wait and see. But the Commonwealth and Canada stood firm at Britain's side, and brighter days dawned.

The effects of the Fall of France on the British Commonwealth Air Training Plan were two-fold. It brought about a tremendous stepping-up in the tempo of the job. It deprived the Plan of much needed supplies in engines and training aircraft guaranteed by Britain under the original agreement. In actuality it completely changed the whole approach to the Plan, for what had been Britain's Plan, carried out on Canadian soil, now became Canada's Plan, pure and simple. Originally the Plan had been geared to Britain's programme of aircraft production and would turn out graduates according to the number of aircraft Britain would be able to supply. The fathers of the Plan had failed, in short, to take account of an unpredictable individual named Adolf Hitler. In May, 1940, however, they were suddenly forced to do so. That they did, that the Plan survived at all, that it came into full flower months ahead of original schedules, is one of the miracles of the war.

Ruin stared the Planners in the face. What could they do with a string of half-completed airfields, with only a few advanced trainers in the country, without an industry geared to produce them here and no more planes to come from Britain? One shipload already had been turned back in mid-Atlantic. Canada was even stripping its own coast defences to send first- and second-line machines to the theatre of War. The Canadian Government offered to send overseas its skeleton crew of instructional personnel if Britain required their aid. Many were sent. Meanwhile Britain urged that no abatement in air-crew production should be contemplated. Speaking in Ottawa on June 3rd, Acting Deputy Minister James S. Duncan outlined the emergency steps taken as follows:

"(1) The 112 Squadron is under notice to proceed abroad, the advance party left Ottawa on the 20th of last month and have arrived in England.

"(2) Further Air Force contributions complete with aircraft, guns and wireless equipment, etc., are now standing by ready to proceed overseas.

"(3) A number of young Pilots just graduated from Camp Borden and who, under other circumstances, would have swelled the ranks of our instructors, are proceeding overseas immediately.

"(4) Fighter and Bomber planes ready for immediate action in France have already been despatched to the United Kingdom and others are awaiting suitable transportation.

"(5) Immediate action is being taken to greatly increase the Canadian aircraft industry not only to take the place, where possible, of the machines which the United Kingdom was to have sent us for the Training Plan, but to provide the Mother Country with an ever-increasing number of Fighter and Bomber aircraft for Active Service.

"(6) In order to obviate inevitable delays, special powers had been granted to the Department of Transport and to the Department of Munitions and Supply which will enable them to proceed with the letting of contracts for the construction of aerodromes, buildings, and for the manufacture and purchase of essential equipment and supplies with a very minimum of delay.

"(7) While maintaining the framework of the British Commonwealth Air Training Plan and proceeding with its development so that at the earliest possible moment it can be geared to capacity again, every effort is being directed towards the maximum output of Pilots, Air Gunners and Air Observers in the shortest possible time for overseas service, and a steady flow of Pilots, and subsequently of air crews generally, will proceed overseas monthly from now onwards to join the operational squadrons of the Royal Air Force.

"(8) Details are being worked out to call up immediately some thousands of young men for service in the Royal Canadian Air Force, and their training for any emergency will be undertaken at the earliest possible moment, thus giving a greater number of these splendid young men the opportunity so ardently sought after by them of serving their country in its time of need."

This was not all. Ministers and Supply officials flew immediately to Washington in search of aircraft, engines, all the things required with which to teach young men to fly. Overnight the Plan was geared to North American production and removed from dependence on British factories. The new Minister of National Defence, Colonel J. L. Ralston, summed up the country's temper when he said in the House: "If we cannot show initiative and resourcefulness in this crisis we are unworthy of the name of Canadians. It does not matter what history says. What counts is that each and every man should feel in his heart that he has done the best he could."

That day in May, 1940, Canada threw the original Plan and its well-timed schedules into the wastebasket. When common sense dictated withdrawal, the Dominion's leaders ordered full speed ahead and more. Without knowing how it was to be done, the Minister of Air, the Minister of Supply and their aides ordered all construction work finished by the end of 1940, whereas originally it had been scheduled for completion in the spring of 1942. Contractors pooled their facilities and went to work on triple shifts. The aircraft industry snapped out of the lethargy into which it had been plunged by what may be termed the original "Old Country Policy" and set to work to produce Canadian machines. Uncle Sam extended the good right hand of neighbourly fellowship, sent to Canada shipments of planes originally intended for France, others on order in Sweden. Instead of killing the Plan, Britain's misfortune gave it new life. The miracle happened. Before the year's end the first graduates of Canada's university of the air were overseas, ready for action if not already engaged.

So passed the first year of war, the year of organisation, of mistakes, of trial and error, the year of disaster and of miracles, the year in which the vast juggernaut of the Air Plan was meshed first in low gear, then in second, only to slip back into reverse before it had really begun to roll. As the year closed, however, the great machine had begun to move inexorably forward in high, gathering momentum as it moved.

The R.C.A.F. goes to War 1940. Major the Honourable C. G. Power, M.C., Ministe[r] National Defence for Air, inspects a Fighter Squadron before it embarks for Britain.

THE PLAN GOES INTO MASS PRODUCTION

ASK the average Canadian citizen to name the greatest single enterprise undertaken in the history of the nation and ten to one he will reply, "The building of the C.P.R."

The answer is eminently reasonable. The first transcontinental railway knitted the patchwork of a struggling country into an entity. It bowled down the mountain barrier, gave access to the western ocean. It bridged the wilderness north of Superior, making the newly-opened prairies one with the industrial east. It changed hamlets into cities overnight. It turned the flow of a young country's commerce from north-south to east-west. It changed Canada from a chain of tuppenny principalities into a thriving young nation. Since then we have builded well.

Today two great transportation systems connect our ocean borders. East and west the country has become a web-like network of feeder lines. Trunk highways span the continent. Passenger planes whisk the traveller from Maritimes to far-away B.C. in the space of hours. And the cornerstone of this huge Canadian edifice was laid on the seventh day of November, 1885, when the last spike of our first transcontinental railway was driven home and a nation was born in fact as well as in name.

Here, then, is something to measure by, the very yardstick of Canadian greatness. How does this vast emprise called the Royal Canadian Air Force, this young behemoth with constant growing pains, compare in scope with the greatest transportation system? How has it met its problems in comparison with the manner in which the builders of the C.P.R. faced theirs? How do the costs rate, side by side? How may we compare the speed with which the railway was flung across the continent with the haste with which the Air Plan was set in productive motion? Let us look back into Canadian history . . .

During the ten years immediately following Confederation, the Founding Fathers and their helpers set about building themselves a railroad to join Atlantic and Pacific. Ten years later they were still fussing with its jigsawed pieces and were constructing a series of lines, which set out from almost anywhere and headed for nowhere in particular. By 1881 the political gentlemen had enough. To the newly-chartered Canadian Pacific Railway Company they handed over 731 miles of railway, bonussed the builders with 25,000,000 acres of colonization lands, handed them a cheque for $25,000,000, and asked them would they please finish the job. The value of all this was set at $77,000,000, that of the finished streaks of rust at $35,000,000. Remember the figure. It will crop up again.

A trifle more than four years later, when the last spike had been driven home, the Rockies conquered, the tundras of Superior bridged, the main line's extremities were 2,894 miles apart, 404 miles of branch lines were completed and 695 miles of track had been leased. $88,321,595 had been spent on the main line. Acquired lines and branches had cost $13,587,127. Equipment (rolling stock, shops, etc.) to a value of $8,960,464 had been purchased. The Company's investment, its cost of building a railway across Canada, had reached a figure of $138,912,251, over and above the Government's gift, then carried at a value of $35,000,000 on the books.

In June, 1886, when through passenger service from Montreal to the Pacific was inaugurated, the job had cost in the neighborhood of $175,000,000, a figure which included the monies spent in the beginning by the newly-formed Federal Government. In other words, the promoters had found and spent the trifling sum of $140,000,000 in five years, the Government a matter of $35,000,000 in ten. The first decade was one of seemingly directionless muddling. The real thrust to the coast did not begin until the company took over in 1881. Then things began

to hum. The promoters couldn't afford to wait. Remember this circumstance, because it forms an integral part of the comparison. These were time and money elements which went into the making of our first trans-Canada railway.

Cut forward now to the end of 1940 and the beginning of 1941, to the Royal Canadian Air Force and its siamese associate, the Commonwealth Air Training Plan.

Experts had begun to think in terms of American production instead of British. The lid was lifted in the recruiting offices. Young gentlemen in Toronto, Montreal and Kamloops who had long since given up hope of being called to the Colours, began to receive wires to report for duty tomorrow. Some day, when time to think comes again, Canada will doff its cap to the men who made the Air Plan tick the day after Dunkirk, and marching in the van of the heroes will be the hard-driving Air Minister Power and the tireless Acting Deputy Duncan.

The problem was not easy of solution. It can find no solution, but Peace after Victory. Bottlenecks abound. One is broken today. A new one appears tomorrow. Aircraft on order from the States went to the coast, instead of to Canadian fields, thence to the United Kingdom. Canadian instructors were uprooted from their training stations, shipped abroad. But with all these strange goings-on to cope with, Minister and Deputy, Staff and administrative people kept turning the head of steam behind the Plan higher and higher. Time, once reckoned our greatest Ally, overnight had become Public Enemy Number One as 1941 dawned. The writer talked with Air Minister Power one day at the year's turn, as he took a brief recess from Parliament in his House office. "We're running 'way out in front of the point we were supposed to pass about this time," he said. "We're miles ahead of anywhere anybody even dreamed we could be six months ago. But Lord knows what'll happen tomorrow. All you can deal with in this game is today . . . and if somebody blows up the bridge in the morning, we'll fix it and go on over the river!"

Here lies the parallel with the C.P.R. which saw ten years of *laissez faire,* followed by the driving days when the railroad thrust through the Rockies and around Superior. These men, Stephen, Van Horne and the others, couldn't wait. In the beginning Time hadn't mattered, because the money came from the taxpayer. Then Time became the essence of the business, because it was get-the-job-done-or-go-broke, as in this other enterprise it became a case of grind out the Pilots, Observers and Gunners, or face the possibility of being driven out of the air.

The impelling urges were identical. The rule-books had to be thrown away. The placid systems of business had to be scrapped. If they hadn't been scrapped in 1884 maybe the railroad would have been, and Canada with it. If the red tape hadn't been thrown away in 1940, maybe everything we fight for would have been lost—and Canada with it. But the job went through.

At the end of May, 1940, as has been noted, slightly more than twenty training establishments of various sorts were in operation in Canada under the Air Plan (exclusive of Service units functioning on the coastal defences). By the end of that year the number had more than trebled. Flying clubs had become Elementary Training Schools; Observers' schools, Bombing and Gunnery schools, Wireless schools, all manner of proving grounds for the combat fliers of tomorrow were in full swing. Throughout the schedules of the Plan operating dates for new establishments were being advanced by units of weeks. On June 2nd, 1940, 1,409 officers and 12,253 airmen were in R.C.A.F. uniforms. On December 9th the figure had become 2,495 officers and 31,890 men. So moved the Air Plan once we knew it had become a matter of sink or swim now, as moved the railroad sixty years

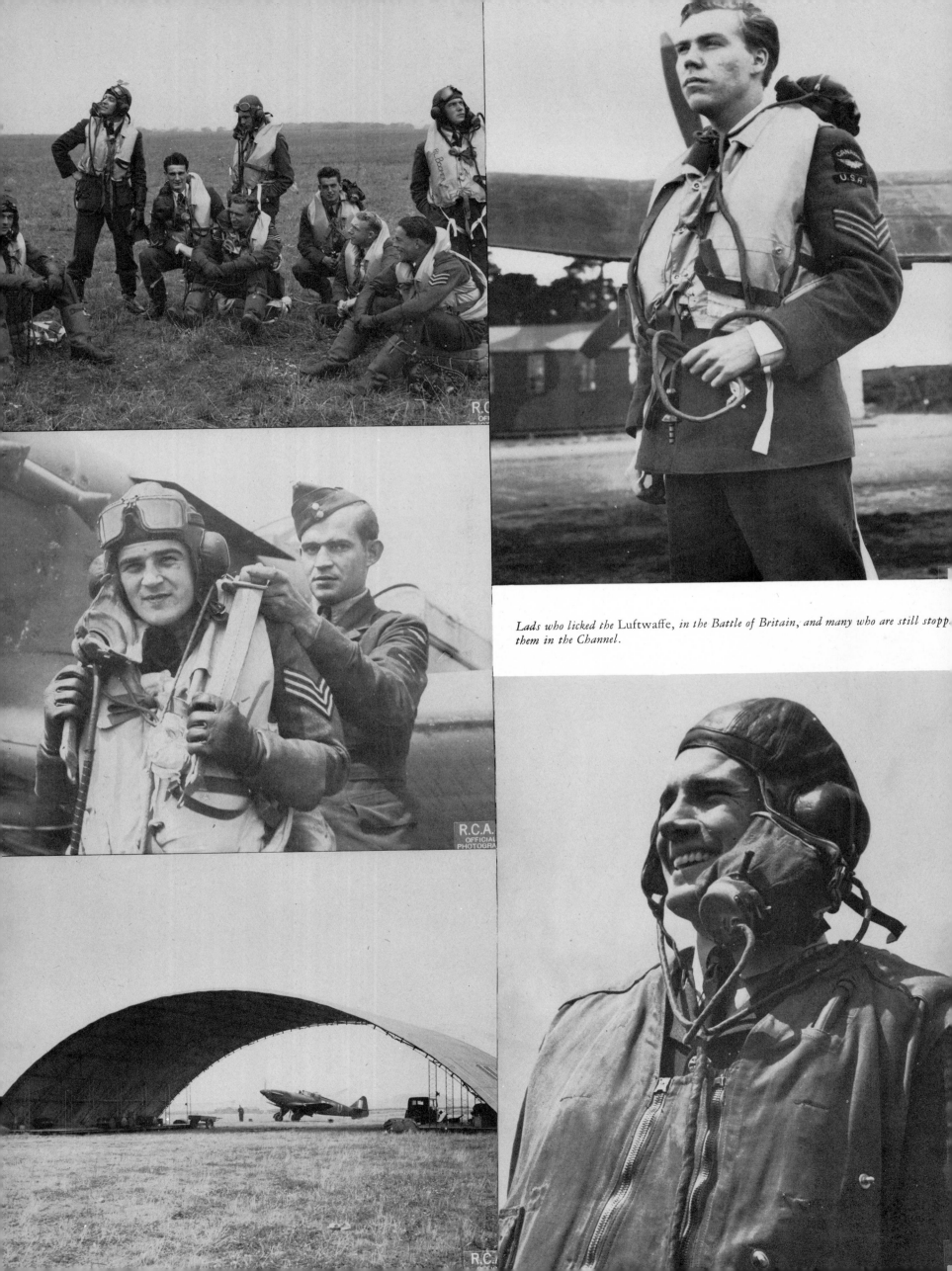

Lads who licked the Luftwaffe, in the Battle of Britain, and many who are still stopp. them in the Channel.

ago, when its builders faced the alternative of get-the-trains-running-or-go-broke. What was to have been done in 1942 was added to the 1941 schedule. Somehow it was done.

One more bracket of comparisons and this phase of the subject is done. When trains began to roll from Montreal to the Pacific in 1886 the task of spanning Canada with steel had cost a matter of $175,000,000. By the end of March, 1941, expenditures on the Commonwealth Air Training Plan had reached a figure of $250,000,000, or almost half as much again as the cost of building our first transcontinental railroad. Today the C.P.R. is rated worth, in round figures, a cool billion. Before the Hun is driven from the skies and peace returns to earth, an equal, or greater, amount will have been expended in producing airmen in Canada. Here, then, is a fair basis of comparison, a yardstick to measure by when you think in terms of the scope of Canada's air effort. When you see the planes overhead in tight formation, heading towards the nearest flying field, what you see is a tiny segment of a vast force, comparable in terms of its relation to the Plan as a whole to an empty freight car on a branch line siding in its relationship to the proportions of the Canadian Pacific. And so it goes from Coast to Coast. Another Canadian Pacific, built in a year and put into full operation in its second twelvemonth !

*   *   *

Where did the Plan stand as 1940 became 1941?

As Parliament met after the New Year, the rising tempo of the Air Plan was clearly visible in the Estimates for the fiscal year. $250,000,000 was the figure set by Air Minister Power for the next twelve months in the air.

The estimates, broadly speaking, divided into three parts. It was proposed to spend during the year 1941-42: on the Home War Establishment $154,000,000 and on the Overseas War Establishment, $15,800,000. Urgent air defence measures pressed at home, over and above the Commonwealth Air Training Plan. Of which more anon.

Of the Plan Major Power told the House in March, 1941, that there had been a great deal of confusion in the minds of the public and of members of the House and in the press. To the House he said:

"It is a huge, complex and complicated undertaking, but in a word it is this: The government of Canada is a contractor for the whole British Empire, to turn out—and this is what I wish to emphasize—an output of air crews, consisting of Pilots, Gunners and Observers. That is the job of work we undertook to do. All else—aerodromes, buildings, aeroplanes, trained technicians, instructors—is only incidental to the process of doing the job we were asked to do, and I submit that we should be judged on the results of the job of work which we have been asked to do.

"We are contracting, but at the same time we are contributing, in that we contribute about 65 per cent of the joint funds and 90 per cent of the raw material, which is the young men who go into the Plan and afterwards become the output, the air crews that are handed over to the Royal Air Force as members of that Force.

"Canada was selected from among the nations of the Commonwealth to undertake this job, partly on account of our freedom from prospective attack, partly on account of our proximity to the United States, which would furnish us with a supply of raw material, and partly on account of our proximity to the United Kingdom, which would also supply us with material, and which was close enough and accessible enough to make delivery of the output easy. Fourth, I suggest that Canada was chosen because of the reputation of Canadian youth for efficiency and gallantry during the last war as members of the Royal Air Force and of the air arm of the Navy.

"A large part of the energies of the officers, staff and men of the Royal Canadian Air Force is devoted to this job. We might have preferred; I imagine that most of the officers of the Air Force would have preferred, a more direct contribution, that is to say, that we send over more all-Canadian Squadrons. We were, however, asked to do this job as a matter of Empire cooperation. It was believed, and I think it will be proved that the belief was founded upon sense and reason, that by pooling the efforts of the Empire to produce these young men and put them in the firing line, we would do much better than if each part of the Commonwealth endeavoured to carry on on its own."

The Plan had passed out of the experimental stage in November, 1940, and could be adjudged a success in that its operators knew what they could produce in aircrew and what might be expected of the months ahead, although the mass production potential still hinged upon supply of flying equipment. But that winter ten production lines (Enlistment to Wings Parade) were functioning and the Plan had brought forth only five per cent less than twice as many Pilots, Observers and Gunners as had originally been scheduled for that date. The Plan had not been doubled in size. It had been accelerated. Courses had been shortened in time. More men had been taken into training than originally planned. At no time was any intent to double the size of the Plan itself anticipated—doubling the number of aerodromes, schools, etc. etc.,—but merely the speeding up of its human production. As construction work ended and schools from coast to coast were completed during 1941, the Plan could be said to have levelled off. Thenceforth it could be expanded without the construction of further aerodromes, by increasing the use of those in existence. The shortening of Pilot courses resulted in the transfer of final-stage training to regions closer to the actual theatre of war. The Pilot-to-be received his wings at the end of S.F.T.S. training in Canada, as originally planned, but crossed the Atlantic for his post-graduate course. Through this method the distance from Manning Depot to operations against the enemy was shortened, though only slightly. On one point Canada and Britain stood firm and in concord: This time young men were not going to be sent into the air against the enemy until they were ready.

In casting about for ways of stepping up the tempo of the schools it was found, particularly in the E.F.T.S., that instructors and machines could be put to more service than originally planned. This was done. On the other hand, although men were ready for training, aerodromes ready to receive them and elementary trainers on the ground awaiting them, other material still remained to be acquired, particularly in the realm of aircraft for advanced training. All very well to call for the opening of a new school by such-and-such a date. But if the Ministry of Supply could not deliver Ansons or Harvards, of what use to open ? In more cases than one E.F.T.S. graduates were forced to await aircraft deliveries before beginning advanced training. So goes the tale of continuing material bottlenecks now, fortunately, almost gone.

Remains, too, the expenditure of machines. An airplane can only take so much and remain airworthy. Then it must go into shops for renovation. Through the early months of the Plan Canada was expending its capital in aircraft. Day and night the machines were aloft. In the Minister's words "We are using these aircraft as hard and as fast as we can. In normal times I could be accused of improvidence." The danger, then, was that too many machines would urgently require overhaul simultaneously. Then, too, a shortage of spares threatened to bog down the Plan. Meanwhile at E.T.F.S. and S.F.T.S. Canada kept 'em flying! Troubles would be faced when they arose, not before.

Beyond all this Canada had been rendering signal service to the War In The Air in other directions. The readers will recall that Britain announced, through Air Vice-Marshal Sir Hugh Dowding, at the beginning of 1941, that the German night bomber had been brought into control, by means of certain scientific devices.

A Fighter Squadron leaves on Patrol: Their ground-crew Pals, wave them on to "Good Hunting".

Canadian and American scientists were honoured in their anonymity as sharing in this contribution and Canada had rounded up many young men of scientific bent who had proceeded overseas post haste. Canadian readers will remember that a nation-wide call for radio mechanics went out at the beginning of 1941 and those who knew any of these young men will recall that they sailed the Atlantic in extremely short time after enlistment. That is where the young radio men went and that is what they were doing.

* * *

Despite all problems, however, twenty-four hundred aircraft were on the aerodromes of the Plan in Canada as the snow went off in 1941. As to training aircraft, the Elementary schools stood slightly over strength as embryo pilots tried their wings over fields from coast to coast. At the Service schools, however, shortages were the order of the day as the nation's infant aircraft industry tussled with the bottlenecks of the hour, particularly with that of providing twin-engined aircraft. Of single-engined advance trainers, notably the Harvard, 89% of requirements had been received. In fine, the shortage was one of reserves. In twin-engined machines, however, only 46% of those needed were on hand and the Plan faced definite future slowdown if the ships could not be rushed through to the young men in training. Air Observers' Schools had only 70% of their needs, Bombing and Gunnery were up to 86% and Wireless Training Schools, where large single-engined ships are used, 82%. The Air Navigation Schools had only 44% of their twin-engine requirements, but the number needed was not great. To meet this crisis Canada had decided in the early summer of 1940 to produce the complete Anson in Canada and to equip it with American engines. The worst bottleneck was to be found in the advanced stages of Pilot training. The Anson would break it, if . . .

In order to co-ordinate the output of Anson parts under the revised plan, Federal Aircraft Limited had been set up as a Government-owned corporation on June 24, 1940, to administer the program and to segregate this work from the remainder of the aircraft production program.

To expedite production, it was decided that, in addition to administering the program, Federal itself would also manufacture fuselages. Premises were leased in Montreal, machinery ordered, and personnel engaged. Three other Canadian companies also were awarded contracts to manufacture fuselages. Other firms undertook to produce wings, spars, and other components of the plane. Federal was empowered to act as a central purchasing agent for other contractors for certain materials, parts, and equipment required.

The first Canadian Anson was not completed and delivered to the Royal Canadian Air Force until the week of September 6, 1941, however, several months behind original schedule, and by the end of September four planes had been delivered. During October an additional 11 were completed, flight tested, and delivered. Twenty planes were delivered during November and an additional 53 aircraft, nearly three times November's output, were produced in December. By this time, the company had attained a satisfactory condition with regard to the delivery of the principal materials and manufactured parts, the requirements for more than 600 aircraft, with few exceptions, being in the contractor's hands or in the companies' stores.

Steps were taken at an early date to provide the large number of spare parts which would be required for normal maintenance of the Ansons produced in Canada. This spares program was well in hand by the end of 1941, and where practicable spares orders were being placed so that spares and production requirements could be combined in the same run by the manufacturers concerned.

The task of getting the Anson into production presented one of the major problems of 1941. That costly mistakes were made no doubt exists, and some of them were almost irreparable. The scheme itself—the creation of a Government company to coordinate the production job—was constantly under fire in the country. Manufacturers from Halifax to Vancouver were impressed into the nation's service to turn out piecemeal the thousands of individual parts called for by the blueprints. It became almost impossible to walk into a major Canadian factory, from sewing machine plant to railway-car shop, in which one did not find Anson bits and pieces in production.

Not merely with respect to the Ansons, expected in April, but not seen until September, was a production "headache" (the term is the Minister's) encountered. The Fleet Fort 60, which is made or assembled by a private manufacturer in Canada, and carries an American Jacobs engine, was another. In order to overcome that difficulty, which was to some extent foreseen, Mr. Ralph Bell (Director General of Aircraft Production), and Mr. Duncan, the former Deputy Minister, had visited the United States and purchased a very large number of twin-engine Cessnas, which were beginning to arrive by Spring and proved to be an excellent machine. Even so, slight delays in the arrival of the Cessnas gave cause for concern, but the production lines made good and in some measure overcame the shortage of Ansons and Forts. But the problems of opening the Service schools were many.

In March, 1941, House and country heard of another "headache", perhaps more difficult of cure than the aircraft pain, because it involved the nation's man-power, the young men who urgently desired to meet the enemy in the air but who could not be trained until the bottlenecks were broken. Of them Air Minister Power said:

"At the beginning of the war thousands of young men desired to join the Air Force, and we were obliged to put them off. We could not take them all in. There was no room for them, either in the training schools which trained the technicians, or at other points. When I refer to training schools I have in mind schools like that at St. Thomas. (N.B. It should be noted, as illustrative of expansion, that at the time this statement was made Canada had 6,000 technicians in training at St. Thomas and other places, and had trained and brought into the Force 10,000 trained mechanics). "If those young men were mechanics before they joined the Force, there was very little difficulty in bringing them in. But if they were not mechanics, they were difficult to handle because we had to open schools for them. If they intended to become air crews—and that includes Pilots, Gunners and Observers—it was still more difficult because, up until April, 1940, we had no schools for them. At that time the schools began, but very slowly. "We were considerably worried as to what we should do. In June, 1940, rather than see these young men go around kicking their heels while waiting, we began taking them in and giving them three months' drill. We took in 5,000 and gave them the drill. Those young fellows are now in the Plan as air crews. "But our difficulty is this:—I do not mind saying that we will require thousands and thousands of air crews. Those young men represent the very flower of the youth of our country. They must be A-plus physically, and they must have educational qualifications equivalent to matriculation from high school. "We will need thousands of these young men. I do not want to say how many thousands a month, but we will need thousands a month. We do not need them all yet. I have in hand a reserve of about six months, but we do not want them to get away from us, if it is possible. That is our problem. "What we are doing at this time is to let them come to our recruiting offices. We enlist them, and let them go away on leave without pay. We tell them to come back in July or August. We say to them, 'Do not give up your jobs; do not give up your schooling;

Building Aerodromes in the Wilderness of Northern B.C. and the Yukon: Huskies b[reak] the trail for the Tractor Train. The Tractor Trail (thread-like line on photo) as [seen] from the air.

we will require you; we will tell you to report in July or August; the day on which we tell you to report will be the day you will report, and there will be no further postponement.'

"The difficulty up to the present time has been that we could not tell a man when he was coming in, because we did not know exactly how our Plan was getting along. But we do know now, with some degree of certainty. We are able to say that a certain number of men shall come in every month, or on such and such a date."

It is not easy to explain to the young man who wants to fight in the clouds, to follow the trail of the Bishops and Barkers, that you have nothing for him to fly, that he must be patient and wait until you have. His own very eagerness to do his part makes him impatient of delay. That was the "human bottleneck" of 1939, of 1940 and, in some degree, of the early months of 1941.

* * *

The $15,000,000 mentioned as earmarked for Overseas War Establishment in the estimates of 1941-2 were set aside for the payment of Canadian aircrew and airmen abroad. Although the British Government undertook under the Plan to pay R.C.A.F. officers and men overseas, the rate was to be that of the Royal Air Force. Canada, however, covers the gap between the British rate and the Canadian, and the $15,000,000 item was to provide for the discrepancy in pay rates.

* * *

Air Force estimates for 1941-42 carried a figure of $154,000,000, as has been noted, for Home War Establishment. Yet in these days of astronomical money-totals little impression was made on the public mind by the sudden upping of the cost of defending the air over Canada (the figures are exclusive of expenditures for the British Commonwealth Air Training Plan). The reason? Quietly, without fuss or fanfare, but speedily, Canada was closing its western aerial door in the teeth of Japan. The development of Canada's Alaska Airway comes under our agreement with the United States for the joint defence of this hemisphere. In November, 1940, the United States-Canada Joint Board on Defence recommended the construction of a chain of air bases linking Alaska with Vancouver and Edmonton. The vast stretch of inaccessible coast line between Alaska and the United States border provided one of the greatest obstacles to an adequate defence of North America's Pacific ramparts. Some system must be provided to permit swift transportation of men and equipment to any point where an emergency might arise. The thousand mile barrier that separated Alaska from the United States has now been bridged by a string of fine aerodromes, established in the wilderness in the face of tremendous difficulties.

By using the new airway, the United States Army today can move fighter aircraft from Seattle, Washington, to Fairbanks, Alaska, in five hours flying time. The short range of fighter planes would have made this impossible before the construction of the airport chain. Troop-carrying transports can fly soldiers over the same distance in about eight hours flying time, instead of the six to seven days occupied in transporting troops by ship from Seattle. That, as well as Canada's defence, is the "why" of the new airway, and the "why" of a major part of those $154,000,000.

An inland route was selected to escape the heavy coastal fogs. It passes over "clear weather" country and is equipped with radio beam stations and other aids to modern air navigation. It follows closely the "Great Circle," shortest route between this continent and Asia.

Over and above its obvious use against the Japanese enemy, the new string of aerodromes offers our shortest cut to contact with our Russian allies.

Canada's old-time bush-pilots had blazed the trail. Years ago one of these, Grant McConachie, began flying into the Peace River country of Northern Alberta. He flew mining machinery and

supplies into the northern settlements and came out loaded with fish from northern lakes for city markets. He flew farther in and established a regular service from Edmonton to Whitehorse. To-day his company, Yukon Southern Air Transport, holds a government mail contract and operates a regular passenger, mail and express service in twin-engined all-metal aircraft of modern type from Edmonton into the Yukon. McConachie pioneered the route and established his own radio stations and landing fields. In 1935 the civil aviation branch of the Transport Department investigated the route, and in 1938 it was inspected by J. A. Wilson, Controller of Civil Aviation. Ground survey parties were sent in the following year, and the new route was recommended to the Joint Defence Board as a channel to Alaska. The plans called for main fields to be established at Grand Prairie, Fort St. John, Fort Nelson, Watson Lake and White Horse. The first two sites were near enough to railways to eliminate any major transportation problem in the carrying in of construction materials. The White Horse site was also close to the rails. But Fort Nelson was 300 miles north of the end of steel and Watson Lake was not even a pin-point on the map of the vast northwest hinterland.

Engineers were flown to Fort Nelson during the winter 1940-41 and started work on laying out the aerodrome. Engineers and clearing crews were also flown to Watson Lake, just north of the Yukon border and about 240 miles by air from Fort Nelson. With building materials for Fort Nelson, a tractor-train started out from Dawson Creek in two sections on February 9, 1941. In the first was a "bulldozer"—an aptly named battering ram consisting of a heavy tractor fitted with great steel blades capable of mowing down trees and slicing the tops off knolls by sheer brute force. Behind it moved another tractor hauling several wooden huts on sleighs containing a combination kitchen and dining room, a "staff quarters", and two bunkhouses for the crew of 28 men. Behind this section was another consisting of a blacksmith's shop and five sleigh-loads of heavy freight hauled by a big tractor. Normally, the train moved ahead four times a day, in the morning, at noon, evening and again at midnight. Hauling of the train was done by the 70 H.P. Caterpillar, taking the cabooses as far as possible then doubling back for the freight and blacksmith shop. In many cases, due to steep grades, bare ground or other forms of heavy pulling, the sleds had to be taken one or two at a time. Regardless of how much this general system varied, it was always planned to have the kitchen up to the bulldozer at mealtimes. The large trailbuilder necessarily was always in the lead. In order to allow passage of the broad sleighs, more than one trip of this machine became necessary to make each leg of road. Thus in the morning it would move ahead for two or three hours, then backtrack to widen and smooth. In the meantime the rest of the train was being brought up until at noon the two met. After lunch, the bulldozer continued making road and the remainder of the train came up to meet the first section. If the type of country permitted, the smaller bulldozer did widening and general conditioning in the rear of its larger mate. Using either method, from one to two miles were averaged per move and on occasion as much as ten miles were covered in twenty-four hours. Far ahead of even the bulldozer, trail-blazers, at first with horses and later using dogteams, chose the route. This followed, generally, an old freight trail to the trading posts on the Sikanni River, but the trail had to be widened to accommodate the larger sleighs and smoothed as trucks were to follow as well. It was, at best, a beginning.

North of the Sikanni only a toboggan or pack trail existed. The train deserted this almost entirely until within a short distance of Fort Nelson, due to its crooked course.

A tremendous project remained behind the bulldozers. More than six hundred tons of general freight, including everything conceivable with which to begin construction of the Fort Nelson

Building Aerodromes in the Wilderness of Northern B.C. and the Yukon: The Bulla breaks trail through bushland on way to Fort Nelson. Tractor Train with cookh caboose follows closely behind.

airport and for the needs of the construction crew, was loaded onto sleighs and trucks. Trains No. 3 and 4, having for power two large Caterpillars—one of them a bulldozer—and co-operating with some twenty trucks shuttled the freight, first to a cache at Nig Creek, then on to the north bank of the Sikanni. Here it was assembled to be brought over the final pull into Nelson.

The hardships endured by the train crews and truck-drivers were tremendous. Yet scarcely had the leading train reached its destination than the heavy freight began to arrive. As the road moved into the last stretch materials were piling up on the north Sikanni bank, approximately one hundred miles to the south of Nelson, waiting for road to be made for the last leg into camp.

As the trains were en route Nature took a hand. Early-breaking Spring descended upon the muskeg. What had been a frost bottomed road quickly became a quagmire, the sticky fingers of which clung tenaciously to caterpillar tracks and dragged trucks down to their hubs. The trail itself became a river of mud and water. Chartered trucks turned back at the Sikanni and raced for civilization while the remaining cars and engines, assisted by those of Train No. 1, worked day and night to bring through all possible freight before break-up. Gradually the material arrived and almost two hundred tons were finally piled at the new airport site before travel was impossible. River ice broke and went out, the trail became a series of roaring torrents, caused by the rapid melting of four to five feet of snow. The earliest break-up on record had disrupted the most carefully laid plans.

Breakdowns delayed the train. Three times in the first week repairs held up progress for a total of twenty-seven hours. On the last occasion the severity of the break necessitated a return, with small tractor and caboose, to the closest blacksmith shop (Fort St. John). Thus seven days found the train only 35 miles beyond the last settlement,—Murdale—a poor beginning.

The second week brought better results. The size of the timber made it possible for the bulldozer to work satisfactorily and the lack of thick underbrush permitted broken trees to be pushed completely from the road. Grades, too, were favourable. February 23rd found Trains 1 and 2 in company and camped alongside a deserted fur-trade settlement at Nig Creek.

The old log buildings, once the nucleus of a thriving trade, stood in a small clearing, monuments to a by-gone day, their weather-beaten sides and collapsing roofs silently hostile to the encroachment of a new era, the era of the diesel tractor and present-day trail building skill.

The crossing of Nig Creek presented an obstacle common to practically all the rivers and creeks. The old trail, accommodating only horse and dog teams, had followed the path of least resistance. Long winding approaches added unnecessary miles and made turns impossible for a connected train of wide sleighs. In many cases the trail lay on the river ice. Hence it became necessary to search for more convenient grades, to cover a minimum number of miles and to make the amount of ice travel as small as possible and to "fill" at the creek crossings. At such points the bulldozer pushed large timbers out on to the ice and piled smaller logs, brush, earth and any available material into the apertures until a ten-foot roadway had been built.

Again and again such "fills" were made. Farther on, the Pine-to-Conroy-Rivers section required no less than four such projects, each presenting individual peculiarities. Up and down the bank went the bulldozer, cutting in where the trail lay across the faces of hills, filling holes and washouts and tearing at the frozen ground to throw it into dry creek-beds and onto stretches of ice. At one place a fifteen-foot fill was put into a fifty-foot river so that a level road lay from one flat to the other. Across this the train pulled two sleds at a time up a grade which a few hours before had been a river valley under four feet of snow and completely filled with trees and underbrush. Now, a twenty-foot

highway led from the stream for half a mile up a ten percent rise. At the Sikanni River crossing, "fill" was out of the question and the only alternative was to use the ice. Cautiously the bulldozer started across the river, feeling its way. Near the opposite shore the ice suddenly gave way. Without warning the massive machine slipped through to the river bottom and began to sink in soft mud. Timbers were jammed under the tracks, but only slowed its descent. The other engines, pulling on the ends of cables, failed to have any effect as quicksand had closed about the tracks.

Working in the ice-cold water, men with shovels dug at the river bottom, slowly releasing the caterpillar tracks from the vice-like grip. At the same time the two tractors, their own tracks slipping and skidding on ice, held cables tight as violin strings. Inch by inch and foot by foot the dead weight began to move as hour succeeded hour. All night long the work continued. Gradually the light of gas lanterns faded before approaching day as the quicksand's death-grip was broken and the trailbuilder rose higher and higher from the water.

Frozen mud caked the tractor tracks in a solid mass. Water had penetrated the engine, necessitating complete cleaning and drying of the lubricating and ignition systems. Against time and bitter weather the repair job went on. The Nelson Trail must be pushed on to journey's end.

The last lap had begun. The Sikanni became a memory. Eyes turned to the last hundred miles of muskeg, of light timber and tangled underbrush. If trucks were ever to come through it meant working and re-working the newly-made road for hours at a time.

The vegetation, for the most part small spruce, birch and poplar saplings and thirty-foot willows, formed a mass so thick as to make impossible the usual procedure of pushing rubble aside from the cleared road. Hence an extra width had to be made; the centre for passage of the train and the sides to accommodate slash thrown aside by the bulldozer blade. No longer did the trailbuilder pit its strength against large trees and send them reeling away from the road. Now it must rip and tear at stubborn saplings that bent before the blade, leaving five or six feet of peeled willow with roots still intact, after the bulldozer had passed. Moss and lichen, shaken loose and falling from the undergrowth, was drawn against the radiator, so that for days it became necessary to stop at two hour intervals to remove the protecting grill and clean away this accumulation, to permit air to reach the overheated engine.

Each night the train's position was reported by radio to the engineer-in-charge, H. P. Keith at Fort St. John. A few entries, culled from the log, will indicate the tempo of average daily progress:

"March 16—Position to-night forty miles north Sikanni. Muskeg country, very rough. Progress slow. Road okay for trucks.

"March 17—Position to-night approximately forty-eight miles north Sikanni."

"March 18—Position to-night fifty-three miles north Sikanni."

"March 19—Position to-night fifty-eight miles north Sikanni."

"March 20—To-night's position sixty-five miles north Sikanni."

Day by day the distance covered increased, until March 27th found the train camped beside the Muskwa River, on the threshold of the Fort Nelson site. Four miles ahead lay the last camp-ground. Warm weather had wrought havoc with the river ice, however. A careful check was made and finally a crossing was chosen which seemed to offer the best support.

At first an attempt was made to pull the bulldozer across on two large skids, but this soon proved impractical. Then it winched itself across (the winch cable was anchored to the opposite bank and with tracks running free the machine began reeling in). Steadily the distance lessened, forty feet, twenty, fifteen—and then misfortune struck.

*Building Aerodromes in the Wilderness: Passing an abandoned Trading Post at Sikar[ ]
River on Way to Fort Nelson. Chief from local Reserve drops in to see Caterpillar Trac[ ]
Train progress. (Lower left) Bulldozer hauls itself out of the Muskwa River. (Lower rig[ ]
This road became roaring stream, two weeks after Tractor Train passed through.*

As if from a blow, the tractor staggered, to one side then the other. Seemingly made of rubber, the ice was bending under the weight. Frantically the operator tried to get his tracks in motion but before they could respond, fifteen tons of metal had plunged to the bottom. Five feet of water closed around its sides, fly-wheel and fan belt sent showers over the cab and with a choke the engine, strangled by ice-cold water, died. Was the game up, with the end of the trail in sight?

The driver, a picture of disgust, extricated himself from the water, expressing in eloquent but unprintable terms his opinion of the combination of heavy machinery and thin ice.

Immediately the task of cutting a channel to shallow water began. All night and most of the next day were spent in cutting free large blocks of ice. These the smaller engine pulled from the water, then at the end of a cable dragged the bulldozer up the slope, until by three o'clock the following afternoon it was in sufficiently shallow water to permit the engine to be started. Once again an overhaul was necessary to remove ice from the machine. Again under its own power the great engine of War-in-the-Bush began to climb to solid footing. Meanwhile a new course had been selected, and over the river flats the train moved on the evening of March 29th, to spend most of the 30th undergoing repairs. Thus on the last day of March the leading train climbed its last hill and camped beside the future Nelson Airport, forty-eight days out from Dawson Creek.

* * *

The equipment and supplies for Watson Lake field could not be moved in until the waterways opened in the spring. A stern-wheel steamer, two tunnel-bottomed boats and a number of barges 55 feet long were built in Vancouver for the job. These and the 800 tons of material for the aerodrome at Watson Lake were shipped up the Pacific coast to Wrangel, Alaska in the spring of 1941, then were freighted 163 miles up the Stikine River to Telegraph Creek, B.C. and hauled 72 miles by truck over a tote road to Dease Lake. Here boats and barges were assembled and, supplemented by local water conveyances, used in freighting the supplies for the trip of 193 miles down the Dease and Liard Rivers. The final stage into Watson is a haul of 25 miles over a road built from the banks of the Liard to the Lake. Aircraft had already taken in a sawmill and planing mill, however, to prepare lumber for the necessary buildings.

Today up-to-date aerodromes span the bush from Edmonton and Vancouver to Whitehorse in the Yukon and on to Alaska on either side of the Rocky Mountain barrier. North of Edmonton, the easterly route runs to Whitehorse, Yukon Territory, with aerodromes at Grande Prairie, Fort St. John, Fort Nelson and Watson Lake. The route on the western side of the Rockies runs north from Vancouver and Kamloops to Williams Lake and Prince George. An aerodrome has also been built at Smithers, near Prince Rupert within operating range of Prince George and coast points.

All these aerodromes are equipped with landing strips 4000 feet long by 500 feet wide to carry the most modern aircraft. They have full lighting equipment for night flying, and a complete radio system to guide aircraft over the route in all kinds of weather.

Construction completed, grading units, bulldozers, ploughs, rollers, and two-ton truck equipment remained in the interior, since it is planned to build intermediate aerodromes in later years. Intermediate fields will be built between Fort St. John and Fort Nelson, between Fort Nelson and Watson Lake, and between Watson Lake and Whitehorse.

So goes the tale which began with the simple announcement of stiffly increased Home-war Air expenditures.

Canada's Burma Road !

Home War activities were by no means confined to the creation of the new Alaska Airway during 1941, however. Construction of new defensive aerodromes on the nation's eastern ramparts and the consolidation of those already started kept those concerned with the nation's defences at full speed ahead. Yarmouth, Shelburne, Dartmouth, Sydney, and, in Newfoundland, Botwood, Gander (constructed by the United Kingdom and Newfoundland authorities) and Torbay provided Canada's eastern defenders with a chain of modern Air Stations. Going north, Canada has established aerodromes and staging facilities at Goose Bay, Northwest River, Labrador, and elsewhere. These are for defence, for ferrying, and for spare aerodromes in case fog or weather conditions make other fields unavailable.

On the west the Dominion carried out a similar programme of developing stations all along the coast, in addition to the Alaska route, at Alliford Bay, Ucluelet, Tofino, Coal Harbour, Bella Bella and other points. The Squadrons on both coasts were increased in numbers, and were equipped with Digbys, Hudsons, Bolingbrokes, and Stranraers made in Canada, and with Kitty Hawks and Catalinas.

"With respect to the personnel of these Squadrons on both coasts, they have a risky, dirty, tiresome and boring task. They may not have all the risk, but certainly they have a large proportion of the risk encountered by those on active service. They serve in lonely places and in dirty weather and patrol work is hazardous in the extreme. Little glamour is attached to it, and yet they carry on day after day without complaint. I therefore wish once more to pay tribute to them and to assure them that, as circumstances permit, it will be my intention to give them an opportunity to do the kind of work overseas which all of them desire to engage in."

The words are those of the Air Minister. That they comprise no exaggeration the writer, after flying with the North Atlantic Patrols, can personally testify. Here is at once one of war's most irksome, at times most dangerous and always most important, aerial tasks. Suppose we turn aside briefly and watch the Atlantic patrols at work . . . . .

The scene is a Canadian port at the time of assembly of a great Convoy of food and the munitions of war for Britain.

The day preceding departure is one of bustling preparation, invisible to anyone but the participants and those who know the signs. At dawn, patrol planes take off out to sea to sweep the waters in relays until darkness falls again. Mine sweepers drag paravanes through the channels of the outer harbor and the path the ships will use to reach the open Atlantic. Skippers go overside for last-minute sessions with their chandlers. The censorship lid clamps down hard on incoming messages and outgoing mail. Finally, toward evening, Masters, Mates and Wireless Operators meet the Naval-Control Officer, the Convoy Commodore, the Commanding Officer of the escort, Pilots and Liaison Officers to discuss the problems of the journey ahead. Every man's credentials are checked before he enters the room. Hundreds of lives, millions of dollars in war materials, tens of thousands of tons of ships depend for their safety during the days immediately ahead on words which will be spoken and orders which will be issued in this meeting. Doors are closed and guards are mounted. A Convoy Conference is in session.

The Naval Control Officer—a Commander of the Royal Canadian Navy—passes a copy of the sailing orders to each Master. "Being in all respects ready for sea," runs the preamble, "you are to sail with a Convoy for your destination, in accordance with the following."

"The following" are the detailed instructions by which every Master must abide at sailing time. In addition, just as he weighs anchor, each skipper will be handed a series of sealed envelopes with definite orders as to when he may use them. These secret

Building Aerodromes in the Wilderness: Supplies and equipment were transported 400 miles of river, lake and portage to the Watson Lake Airport—on the newly devel- Alaska Airline. Aircraft and troops can now be flown from Seattle, Washington Alaska, in a few hours (Top right and Centre right—Whitehorse Airfield).

orders show the route to be followed, day by day, the place of rendezvous and that of dispersal. At his first port of call after leaving the Convoy, each Master must return all papers to the Naval-Control Officer on duty there.

Discussion turns to the subject of departure. Ships will fly a specified flag at their anchorages to indicate their need of pilots; each will run up another flag as soon as the pilot is topside. Ships may show name boards to facilitate placing pilots on board, but names will come down and stay down as soon as anchor is weighed. Thenceforth everyone is anonymous. Each ship will move from its anchorage at a specified moment and will pass control stations at stipulated times and stated speeds, picking up pace as the Convoy steams in line toward the submarine nets and again after pilots are dropped. Ships will then continue in line out to sea to an appointed rendezvous, where they will form into Convoy pattern as laid down in cruising orders; unless fog is encountered on leaving port, in which case they will continue in line until the fog clears and new orders are received from the Commodore. Thereafter they will sail 3000 miles through sleet, fog, gale and whatever else the North Atlantic has to offer. Nobody will shift position in the flotilla. No lights will be shown. Wireless will keep silence. All very simple.

The Convoy leaves. As it steams out toward its rendezvous at sea in single file, Destroyers shake off their hawsers, pressure is raised in battleship boilers, and Flying Boats take off from their moorings in a quiet arm of the harbor to relieve aircraft already sweeping the sea. By the time the merchantmen form up outside, their defense force will be in place, ahead of, beside and above the Convoy.

Its occupants swathed in heavy fleece-lined flying gear, a twin-motored flying boat taxied toward open water for its take-off. As it left the mooring cove, motors came in with a roar. The submarine boom and its gate vessels passed under the wings. On near-by headlands coastal-battery emplacements could be made out. Ahead lay the gray Atlantic.

The roar of the engines echoed back from the hull of the great Flying Boat, reinforced to withstand the buffeting of the sea in the event of forced landing. The Pilot turned in the cockpit seat and shouted, "Fuse the bombs!" A Machine Gunner wriggled forward and opened the gun hatch in the nose. Another took up his position in the after hatch. The Navigating Officer sat in the cabin, plotting position and course. The wintry Atlantic wind blew in the front hatch, whirled through cockpit and cabin and out the back way. Helmets were snugged down over ears.

Half an hour passed. The Pilot pointed ahead to a group of dots against the colorless background of sea. Down below, the Convoy was taking shape, as tramps and tankers rolled in the heavy swell as they jockeyed into their positions. On the port hand, a tanker seemed to be having trouble getting into its appointed place in the column. Five columns to starboard a freighter straggled in the rear. Just about now the Commodore would be pacing the bridge of his ship in the lead of the centre column, delivering his elderly soul on the subject of freshmen Convoy Skippers.

The flying boat dipped low over scurrying destroyers which were sweeping wide arcs across the path of the merchantmen. Ice would be coating decks, rails and cables from that freezing spray from their bows. Soon Convoy and destroyers were left far astern as the plane flew on to take up its reconnaissance position far in advance of the armada. Another half hour passed. The Navigating Officer came forward and handed a pencilled course to the Pilot, who read it carefully and fastened it against the panel. The big boat came over in a steep bank and, repeatedly changing direction, began to fly long tangents back and forth over the ship lane and far out on its flanks.

The plane circled low over the flotilla. Its tramps and tankers were heeling over on the rising swells. White spray broke over

every bow. Destroyers knifed back and forth ahead. Back toward the coast, what had been a speck against the gray began to take shape as a ship, quickly to be identified as the great battleship which would act as principal escort throughout the crossing. The plane swooped down almost to the wave tops as the big battle wagon came thundering into the center of the Convoy, slackening pace and taking up position at the head of centre, three cables to starboard of the freighter in which the Commodore rode. From that position she could manoeuvre most handily for defense of the whole. There she would be protected on either flank from attack, could attack an enemy over, or through, screening merchantmen. Guns bristled from the turrets. Decks were swept clear. The appearance of action, of readiness, could be read in every line as her bows flung back their high spume.

The Flying Boat turned out to sea again and began to climb. Through the long afternoon its crew searched the waters for untoward signs, changing altitudes as ice began to form on the wings—the first fear of all the Convoy fliers—now climbing to study the meaning of a distant wisp of smoke, now swooping down almost to the surface of the sea to examine an irregularity in its white-capped expanse. Out ahead and back again, ahead and back, out to the flanks, and back to the Convoy, the big ship flew through the long, cold afternoon.

Dusk began to close in, the urgent hour which gives added advantage to a quick-striking undersea enemy. Low skimmed the great Flying Boat, every eye aboard peering into the sea. Destroyers whisked back and forth, ahead, astern and along the flanks of the armada. Freighters, tankers and battleship escort veered from their earlier course to sail long and short zigzags on the Commodore's signal. Slowly darkness fell, until only a dull glow remained in the west. The Convoy turned back to its normal course, straight ahead at eleven knots. As the Flying Boat left the ships, all that could be seen beneath its wings and fuselage was the white of streaming wakes and bow waves as the merchantmen steamed slowly toward distant Europe in their first of many blackouts. The Flying Boat turned back toward the coast. Three-quarters of an hour later a light blinked weakly in the distance. Five minutes later another light broke through on another cape, winked, went out, winked again. The plane droned on. Other lights began to join those which had shown at first, until the black of the land stood like an escarpment against the opaque sea. The Pilot shouted back an order, "Defuse the bombs!" Gun hatches were closed and half-frozen gunners wriggled through to the cabin. The plane lost height, and more lights came into view behind a headland. The Navigating Officer flashed a light to watchers on the water below. The answering signal—"O.K. to land"—came back. The roar of the motors died to a chuckle and the nose dipped down. The big ship came about in a steep bank, levelled off, skimmed the harbor surface, settled on the water, ceased to be an aeroplane and became a boat. Convoy Patrol was finished for the night, but at dawn tomorrow other aircraft would be in the air again, flying out to sea to pick up the merchantmen and fighting ships, and act as their eyes through another long day.

As the tender slipped across the harbor the black hull of an inbound freighter lumbered toward the inner basin. Beside a near-by dock two ice-sheathed Destroyers had just tied up, home from an earlier Convoy and hurriedly readying themselves for sea again. On the capes gun crews were changing, huge search-lights were mounted. In a hundred coves along the coast, ma-chine-gun crews were at their stations. Thus Canada at War on its Home front.

Quietly and unostentatiously, ever since the day in 1939 when the conflagration of war struck again, the Squadrons of Canada's coast defences have gone about their urgent tasks from the fjords of Alaska on the west to the river-mouths of Labrador in the east

*Atlantic Convoy: Vickers "Stranraer" Flying Boat, taking off . . . The Convoy .
Corvettes on escort duty . . . A Sunderland Flying Boat, "Battleships of the Air"; the
long range Flying Boats, spot and sink submarines and locate enemy warships. (Lower lef
Part of the sting in a Catalina Flying Boat (see page 77), used on Atlantic and Paci
Patrol. . . The Ships of the Convoy viewed from a Sunderland.*

and far out over the seas. In 1942, as German submarine wolf-packs hunt off North American shores and Japanese marauders look with yearning eye towards the islands of the west, the value of the tasks which these gallant men of the Air Force fulfil is beyond measure.

A hard, thankless job. Yet it is one which brings its own reward, not in enemy aircraft sent spinning into the sea, it is true, but apart from the submarine hunt, in the succour which air crews are constantly able to bring to the men who sail with the Convoys. Here, for example, is one day's work, off Canada's east coast. The day was January 24th, 1942. It might as well have been almost any other.

That morning a Catalina flying boat of the R.C.A.F. came upon two freighters which had lost their places in Convoy and, finally, had lost their Convoy altogether. It gave the masters new courses enabling them to rejoin the main body. The same day a Canso of the R.C.A.F. found another straggler which had fallen back, due to poor coal. It brought a destroyer to the scene and the destroyer gave assistance to the limping merchantman. During the same day two other R.C.A.F. Catalinas gave aid to survivors of torpedoed vessels. In the first case a lifeboat and five survivors were found. Food and water were dropped in dinghies and occupants of the lifeboat were instructed to tow the dinghies because of their bright colour. A rescue ship was sent out to bring the mariners to port. The second Catalina found two life-boats and twenty survivors of an east-coast torpedoing. Signals were exchanged and a corvette was sent to the rescue. Such jobs are all in the day's work to the crews who fly the aircraft off our Canadian coasts. No glory. But plenty of muck!

* * *

Amongst the extremely important developments of 1940-41, although it is not actually of Canada, but of the R.A.F., was the establishment on Canadian soil of the headquarters from which a constant flow of Bombers has been funnelled through to Britain. Organised in the first instance as the Canadian Pacific Air Service at request of Morris W. Wilson, President of the Royal Bank of Canada and British Ministry of Aircraft Production representative in Washington, the Atlantic ferry became an accomplished fact in short order. As the Bombers began to move in increasing volume, calling for greatly increased terminal facilities on Canadian soil, Harold M. Long, hard-hitting Montreal business man, was impressed into service by Wilson and the Ferry operated from the end of February to August 1st, 1941, under the name and style of Atfero. Thanks to Long's driving personality and the operating genius of Captain C. H. (Punch) Dickins, renowned Canadian bush-pilot, hangars, repair shops and all necessary buildings went up in rapid fashion as material bottlenecks were broken with priority orders and constant riding of producers, as Dickins made the urgently needed aircraft move. Soon a stream of medium and, later, four-engined Bombers were flying east from Dorval (Montreal), through Newfoundland to Britain, piloted in the main by veteran pilots of the Canadian bush and by commercial fliers from the United States. Their record of success in the one job that counts, deliveries beyond the ocean, has been outstanding and reflects great credit on the "business fliers" of North America. In all this the R.C.A.F. and the Depart-ment of Transport cooperated in the fullest degree, providing all western bases with the exception of Gander, Newfoundland. Atfero was replaced by the R.A.F. Ferry Command under Air Marshal Sir Charles Bowhill in August 1941. To-day the job is handled by a combined Civilian-R.A.F. organisation, the great majority of its Pilots still being veteran civilian fliers.

During 1941 the Atlantic Ferry provided transportation for many distinguished passengers travelling on war missions for the United Kingdom, the United States and Canada. Amongst the Canadian passengers were Prime Minister W. L. Mackenzie

King and Air Minister Power, each of whom visited Britain to inspect Canadian military formations overseas and for consulta-tions with the British Government on the Canadian war effort. In the Prime Minister's case the eastbound flight was his first journey aloft. Leaving Canadian soil on July 20th, Mr. King reached Britain without incident after a refuelling stop in New-foundland. While in England, Mr. King visited Canada's air fighters at their stations, joining their officers at mess and chatting informally with non-commissioned flying men. He returned to Canada on August 8th to report "all's well" with the graduates of the Air Plan.

Major Power's visit, which began on July 1st and was completed with his return to Canada by air on the 25th, was more particu-larised as to its purpose, that of visiting "his boys" in Britain and of discussing with the Air Ministry of the United Kingdom various aspects of the Air Plan and its operation in action, concerning which the Minister reported to Parliament on his return in the following terms:

"Anyone who has been overseas knows that our boys are there. They are not there in speeches; they are not there in the papers, but they are there in Bombers, there at their stations, and there over Germany every night. They are there in Tripoli and Libya and Russia—and everywhere. Wherever the Royal Air Force is, there they are.

"Last year someone asked in the House what the position was, and I said we would be judged by the results of our plans. I can say now that that Honourable member need not ask me; he could ask Hitler. Hitler knows, and he is going to know more and more, as this war goes on. The other answer is to read the daily press. There is no doubt that we can say that the Royal Canadian Air Force pupil graduates are coming into their own. There were those who jeered when we began eighteen months ago with the first class of 168 men and said that we could not win wars on schedules. That class of 168 men has been multiplied one-hundred-fold, and today I think we can safely say that the Empire Training Scheme has won its wings.

"Overseas we have sixteen Squadrons in active operation. They are of all types and categories, Fighter, Night Fighter, Army Co-operation, Bomber and so on. Besides that, thousands of our men are in the Royal Air Force wherever the Royal Air Force is fighting. We have also supplied radio mechanics and ground crews. As yet we have not sufficient ground crews, but we are sending them over all the time and before long we expect to equip the numerous Royal Canadian Air Force Squadrons there now and whatever Squadrons we may be able to send over later with our own ground crews.

"The purpose of my trip overseas was to see and hear from our partners in the Joint Air Training Plan just how our boys were shaping up, to see the boys themselves, and as the Plan was in full operation to ascertain what modifications and improvements could be made, particularly what improvements could be made in Canada. I stressed particularly the lot of our graduates, those men who are not formed into Royal Canadian Air Force Squa-drons. A vast majority of them are attached to the Royal Air Force. "Perhaps it would have been better if we had been able to keep them together as Canadians, but the circumstances were such that we had to sacrifice national pride to efficiency and expedition. In order to produce more of them more quickly and get them into the fighting line, we placed them in a joint pool with the other young men of the Commonwealth. I do not think that will do them any harm. There has been no difficulty in getting them to fight alongside men of other lands. The cause is such and the enemy is such that all sons of freedom can very well combine to fight against this common enemy. But the boys themselves, and their parents as well, like to think that they are with pals, and it was in order to keep them together as much as possible, whether

Ferry Command: The Rt. Hon. W. L. Mackenzie King shaking hands with Air C
Marshal Sir Frederick Bowhill. (Top right) Pilots and Navigators of the Ferry Comm
have a conference before taking off. (Lower left) Prime Minister chats with Capt. L
Messenger, Pilot of the aircraft that took him to Britain . . . visiting the Night Fig
in Britain.

in Canadian or British formations, that I made representations to the British government.

"As time goes on, more and more Canadians will be grouped together in Squadrons, at stations, in Groups and in Commands, and our men will assume higher and higher responsibilities.

"There is little else I have to say with respect to my visit. I saw the boys. I was impressed by their morale, their gayety, their brave comradeship, their sportsmanship and their keenness to get at their job. I do not know that there is anything of particular interest for me to tell with respect to my visits to the different stations. I saw a very large proportion of the stations where our Canadians were congregated in any degree, and all I can say is that I hope we were in some manner successful, not in raising their morale, because that is not needed, but in impressing on our boys that the people of Canada are back of them right through to the end. There are many of them, and there will be many times more—how many I am not permitted to say. I can give no figures, no statistics. I do not need to, because their deeds are written large across the blazing skies of Africa, Europe and Asia; they are being seared into the minds of the people of Germany and are being written gloriously into the pages of the history of Canada and the Commonwealth. Unfortunately they are being written, too, on the hearts of the afflicted parents of those who become casualties. There is little I can say to alleviate their grief, and I can promise no relief except this, that those who say the Canadian people cannot take it do not know whereof they speak. May I say that in the communications received from the afflicted parents there is a note of pride, of nobility, of patience and of strength. For the moment it is these individuals who feel the blow. It will be only after this accursed conflict has been liquidated and we have attempted to take stock of our national assets, when we shall require in our post-war struggle for existence in a newer world all the strength of will and brain inherent in our national character, that the Canadian people will be aware of the grievous blow and of the sacrifice which it has suffered through being deprived of the most noble, the most brilliant and the most able young men of this generation."

* * *

The personnel of the Royal Canadian Air Force in Canada and overseas on the 1st of November, 1941, was approximately 90,000, this in addition to pupils attached to the Royal Canadian Air Force but belonging to the Royal Air Force, the Royal Australian Air Force and the Royal New Zealand Air Force. It was also in exclusion of 11,000 civilians, about half of whom were taking the places of Service men who had been released for more active duty. Thus, all told, there were under the control of the Department of National Defence for Air well over 100,000 persons. At the beginning of February, 1942, the figure had reached 106,000 men in uniform and more than 13,000 civilians, or virtually 120,000 all told. From the insistent upward movement in Air Force enlistment figures, whenever facilities for increase offer, it becomes apparent that young Canada insists that the heritage of flight is his. Particularly there is that field between 18 and 25, wherein, without any particular efforts on the Recruiting Officers' part, without any propaganda, there will always be priority for the Royal Canadian Air Force. Whether the authorities like it or not, whether Canada takes other steps, selective or otherwise, the young men of the Senior Dominion want to join the Royal Canadian Air Force; and it does not matter what anybody does about it, they are going to join it anyway. The writer once asked the Air Minister to state an objective. The reply? "In so far as the Air Force is concerned the sky is the limit. We will take as aircrew all the young men of Canada who are willing and able to serve, and we make no limit anywhere. I do not even follow the example of the Minister of National Defence for the Army. If anyone wants to enlist in our Air Force, whether his employer likes it or

not, whether his employer calls him a key man or not, if he wants to come in the Air Force he comes in, and that is all there is to it.

"With respect to the higher strategic aspects of the war", Major Power continued, "namely as to with what particular branch of the Service the War is eventually to be won, I am not prepared to discuss that, because I do not know. But I will say this: you may need the Army to win the war, but you will lose the war without the Air Force. That has been patent to everybody since the War started, and that condition is going to obtain to the end of the War. The experience of this War has shown that, even with her mighty mechanized forces, Germany made no advances whatsoever until she obtained air superiority."

If one were to think in terms of days gone by, probably he would say, that this War has shown that Providence is on the side of those who have air supremacy. Up to this time there has been no doubt of that.

* * *

It is no longer merely a young man's force, this R.C.A.F., but that of young women as well. In connection with the Home effort, Canada instituted in 1941 a corps first known as the C.W.A.A.F., The Canadian Women's Auxiliary Air Force, and now as the R.C.A.F. Women's Division. A commission was given the original commanding officer, Mrs. Walker, and two others to female medical doctors. All others have been trained at its school in Toronto, where Havergal Ladies' College was taken over as a training centre. A beginning was made by selecting for training, to be turned out in accordance with the marks obtained, either as non-commissioned officers or officers, 150 women from across Canada. These form the nucleus of the officers and non-commissioned officers of the Division. Canadian young women rushed to the colours as soon as it was created. The first graduates, 126 strong, reported to the S.F.T.S. at Uplands (Ottawa) on January 5th, 1942. A similar group arrived at Brantford on the 12th, others at Moncton, Dunnville and Saskatoon on succeeding Saturdays. These patriotic young women serve in many capacities; as drivers, clerks, parachute packers, switchboard operators, etc. As this is written 600 were at Havergal qualifying for their future duties. Women cooks are trained at the R.C.A.F. School of Cookery at Guelph.

* * *

In addition to the organization of the Women's Division, the Air Cadet League of Canada was inaugurated in June, 1941. The president is George B. Foster, K.C., D.F.C., of Montreal, and a list of prominent men was chosen from all over Canada to act as directors. These were:

"Hon. F. P. Brais, K.C.; H. R. Carson; A. W. Carter, M.B.E.; D.S.C.; Pierre deVarennes, K.C.; H. E. Drope; Gilbert M. Eaton, John D. Eaton; Sir Ellsworth Flavelle; G. B. Foster, K.C., D.F.C.; Chas. A. Gray; Geo. R. Hodgson; Major R. H. B. Ker; D. R. MacLaren, D.S.O., M.C., D.F.C.; Arthur L. Melling; W. W. Rogers; Hon. Ivan Schultz, K.C.; Earle Spafford; Terrence M. Sheard. The honorary secretary is Arthur L. Melling, and Squadron-Leader R. W. Frost, R.C.A.F., is acting National Director.

There were enrolled in Canada at the beginning of 1942, something like 14,000 air cadets in units divided approximately as follows:—British Columbia, 2,500 in nineteen units; in Alberta 1,200 in eleven units; Saskatchewan, 2,400 in eighteen units; Manitoba, 700 in three units; Ontario, 1,000 in eight units; Quebec, 5,000 in thirteen units; Nova Scotia, 200 in three units; Prince Edward Island, 100 in two units. The age limit is 18, at which time the young men are ready to try their wings.

In many instances former Royal Canadian Air Force or Fleet Air Arm officers have turned out to help the boys by giving them their drill and training. The Air Cadet Training Programme is a basic

(Top left) Prime Minister congratulates a Fighter Pilot. (Centre left) Prime Mini[s]ter has late snack in the mess of an R.C.A.F. Fighter Station—on his right, Air Vice Mars[hal] R. E. Saul, C.B.E., D.F.C., on left, Group Captain S. P. Campbell, (Hamilton, On[t]. Other pictures show Hon. C. G. Power, Air Minister, visiting his "Boys" overseas.

programme and is similar to the elementary ground training received in R.C.A.F. schools. In addition a system of university training for future air crew recruits was inaugurated in 1941. It is not a C.O.T.C. It does not give or promise commissions, but it is a university air training course. A number of Canadian universities have made arrangements to provide what is called pre-flight training on the Royal Canadian Air Force syllabus as an alternative to Army training. Only university students who can meet the medical requirements for air crew training and who sign a statement of honourable intention to join the Royal Canadian Air Force at the completion of their university course are accepted. Medical examination and uniforms are provided by the Royal Canadian Air Force, which also makes available the necessary training equipment and instructional assistance. Students completing this course are recognized as having fulfilled the requirements of the National Resources Mobilization Act.

The course is equivalent to the course of training at Initial Training Schools of the Royal Canadian Air Force in connection with the British Commonwealth Air Training plan. The university course provides 200 hours of similar instruction in mathematics, armaments, Air Force law, airmanship, theory of flight, et cetera and is followed by two weeks of summer camp at one of the Service Flying Training Schools, where this ground instruction in Air Force life is continued under Service conditions.

Besides this, as a man-power salvage job, a Cease Training school has been opened at Trenton, Ontario, primarily for student Pilots who fail to make the going through no fault of their own, perhaps on account of physical defects or because they just naturally cannot fly a machine. This is a reorientation school, or rehabilitation school, wherein these young men are assisted in finding some other trade within the Service. It may be a man would not make a good Pilot but has the educational qualifications to be an Observer, or if he has a good educational background he may make a ground instructor in one of several categories. The school has been placed under the care and command of Wing-Commander Denton Massey, M.P.

All boys 'washed out' as Pilots, go to this school to be re-selected for some other branch of the Service.

*   *   *

The Air Plan was thought of such importance in the British grand strategy that a member of the Royal Family, His Royal Highness the Duke of Kent, visited the schools of the Training Plan in Canada, including those belonging to the Royal Air Force, during the summer of 1941. He came as an Air Commodore in the Royal Air Force and flew from one end of the country to the other. He arrived after all the flying stations in Canada had been selected and a great majority were in full operation.

British Commonwealth Air Training Plan establishments as at February 1st, 1942, were as follows:

Elementary Flying Training Schools: Malton, Ont.; Fort William, Ont.; London, Ont.; Windsor Mills, P.Q.; High River, Alta.; (Relief—Frank Lake, Alta.); Prince Albert, Sask.; Windsor, Ont., Vancouver, B.C.; St. Catharines, Ont.; Hamilton, Ont.; Cap de la Madeleine, P.Q.; Goderich, Ont.; St. Eugene, Ont.; Portage la Prairie, Man.; Regina, Sask.; Edmonton, Alta.; Stanley, N.S.; Boundary Bay, B.C., (Relief—Langley, B.C.); Virden, Man., (Relief—Hargrave, Man.); Oshawa, Ont., (Relief—Whitby, Ont.); Chatham, N.B.; Quebec City, P.Q.

Air Navigation Schools: Rivers, Man.; Pennfield Ridge, N.B.
Air Observer Schools: Malton, Ont.; Edmonton, Alta.; Regina, Sask.; London, Ont.; Winnipeg, Man.; Prince Albert, Sask.; Portage la Prairie, Man.; Quebec City, P.Q.; St. Johns, P.Q.; Chatham, N.B.

Bombing and Gunnery Schools: Jarvis, Ont.; Mossbank, Sask.; Macdonald, Man.; Fingal, Ont.; Dafoe, Sask.; Mountain View,

Ont.; Paulson, Man.; Lethbridge, Alta.; Mont Joli, P.Q.

Service Flying Training Schools: Camp Borden, Ont.; (Relief No. 1—Edenvale, Ont.; Relief No. 2—Alliston, Ont.) Ottawa Ont.; (Relief No. 1—Pendleton, Ont. Relief No. 2—Edwards, Ont.); Calgary, Alta. (Currie barracks); (Relief No. 1—Shepard, Alta.); Saskatoon, Sask., (Relief No. 1—Vanscoy, Sask. Relief No. 2—Osler, Sask.); Brantford, Ont., (Relief No. 1—Burtch, Ont.); Dunnville, Ont., (Relief No. 1—Welland, Ont.); Macleod, Alta., (Relief No. 1—Granum, Alta.); Moncton, N.B., (Relief No. 1—Scoudouc, N.B. Relief No. 2—Salisbury, N.B.); Summerside, P.E.I., (Relief No. 1—Mount Pleasant, P.E.I. Relief No. 2—Wellington, P.E.I.) Dauphin, Man., (Relief No. 1—North Junction, Man. Relief No. 2—Valley River, Man.); Yorkton, Sask., (Relief No. 1—Sturdee, Sask. Relief No. 2—Rhein, Sask.); Brandon, Man., (Relief No. 1—Chater, Man. Relief No. 2—Douglas, Man.) St. Hubert, P.Q., (Relief No. 1—St. Johns, P.Q. Relief No. 2—Farnham, P.Q.); Aylmer, Ont., (Relief No. 1—St. Thomas, Ont.); Claresholm, Alta., (Relief No. 1—Woodhouse, Alta.); Hagersville, Ont., (Relief No. 1—Kohler, Ont.); Central Flying School: Trenton, Ont., (Relief No. 1—Mohawk, Ont.).

Wireless Schools: Montreal, P.Q.; Calgary, Alta.; Winnipeg, Man.; Guelph, Ont.
Initial Training Schools: Toronto, Ont.; Regina, Sask.; Victoriaville, P.Q.; Edmonton, Alta.; Belleville, Ont.; Saskatoon, Sask.
Technical Training School: St. Thomas, Ont.
Technical Detachments: Toronto, Ont.; Montreal, P.Q.
Composite Training School: Trenton, Ont.
School of Aeronautical Engineering: Montreal, P.Q.
Holding Unit: Moncton, N.B.
Air Armament School: Mountain View, Ont.

Depots: Trenton, Ont.; Winnipeg, Man.; St. Johns, P.Q.; Calgary, Alta.; Toronto, Ont.; Montreal, P.Q.; Ottawa, Ont.; Brandon, Man.; Edmonton, Alta.; Quebec, P.Q.; Lachine, P.Q.; Camp Borden, Ont.; Regina, Sask.; Halifax, N.S.; Rockcliffe, Ont.

*   *   *

The Plan is never static. It lives in a state of flux. In the beginning the call was all for Pilots. At the time of closing these pages there was a special call for Observers and Bombers. Accordingly difficulties must always be met as they come. Schools must always be kept up to date, so that the Plan may be able to produce the men who are most required at a given time. For this reason it has been necessary to increase the number of Manning Depots and Initial Training Schools to a considerable degree over that which was anticipated at the beginning.

As to the future of the Plan, Air Minister Power stated at the end of 1941 that there is a proposal for its continuance after 1943, this being one of the matters which the Minister discussed while on the other side. As to whether Australia and New Zealand will continue on the same basis as in the beginning in an extended Plan, or whether they may prefer to do their own training, in view of the fact that to a considerable extent they have now developed their own schools, had not been determined at the end of Winter 1941-2.

The personnel the sister Dominions have sent has been outstanding in the Canadian schools. Australian and New Zealand pupils have made names for themselves in the way of discipline and energy, and the enthusiasm they show in their work.

Apart from these Joint Training Plan Schools there are a number of schools manned by Royal Air Force personnel and utilized for the purpose of training Royal Air Force pupils. No authority from the United Kingdom officials to give information respecting the location of these schools, the number of personnel or pupils is available. It can be said, however, that these courses are under the control and administration of the Royal Canadian Air Force,

The Air Minister Overseas: (above) with Air Marshal A.G.R. Garrod, C.B., O.B.E., M.C., D.F.C. (Centre left) First Anniversary Dinner of No. 1 Fighter Squadron, May 1941. (Centre right) The Minister with Staff Officers. (Lower left) Air Vice Marshal G.O. Johnson, Air Marshal A.G.R. Garrod, Air Marshal L.S. Breadner, Air Commodore Hon. R.A. Cochrane, Air Chief Marshal Sir Frederick Bowhill, the Air Minister, Air Vice Marshal N.R. Anderson, Air Commodore A. Durston. (Lower right) The Air Minister, Hon. Vincent Massey, Rt. Hon. Winston Churchill, Hon. Ian Mackenzie

and constitute a most important addition both in schools and in the responsibilities of the Staff of the R.C.A.F.

Canadian government facilities have been used entirely in connection with the selection of sites for the R.A.F. schools, the development of aerodromes, and the construction of buildings and runways. All projects contemplated were being proceeded with expeditiously at the end of 1941. The additional burdens placed upon the various Departments, as well as the Royal Canadian Air Force, have been met without difficulty. The estimated cost of the transfer school policy to March 31, 1942, is $105,-000,000.

* * *

Aircraft in hand at the end of 1941 were double in number those available at the end of 1940, most of them Elementary Trainers. They were coming in on time, in virtually every type, but the need was much greater than a year before. The Ministry of Supply was honouring its commitments, but the R.C.A.F. was asking for more, and apparently will continue to ask for more. There is no use in extending in one direction without extending in others at the same time, so that a man's training can be carried right through. Some types of aircraft are harder to get than others. They must have special qualities and performance. This applies particularly to the training aircraft in the Bombing and Gunnery schools.

Equipment was again being received from the United Kingdom at the end of 1941. Technical Officers were experimenting, substituting and modifying, in the hope of adapting certain types of aircraft built in Canada to special training tasks and substituting these for aircraft most difficult to get from the other side. Granted success in these and similar experiments the Plan will be able to increase considerably its output of a certain type of pupil, the straight Air Gunners—tail-end Charleys.

Overhaul has been a major problem from the beginning. After two years it showed no sign of abatement. On the contrary, according to the Minister for Air:

"Overhaul last year was a headache; this year it has been Arthritis, Phlebitis, St. Vitus Dance and everything else put together. The cause of the disease is a shortage of spares. There is a world shortage of spares, and particularly of engine spares. Naturally it arises from the urgent demand for engines for operational aircraft. What spares can be made here we will make, but there are limits in that regard. It is a difficult art, calling for special tools which may be needed elsewhere. The answer is to extemporize, substitute and multiply. We are doing all this. So far there has been no hold-up, and we hope there will not be. But I do not wish to disguise that the going is pretty tough, and that we shall have a hard time to keep our planes in the air."

There will always be bottlenecks until the day of Victory!

* * *

The following flying statistics will be of interest to the reader:

1. Hours flown by Air Plan Schools to September 30, 1941.................... 1,795,893
   At 125 miles per hour this represents... 224,486,625 miles
   Number of fatal accidents.............. 157
   Number of hours flown per fatal accident 11,438 hours
   Number of miles flown per fatal accident 1,429,851 miles

2. United States civilian flying in 1940 show 1,269,231 miles flown per each fatal accident.

3. The fatal accident rate of Plan schools has come down from November, 1940, when it was .17 to September, 1941, when the rate was .067 or 1 fatal accident to 1,818,279 miles flown, but we must expect an upward trend during the winter months.

4. Total flying time for September, including home war establishment and Royal Air Force in Canada.................... 253,490 hours
   Total flying time since April, 1940...... 1,887,130 hours
   Total flying time since Sept. 30, 1940 to Sept. 30, 1941...................... 1,760,640 hours
   Total flying time since Jan. 1, 1941—that is for nine months of the present year.. 1,596,680 hours
   This latter figure indicates that the total flying time for the present calendar year will be about...................... 2,250,000 hours

5. If the average flying speed is taken at 125 miles an hour, then we are exceeding 31,686,250 miles a month, or over 1,000,000 miles a day.

* * *

What are the graduates of Canada's Air Training Plan meeting in combat overseas? Man for man, no doubt has ever existed in Canadian minds that we are more than a match for the enemy. Aircraft for aircraft we are catching up numerically; in quality we are better in our top-flight machines. But what is the enemy force against which our young men are pitted? Is Germany's *Luftwaffe* of similar physical construction to the Royal Air Force, or to the R.C.A.F.? How does Germany's concentration of air power work?

From what he has read the Canadian reader is posted as to the air-fighting methods of the British nations. He knows that the War In The Air overseas is carried on through a series of Commands (Bomber, Coastal, Fighter, etc.) and that each of these specializes in its own branch of aerial warfare. Let us look for a moment, then, at Germany's air-war organisation, in order that it may be possible to compare methods, as well as to be familiar with the structure of the German air-arm.

Many senior officers of the present German Air Force, notably Field Marshal Goering, were members of the German Air Force in the war of 1914-1918. It may be of interest, therefore, to review briefly the lessons of the last war with regard to the German Air Force.

In the last war Germany had naval and military air services, and her Air Force to-day retains military titles in the ranking of its officers. The General Staff, with control of the military Air Service, never asked of it the costly offensive efforts that were asked of the Royal Flying Corps. Then, as now, the Germans regarded their Air Force as a weapon of strategical rather than tactical offense. To-day the *Luftwaffe,* (Air Arm) as the German Air Force is named, is the Senior Service. Goering is its Air Minister and Commander in Chief; and his personal power places the German Air Force in an advantageous position in relation to the Army and the Navy in the *Oberkommando der Wohrmacht,* or Supreme Command of Reich Armed Forces, Hitler's Defence Council. Operationally, the *Luftwaffe* retains control of almost all except shipborne aircraft.

It was the policy of the German General Staff during the last war to use the military air service sparingly and mainly defensively, using high land-moored ballons as much as possible for observation, thereby saving the effort of the Air Force for critical times by keeping flying to a minimum on quiet days, as was inferred above. On the other hand it should be noted that when Goering, who now commands the *Luftwaffe,* took over the command of the Richthofen squadron in June 1918, he showed himself to be prodigal of his resources of men and machines, and inspired such supreme and continuous effort during the Amiens offensive of August 1918 that the Richthofen squadron virtually ceased to exist and had to be withdrawn from the battle front for reconstitution.

The Ships the Angels Fly—(Top left) Hurricane 11 B; (top right) Cannon-mounted Sp... (centre left) Guns on Hurricane 11 B; (lower left) Curtis Kitty Hawk; (lower ... formation of Lockheed Hudsons over England.

When the German Air Force undertook offensive bombing operations in the last war, they usually chose strategically important targets and concentrated their forces in attacks against them until destruction had been achieved. There was relatively little spasmodic bombing, and dispersal of air effort in invariable and considerable close tactical support of ground operations was frowned on as a costly and relatively ineffective use of the air weapon. The organization of the German Air Force to-day is designed to allow an even greater concentration of effort, as will be explained later, against strategically rather than tactically important targets, as the operations in the invaded countries have shown.

In the last war the German scheme of allotting air units to Army formations was more elastic than that in the British forces, and enabled the Germans to pursue a policy of ruthlessly denuding inactive fronts in order to concentrate air power in critical areas. This power of rapid concentration enabled the Germans to withstand the numerical air superiority of the Allies in the last year of the 1914-18 war, being especially marked at Cambrai in November, 1917, and before the German offensive of March 1918.

Again in the 1940 breakthrough in France, the same power of concentration, allied with extreme mobility, accentuated the existing numerical inferiority of the Allies. It is important to note that superior mobility and power of concentration can in a considerable degree compensate for inferior numerical strength. In the last war Germany did not follow the policy that the Western Front should absorb all the latest aircraft types. Subsidiary theatres generally received samples of these, which often enabled the Germans to enjoy a measure of local air superiority even when numerically inferior.

The organization of the German Air Force to-day is designed to enable its whole weight, if necessary, to be concentrated on any desired area at the shortest notice. The main features of the organization making for this power of concentration of force are; —(1) Unity of Command and Operational Control. (2) Offensive Forces organized separately from Non-Offensive. (3) Offensive Forces organized into complete Air Forces. (4) Organization of the Offensive Forces on a basis of extreme mobility. (5) Organization of the Non-Offensive forces on a territorial basis.

Due partly to the personal position of Field Marshal Goering, and partly to the Nazi belief in the decisiveness of air power, the German Air Force enjoys a unity of command and independence of policy which is not paralleled in the Allied Air Forces. The *Luftwaffe* has retained operational control of almost all aircraft except shipborne aircraft, and even these come under the Air Force when they are based away from their ships. Coastal units come under the command of the *Luftflotte* in whose area they are operating. Army Co-operation units, though attached to Army formations, are under the operational control of an Air Force officer who acts as Air Adviser to the Army Commander to whose formation he is attached. The entire active and passive Defence Forces of the Reich, including Anti-Aircraft and Air Raid Precautions, come under the Air Force. There is nothing in Germany to parallel the Fleet Air Arm of the British Admiralty, or the position of the Admiralty in relation to the R.A.F.'s Coastal Command, nor even the newly formed Army Co-operation Command of the R.A.F. The position of the *Luftwaffe* is, as has been indicated above, very strong, in that, in addition to retaining this unity of command and operational control over almost all aircraft, its commander, Reich Marshal Goering, is the most powerful member of the Supreme Command of German Armed Forces. This body, under Hitler, co-ordinates and allocates tasks to the three Services of whose representatives it is formed. This strong position, especially in unity of command and operational control, is an important factor in the achievement of extremely rapid and heavy concentration of force, especially in combined operations.

Under the German Air Ministry the organization of the German Air Force is divided into two sections (1) The Offensive or Striking Forces, organized under the *Luftflotten*, or Air Fleets (2) The Non-Offensive (i.e. non-operational and purely defensive) Forces, organized under the *Luftgaue* or Regional Commands. These two parts of the German Air Force are quite distinct in their organization.

The Offensive or Striking Forces are organised under five *Luftflotten*, or Air Fleets, which are Air Striking Commands whose function is to operate the *Fliegerkorps* (Flying Corps or Divisions) of which the Airfleet is made up, from the operational area assigned to the Airfleet. That is, the *Luftflotten* are Operational Airfleet Headquarters with Staffs, Flying Divisions, etc.

In any emergency, a *Luftflotte* on an inactive front might be stripped of almost all its fighting units to reinforce the critical area; but the *Luftflotten* Headquarters will remain ready to function again if necessary. The organization of the *Luftflotten* is not concerned with non-operational matters such as administration, training, supply, and so on, so long as these are working satisfactorily; these are the responsibility of the *Luftgaue*, or Regional (Non-Offensive) Commands.

In every *Luftflotte* operational area there are two or more of these Regional (Non-Offensive) Commands to provide defended base facilities for the Offensive Forces. In this function of provision the *Luftgaue* communicate direct with, and receive their orders direct from, the Air Ministry, and the subordination of the *Luftgaue* Commander to the *Luftflotte* Commander would therefore appear to be, apart from any question of rank, no more than a device to enable the operational commander to get from the non-offensive ground organizations what operational requirements dictate, without fear of delay or obstruction.

Thus those responsible for the conduct of operations are largely freed from preoccupation with matters of administration and supply and training etc., and can concentrate on the essential business of operations in the knowledge that the facilities they require are being provided by the non-operational branches of the service. This division of the organization of the *Luftwaffe* obviously makes for a high degree of flexibility and speed in the conduct of operations; and, together with the features discussed below, with which it is bound up, it is the essence of the remarkable power of rapid concentration of force possessed by the *Luftwaffe*.

Unlike the Offensive Forces of the R.A.F., which are organized into functional commands—Bomber Command, Fighter Command and Coastal Command—those of the *Luftwaffe* are organized under the *Luftflotten*, or Air Fleets, into Flying Divisions, *Fliegerkorps* or *Fliegerdivisionen*, which are in fact complete Air Forces with their own Headquarters, Bomber, Fighter, Reconnaissance and Transport aircraft. There are at the present time eleven of these divisions, including the fully operational Tactical Development Division, and one Division of Parachute Troops and Air Transport Units for them. Thus, the rapid reinforcement of a critical area can be achieved with the maximum speed by a simple order moving up a number of these self contained, completely mobile air forces to the *Luftflotte*—Air Striking Command—in whose operational area the critical position exists, where the reinforcing divisions will find awaiting them orders from the Command and secure bases provided independently of the Striking Command by the *Luftgaue* (Administrative and Defensive Commands). War experience in fact caused the Coastal Command of the R.A.F. to develop from a mainly reconnaissance Command to a Striking Command similar to the *Luftflotten*, equipped with its own Fighter and Bomber aircraft as well as Reconnaissance machines and Flying Boats. The German organ-

The Ships the Angels Fly—(Left to right, top to bottom) Bristol Beaufort, Douglas Havoc, Boeing Flying Fortress B 17 E, Vickers Wellington, Consolidated Liberator, and Bristol Beau Fighter.

ization is plainly effective in allowing rapid concentration of force.

The fact, discussed above, that the Striking Forces are relieved as far as possible of responsibility for non-operational matters of ground organization, and are organized as complete Air Forces, are important factors, in making them mobile. The *Flieger Divisionen* can move from the operational area of one Striking Command (*Luftflotte*) to that of another, at shortest notice, knowing that they will find the same necessary base facilities in the area to which they are proceeding, as they have enjoyed in the one they left, though provided by different *Luftgaue* —Regional Commands. The base facilities in the *Luftgaue* covering all German occupied Europe are provided independently of the Striking Forces which are thereby given freedom of movement in themselves, and a wide range of bases from which to operate. In addition, everything has been done to enhance the mobility of the Striking Forces. The largest mobile unit is the *Flieger,* or Flying Division. This consists of a Headquarters and a variable number of *Geschwader* or Groups of Bomber, Fighter, Reconnaissance, etc., Aircraft. Divisional Headquarters, and every *Geschwader* (Group Headquarters) has a number of transport aircraft attached to provide maximum mobility, and every formation below the *Geschwader* or Group has its Staff Flight of three to six aircraft. Bomber and Fighter Squadrons may each have one or two transport aircraft for mobility purposes. Thus the whole of a *Flieger* Division is organized for air transport. There are twelve of these divisions, and it is easy to see how, with the mobility described above, these air divisions can rapidly be concentrated on one decisive area if necessary.

It would not be accurate to describe the Non-Offensive Forces, in contrast to the Striking Forces discussed above, as non-operational; for the *Luftgaue,* into which they are organized (Air Regions, literally) are responsible for certain operational formations of fighters for purely defensive purposes, as well as for Anti-Aircraft Artillery and all other forms of active and passive air defences. It is the essence of the function of the Non-Offensive Organizations to provide secure bases for the Striking Forces in every operational area. The Non-Offensive Forces are therefore organized within those operational areas. In every Air Striking Command (*Luftflotte*) area there are two or more *Luftgaue,* whose commanders and staffs are responsible to the Air Ministry for Supply and Maintenance, Training, Armament, Air Defence, and so on. The complete picture. therefore, is of a number of stations, stretching across German-occupied Europe, regionally organized, providing bases for Flying Divisions which can fly from one Striking Command area to another according to strategical requirements. This territorial organization of commands is ideally suited to German geography, in that it enables full use to be made of Germany's natural advantage of interior lines of communications, and also to German strategy, which has always leaned to the "lightning stroke" type of doctrine. It gives a much greater degree of mobility than does the organization of the Royal Air Force; but it must be remembered that the Royal Air Force has very different geographical conditions to cope with, and its organization has not had the advantage of the German of being set up in a very short time (1933-5) by one man with dictatorial powers delegated to him—Goering; but has grown up, sometimes slowly, sometimes fast, and much of its organization has therefore been dictated by compromise.

The two methods may be described then, as horizontal (the German) and perpendicular (the British). In the German groups each is self contained as to types, whereas in the R.A.F. (and, therefore, in the R.C.A.F. Squadrons overseas) forces are grouped in Commands according to specific types of operational duties. The object of these paragraphs is not to draw a comparison based on merit of methods, but to delineate the German approach to aerial warfare in its variances of organization from our own, in order that the reader may visualise the organization of the enemy to be vanquished.

*   *   *

So drew to a close two years of War In the Air. From a standing start Canada had fashioned the great university of flight making use of existing Air Force and Civil Aerodromes and every other facility at hand, carving new Stations out of prairie farmland and virgin forest, finding somewhere the thousands of aircraft needed to produce the constant stream of Pilots, Observers and Gunners who soon would knock the Hun from the skies of the War Fronts. In their teeming thousands young Canadians had passed through the schools and had gone to war, bright wings on their breasts. Overseas more than twenty Canadian Squadrons were fighting as units, thousands of other young graduates were making their mark in the R.A.F. Ground-crew men were "over there" in thousands. On the Home Front the schools ran full out, the Recruiting Offices were still bringing in young men as rapidly as they could be absorbed into the Plan. We had fashioned a great air-defence chain behind our Pacific Coast to protect Canadian homes and soil from potential invaders. On the east the R.C.A.F. sought submarines, escorted the great Convoys of supply en route to beleagured Britain. So ended the second year of Canada's War in the Air, the year of mass production, the year during which the youth of a nation passed from the halls of aerial learning into the sterner role of the Fighting Flier. The legendry fashioned by the Bishops, the Barkers and the Collishaws goes on, its golden pages written in filmy cloud and the spray of lead.

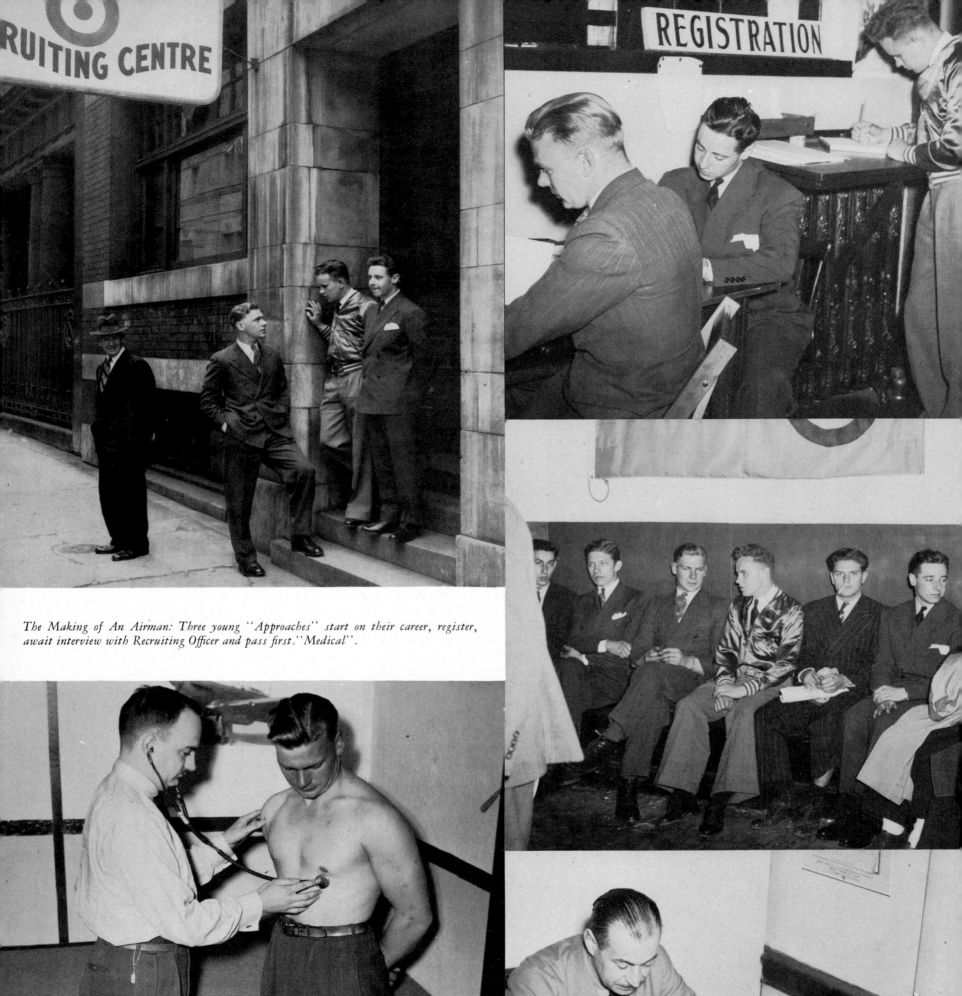

The Making of An Airman: Three young "Approaches" start on their career, register, await interview with Recruiting Officer and pass first "Medical".

THE MAKING OF AN AIRMAN

"WE have taken the very cream of the youth of Canada. We have taken these youths from our schools, our colleges and our universities. I think these men are the most truly Canadian body that exists anywhere in the world. I would say that as a body they are more Canadian than even this House of Commons. There has been no great tide of immigration from the other side, from Great Britain, or anywhere else during the past twenty-five years. These boys are mainly third, fourth and fifth generation Canadians, bred in Canada, schooled in Canadian schools and with an intensely Canadian viewpoint. Their viewpoint is far removed from that of most of us who are perhaps more closely connected with the old land. They are more Canadian by far than was the Canadian army in the last war, in which was a large proportion of men born on the other side of the water. As I say, these men have the Canadian viewpoint, if it exists anywhere. They are the future leaders of this country and the destiny of Canada will some day be in their hands. Therefore it behooves us to see to it that these men do not return from overseas with the same sense of disappointment, disillusionment and discontent as did the men who returned from the last war."

* * *

The speaker is a man who knows whereof he speaks, Canada's Minister of National Defence for Air, Major the Hon. C. G. Power, M.C. The words were spoken during the course of a review of Canada's war in the air before the Commons in Ottawa on November 6th, 1941, immediately following the Minister's tour of inspection in Britain of Canada's contribution to aerial warfare in the R.C.A.F. and the R.A.F. overseas. At that time more than 90,000 young Canadians were serving in the Air Forces at home and beyond the ocean. As this is written, a few weeks later, the number is in excess of 100,000. More are joining the colours as rapidly as trained men graduate and proceed to the coasts of the Dominion to embark for Active Service abroad. Thousands were in action as these paragraphs were penned.

Where did they come from? What urge drove them to volunteer for the knight errant's role high above the clouds? What manner of lads are they? Can we continue to find them, *ad infinitum,* or shall we reach saturation point one day soon? These and a score more are questions stemming from the phrase which constitutes the title of this chapter.

They came from the farm, from the university campus, from the country town garage, from the counting house, from all the places and trades and walks of life whence come gallant youngsters to defend the cause of liberty. They came in droves, not in a trickle of hundreds, but in thousands and tens of thousands, with one cry on their lips: "Let me at 'em!" Here was Romance, yet Romance with a purpose, that purpose the highest which can beat in young breasts, the determination to do battle for a cause that is just. This time we must not let them down. When they return to the homeland, with Victory shining on them, our's the job to see that the Peace, too, is won this time, that we are ready to go forward with them to lay the foundations and erect the pillars of a better world, a truly free Canada.

They came from the deep French country below Montreal, and many of them went home with sore hearts, for their lack of fluency in a language common to their brothers from the other provinces. Time and experience have provided a cure for that, but it was a grievous sore to many for long months. It was French Canada's late, beloved Minister of Justice and successor to Laurier in the hearts of his people, Ernest Lapointe, who summed the problem of the young French-Canadian to the writer shortly before his death: "We have discovered that you can't fight a bilingual war in this day of machines and science!" That day is

behind us now. Young French-Canada takes to his wings with English on his lips, and a new unity is growing between the sons of the seigneurs of Quebec and the plainsmen of the west. Would it might grow everywhere! But of such matters more anon . . .

They came from the mountains and they came from the plains. They came with dirty hands and they came with manicured fingers. They came early and they came late. And for months many of them were sent back whence they came. "We'll send for you when we need you," was the slogan then. Many of them went home vowing never to return. Not all the Recruiting Sergeants are Ph.D's. and not all the officers they met and talked to were men of far-seeing vision or discernment. Or perhaps the load was too great on such as these. The stream was constant and unending. The applicants sought letters from Members of Parliament, from the Friend Who Knows A Minister, from the Uncle Who Is In Politics, seeking favours not with the desire uppermost in the pre-war democratic heart, self-interest, but in the hope that such influence as the individual could bring to bear might carry the applicant into the skies over Dortmund or Essen that much more quickly. And long months passed for many of these before they found themselves in their country's uniform.

In a people's anxiety to spring to arms, Patience is a virtue seldom shown, a virtue not consonant with any term which implies willingness to serve. But several factors could not be avoided in enlisting our young manhood to fly. The first was our definite unpreparedness, although for five years gradual expansion of our Air Force had been under way. The second, to which considerable space has been devoted in an earlier chapter, is that we had not determined for ourselves or with our Allies, what form our air training should take. Third, once our decision had been taken, the facilities still remained to be created and established before any major Plan could be undertaken. From such factors arose the impatience to be seen and heard on every side, in every Canadian village and city, during the months while we were building aerodromes and creating the great training personnel under which the Plan functions.

It must not be thought, however, that Canada waited for consummation of the Air Training Plan before setting to work to assemble personnel, particularly in instructors and ground crew, to man the existing stations in the country, plus those which could be borrowed in whole or in part from amongst existing air stations, and those which would shortly come into being through the race-against-the-clock of Canadian industry. Already the manner in which schools were brought into operation under the staggered plan essential to such a gigantic task has been reviewed. Suffice to say again that the fullest possible use was being made of the great fields already in existence at Trenton and Borden and elsewhere for the training of instructors in the early weeks of war. But it must be remembered that total strength of the Royal Canadian Air Force, all ranks, including the Reserve, totalled only 4,000 when war began. Of these virtually ninety percent were drafted at once into the shaping of the plan. The beginnings were small.

But the Plan, received with acclaim in December, was the object of severe criticism before its first winter was out. The fact that a Federal General Election intervened before actual training (beyond that of permanent cadres) could be undertaken, did not help allay the nation's concern, for the Government's critics, quite naturally, took full advantage of our lack of schools, aircraft, equipment, and our inability to enlist men in large numbers, when shaping their hustings speeches. Nor did editors of the

The Making of An Airman: Attestation, testing good lungs, the big moment of swearing in, finger printing—and so to Manning Depot.

anti-Government press hold their fire. Thus as Government officers on the one hand and Service personnel on the other worked day and night to bring order out of the chaos of the organization period, they were bombarded from all sides with the demand for production of airmen graduates. The sending overseas, early in 1940, of three "token" squadrons, one of fighter pilots and two composed of army co-operation officers and men, did little to allay the temper of the critics. (These squadrons were made up from pre-war R.C.A.F. officers and airmen and arrived in Britain prior to the opening of the first classes in Canada under the Plan). Not until April, 1940, did the first class of flying-men-in-the-making report to the Initial Training School in Toronto (situated at the former Eglington Hunt Club), at approximately the hour when Germany struck west through Belgium and into France, and the whole approach to War changed, as did our sources of supply for equipment which the United Kingdom mission had undertaken to deliver to Canada to set the Plan in motion.

Now the hour of blood, sweat and tears was upon the continuing free peoples. Canada had not yet been able to equip and open its first Elementary Flying Training School. Yet Canada promptly offered Britain the services of men ready for action intended primarily to serve as instructors in the Dominion. But Britain said "Stick to the scheme. We can take it!' The request, then, was rather for all possible acceleration without reducing the quality of human output, although an immediate contribution of qualified men and of available aircraft was made, as noted in Chapter III.

Canada accelerated. All through that summer the rivetters and the great machines of construction roared through the day and the night throughout the country. Although there was not at any time an acute shortage of elementary training aircraft in the country, vital shortage *did* exist in advanced trainers, a shortage which became infinitely critical when the Fall of France cut off supplies (as, for example, the British Anson) from the United Kingdom. But the difficulties were faced and overcome. The schools opened. The advanced trainers were found, though in more than one case classes ready to graduate from Elementary Schools perforce had to be kept on, in order that pupils might not go stale while waiting for available S.F.T.S. training, with resultant back-up into Initial schools, Manning Depots and, therefore, at the counters in the Recruiting stations.

* * *

Pictorialised in adjacent pages is the story of the making of an airman, be he Pilot, Observer or Wireless Air Gunner. So let us visualize the life of these lads from farm, factory, office and school as they undertake the courses which lead to winged graduation, thence to docksides somewhere in Eastern Canada and across the seas. In the first picture the reader will have noted three young men, eager of mien, standing in the doorway of a Royal Canadian Air Force Recruiting Centre. This is the day each has been awaiting. Until today these young men have been only what the R.C.A.F. calls "approaches", that is to say they have visited Recruiting Centres in search of information. Now each has signified his desire to join up and has been called. One has made application for Pilot, and therefore must be somewhere within the age bracket 18 to 31. A second will follow the course leading to the degree of Air Observer in the university of the skies. He must fall within the 18-32 years age group. The third, accepted to train for the wing of a Wireless-Air Gunner, must also come within the latter age limit.

They enter, sign the register and adjourn to a waiting-room to take their turns before the Recruiting Officer. Next comes the stethoscope-equipped doctor, all the deep breaths and coughings of routine physical examination, thence to completion of the rigorous "medical" required of potential air-crew recruits, then finger-printing and, finally, the taking of the Oath. Now yesterday's young civilian is today's AC2 (Aircraftman, 2nd Class), ready for the Manning Depot and the discipline of parade ground and barracks.

At the Depot the young man, no matter his final ambition, gets his first taste of the life of the airman-to-be, a life which varies only slightly from that of the army's raw recruit. He drills, marches the square for what seem to be endless hours. He learns to accept the acid comments of the drill instructor with level gaze and stony mien, to pull in his abdomen and throw out his chest, push back his shoulders until the blades are rubbing. He discovers muscles he had not dreamed existed before, makes his discovery when sinews begin to complain of this unexpected toughening treatment. He learns how to march, how to salute and to bring his eyeballs around with a click. He becomes the proud owner of boots, tunic, fatigue pants, cap, three pairs of sox, two suits of underwear, four shirts and all the odds and ends which comprise the equipment of the fighting man in embryo. He earns $1.30 a day. He sleeps upper or lower, according to liking or luck, in a double-deck bunk. He learns that boots must be kept well-shined, buttons polished, face clean shaven at peril of his liberty in such hours of leisure as will come his way at end of an arduous day. He breakfasts at six-thirty, discovers that cereal, sausages or eggs, bread and coffee provide a sound foundation for a long morning's drill. When the day's work is done he is often free to go "downtown". When funds have run out he can find plenty to do with his leisure in barracks; free movies, a sing song, a book from the library. But sleep is usually all he thinks of during the first few evenings of his three weeks' course in the R.C.A.F. kindergarten. By the end of his stretch the rough edges have been filed down smooth on the grindstone of discipline and the young man is ready to move a step higher on the ladder. If he is Pilot or Observer material he passes along to an Initial Training School, of which six are situated at strategic points throughout the country (at Toronto, Regina, Victoriaville (Quebec), Edmonton, Belleville (Ontario) and Saskatoon, within reasonable travelling distance of the Manning pools. Candidates for the Wireless-Air Gunner's role part company with Pilot and Observer partners and pass along to Wireless Schools, located at Montreal, Calgary, Winnipeg and Guelph (Ontario). But of the WAG candidate, more anon . . .

Life at the I.T.S. is lived in an atmosphere more rarified than the rough-and-ready, hop-to-it air of recruit days. The young gentleman's bed now boasts clean white sheets. His réveille is half an hour later, 6.30 as against 6. During the daylight hours he attends classes in mathematics, accounts, armament, personal hygiene, Air Force law, all manner of things. The biggest moment of all comes when he fits himself into the "office" of the Link Trainer in which, though it is appended to the ground, he senses all the thrills of flight and learns the rudiments of the job ahead.

The Link Trainer does everything but fly. It lives in a circular room, the painted walls of which show a landscape of mountains, lakes and fields. Within this orbit the machine moves on sockets. It can be dived and spun. It can do virtually anything within the realm of flight. And it can give the nervous pupil the jitters, as many a young man presently dropping bombs on the invasion coast can testify. In it the nervous and tightened-up young pilot-to-be turns into an automaton, or even freezes to the controls, while his more blithesome brother "flies through the room" with all the abandon of a veteran. Some descend from its cockpit never to fly again, washed out by psychological and physical reactions to the conditions of flight which prove them unfitted for the tasks for which they have volunteered.

The Link is not the only innovation the student encounters after entering his Initial Training School. In the decompression

The Making of An Airman: The rookie learns the answers, loses his civilian identity, discovers it's a good life.

chamber he will face conditions identical with those he will meet later 25,000 feet above Mother Earth. Here his reactions to power dives, sharp climbs, his responses to varying atmospheric conditions, with and without the aid of oxygen, are recorded. The incurably air-sick are weeded out, to fly no more. Physical defects not discoverable in the stiffest "medical" are run to earth. Only the sound and the strong survive this first test of every individual's reaction to the actual conditions of War in the Air. Here the electrocardiograph tests the young man's heart, electroencephalography the reactions of his brain. Many of these developments came to the Air Force from the Banting Institute, named for the late Sir Frederick Banting, knighted between wars for his contribution to medical science as co-discoverer of insulin, himself killed in an air accident in Newfoundland while flying on a special war mission. Thus the Institute, working in conjunction with the Royal Canadian Air Force Clinical Investigation Unit, has gone far in the role of saving young men's lives by weeding out the unfit-to-fly through the medium of scientific examination. Last time, in the words of the men from the submarines, airmen were chosen "By Guess and By God" and young men whose psychological or physical kinks rendered them unfit to fly often communicated their unfitness only when they buried aircraft noses into Mother Earth. Today, though science may break young hearts, by grounding their owners for life, its strange devices are saving lives by the hundreds by seeking out under conditions of safety, reactions and reflexes which function only under actual conditions of flight.

Life on an I.T.S. station is not all work and psychoanalysis, however. Evenings are free and social relaxations handy. On the Station itself, as at the Depot, movies, softball games and other sports are at hand. Here the young man is given the prized white ribbon to sew on his cap, the ribbon which indicates he is no groundsman. In adjacent towns homes and hostels are opened to him, many a lifetime love-affair has its beginnings. Nevertheless the seven weeks at his I.T.S. comprise a vital period in the ex-recruit's air life. From it he will emerge as sure-fire Pilot material, or as an Observer-in-the-making . . . or find himself relegated to the ground by an hitherto unsuspected kink in his make-up. The seven weeks on his Initial Training Station, then, are make-or-break weeks. Nobody knows to this day, at first sight, which man is the Pilot of tomorrow, which the Observer, which the groundling. In the main the reckless, physically perfect youngster makes the ideal Pilot, the cool, calculating fellow with the flair for mathematical matters, the Observer. Each, however, is equally important in the War In The Air. At I.T.S. science deals the hand and picks the winners.

At the end of the I.T.S. course, Pilot and Observer part company, the one to report to Elementary Flying School, the other to Air Observers' School. Each now moves up a peg to LAC (Leading Aircraftman), steps up in pay to $1.50 per diem, plus 75 cents Flying Pay. The boys are on their way. Now, let us follow our young Pilot-to-be as he leaves the ground for the first time.

*   *   *

The young man reports to one of twenty-two Elementary Flying Training Schools (EFTS in the parlance of the Force) now in operation throughout the Dominion from Stanley, Nova Scotia, in the east to Boundary Bay in British Columbia.

In appearance at least he is now the full-fledged airman, possessor of flying suit and boots, gauntlets, goggles and helmet. His working hours are divided as evenly as possible into classroom work and actual flight, or activities closely associated with it. His first journey aloft is purely a sight-seeing expedition with his future instructor. Soon he is putting hands and feet on the dual-control equipment and getting the feel of actual flying. Little by little his instructor breaks him in, according to the pupil's aptitude. He comes to feel at home with the "stick" in his hands and to move it through its arc. He has learned on the ground that if the stick is pushed forward, the nose of the plane goes down, that if you pull it back the nose will rise. He knows that to move the stick to right or left will bank his ship, right or left wing down. He knows the relationship of these stick-movements to the control-cables leading out to movable parts of wings and tail-assembly. He has learned the whys and wherefors of left and right rudder movement and what happens when these are correlated with movements of the stick (and what can happen when they are not correlated!). Now he begins to translate theory into practice. The young fledgling is making ready to leave the nest, but meanwhile the parent-bird is showing him how to use his wings . . . and is bringing him home in safety until he can learn to fly alone.

Soon the student begins to be bored by the day in and out routine of circuits and landings, circuits and landings, with the feeling growing in his mind that he can do this job every whit as well as the instructor who is always at hand to pull him out of trouble. A few days ago even to touch the controls of a plane was life's greatest thrill. Now the thrill has worn threadbare and he longs for the time when he can try it alone. The instructor watches the student carefully. The lad must not Solo before he is ready, nor while he is too cocksure, nor when he is jittery, nor must he wait too long and go stale at the stick. Usually somewhere between eight and twelve hours of dual-control are over the horizon when the instructor checks his pupil as ready to Solo and the young man goes it alone.

The first Solo remains the greatest thrill of every flying man's career, something he remembers for the rest of his days as he tells of his squeegee take-off and the hop, skip and jump landing which, when he made it, brought him the greatest glow of pride of his young airman's life. But the pre-Solo moments are long as hours. This is it. This is what he came here for. This is make or break. He taxies out and turns nose into wind, lets in throttle and roars off towards the field's distant edge, realising on the instant that the plane he flies is every bit as much an individual as he is. The tail comes up into flying position at last. He had been wondering about that through seconds that were days, as he tried to remember how to correct his ship's apparent determination to yaw. Wheels bounce and then begin to skim the ground. He feels the sensation of flight. Keep your nose down, laddie, or else . . . The speeding little ship climbs gently away from the field. Left stick, left rudder. Over she goes into a gentle bank. A short straightaway, another turn and up the backstretch out beyond the limits of the field. He comes about and turns into the wind for home. Throttle back and nose down into a gentle glide. He begins to feel the thrill of supermanhood. Down, down, down. Take it easy. Mustn't undershoot. Mustn't overshoot. As he comes closer to the ground he begins to wonder again. Is he going to make it? Had he better take no chances, give her full throttle and go around again to make sure of a safe landing? The ground is coming up at him. He levels off and lands. Maybe he makes a "perfect landing" five feet above the ground and pancakes the rest of the way. Certainly he wasn't going to make the mistake of flying into Mother Earth! But these elementary trainers are birds with tough underpinnings. They need their toughness to take the beatings of the First Soloists! Anyway ship and Pilot are down and it is a conquering hero who taxies up to the Tarmac in front of the hangar. Here comes a Pilot, brothers! take off your hats!

Now the young man really begins to go to town! Soon he is trying the gentler species of Spins, short Cross-Country flights. Off comes the red band which marks the un-Soloed flier, though the red pennon may still be tied to his plane, warning other fliers to give the young man all the sky he needs. After twenty hours of Solo flying the Training Officer gives him his first test.

The Making of An Airman: Inoculation, canteen, guard duty and recreation.

If he shows promise he goes on. If not he may be changed over into Observer or Gunner, or assigned to training in one of the seventy-two trades which comprise the ground chores of the R.C.A.F. Granted good fortune and better than average skill he moves along into more advanced flying. Classroom work occupies his out-of-the-air hours, studying for the morrow his evenings . . . navigation, theory of flight, airmanship, engines, airframes, Morse, Weather. The flying hours pile up. When they reach the fifty mark his work is examined again. If he makes the grade he passes on from aviation's high school into its university course at a Service Flying Training School, after seven weeks of the hardest work he has ever done in his young life. Another Spitter Pilot, or another young man to lug big loads of bombs to Cologne and Brest is on his way!

The sixteen Service Flying Training Schools are divided as to the pilot types they produce. At some Ansons and Cessnas produce the twin-engine Pilots of tomorrow. At others Harvards and Yales develop future single-engine Pilots. Into which of these the candidate is to fall is a question decided by the examining officer at the close of the young man's seven weeks' training at his Elementary School. By and large the lads with the hair-trigger minds and the devil-may-care hearts are the ones destined for the Fighters, the do-or-die-if-it-takes-until-Christmas fellows wind up with the Bombers, where steadiness is a virtue. The Fighter Pilot flies by instinct, the Bomber Pilot more by the book. But there are no fixed rules of selection, because no two candidates have ever been identical human beings. In fine, there is no perfect Fighter Type, no perfect Bomber Type which makes each identifiable on sight.

First Solo is the student's preliminary destination at his Service School, as at Elementary, but the wait is not likely to be so long, nor the tour of dual so arduous. The young man already is airwise, well-schooled, knows many of the answers of his new calling. Though he goes dual again with an instructor, in double-quick time he is away alone in his Anson or, if he is bound for the Fighter Squadrons, in the cockpit of a Harvard. His day may begin at 2 a.m., for he is an all-hours flier. Inclement weather does not keep him ground-bound, as at his Elementary School. In classrooms he must bone again through higher courses in navigation, engines, airframes, airmanship, meteorology, armament, wireless and aerial photography. In his leisure he studies. His flying tests, beyond the realm of aerobatics take in all manner of landings; forced, power, gliding, rough ground. He must become acquainted with all the wrinkles of trick take-offs. He must pass navigation tests in which, say, he must fly for ninety miles on a given bearing, change course and fly hooded, on instruments, for another distance then, with the aid of a map, fly home by checking objects, such as rivers and towns, on his map. All very easy. Through all this he wears his parachute, but makes no jumps, for the excellent reason that the gentlemen who wrote the course decided long ago that the test jump is one hazard it is not necessary to ask the youngsters to take. A jump is just as hard to take over Ontario's Prince Edward county as it is over the suburbs of Essen. So his instructors show the young man how to bail out, tell him how many to count, what to do about the ripcord and let it go at that. He has enough to learn, and learn quickly, in any case.

The S.F.T.S. course runs through ten weeks and it ends with the ceremonial parade on which the coveted wings are pinned to the young Pilot's bosom. Now the L/AC disappears and is replaced by the gallant Sergeant Pilot at $2.70 a day, plus $1 Flying Pay. Be-winged and be-striped the newly fledged flying man is on the next train for home and ten days leave, at the end of which he reports to his Embarkation Camp to await his turn to move down to the coast and catch his troopship for the actual theatre of War. There he will complete his training with 25 hours of flying the actual combat craft he will take into battle. Of his graduating class approximately one-third will be commissioned at Embarkation Camp. More will be promoted on arrival overseas. The others, the lads who do not appeal to their superiors as "officer material", who lack, it may be, the necessary qualities of leadership, who may have "a spot of trouble" on their records, must wait to win their spurs in battle. Many do. The new promotion means $4.25 a day, plus $2 Flying Pay, plus uniform allowance of $150. Needless to say, it is highly coveted and highly prized.

So comes the young Pilot to the wars through the hard grind, but grand fun, of the British Commonwealth Air Training Plan, the world's greatest university of the air.

* * *

Meanwhile what of our Observer-to-be? What has happened to him since he left I.T.S., or was he dropped from the Pilots' ranks during his Elementary course?

The operation by civilian companies of the Air Observers' Schools, situated at Malton (Toronto), Edmonton, Regina, London, Winnipeg, Prince Albert, Portage la Prairie, St. Johns (Province of Quebec) and Chatham (N.B.), has already been described in a previous chapter. The priceless value of these scientifically trained young men, graduates of the AOS, is something which cannot be overstressed. Given the best Pilot in the world, the most deadly-eyed Gunners, the great Bomber and its cargo of sudden-death-to-the-enemy lose all value, as may the lives of the crew, should the young man in the navigator's seat, the Air Observer, be improperly trained, slipshod or inaccurate in guiding the ship to its target and bringing it home again. That is often overlooked by the uninitiated. The best Bomber Pilot in the R.C.A.F. is just as good as his Navigator.

Maps, charts, compasses, bomb-sights and cameras become the undergraduate's tools from the moment he reports from Initial Training School, or from the Elementary Flying School which has retired him from a Pilot's course, to his Air Observers' station. He must learn to send or receive eight words of Morse to the minute on the buzzer and six on the Aldis lamp. He learns aerial-photography in terms of modern warfare, which means, *inter alia,* that he must know how to record bomb destruction, troop placements, railway yards, etc. He must know how to place a stick of bombs neatly astride a target from a mile to four miles aloft. That means knowing how to calculate the speed of his own craft, the windspeed and that of his target, if it should be a moving object. This he learns on the bombing range adjacent to his school, over which students practice under actual conditions to be met later. He must know what to look for as he flies, how to report it to his station and to other members of his own crew. He does not learn to fly. Where would he find time? But the reader may rest assured that as he bites into the job of becoming the scientist aboard a big Bomber the young gentleman loses any sense of inferiority he may have picked up when he discovered he couldn't be a Pilot. He realises what his responsibilities are, soon learns that the Bomber Command would be nowhere without his kind.

During the scores of flying hours the Observer candidate puts in at his first school, of which ten hours are night-flying, he is tested periodically and, on graduation, must be able to direct the flight of a ship under varying methods of navigation. Fourteen weeks elapse while this schooling proceeds, after which he is transferred to a Bombing and Gunnery School to continue training in the fine arts of placing high explosive missiles where they will do the most harm, by night or day, from high altitude or low. After twenty hours' flying experience in this branch of his future job the young man puts up the single wing of Air Observer and the coveted Sergeant's stripes. Now he moves along to postgraduate work at one of the two Air Navigation

The Making of An Airman: Dates, lectures, Link Trainer, kit inspection, revolver practice.

R.C.A.F.
OFFICIAL
PHOTOGRAPH

Schools, situated at Rivers, Manitoba, and Pennfield Ridge, N.B. Astronomical navigation occupies an important part of the latter-stage training of the young Observer. Aboard the Bombers he will ride high above the clouds until approaching his objective, then seek a hole through which to slice down upon whatever may be his target for tonight. The job, therefore, is to come upon the enemy unseen, pounce and get away. Hence he must be a Navigator *par excellence.* Already he has had weeks of schooling in getting-there-and-coming-back at his Air Observers' School. Now the final touches are added, with the Stars and the Moon as his working tools for eighteen hours of night flight, the Sun for twelve by day. To this is added advanced bombing instruction and Morse practice. Then comes Embarkation Leave (during which, as in the case of Pilots, approximately one-third of the members of every graduating class are commissioned) and departure for overseas. On reaching Britain another seventeen per cent are stepped into the commissioned ranks. For the rest the combat record must tell the tale.

*   *   *

The third member of our trio, the Wireless Operator-Air Gunner in the making . . . WAG to his associates . . . is not merely enlisted as "aircrew" but is a specialist from the day of enlistment. Once converted from civilian ways to those of the Air Force at Manning Pool, he moves in a straight line towards his final goal. He never sees an Initial Training School, but, once the rough edges are off him, moves straight into training for his own chosen craft. From the Manning Depot he is sent direct to one of four Wireless Schools, situated at Montreal, Calgary, Winnipeg and Guelph. Education requirements are not set as high for him as for his future crew-mates, only two years of high school being demanded, whereas junior matriculation is the lowest qualification Pilot or Observer candidate may offer.

At Wireless School the WAG first tackles seventeen strenuous weeks of classroom work on Morse code, Morse signalling by buzzer, semaphore and lamp, radio theory, gunnery instruction, plus a general round-up of the subjects taught in Initial Training Schools. The core of his training is to learn to handle signals from the ground which will enable his Pilot to make a blind approach and to conduct two-way communication between plane and ground. After his long tour of instruction in the classroom he goes aloft in the cabin of a Noorduyn Norseman, carrying Pilot, Instructor and four students. Four hours of this, then six hours in a DeHaviland Moth, alone with his Pilot, qualify him, if he has learned truly and well, for his "sparks", the badge which declares him a qualified Wireless Operator. Principally his examination consists of maintaining two-way communication with the ground during triangular cross-country flights of varying length. The Wireless Operator part of him is now equipped. Next comes the job of adding the Air-Gunner half, for which purpose he is shipped to one of nine Bombing and Gunnery Schools, situated in open country districts at Jarvis (Ontario), Mossbank (Saskatchewan), Macdonald (Manitoba), Fingal (Ontario), Dafoe (Saskatchewan), Mountain View (Ontario), Paulson (Manitoba), Lethbridge (Alberta) and Mont Joli (Quebec). Here he receives four weeks of concentrated training in machine-gun firing, the handling of 20-millimeter cannon and knowledge of ammunition, gun-turret manipulation, theory of sighting, range estimation, recognition of aircraft and the handling of pyrotechnic signals. He begins his shooting on the ground, then aloft with the camera-gun, which fires no ammunition but which proves by photography whether or not he has

missed or scored on his targets. Then real shooting begins, first at buoys moored in the water, then at linen sleeve-targets, twenty feet in length, towed approximately 1,000 feet behind another aircraft. His Pilot brings him to within 200 yards of the sleeve. Then the gunner lets go. The aircraft used in this highly exhilarating pastime are Fairey Battles, in each of which two pupils ride. One shoots plain machine-gun ammunition, the other fires red painted bullets which leave coloured marks when they puncture the cloth, thereby giving each pupil credit for his own hits and a check against his misses. In all the Air-Gunner fires several thousand rounds of live ammunition at ground and air targets during the course.

Graduated as Operator and Gunner combined, the young man is promoted to Sergeant's rank and receives the Air-Gunner's single wing. Then, as in the case of his fellows from the Service Training Schools and the Air Observers' stations, he goes on Embarkation Leave and is ready for overseas. Only about five per cent of each graduating class are commissioned before leaving Canada, however, and a further percentage after some experience in operational work overseas, a circumstance which doesn't sit too well with the WAGS. So comes to an end the tale of the making of an airman, be he Pilot, Observer or Wireless Air-Gunner. Beyond the seas they come together again, this time as teams who train together in Bombers of the types they will actually fly as teams into the enemy's camp and back. As Teams they will continue until casualty, illness or promotion breaks up the triumvirate.

At this writing plans are under way for the training in Canada of the straight Air-Gunner, the Tail End Charlie who sits alone in the rear turret "with all Heaven above him and all Hell below" doing a job which, in Air Minister Power's words to Parliament in November, 1941, calls for "clear grit. They must have nerves of steel and a clear eye. We have in Canada men of that kind we could train, when we get the necessary extra aircraft to do it."

So goes the tale. So come into the Plan and pass along to the glory of battle the youngsters from farm and factory, office and school, who are the blood and bone and sinew of Canada's War In the Air.

In closing, to round out the picture, it must be remembered by the reader that a training establishment does not consist merely of students and instructors. Fifteen men on the ground to keep one man in the air is a fair yardstick of the war-flying job. Staff personnel of the British Commonwealth Air Plan, as this chapter is written, totals more than 53,000 men from welders, parachute riggers, metal workers, tractor operators, meteorologists, instrument makers, draughtsmen and fitters to hospital orderlies, tailors, policemen, interpreters, masseurs, firemen, clerks and cooks. Now young women are being enrolled and performing duties at training stations to release men for more arduous service. As Canada saw the job at first, only aircrew would be trained in the Dominion and sent across the seas, our Allies to provide the ground-operational personnel. The demands and exigencies of rapidly expanding warfare have changed this, as all other, plans, however. Thus, at the end of 1941, thousands of ground-crew personnel already had been sent abroad, with more to follow. The first all-Canadian Squadrons, of which at least twenty-five will be fully equipped with young Canadians from A.O.C. down to the boys on sentry-go, already had been formed in Britain. So the Plan expands. Young Canada still storms the gates, seeking entry. This time, as last time, the sons of the senior Dominion seek to fight their way *per ardua ad astra.*

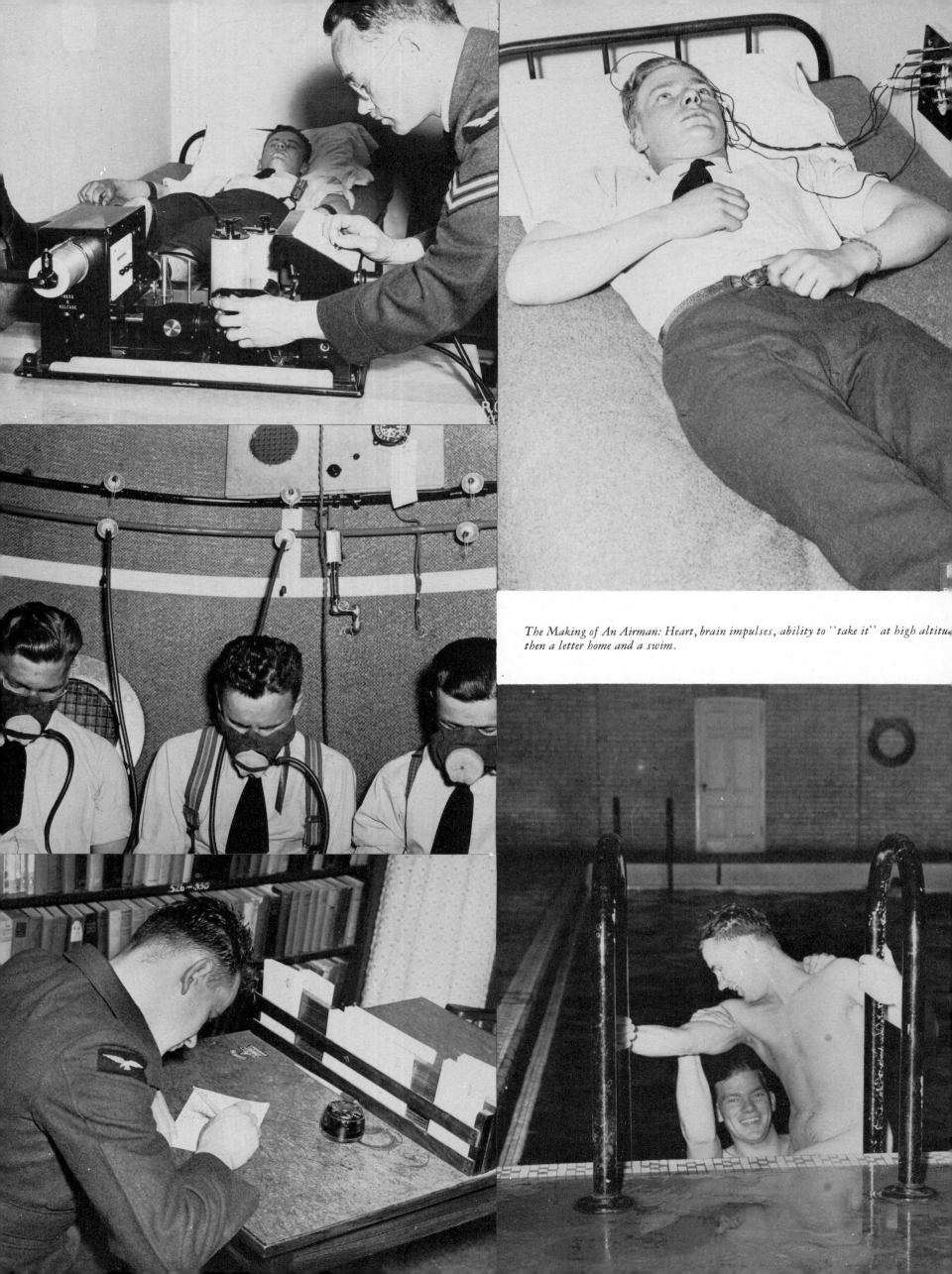

The Making of An Airman: Heart, brain impulses, ability to "take it" at high altitude, then a letter home and a swim.

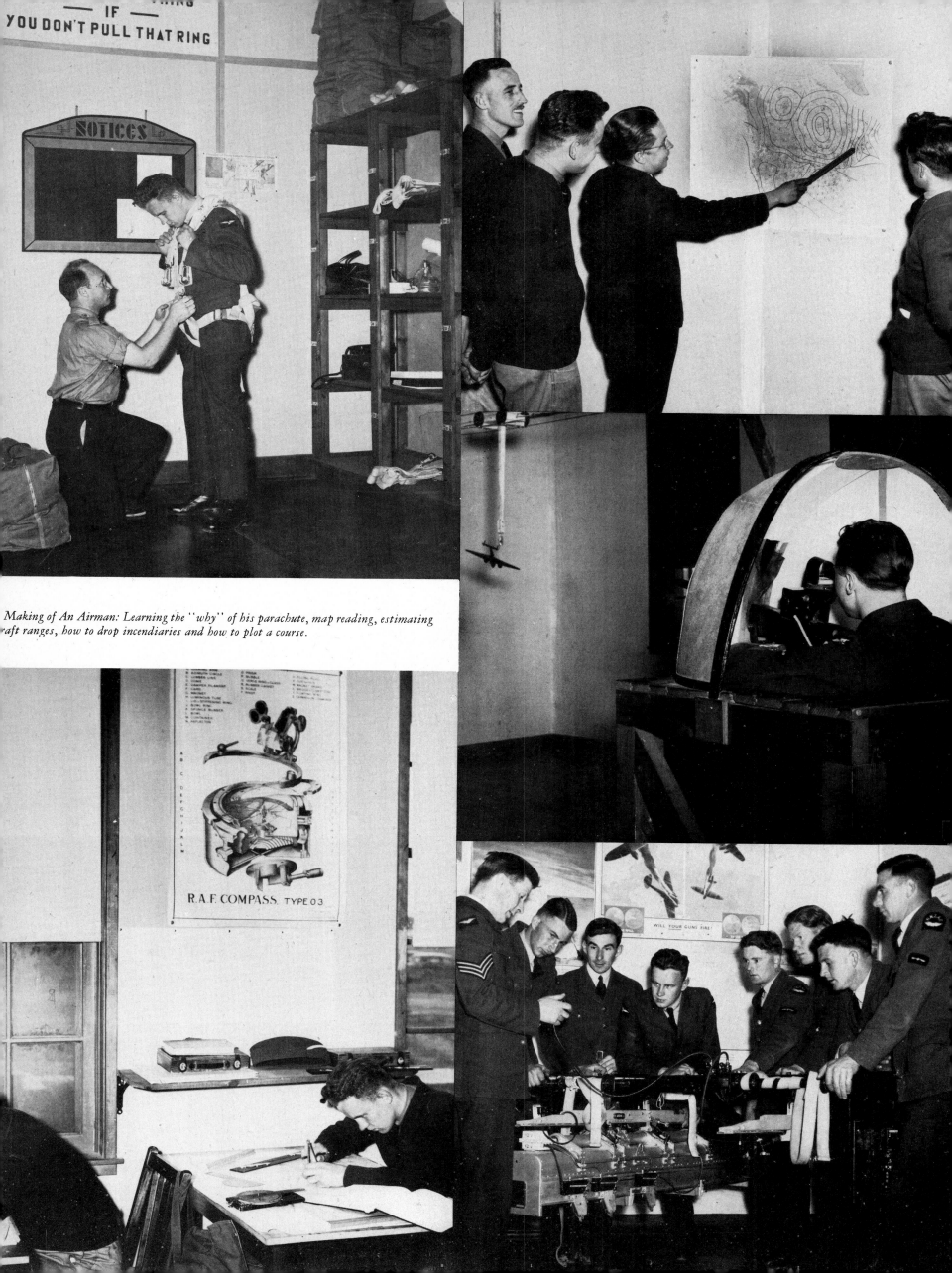

Making of An Airman: Learning the "why" of his parachute, map reading, estimating aircraft ranges, how to drop incendiaries and how to plot a course.

The Making of An Airman: Compass, Bombsight, Camera and Wireless instructio

The Making of An Airman: How to be a navigator in five easy lessons!

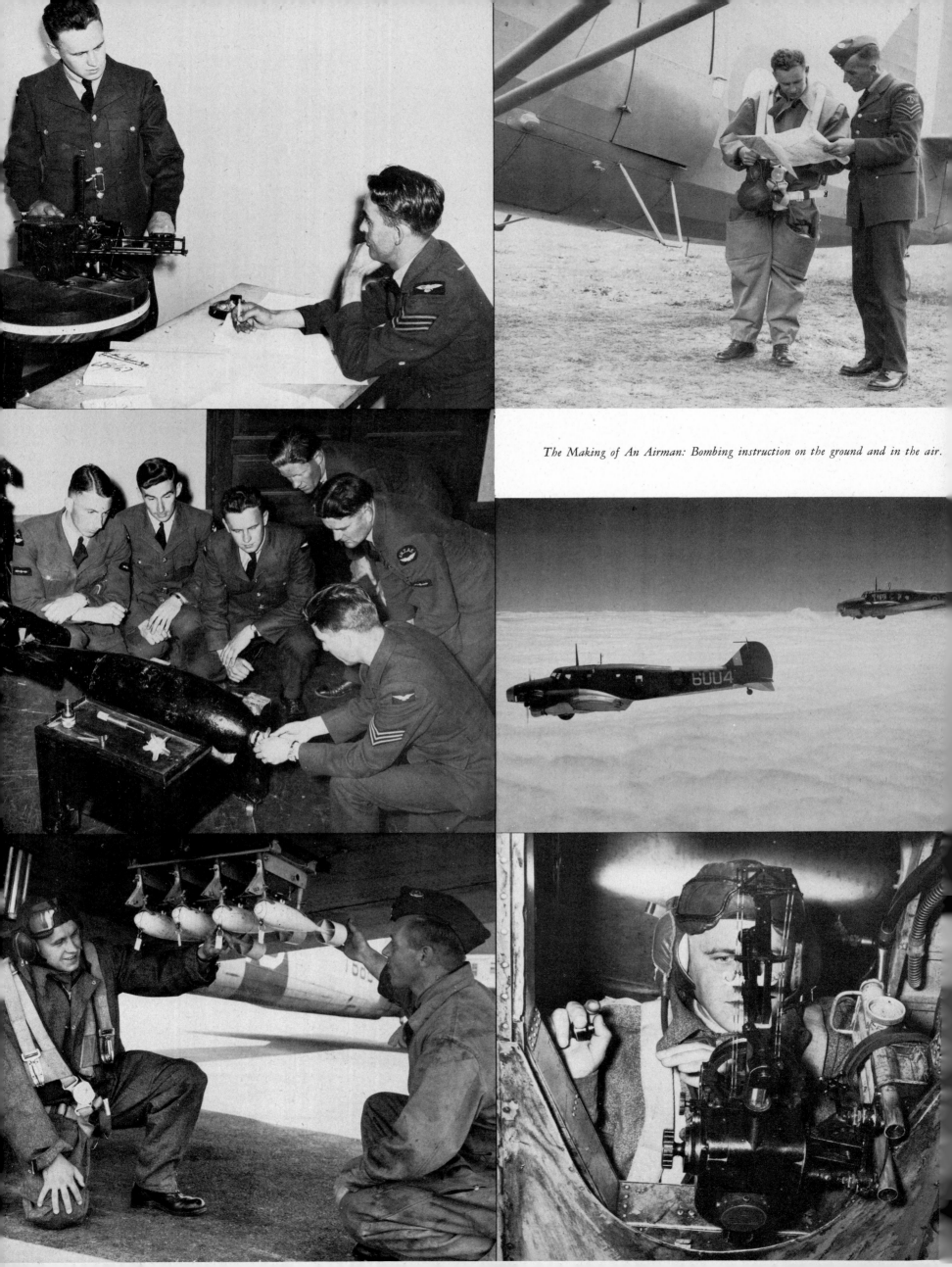

The Making of An Airman: Bombing instruction on the ground and in the air.

The Making of An Airman: The Pilot of tomorrow is shown the ropes at E.F.T.S.

The Making of An Airman: The Pilot of Tomorrow before and after (lower left) his solo, at S.F.T.S.

Making of An Airman: Formation flight of Harvards. A Fleet in the air. The Pilot
as his enemy in silhouettes, and the Gunner his guns, on the ground and aloft in a Fairey
le (lower right).

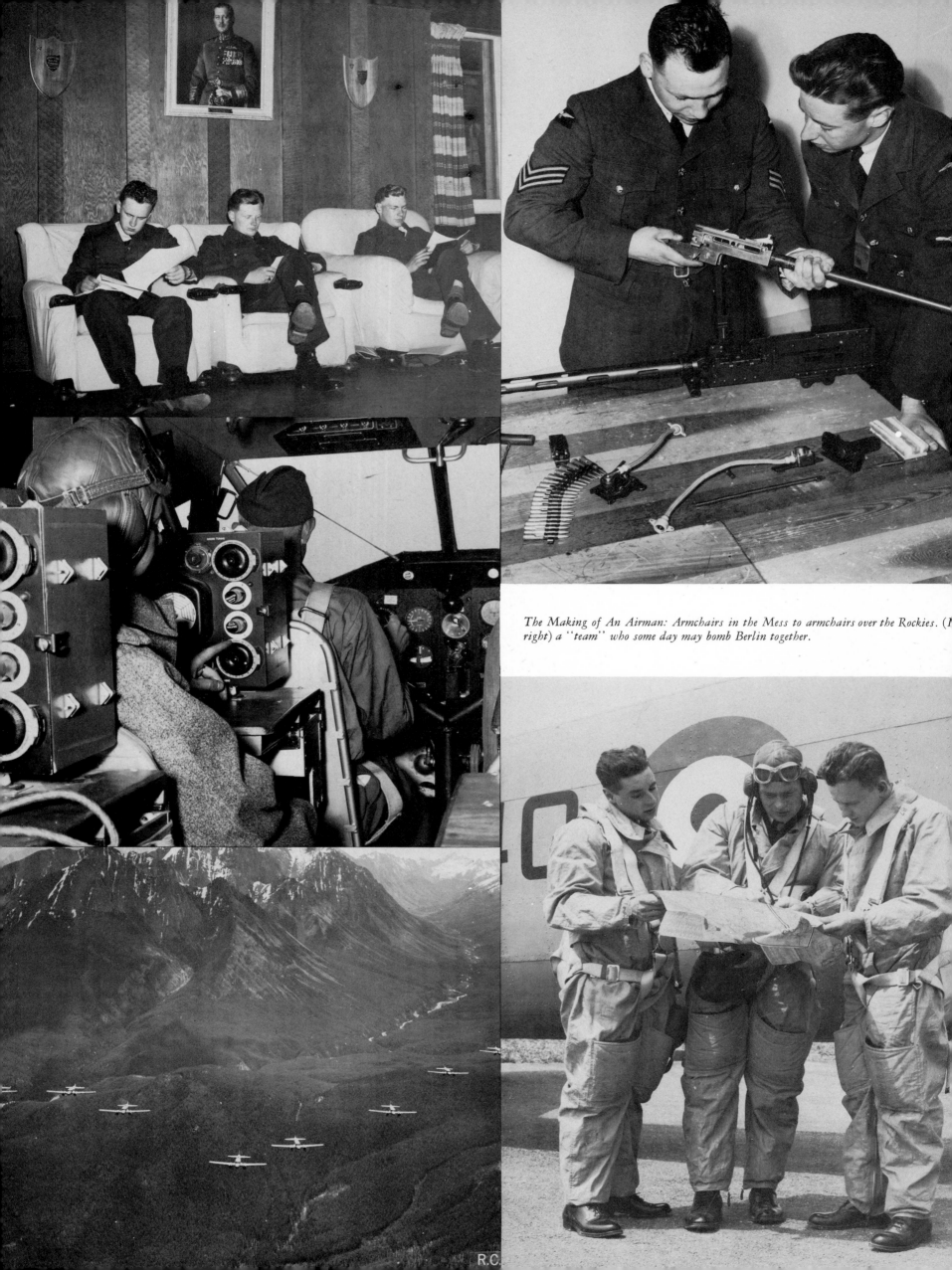

The Making of An Airman: Armchairs in the Mess to armchairs over the Rockies. (N
right) a "team" who some day may bomb Berlin together.

The Making of An Airman: Down the Home Stretch—Air Marshal W. A. Bishop, V.C., presents wings to the Airmen of tomorrow.

The Making of An Airman: We're on our Way!

The Making of An Airman: A welcome to Britain, complete with Escorts.

Canadian Bombers hold a Briefing. Wing Commander R. M. Fenwick-Wilson A.
(Rock Creek, B.C.) and Squadron Leader W. B. Keddy, D.F.C. (Cornwall,
chat with a Bomber Pilot before the "Raid"—The Wing Commander and Squadron L
R. C. Bissett, D.F.C. (Edmonton, Alta.) talk over the Target. Other photos show C
before and after Raiding enemy objectives.

R.C.A.F.
OFFICIAL
PHOTOGRAPH

CANADA'S CONSTRUCTION MEN DO THE IMPOSSIBLE

IN PRECEDING chapters emphasis has been laid on the estimate that the British Commonwealth Air Training Plan comprises Canada's greatest single achievement as a nation. Viewed against the backdrop of 1939 a miracle has been wrought in the northern half of North America in the space of two years. On the outbreak of war the Royal Canadian Air Force was a combatant force in name only, operating a few obsolete aircraft, two first class inland stations at Trenton and Borden, a handful of minor fields and coastal bases, the whole manned by 4,000 officers and airmen, including reservists. As this work is completed approximately 125,000 men are in the service of the R.C.A.F. overseas and on more than 100 stations in the Dominion. Judged on a population basis, the United States would require an enlistment of 1,875,000 airmen, on 1,500 fields, to equal the Canadian effort. Yet this strangely modest people living north of the 49th Parallel, who carry their modesty even to the point of speaking as if they have no War Effort, as if no group in the country, other than that of which the individual is a member, had any stomach for the grisly business, have somehow failed to grasp the import of events which have happened on their own soil these past two years. From what point of the United Nations' compass the final air victory will come it is not possible, at this writing, to predict. But for what will emerge in 1942 and 1943 in the War In The Air, much of the credit for production of the human output must be given to the training fields of Canada, on which not merely tens of thousands of young Canadians, but thousands of Englishmen, Scots, Welshmen, Australians, New Zealanders and Americans have already won, or will win, their coveted wings. Nowhere in the glowing history of flight can a brighter page of achievement be read.

All this, primarily, is the achievement of the young men who have gone out to meet the enemy wherever he may be found. To them belongs all the glory for what has been done and for the victory which will be theirs. But there is another facet to the picture. How were the facilities provided by means of which these brave men became Combat Pilots, Observers and Gunners? It has been a gigantic task to equip this Air Training Plan with aerodromes, hangars, barracks, aircraft, machine guns, bombs, all the assortment of bits and pieces which, added together, become the physical properties of the Commonwealth Plan. The fields and pastures of 1939, not in one place but in many, are the sites of huge industrial structures and of new towns which have grown up about them as, at the other end of the Air Plan funnel, yesterday's forest is today's great aerodrome. For all the modesty of its people, for all the debate and bickering which goes on in the country (a performance which has been continuous since September, 1939), the industrial aspect of Canada's War In The Air is a phenomenon which completely merits such adjectives as magnificent and miraculous.

Here and there, interspersed through previous chapters, the reader has read of the problems of getting the Air Plan started. He has read the report of such an authority as J. A. Wilson, Director of Civil Aviation, concerning the selection of aerodrome sites and the construction of fields. It is the purpose of this chapter, then, to show how it was done; how the aerodromes were made, the buildings erected. What is proposed is a bird's-eye view of how the physical equipment of the construction phase of the Plan was faced. First, then, let us examine how this continent-wide chain of aerodromes, hangars and shops was conjured into being.

In this direction, although the job the Construction Industry did must appear as a miracle to those who do not know this Canada, tasks were undertaken which, in their own parlance, were "right up the alley" of the men who did them. The reference is to the remarkable gentlemen who provided the aerodromes, the hangars, the barracks, the storehouses, the buildings which house the machine-shops, all the basic immovables of the British Commonwealth Air Training Plan . . . and to the Sons of Martha who work for them. When the Plan was tossed into the laps of the Dominion's construction industry what was expected was a hoarse cry of "It can't be done in that space of time!" Instead the answer was "Okay, mister. Your job will be done!" It was. Ahead of schedules in scores of cases.

Those who thought, late in 1939, that it would be a physical impossibility to provide the physical assets required . . . all the flying fields, the Relief Stations, the runways, the hangars . . . and get the Plan going during the Summer of 1940, did not know the capacity for getting things done which is the essence of the construction trades in such a country as Canada. For decades the Canadian builder has constantly been moving into the northern wilderness, equipped with whatever machinery might be at hand, to raise huge dams in canyons a hundred miles from the nearest settlement, to build vast smelters in the heart of the northern forest, to sling railways across the virgin wilderness into a Flin Flon or a Rouyn. Getting jobs done that couldn't be done has always been the stock in trade of Canada's construction men, since the day when the idea of bridging northern North America with a transcontinental railway was first conceived and a nation was born.

To the men who have done this job it has been all in the day's work, tackled as impersonally as they would undertake construction of a new grain elevator, or a bridge to coax tourists over the river into a new sportsman's paradise in the wild-and-woolly north. The official records may almost be said to reflect the nature of the men who did the job, for the records are plain matter-of-fact statements of what was wanted, who was hired and how much he was paid. But these Service Flying Training Schools, these Bombing and Gunnery stations, these Air Navigation Schools, in many cases were carved out of virgin wilderness, to become svelte air stations, directed by young men with ramrod spines and eyeballs that come round with a click whenever a senior officer goes by, and they were built in some cases between the time the recruit passed from civilian clothes through Manning Depot, I.T.S. and Elementary Training School by gentlemen who wouldn't click an eyeball for Royalty itself. That may be drawing a long bow, for emphasis' sake. The point is that it happened with considerable speed. It had to. There was a Plan coming up. The fields had to be ready. They were.

*   *   *

Somewhere out beyond the thriving port of Saint John, today's visitor, if he has the necessary credentials, may pass through the gates leading into No. 2 Air Navigation School. It is an extremely military-looking place, about it an air of orderly coming-and-going. Aircraft skim its asphalt runways in constant take-offs and landings, as expert navigators instruct the young men of tomorrow's Bomber crews in the fine art of how to get there and how to get back. The uninitiated visitor from distant parts might be excused if, looking at today's R.C.A.F. station at Pennfield Ridge, he marvelled aloud at the gentlemen of vision who, years ago, had seen the wisdom of placing such a school in a spot so ideal. More than one visitor from beyond the Atlantic has done so. Today it is that sort of place.

But if the same visitor had flown over what is now No. 2 A.N.S. in, say, the early summer of 1940, he would have seen on every hand only the coastal wilderness. In sight, not a building, not a clearing, not a runway. Just trees. And over there, somewhere in

Another Bomber Squadron Briefing. (Top right) One Team which has just given "The Works"—Planning and ready to take off with their Bombs. Giving the "Folks Home" a thrill over the Air.

the distance, the implacable sea. Then things began to happen. Rough-looking men turned up with machines of weird appearance. Others carried axes, and pretty soon the cry: "*Timber-r-r-r!*" echoed through southern New Brunswick as the well-felled trees began to topple into the snow, in the exact places where the axe-men wanted them to fall. The slash was cut and piled. The logs were dragged to the edge of the clearing. Then, come Spring, the strange diesel-powered machines, the bulldozers, went to work. They moved up on the stumps, dragging them out by the roots and tossing them aside. In a matter of weeks yesterday's forest primeval was today's clearing. But still it bore no resemblance to a modern airport.

Soon the grading and levelling machinery moved in and new crews, new experts, took up the task where it had been left off when the bulldozers and the stumpers finished last night. A few days more and the rough clearing began to assume an orderly aspect. Seen from the air the aerodrome-to-be looked like a well-harrowed field of gigantesque proportions. But still more crews were moving in. Along the rim at one side the skeleton frames of buildings began to rear skywards. The boundary marks of tomorrow's smooth runways were laid. Huge rollers began to pack down the virgin earth, earth which only a few weeks ago had been a maze of stumps and boulders. Graders, all manner of juggernaut equipment, scraped the place level, powdered its topsoil fine. Seeders travelled up and down the inner-triangles between the highways where the aircraft would come and go with their loads of student Navigators. Living quarters for officers, pupils, groundcrew, sprang up almost overnight. The hangar roof went on over the beams and girders. The cement mixers poured the floor while hustling asphalting crews were top-dressing the level runways. Air Force schedules of September 30th, 1940, mentioned Pennfield Ridge tersely. The site of the school had been selected, they said, and a contract awarded for the construction of buildings. In another column July 21st, 1941, was mentioned, with casual *sang froid* as the opening date. The specific hour was not disclosed, but it might as well have been. A little later another memorandum mentioned Pennfield as being under construction, and all through the bleak Atlantic winter the site was being readied for summer occupation. Meanwhile, over at Transport, other files noted that Dexter Construction of Fairville, Storms of Toronto and Acme Construction of Saint John had the job in hand, that it would cost half a million dollars, that the original development would be finished by the end of May and all the fancy trimmings mopped up in July. And so it came to pass.

The same story could be written a hundred times over. It could be told of the job Bird of Winnipeg did at Saskatoon during the spring and summer of 1940, of the Relief Field at Rhein, Saskatchewan the same people made that summer, before moving on to Weyburn, Saskatchewan, for another half-million dollar chore, and of the job they are doing, as this is written, over at Halbrite. It could be told of the numerous Dutton Brothers' jobs at Shepard, Granum, Dewinton, Airdrie and Calgary, all in the sovereign province of Alberta, or of Carter-Halls-Aldinger of Winnipeg, who did the work at Estevan, Hartney, Macdonald, Yorkton and, in part, at Regina, before swinging north into the vastnesses of northern B.C. to tackle two of the key problems of the Alaska Airway at Prince George and Smithers. Or there is Tomlinson Construction. Tomlinson handled Carberry, Chater, Dauphin and Petrel, all in Manitoba, in the early stages of Plan-building, with smaller chores at Winnipeg and North Bay. Then the crews were rushed north and created the Fort St. John, B.C. link in the Alaska lifeline. This year (1942) the gangs are at points as widely separated as Yarmouth, Nova Scotia (a key field of Canada's eastern defences), Souris, Manitoba and Kirkcaldy, Alberta; every one a major job. These, and many like them, laid the ground

floor of the Air Plan. They laid it well, and they laid it on time. The tale of the exploits of these builders, the Frontier Busters of the 1920s and 1930s, is almost endless. Here and there a little fellow, unused to the ways of the back-country, to the hazards of building things in the wilderness, fell behind schedule, or even fell down. But when that happened there was always one of the true northern construction giants to step into the breach, to swing in new crews, to bring machines, to do anything to assure completion of the job according to the schedule. It has been a grand job, done in the grand manner, by men not addicted to counting pennies, by men ready and willing to pool every last resource in their mutual possession to make sure no man would ever be able to point the finger of scorn at Canada's construction industry and say "You held up the coming into production of this great Air Plan!" It happened everywhere simultaneously, from B.C. to P.E.I. It succeeded because men laid aside the ideas of 1939 and pooled their machines in common cause. It wasn't the only job to be done. In other directions great military encampments and huge war-industry plants had to be built almost overnight. It is the record, then, of a great communal achievement.

To cite them all here, to tell what they did and how they did it, is out of the question. But, in order that the reader may sense the size of the project by the number of stations involved and the number of contractors named in the record as participants, the list of schools and other establishments built, or enlarged, under the Plan is appended, with the corporate names of those who did it, as revealed by the records of the Department of Transport. The list speaks for itself.

SERVICE FLYING TRAINING SCHOOLS

No. 1, CAMP BORDEN, ONT.: Permanent Station pre-dates war. Other construction by Maguire Contracting Company, Toronto, Ont., Bennett-Pratt, Limited, Toronto, Ont. EDENVALE, ONT. (Relief Station No. 1 for No. 1 S.F.T.S.) Law Construction Company of Toronto. International Water Supply, Limited, London, Ont. ALLISTON, ONT. (Relief Station No. 2 for No. 1 S.F.T.S.) Armstrong Brothers Construction Co., Brampton, Ont. No. 2, OTTAWA, ONT.: Dibblee Construction Company, Ottawa, Ont.; Patterson Construction Company, Ottawa, Ont.; Albert and Thomas Adams, Ramsayville, Ont. PENDLETON, ONT. (Relief Station No. 1 for No. 2 S.F.T.S.) Dibblee Construction Company, Ottawa, Ont. EDWARDS, ONT.: (Relief Station No. 2 for No. 2 S.F.T.S.) Whitmore and McArthur, Russell, Ont.

No. 3, CALGARY, ALTA.: Buchan Construction Company, Calgary, Alta.; H. G. Macdonald Company, Edmonton, Alta., Dutton Brothers and Company, Calgary, Alta., Fred Mannix, Vancouver, B.C. SHEPARD, ALTA. (Relief Station No. 1 for No. 3 S.F.T.S.) Dutton Brothers and Company, Calgary, Alta.

No. 4, SASKATOON, SASK.: Bird Construction Company, Winnipeg, Man.; Evans Gravel Surfacing Company, Saskatoon, Sask. W. C. Wells, Wilkie, Sask., Smith Bros. and Wilson, Saskatoon, Sask. VANSCOY, SASK. (Relief Station No. 1 for No. 4 S.F.T.S.) Western Construction Company, Edmonton, Alta. OSLER, SASK. (Relief Station No. 2 for No. 4 S.F.T.S.) Saskatoon Contracting Company, Saskatoon, Sask.

No. 5, BRANTFORD, ONT.: Standard Paving Company, Limited, Toronto, Ont., Colas Roads, Limited, Toronto, Ont., Ontario Construction Company, St. Catharines, Ont. Frid Construction Company, Hamilton, Ont. BURTCH, ONT. (Relief Station No. 1 for No. 5 S.F.T.S.) George W. Porter Construction Company, Toronto, Ont. Roy Beattie, Islington, Ont.

No. 6, DUNVILLE, ONT.: Dufferin Paving and Crushed Stone, Limited, Toronto, Ont. Timms Construction Company, Welland, Ont. Pigott Construction Company, Hamilton, Ont. WELLAND, ONT. (Relief Station No. 1 for No. 6 S.F.T.S.) Scott Jackson Construction Company, Toronto, Ont.

No. 7, MACLEOD, ALTA.: Western Canada Construction Company, Edmonton, Alta. Bennett and White Construction Company, Calgary, Alta. Fred Mannix, Vancouver, B.C. GRANUM, ALTA.: (Relief Station No. 1 for No. 7 S.F.T.S.) Bennett and White Construction Company, Calgary, Alta. Dutton Brothers, Calgary, Alta. General Construction Company, Vancouver, B.C. and International Water Supply Limited, London, Ont.

Fighters arrive at 'drome. Cleaning the Guns of a Night Fighter . . . Off to hara[ss] Nazis . . . Warriors of the Skies await the call to action . . . later, a swim an[d] practice in the Pool.

No. 8, MONCTON, N.B.: Rayner Construction, Limited, Toronto, Ont. Wheaton Brothers, Limited, Moncton, N.B. M. A. Condon and Son, Kentville, N.S. Acme Construction, Saint John, N.B. Ambrose Wheeler, Moncton, N.B. SCOUDOUC, N.B. (Relief Station No. 1 for No. 8 S.F.T.S.) Dexter Construction Company, Fairville, N.B. SALISBURY, N.B. (Relief Station No. 2 for No. 8 S.F.T.S.) Rayner Construction Company, Toronto, Ont.

No. 9, SUMMERSIDE, P.E.I.: Curran and Briggs, Limited, Toronto, Ont., M. F. Schurman Company, Summerside, P.E.I. MOUNT PLEASANT, P.E.I. (Relief Station No. 1 for No. 9 S.F.T.S.) Curran and Briggs, Limited, Toronto, Ont. Municipal Spraying and Contracting, Limited, Halifax, N.S. WELLINGTON, P.E.I. (Relief Station No. 2 for No. 9 S.F.T.S.) Morrison and McRae, Limited, Summerside, P.E.I.

No. 10, DAUPHIN, MAN.: Tomlinson Construction Company, Toronto, Ont. P. W. Graham and Sons, Moose Jaw, Sask. Fraser Macdonald Company, Winnipeg, Man. NORTH JUNCTION, MAN.: (Relief Station No. 1 for No. 10 S.F.T.S.) Manitoba Engineering Co., Winnipeg, Man. VALLEY RIVER, MAN.: (Relief Station No. 2 for No. 10 S.F.T.S.) Barager Brothers, Elm Creek, Man.

No. 11, YORKTON, SASK.: Carter Halls Aldinger Company, Winnipeg, Man.; Saskatoon Contracting Company, Saskatoon, Sask., Poole Construction Company, Regina, Sask. STURDEE, SASK.: (Relief Station No. 1 for No. 11 S.F.T.S.) Nelson River Construction Company, Winnipeg, Man. RHEIN, SASK.: (Relief Station No. 2 No. 11 S.F.T.S.) Bird Construction Company, Winnipeg, Man.

No. 12, BRANDON, MAN.: Long Lac Construction Company, Port Arthur, Ont. Bond Construction Company, Kenora, Ont. Bird Construction Company, Winnipeg, Man. Dorosz Brothers, Brandon, Man. CHATER, MAN.: (Relief Station No. 1 for No. 12 S.F.T.S.): Tomlinson Construction Company, Toronto, Ont. Henry Borger and Sons, Limited, Winnipeg, Man. DOUGLAS, MAN.: (Relief Station No. 2 for No. 12 S.F.T.S.) Long Lac Construction Company, Port Arthur, Ont.

No. 13, ST. HUBERT, P.Q.: Celestin Simard, Montreal, P.Q. Raymond McDonnell Company, Montreal, P.Q. L. G. Ogilvie and Company, Montreal, P.Q. Bremner, Norris and Company, Montreal, P.Q. Cook and Leitch, Montreal, P.Q. Walter G. Hunt Company, Montreal, P.Q. ST. JOHNS, P.Q. (Relief Station No. 1 for No. 13 S.F.T.S.): Dibblee Construction Company, Montreal, P.Q. William H. Kelly, Hawkesbury, Ont. FARNHAM, P.Q.: (Relief Station No. 2 for No. 13 S.F.T.S.) Roy and Brassard, Lac Megantic, P.Q.

No. 14, AYLMER, ONT.: Towland Construction Company, London, Ont. International Water Supply Limited, London, Ont. Johnson Bros., Brantford, Ont. Timms Construction, Welland, Ont. ST. THOMAS, ONT.: (Relief Station No. 1 for No. 14 S.F.T.S.) Armstrong Brothers, Brampton, Ont. International Water Supply, Limited, London, Ont.

No. 15, CLARESHOLM, ALTA.: General Construction Company, Vancouver, B.C. Bennett and White Construction Company, Calgary, Alta. WOODHOUSE, ALTA.: (Relief Station No. 1 for No. 15 S.F.T.S.): General Construction Company, Vancouver, B.C.

No. 16, HAGERSVILLE, ONT.: Dufferin Paving and Crushed Stone, Limited, Toronto, Ont. Russell Construction Company, Toronto, Ont. Brennan Contracting Company, Hamilton, Ont. KOHLER, ONT.: (Relief Station No. 1 for No. 16 S.F.T.S.): Law Construction, Limited, Toronto, Ont.

CENTRAL FLYING SCHOOL, TRENTON, ONT.: Brennan Contracting Company, Limited, Hamilton, Ont. Hill-Clark-Francis, Limited, New Liskeard, Ont. MacFarland Construction Company, Picton, Ont. MOHAWK, ONT.: (Relief Station No. 1 for C.F.S.): King Paving Company, Oakville, Ont. H. A. Brazier, Toronto, Ont.

ELEMENTARY FLYING TRAINING SCHOOLS

No. 1, MALTON, ONT.: Brennan Contracting Company, Limited, Hamilton, Ont. Godson Contracting Company, Toronto, Ont. A. Cope and Sons, Limited, Hamilton, Ont., H. A. Wickett Company, Toronto, Ont.

No. 2, FORT WILLIAM, ONT.: E. A. Bell, Fort William, Ont. Sterling Construction, Windsor, Ont. Claydon Company, Fort William, Ont.

No. 3, LONDON, ONT.: Johnson Brothers Company, Brantford, Ont. Canadian Bitumuls Company, Toronto, Ont. John Bremner, London, Ont. Central Construction Company, London, Ont. Towland Construction Company, London, Ont.

No. 4, WINDSOR MILLS, P.Q.: Union Quarries and Paving, Quebec, P.Q. Armand Sicotte and Sons, Montreal, P.Q. Newton Construction Company, Sherbrooke, P.Q.

No. 5, HIGH RIVER, ALTA.: Western Canada Construction Company, Edmonton, Alta. Buchan Construction Company, Calgary, Alta.

No. 6, PRINCE ALBERT, SASK.: Mamczasz and Rollack, Prince Albert, Sask. Dorosz Brothers, Regina, Sask. National Contracting, Prince Albert, Sask.

No. 7, WINDSOR, ONT.: Dinsmore, McIntyre, Limited, Windsor, Ont. Ryan Contracting Company, Windsor, Ont. Colas Roads, Limited, Toronto, Ont. Sterling Construction Company, Windsor, Ont.

No. 8, VANCOUVER, B.C.: Dawson Wade and Company, Vancouver, B.C. General Construction Company, Vancouver, B.C.

No. 9, ST. CATHARINES, ONT.: Ontario Construction Company, Limited, St. Catharines, Ont.

No. 10, MOUNT HOPE (HAMILTON) ONT.: Hadley, McHaffie Construction Company, Hamilton, Ont. Scott-Jackson Construction, Limited, Toronto, Ont. Brennan Contracting Company Limited, Hamilton, Ont.,

No. 11, CAP DE LA MADELEINE, P.Q.: E. Massicotte and Sons, Cap de la Madeleine, P.Q., La Compagnie de Construction Laviolette, Trois Rivieres, P.Q. Page Equipment Company, Trois Rivieres, P.Q.

No. 12, GODERICH, ONT.: Tope Construction Company, Hamilton, Ont.

No. 13, ST. EUGENE, ONT.: Bertrand Brothers, L'Orignal, Ont. Alex J. Garvock, Ottawa, Ont.

No. 14, PORTAGE LA PRAIRIE, MAN.: Nelson River Construction Company, Winnipeg, Man. Hewitson Construction Company, Port Arthur, Ont. Rayner Construction Company, Toronto, Ont. Claydon Company, Winnipeg, Man.

No. 15, REGINA, SASK.: Carter-Halls-Aldinger Company, Winnipeg, Man. Traub Construction Company, Regina, Sask. Smith Bros. and Wilson, Regina, Sask.

No. 16, EDMONTON, ALTA.: Bennett and White Construction Company, Calgary, Alta. Crown Paving and Construction, Limited, Edmonton, Alta. Northern Boat Building Company, Edmonton, Alta.

No. 17, STANLEY, N.S.: Municipal Spraying and Contracting, Limited, Halifax, N.S.

No. 18, BOUNDARY BAY, B.C.: Dawson Wade and Company, Vancouver, B.C. Northern Construction Company and J. W. Stewart, Vancouver, B.C.

No. 19, VIRDEN, MAN.: R. A. Kenney, Winnipeg, Man. Dorosz Brothers, Brandon, Man. Bird Construction Company, Winnipeg, Man.

No. 20, OSHAWA, ONT.: Don Construction Limited, Toronto, Ont. International Water Supply, Limited, London, Ont. Sterling Construction, Windsor, Ont. H. A. Wickett Company, Toronto, Ont. WHITBY, ONT.: (Relief Station for No. 20 E.F.T.S.) Armstrong Brothers, Brampton, Ont.

No. 21, CHATHAM, N.B.: Armstrong Brothers, Perth, N.B. John Flood and Sons, Saint John, N.B.

No. 22, L'ANCIENNE LORETTE, (NEAR QUEBEC) P.Q.: Belmont Construction Company, Montreal, P.Q. International Water Supply Company, London, Ont. A. Deslauriers et Fils, Quebec, P.Q.

N.B.—Schools Numbers 5, 18, 19 and 20 are double-size, thus completing the total of 26 E.F.T.S. called for under the Plan.

AIR NAVIGATION SCHOOLS

No. 1, RIVERS, MAN.: Nelson River Construction Company, Winnipeg, Man. Barnett-McQueen Company, Fort William, Ont. North American Lumber Supply Company, Winnipeg, Man.

No. 2, PENNFIELD RIDGE, N.B.: Dexter Construction, Limited, Fairville, N.B. Storms Contracting Company, Toronto, Ont. Acme Construction, St. John, N.B.

AIR OBSERVERS' SCHOOLS

No. 1, MALTON, ONT.: Frid Construction Company, Toronto, Ont.

Flares, Drift, and Submarine Markers on Active Service: (Top to bottom, left) Ch
course by dropping Sea-Marker. Carrier Pigeon about to be released. Demonstrati
how to keep afloat in a "rubber doughnut." (Top to bottom, right) A Flare and M
being released. A Canadian Bomber Pilot shows us his "Gadget Board."

No. 2, EDMONTON, ALTA.: Bennett and White Construction Company, Edmonton, Alta.

No. 3, REGINA, SASK.: Smith Bros. and Wilson, Regina, Sask.

No. 4, LONDON, ONT.: Johnson Bros. and Company, Brantford, Ont.

No. 5, WINNIPEG, MAN.: Claydon Company, Winnipeg, Man. Tomlinson Construction Company, Toronto, Ont. Dominion Bridge Company, Montreal, P.Q.

No. 6, PRINCE ALBERT, SASK.: National Contracting Company, Prince Albert, Sask.

No. 7, PORTAGE LAPRAIRIE, MAN.: Claydon Company, Winnipeg, Man.

No. 8, QUEBEC, P.Q.: Komo Construction Company, Quebec, P.Q.

No. 9, ST. JOHNS, P.Q.: Newton Construction Company, Sherbrooke, P.Q.

No. 10, CHATHAM, N.B.: Armstrong Bros., Perth, N.B.

BOMBING AND GUNNERY SCHOOLS

No. 1, JARVIS, ONT.: Dufferin Paving and Crushed Stone, Limited, Toronto, Ont. Grant Construction Company, Toronto, Ont. Colas Roads, Toronto, Ont. Johnson Brothers, Brantford, Ont. Frid Construction Company, Toronto, Ont. Sterling Construction, Windsor, Ont. Schultz Construction, Brantford, Ont.

No. 2, MOSSBANK, SASK.: Sutherland and Berry, Moose Jaw, Sask. Evans Gravel Surfacing Company, Saskatoon, Sask. Poole Construction Company, Regina, Sask. R. B. McLeod, Saskatoon, Sask. Poole Construction, Regina, Sask.

No. 3, DAFOE, SASK.: Dawson Wade and Company, Vancouver, B.C. Gibbs Brothers, Lumsden, Sask. International Water Supply, Limited, London, Ont. Shoquist Construction, Saskatoon, Sask. W. C. Wells, Wilkie, Sask.

No. 4, FINGAL, ONT.: Ryan Contracting Company, Windsor, Ont. Scott Jackson Construction Company, Toronto, Ont. Industrial Construction Company, Windsor, Ont. International Water Supply, Limited, London, Ont. Russell Construction Company, Toronto, Ont. General Engineering Company (Canada), Toronto, Ont.

No. 5, CHARLOTTETOWN, P.E.I.: Storms Contracting Company, Toronto, Ont. Hooper Contracting Company, Charlottetown, P.E.I. Phillips and Matheson, Charlottetown, P.E.I.

No. 6, MACDONALD, MAN.: Carter-Halls-Aldinger Company, Winnipeg, Man. Tomlinson Construction, Toronto, Ont. Assiniboia Engineering Company, Winnipeg, Man. Dutton Bros., Calgary, Alta.

No. 7, MOUNTAIN VIEW, ONT.: H. J. McFarland Construction Company, Picton, Ont. Armstrong Brothers, Brampton, Ont. Ontario Construction, St. Catharines, Ont. Pigott Construction, Hamilton, Ont.

No. 8, PAULSEN, MAN.: Manitoba Engineering Company, Winnipeg, Man. P. W. Graham and Sons, Moose Jaw, Sask. Claydon Company, Winnipeg, Man.

No. 9, LETHBRIDGE, ALTA.: Western Canada Construction, Limited, Edmonton, Alta. General Construction Company, Vancouver, B.C. Doncaster Construction Company, Lethbridge, Alta. Bennett and White, Edmonton, Alta., Shoquist Construction, Saskatoon Sask.,

No. 10, MONT JOLI: Construction Nationale et Chemins Limitée, Quebec, P.Q. Cartier Construction, Montreal, P.Q. Collet Freres, Mont Joli, P.Q.

* * *

HOME WAR ESTABLISHMENT

(a) Western Command

ALIFORD BAY, B.C.: Northern Construction and J. W. Stewart, Vancouver, B.C.

BELLA BELLA, B.C.: Coast Construction, Vancouver, B.C.

COAL HARBOUR, B.C.: Northern Construction and J. W. Stewart, Vancouver, B.C.

GRANDE PRAIRIE, ALTA.: Western Construction and Lumber Company, Edmonton, Alta. Turner, Remple and Donald, Grande Prairie, Alta.

FORT ST. JOHN, B.C.: Tomlinson Construction Company, Toronto, Ont. Western Construction and Lumber Company, Edmonton, Alta.

FORT NELSON, B.C.: Western Construction and Lumber Company, Edmonton, Alta.

WATSON LAKE, Y.T.: General Construction Company, Vancouver, B.C.

WHITE HORSE, Y.T.: British Yukon Navigation Company.

SMITHERS, B.C.: Carter-Halls-Aldinger Company, Winnipeg, Man.

PRINCE GEORGE, B.C.: Carter-Halls-Aldinger, Winnipeg, Man.

PRINCE RUPERT, B.C.: Ryan Construction Company, Vancouver, B.C.

TOFINO, B.C.: Coast Construction Company, Vancouver, B.C.

PATRICIA BAY, B.C.: General Construction Company, Vancouver, B.C.

OLD GLORY MOUNTAIN (NEAR ROSSLAND) B.C.: Lazareff and Company, Trail, B.C.

GEORGIA POINT ACTIVE PASS, B.C.: Marwell Construction Company, Vancouver, B.C.

UCLUELET, B.C.: Coast Construction Company, Vancouver, B.C.

WASA, B.C.: Marwell Construction Company, Vancouver, B.C.

VICTORIA, B.C.: G. H. Wheaton, Victoria, B.C.

(b) Eastern Command

SAGUENAY, P.Q.: Local Construction Company, Montreal, P.Q.

SAINT JOHN, N.B.: Coastal Asphalt Products, Limited, Saint John N.B.

DARTMOUTH, N.S.: Acadia Construction Company, Halifax, N.S. Standard Construction Company, Halifax, N.S. Newton Construction Company, Sherbrooke, P.Q. Jas. N. Kenny, Halifax, N.S.

MAUGERS BEACH, N.S.: James P. Kelly, Halifax, N.S.

SHELBURNE, N.S.: T. C. Gorman (Nova Scotia) Limited, Halifax, N.S. Tomlinson Construction Company, Toronto, Ont. Stewart Construction Company, Sherbrooke, P.Q.

GREENWOOD, N.S.: Municipal Spraying and Contracting Company, Halifax, N.S.

YARMOUTH, N.S.: Tomlinson Construction Company, Toronto, Ont. Standard Construction Company, Halifax, N.S.

CHEBUCTO, N.S.: James P. Kelly, Halifax, N.S.

NORTH SYDNEY, N.S.: Stewart Construction Company, Sherbrooke, P.Q.

SYDNEY, N.S.: Standard Paving Maritime, Limited, Halifax, N.S. J. W. Stephens, Limited, Sydney, N.S. Fundy Construction Company, Saint John, N.B. M. R. Chappell, Halifax, N.S. Standard Construction Company, Halifax, N.S.

TOR BAY, NFLD.: McNamara Construction Company, Toronto, Ont.

BOTWOOD, NFLD.: Atlas Construction Company, Montreal, P.Q.

NEWFOUNDLAND AIRPORT, NFLD.: Atlas Construction Company and Atlas Polar Company, Montreal, P.Q.

NORTHWEST RIVER, LABRADOR, NFLD.: McNamara Construction Company, Toronto, Ont.

(c) R.A.F. Ferry Command

DORVAL, P.Q.: Dibblee Construction Company, Montreal, P.Q. J. E. Brazeau, Limited, Montreal, P.Q. J. A. A. Leclair-Dupuis, Limited, Montreal, P.Q. L. Gordon Tarlton, Limited, Outremont, P.Q. Canadian Comstock Company, Montreal, P.Q. International Water Supply, Limited, London, Ont.

* * *

The construction of runways, hangars and housing for the trainees of the Commonwealth Air Plan, the creation of ground facilities for the nations coastal defences and the building of the aerodromes of the Alaska Airway have not been the beginning and ending of the amazing job done by Canadian construction men, however. Before the Plan itself had set in the mould, Canada was asked to provide space for great numbers of Royal Air Force airmen in training. That meant more fields, more schools, more relief aerodromes and many of them. The facilities of the nation's own coast-to-coast airway had to be stepped up. Test-fields had to be made alongside the aircraft plants which were springing up throughout the country. The Plan called not merely for Flying Stations but for all the supporting Ground Establishment and Depots required in so vast a project. At peril of fatiguing the reader with the apparently endless list of what these men, the builders of Canada, have done, the list of supernumerary tasks

The *Air Gunner's Pet, his Gun:* A few of the guns used by Canadians in combat, to the Hun off the tail of their Pilots.

performed during the war period, over and above those of the Air Plan and Home Defence, is appended. It is classified alphabetically, without detail. Many of the jobs, it may be said, were as big as any of those which come under the Plan proper.

AIRDRIE, ALTA.: Dutton Brothers, Calgary, Alta.

AMHERST, N.S.: B. H. Williamson, Saint John, N.B.

ARNPRIOR, ONT.: H. J. McFarland Construction Company, Picton, Ont.

ASSINIBOIA, SASK.: Nelson River Construction, Limited, Winnipeg, Man.

BLISSVILLE, N.B.: Canada Construction Company, Fredericton, N.B.

BOWDEN, ALTA.: Western Canada Construction Company, Edmonton, Alta. International Water Supply, Limited, London, Ont.

BOHARM, SASK.: Western Construction and Lumber Company, Edmonton, Alta.

BRADA, SASK.: H. S. Stewart, North Battleford, Sask.

BUTTRESS, SASK.: Evans Gravel Surfacing Company, Saskatoon, Sask.

CALGARY, ALTA.: H. G. Macdonald Company, Edmonton, Alta. Bennett and White Construction Company, Calgary, Alta. Buchan Construction Company, Calgary, Alta.

CARBERRY, MAN.: Tomlinson Construction Company, Toronto, Ont. International Water Supply, Limited, London, Ont.

CARON, SASK.: Saskatoon Construction Company, Saskatoon, Sask. Evans Gravel Surfacing Company, Saskatoon, Sask.

CARTIERVILLE, P.Q.: Armand Sicotte and Sons, Montreal, P.Q.

CENTRALIA, ONT.: Warren Bituminous Paving Company, Toronto, Ont. International Water Supply, Limited, London, Ont.

CLEAR CREEK, ONT.: R. N. Southen, London, Ont.

CLINTON, ONT.: Pigott Construction Company, Hamilton, Ont.

CRESCENT VALLEY, B.C.: R. C. Moncrieff, Vancouver, B.C. F. R. Charles, Nelson, B.C.

DAVIDSON, SASK.: Evans Gravel Surfacing Company, Saskatoon, Sask. R. B. McLeod, Saskatoon, Sask. International Water Supply, Limited, London, Ont.

DEBERT, N.S.: Storms Contracting Company, Toronto, Ont. Acme Construction Company, Saint John, N.B. Tomlinson Construction Company, Toronto, Ont. R. A. Corbett and Company, Truro, N.S.

DEWINTON, ALTA.: Dutton Brothers and Company, Calgary, Alta., F. R. Gibbs, Medicine Hat, Alta.

EARLTON JUNCTION, ONT.: Hill-Clark-Francis, Limited, New Liskeard, Ont.

ELGIN, MAN.: McCormick Construction Company, Winnipeg, Man.

ENSIGN, ALTA.: W. H. Reed, Edmonton, Alta.

ESTEVAN, SASK.: Carter-Halls-Aldinger Company, Winnipeg, Man. Dominion Construction Company, Winnipeg, Man.

GANANOQUE, ONT.: King Paving Company, Oakville, Ont. Harvey Construction Company, Toronto, Ont. Storms Contracting Company, Toronto, Ont.

GRAND BEND, ONT.: Towland Construction Company, London, Ont.

HALBRITE, SASK.: Bird Construction Company, Winnipeg, Man.

HAMILTON, ONT.: Frid Construction Company, Hamilton, Ont.

HALIFAX, N.S.: Stewart Construction Company, Sherbrooke, P.Q.

HAMLIN, SASK.: McNamara Construction Company, Toronto, Ont.

HARTNEY, MAN.: Carter-Halls-Aldinger Company, Winnipeg, Man.

HOLSOM, ALTA.: General Construction Company, Vancouver, B.C.

INNISFAIL, ALTA.: Crown Paving and Contracting Company, Edmonton, Alta.

INVERLAKE, ALTA.: Western Construction and Lumber Company, Calgary, Alta.

KENORA, ONT.: Bergman and Nelson, Limited, Kenora, Ont.

KIMBERLEY, B.C.: Bennett and White Construction Company, Calgary, Alta.

KINGSTON, ONT.: McGinnis and O'Connor, Kingston, Ont. Grant Contracting Company, Toronto, Ont.

KIRKCALDY, ALTA.: Tomlinson Construction Company, Toronto, Ont.

MEDICINE HAT, ALTA.: General Construction Company, Vancouver, B.C.

MONTREAL, P.Q.: Duranceau and Duranceau, Montreal, P.Q.

MOOSE JAW, SASK.: Wm. C. Wells, Regina, Sask. Bird Construction Company, Winnipeg, Man.

MONCTON, N.B.: Ambrose Wheeler, Limited, Moncton, N.B.

NEEPAWA, MAN.: Manitoba Engineering Company, Winnipeg, Man.

NORTH BATTLEFORD, SASK.: W. C. Wells, Wilkie, Sask. McNamara Construction Company, Toronto. H. S. Stewart, North Battleford, Sask.

NORTH BAY, ONT.: Angus and Taylor, Limited, North Bay, Ont. Tomlinson Construction Company, Toronto, Ont.

OBERON, MAN.: Baragar Brothers, Elm Creek, Man.

OTTAWA, ONT.: Simard Bros., Montreal, P.Q.

PATRICIA BAY, B.C.: Marwell Construction Company, Vancouver, B.C.

PEARCE, ALTA.: Columbia Bitulithic, Limited, Vancouver, B.C. Fred Mannix, Vancouver, B.C.

PENHOLD, ALTA.: Doncaster Construction Company, Edmonton, Alta. Crown Paving and Construction Limited, Edmonton, Alta. Fred Mannix, Vancouver, B.C. Poole Construction Company, Edmonton, Alta.

PENTICTON, B.C.: Williams and Carruthers, Limited, Vancouver, B.C. Kenyon-Killack, Limited, Penticton, B.C.

PETREL, MAN.: Tomlinson Construction Company, Toronto, Ont. International Water Supply, Limited, London, Ont.

PICTON, ONT.: King Paving Company, Oakville, Ont. Hill-Clark-Francis, New Liskeard, Ont.

PORT ALBERT, ONT.: Warren Bituminous Paving Company, Toronto, Ont. Brennan Contracting Company, Brantford, Ont. Johnson Bros., Brantford, Ont.

QUEBEC, P.Q.: F. X. Lambert, Quebec, P.Q.

RALPH, SASK.: Baragar Brothers, Elm Creek, Man.

REGINA, SASK.: Bird Construction Company, Winnipeg, Man. Waterman-Waterbury Mfg. Company, Regina, Sask.

ST. ALDWYN, SASK.: Saskatoon Contracting Company, Saskatoon, Sask.

ST. JOSEPH, ONT.: Johnson Brothers Company, Brantford, Ont.

ST. THOMAS, ONT.: Schultz Construction Company, Brantford, Ont.

SANDHURST, ONT.: Angus and Taylor, Limited, North Bay, Ont.

SOURIS, MAN.: Tomlinson Construction Company, Toronto, Ont.

SUFFIELD, ALTA.: Nelson River Construction, Limited, Winnipeg, Man.

SWIFT CURRENT, SASK.: Dufferin Paving Company, Toronto, Ont. Bird Construction Company, Winnipeg, Man. A. W. Heise Company, Saskatoon, Sask.

TORONTO, ONT.: Carter-Halls-Aldinger, Toronto, Ont.

VICTORIAVILLE, P.Q.: Dansereau, Limited, Montreal. P.Q.

WEYBURN, SASK.: Bird Construction Company, Winnipeg, Man. Saskatoon Contracting Company, Saskatoon, Sask.

WHITLA, ALTA.: George Smith, Maple Creek, Sask.

WINNIPEG, MAN.: Bird Construction Company, Winnipeg, Man. G. A. Baert, St. Boniface, Man.

The Stuff Young Canada Gives 'Em: ''Eggs'' up to 500 lbs. each for Hitler's midn̲
supper or breakfast, and the brave lads who deliver them. (Lower right) The Hon. Vi̲
Massey visits a Canadian Bomber Squadron ''Somewhere in Britain.''

THE THIRD YEAR ENDS

SINCE the First Edition of this book went to press many new developments have taken place which have added to the scope of the Plan as it looks down the future towards Victory. Although at the outset the two major developments of 1942's summer may appear apart as the poles, nevertheless each had the same final objective . . . the fashioning of a greater and more powerful Plan.

These two major items are:

The Agreements emerging from the United Nations Air Training Conference which sat in Ottawa on May 19th through May 22nd, attended by delegations from Canada, the United Kingdom, the United States, South Africa, Australia, New Zealand, Belgium, China, Greece, Norway, the Netherlands, Poland, Czechoslovakia and Yugoslavia. It opened the way through standardization of training to greater Allied cohesion in air fighting.

The new Plan, signed by the original signatories, which projected the Plan into 1945 and amended the original in the hard light of experience.

. . .

At the opening Plenary Session of the United Nations Conference the Canadian Prime Minister, in welcoming the delegates and keynoting the conclave, said in part:

"I should like, at the outset, to say a word as to the origin of the Conference. The proposal to hold the Conference grew out of the preliminary consideration which the Canadian Government had been giving to the terms upon which the British Commonwealth Air Training Plan should be extended when the existing agreement expires on March 31, 1943. We felt that it would be an advantage to the common cause to have the widest possible use made of the experience gained in Canada, in co-operative air training, by the nations of the British Commonwealth. It was also felt that the fuller the knowledge on the part of those engaged in air training, both in the United States and Canada, of existing conditions in our respective countries and of probable future developments, the better it would be for our joint efforts. The other British nations participating in the Plan shared the view of the Canadian Government.

"Accordingly, during my visit to Washington in April, I discussed the proposal with Mr. Roosevelt. As to the advantages of a Conference, the President expressed himself as being in whole-hearted agreement. Mr. Roosevelt made important suggestions as to the scope of the Conference and its agenda. The announcement that, at Canada's invitation, an Air Training Conference would be held at Ottawa was made immediately thereafter from the White House by the President and myself.

"It was originally contemplated that the Conference would be confined to those of the United Nations with air training programs actually under way on the North American continent. It was realized that the North American training problems to be discussed might not be of immediate concern to the other United Nations. It was felt, however, that it would be to the general advantage to invite to the Conference representatives from all the United Nations who are actively participating in combat in the air. To-day, only one month after the Conference was announced, the delegates of fourteen nations are assembled here to begin its deliberations.

"It is a matter of regret to the Canadian Government, as I am sure it is to all present, that circumstances have made it impossible for the Union of Socialist Soviet Republics to be represented. The magnificent effort and achievement of the Soviet Air Force in actual combat would have ensured for its representatives the warmest of welcomes.

"It will, I am certain, not be regarded as invidious if I extend a word of special welcome to the Chinese delegation. We are proud to be associated with China in the struggle for freedom which that country waged alone for so long, and has continued so heroically. None know better than our Chinese allies how vital to ultimate triumph is supremacy in the air.

"It was the same appreciation of the need for superiority in the air that brought about the British Commonwealth Air Training Plan. The negotiation of an agreement to establish a joint air training plan was begun in Canada at the very commencement of the war. The agreement establishing the plan in Canada was reached by the United Kingdom, Canada, Australia and New Zealand, in this city, on December 17, 1939. The plan has now been in operation for over two years. In that time, Canada has become one of the greatest air training centres in the world. The Plan has already far exceeded its original objective. Thousands of pilots and airmen trained in its schools are engaged in combat with the enemy. They are serving in every theatre of war. The Plan has been so designed and developed that its output can be readily and speedily increased.

"The aim of the British Commonwealth Air Training Plan was stated, at the outset, to be the achievement, for the nations of the British Commonwealth, by co-operative effort, of air forces whose co-ordinated strength would be overwhelming. Since the Plan was inaugurated, the scope and, to some extent, the character of the war has changed. To-day the whole world is involved in a universal conflict. The success of the United Nations will depend, in large part, upon the development of unified planning and of organization of all their activities directed towards the common aim of winning the war.

"In many fields, the means of achieving common unified action in the prosecution of the war have already been devised. There is a unified organization for the strategic direction of the war, for common planning, for the allocation of finished munitions and of raw materials. This common organization is evidence of a growing realization that there is but one war, in which the fate of all alike is at stake.

"It is not unnatural that, in the wider co-ordination of air training, Canada should take the initiative. In this field, we have already met and successfully overcome many of the problems of rapid expansion under pressure of time.

"The aim of the Air Training Conference is, however, not merely the discussion of problems. It is proposed to explore all possible avenues of co-ordination in the field of air training, with a view to planning the best and speediest use of all existing facilities. It is our hope that the Conference will make a definite contribution to the air strength of the United Nations.

"In the joint announcement by President Roosevelt and myself, the broad purpose of the Conference was set forth in these terms:

"'Plans for the Conference developed out of the recognition of the desirability of more closely co-ordinating the British Commonwealth Air Training Plan with the greatly extended air training program undertaken by the United States and others of the United Nations.

"'The purpose of the meeting lies along the lines of further united military efforts. The meeting in Ottawa would extend the Air Programs to take in the training of personnel to operate the military aircraft to the end that the most effective use will be made of all resources of personnel.

"'Great progress has already been made in pooling the aeroplane production of the United Nations.'

"The holding at Ottawa of the present Conference is a recognition of the imperative need of co-ordinated air strength as an

At the United Nations Air Conference in Ottawa:—(Top left) Captain Balfour of the United King and Air Minister Power in centre. (Top right) Conferees visit the Link Trainer Room at Upla (Centre left) Prime Minister King chats with China's Major General Shen. (Centre right) ". the result of our labours be determination to build up our air power to overwhelming strength." (L left) The United States delegation arrives. (Lower right) Chief Delegates at work.

element, perhaps the vital element, in victory. But it is more than that. It also marks a recognition of the central position which North America has come to occupy geographically and strategically in a world-encircling war in the air. In relation to the great areas of combat, Canada and the United States are coming to have interior lines of communication. This continent is at the very centre of a war which is all around us. In aerial warfare on a global scale, we of the North American continent have a distinct advantage in that we are able, in the disposition of our forces, in relation either to the Atlantic or Pacific oceans, freely to cross the continent itself.

"It is imperative to keep in mind that air training is directed to actual combat in the air. The ultimate purpose all have in view is the attainment of overpowering and decisive air strength. The magnificent contributions already made to that end by the United Kingdom and the United States are the pride of all who love valour and who cherish freedom.

"Canada's contribution is not to be measured by the extent of our population. In numbers we are a small nation. Planning and experience during two years of war have combined with geography to make Canada, in terms of the development of air strength, a world power. These advantages of planning, experience and geography, the Canadian people are proud to have an opportunity to share."

. . .

The Canadian Prime Minister's address was followed by others in like vein by the chief delegates of all the attending nations. Thereafter a number of special Committees were set up to deal with specific problems of air training. A Conference Committee acted as a channel of communication between the Conference and the Special Committees and Reports were presented at the concluding session.

The Conference provided a splendid opportunity for a complete exchange of information on every phase of air training between the United Nations.

The training of pilots, air navigators, bombers, air gunners, wireless air gunners and flight engineers; the selection of aircrew personnel; the interweaving of various types of flying; the functions and organization of operational training units; the composition of aircrew; these and many other subjects were fully examined.

Each delegation learned from the experiences of the others in the field of air training and went home anxious to put the knowledge gained to good use. The primary result will be closer approach to standardization of air training methods than was previously possible, making easier and more effective the co-ordination of the air activities of the United Nations.

A careful survey of the aircrew resources of the various countries represented was made in respect to the United States and the nations of the British Commonwealth. The result was encouraging, but it must be recognized, however, that the aircrew situation of the countries temporarily under enemy occupation presents a special problem. The difficulties in the way of solution of this problem are great, but courage and resolution are being shown by those countries.

The Conference gave careful thought to the means by which the training capacity of the United Nations can be co-ordinated. Alterations in requirements, some of which cannot be foreseen at this writing, may alter the circumstances at any time, involving adjustments. With this probability in view, and with the further object of ensuring a rapid and effective interchange of information regarding training generally, the Conference approved formation of a Combined Committee on Air Training, known as the Combined Committee on Air Training in North America, to consist of representatives of the United States, the United Kingdom and Canada, the headquarters of which are in Wash-

ington. The Committee is advisory and its duties include the exchange of information on air training questions, advice on standardization of training methods, and advice on measures to be taken to ensure that the most effective use is made of the air training facilities of the United Nations in North America.

. . .

The United Nations Conference was followed by the meeting between the members of the British Commonwealth Air Training Plan, Canada, Great Britain, Australia and New Zealand, to review the period since the Plan had been created and to amend existing contracts. Under this new Agreement the life of the Plan was extended into the spring of 1945. The new Agreement recognized the increased necessity for Canada's own defence and made suitable arrangements for the retention in Canada of a greater number of aircrew for this purpose. In addition what has since come to be known as the "Canadianization" of the R.C.A.F. overseas was canvassed and essential rules governing the placing of Canadians in their own formations set up. The Conferences closed, it could truthfully be said, in an atmosphere and concord of higher quality than that in which the Plan itself had been hammered together in December 1939. They had travelled a long and arduous road together, these Planners. Now each knew the others' value as partners.

A considerable expansion in the number of aircrews trained was provided for under the new agreement, but the machinery, in terms of aerodromes and major physical structure, already had the potential capacity to meet this increase, thanks to the drive of those who heroically built the Plan. The greater output of men, however, meant reorganization of training facilities. Doubling the capacity of certain schools called for additional aircraft and additional accommodation. Some schools moved, bag and baggage, to new locations to make way for schools of different types.

Outstanding factor in this reorganization was the new emphasis on the training of specialists who, with the Pilot, form the modern, efficient aircrew. Originally the Air Observer was the navigator, the bomb aimer, the observer and the aerial photographer of aircraft that carried crew in addition to the Pilot. Larger aircraft have accommodation for more specialists, however. Hence new "trades" arise, such as Navigators, Air Bombers, Wireless Air Gunners, Observers W/T (Wireless Telephone), Air Gunners, and Air Observers. The latter continue their former functions in smaller aircraft. These new trades called for greatly increased capacity at the Air Observers Schools, which meant that in doubling the capacity of such schools, Elementary Flying Training Schools previously sharing the same aerodromes had to be moved to other sites.

Similarly the expansion in volume of aircrew to be trained called for an increase in manpower.

Under the original Plan Canada provided about 80 per cent of the men to be trained as Pilots, Air Observers and Wireless Air Gunners. The United Kingdom, Australia and New Zealand provided the remaining 20 per cent. Later, the Royal Air Force established a number of its own schools in Canada, which, although distinctively R.A.F., came under the British Commonwealth Air Training Plan for administrative purposes. These special R.A.F. schools continued to retain their identity as R.A.F. schools under the new agreement, but, as from the signing of the new Pact, all future schools, whether of R.A.F. origin or otherwise, would be designated as R.C.A.F. units.

The new agreement provided that the United Kingdom will supply at least 40 per cent of aircrew students to be trained in Canada, leaving 60 per cent to be supplied jointly by Canada, Australia and New Zealand. Students from other United Nations

WOMEN AT WAR: The R.C.A.F. Women's Division grows constantly in stre... (Top left) On Parade. (Top right) Milady is togged out for war. (Centre) Opera... room crew at work. (Lower left) A detachment of Canadian girls arrives in Newfound... (Lower right) An Airwoman polishes up the "office window" prior to an operat... flight.

would come to Canada as part of the United Kingdom contribution.

In line with the Canadianization policy for R.C.A.F. men overseas, new moves toward maintaining the identity of the R.C.A.F. were reflected in the provision that, as far as possible, additional R.C.A.F. squadrons formed in the immediate future should be bomber squadrons and attached to the same group as the existing R.C.A.F. bomber squadrons. In that way, it was planned to move more rapidly toward formation of a Canadian Bomber Group.

R.C.A.F. personnel placed at the disposal of United Kingdom will continue to be attached to the R.A.F., but the R.C.A.F. was conceded the right to recall them, subject to operational expediency.

In the new provisions governing the conditions of service of R.C.A.F. aircrews overseas considerably larger opportunity for winning commissions on the field was created. Previous ratios were abolished so far as Pilots, Observers, Navigators and Air Bombers are concerned and all those who are considered suitable to the standards of the Canadian Government and who are recommended for commissions are commissioned.

The reader who chooses at this point to look back to the early production stage will quickly discern, then, how far we had come in many directions since the first Pilots and Observers emerged from the schools.

. . .

No last look at the third year's end would be complete which fail to note the great part being played by Canadian women in the Air Plan of 1942.

The R.C.A.F. Women's Division came into being on July 2nd, 1941, its purpose being to release manpower of the R.C.A.F. ground staff for more urgent duties, notably that of aircrew. Originally titled "Canadian Women's Auxiliary Air Force," as noted in an earlier chapter, the Division patterned its organization and training on that of the W.A.A.F., auxiliary to the RA.F. To assist in organization and training, four officers of the W.A.A.F. were sent to Canada, remaining in an advisory capacity for a year.

During that year expansion was rapid. Starting with nine "trades," or categories of work, the list grew quickly as the Division proved its worth, and on February 2nd, 1942, recognition of it as an integral part of the R.C.A.F. and not an auxiliary was marked by a change of name to the present title. The original trades of the Women's Division were basically "woman's work" and included replacement of men as cooks, waitresses, clerks (stenographer, accountant, general, medical), equipment assistants (storewomen), dental assistants, hospital assistants, telephone operators and "general duties"; along with motor transport drivers and parachute riggers.

Canadian girls quickly proved their ability to take over more duties of essential ground staff work, so that mid-1942 found included among their trades those of teleprinter, instrument maker, dispenser, laboratory assistant, photographer, radiographer, meteorologist, postal clerk, wireless operator (ground), and the responsible, secret work of the operations room.

Airwomen are not enlisted for flying duties, and apart from flights made in the course of duty and a familiarization flight, taken as part of their basic instruction or shortly thereafter, are not permitted to fly in service aircraft.

Canada's young womanhood answered the call to the nation's service in its Air Force in great numbers. To the life of the stations in the Training Commands they have adapted themselves with ease. In thousands they perform difficult duties which release young men for the still more arduous tasks of flight. Many groups had proceeded overseas prior to the end of the third summer of war. Recruits were then still hammering on the Recruiting Centre doors.

. . .

As the third year of war ended, then, Canada's War In The Air continued to reach to greater heights. The young North American nation had clearly established itself as the great aerial training centre of the United Nations, as the pattern provider, too, for newcomer Allies, as well as the home-from-home for young fledglings escaped from the occupied lands, anxious to return to the defence of their homelands through the medium of flight.

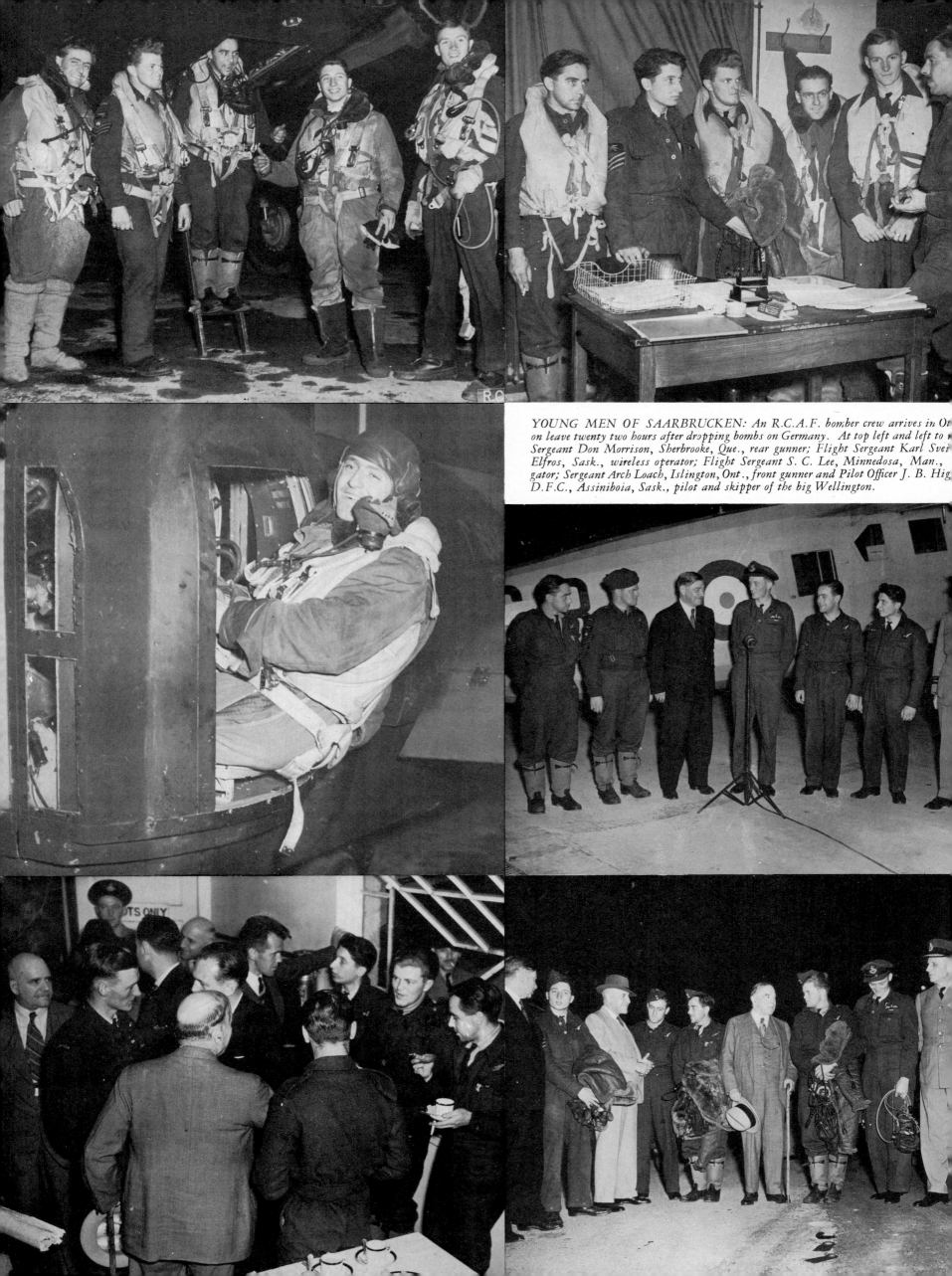

YOUNG MEN OF SAARBRUCKEN: An R.C.A.F. bomber crew arrives in Ot~~~ on leave twenty two hours after dropping bombs on Germany. At top left and left to ~~~ Sergeant Don Morrison, Sherbrooke, Que., rear gunner; Flight Sergeant Karl Svei~~~ Elfros, Sask., wireless operator; Flight Sergeant S. C. Lee, Minnedosa, Man., ~~~gator; Sergeant Arch Loach, Islington, Ont., front gunner and Pilot Officer J. B. Hig~~~ D.F.C., Assiniboia, Sask., pilot and skipper of the big Wellington.

THE PLAN IN FULL STRIDE

When the First Edition of Canada's War In The Air went to press, the British Commonwealth Air Training Plan was in full swing of production, but still reaching to new heights. That was in the spring of 1942. At that time the sign-off was couched in these words:

"Canadians have been at war two and one half years. During those years their whole approach to life, their way of life itself, has changed sharply. Day by day the war has come nearer to these shores. Day by day we have begun to feel the tightening of the nation's belt, slowly, but inexorably. But Canadians, their homeland still isolated from the battlefields of Armageddon (for how long no man knows) are ready for whatever issue the hour may bring forth, welcome each new restriction which means a greater contribution to victory. The restricted use of gasolene means more flying-time for the boys who make ready to fight the Hun. The rationing of foods means more farm-produce for the convoys to carry, the shortening of clothing materials more man-power for war industries, more men for the armed forces. The folk of this land may argue and disagree amongst themselves, even in the hour of peril, for this is a land of complicated problems many of which predate the war. But the heart of these people is sound. They know what they are fighting for and what issues are at stake. They will not fail their kind. They have not failed yet. The record glows with their spirit and with their achievements, greatest of which (in one man's opinion) is this streamlined edifice called the British Commonwealth Air Training Plan. That is the message the writer hopes and believes this work will carry to Canadians and to their friends everywhere in the world.

"To tell of this great job has been as fascinating an experience as ever came a writing man's way. To visit the great schools and chat with the lads who have gone or will soon go out to meet the enemy has been an inspiration and a joy, not untinged with prideful sorrow that such things must be. If the book reflects these things it has been worth the months of work."

Not one line of that finale calls for change. A year has passed since it was written, a year of trial and storm, but a year which, as it ends, brings sunrise in sight at last. Meanwhile what has happened? How did this great adventure in the skies stand as the fourth year of war drew to a close?

1. No further expansion of the Air Training Plan was intended. In the physical sense of the term it had reached its peak.

2. Instead of 74 schools, as originally contemplated in 1939 (at which time many experts believed that we had set our sights too high), the number of schools was 154.

3. The total output of aircrew under the Plan in the spring of 1943 exceeded 50,000 flying warriors.

4. There were 40,000 R.C.A.F. personnel of all categories overseas.

5. 38 R.C.A.F. Squadrons had been formed overseas, or were in the final stages of formation, in addition to operational units serving on the defences of North America and over Canada's two ocean fronts.

6. For every Canadian with the R.C.A.F. outside Canada, eleven were serving with the R.A.F.

7. Cost of operating the Air Training Plan exceeded $40,000,000 a month . . . almost half a billion dollars a year.

8. More than 2,000,000 miles were being flown every day in Canada to train youngsters for the air-fighting jobs of to-morrow.

9. More than 10,000 aircraft were in service under the Plan.

10. Due to greatly increased and improved equipment (such as the Catalina flying-boat, now being manufactured in quantity in Canada) R.C.A.F. operations over the North Atlantic had been greatly stepped up, with highly beneficial results to the anti-submarine score. Canadians were participating in the job of driving the Jap from the Pacific gateway.

11. At the close of four years of war the monthly output of the Plan was still increasing and would continue to rise for several months to come, although the peak had been reached in the field of equipment. The press announced early in June 1943, for example, that the greatest aircrew draft of the war had just reached Britain in safety.

12. Canadian young women in thousands had entered the service, completed training in numerous branches of work and were serving at home and overseas. Every recruit signing to serve with the Women's Division released a man for combatant duties. Such were the straws in the wind as the fourth year of war drew to a close. When Peace returns to earth and the whole story of war's achievement is viewed in its true perspective, it will be in no way surprising if the discovery is made that the carrying out of the Plan after the Fall of France and through the months when the Commonwealth stood alone against all comers proved to be a deciding factor in the saving of free civilisation. Whether or not such is the case, of this you may be sure: without the men who went through the mill of the Plan on Canadian aerodromes, British (and finally United Nations) superiority over the *lufftwaffe* would not have been achieved in twice the time.

A salute, then, to those who fly, to the fledglings of other days from the prairies and the mills of Sydney, from the gold mines of Kirkland and the counting houses of Montreal and Toronto. This book is for them . . . nobody else.

INSIGNIA AND BADGES OF THE R.C.A.F.

OFFICERS' PEAKS & BADGES

Air Officers

Group Captains

All other Officers

Service Forage Cap

CAP BADGES

Officers of Air Rank

Officers below Air Rank

Pilot Badge

Chaplain's Cap Badge

Medical Officer's
Collar Badge

(*Also worn by Airmen
of the Medical Services*)

WARRANT OFFICERS & N.C.O.s

Warrant Officer

W.O. 2nd Class

Flight Sergeant

Sergeant

Corporal

Drum Major

Physical Training
Instructor

Cap Badge
(N.C.O.s. and Men)

Leading Aircraftman

Wireless Operator

Airman of Central Band

(*This badge without
the crown is worn by
Voluntary Bandsmen*)

Air Observer

Air Gunner

Ensign of the R.C.A.F.

COMPARATIVE RANKS

NAVY	R.C.A.F.	ARMY
ADMIRAL OF THE FLEET	MARSHAL OF THE ROYAL AIR FORCE	FIELD-MARSHAL
ADMIRAL	AIR CHIEF MARSHAL	GENERAL
VICE-ADMIRAL	AIR MARSHAL	LIEUTENANT-GENERAL
REAR-ADMIRAL	AIR VICE-MARSHAL	MAJOR-GENERAL
COMMODORE 1st Class 2nd Class	AIR COMMODORE	BRIGADIER
CAPTAIN	GROUP CAPTAIN	COLONEL
COMMANDER	WING COMMANDER	LIEUTENANT-COLONEL
LIEUTENANT-COMMANDER	SQUADRON LEADER	MAJOR
LIEUTENANT	FLIGHT-LIEUTENANT	CAPTAIN
SUB-LIEUTENANT	FLYING OFFICER	LIEUTENANT
COMMISSIONED GUNNERS, BOATSWAINS, AND THEIR EQUIVALENT RANKS (DISTINCTIVE BADGE AS SUB-LIEUTENANT)	PILOT OFFICER	2nd LIEUTENANT

Courtesy R.C.A. Victor Co., Limited

INDEX TO BOOK ONE — PER ARDUA AD ASTRA

THAT MEN MAY FLY

When Peace returns to our world and you of the Royal Canadian Air Force Women's Division resume the way of life that was yours before you answered your country's call, you will do so secure in the knowledge that the young womanhood of Canada will have played a gallant role in winning the victory. Of you it has been said time and again that your enlistment has released an equal number of men for combatant jobs from the duties now taken over by young women on the air stations of Canada and those beyond the seas. That is indeed truth, but it is not the be-all and end-all of the story of your contribution.

Many's the duty you have taken over to which women are peculiarly suited . . . jobs which call for the delicate sense of precision which is in your fingertips, others which bring out your sense of responsibility for accuracy and detail. In these and many another, raising the standards of the Service to heights never known before you came, you of the Women's Division have made an outstanding contribution to the job Canada has on its hands.

It is not summed up in the statement that your coming releases men to fight . . . Today men fly and fight because of the duties you perform, whether in packing their parachutes, in the Operations Room, or in the hundred-and-one other tasks which you do. Truly indeed, you serve that men may fly . . . Canada and her partners and allies owe you a debt which can never be paid. And yours will be the job in the world of tomorrow of making sure that we build a better and finer Canada for the Children of today.

RCAF
ROYAL CANADIAN AIR FORCE

To Canada's FIGHTING COMRADES OF THE SKIES

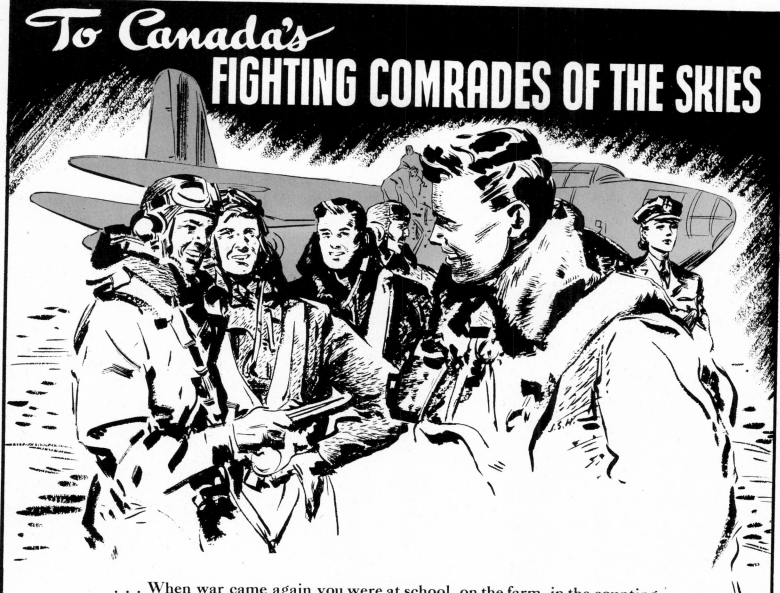

. . . When war came again you were at school, on the farm, in the counting house. You forsook the ways of peace and came clamouring to the Recruiting Centres, demanding opportunity to play your part in driving the enemies of Freedom from the skies of the world. From the Training Schools of Canada you went forth to fight the good fight. You have fought it over the Occupied Countries, in the Far East, over the deserts of Africa, at Malta, deep into Germany itself, wherever the enemy could be found. You have played a role unexcelled by the youth of any nation. Canada will not forget.

. . . Today the young brothers of yesterday's fledglings in turn are joining the gallant brotherhood of the skies. Tomorrow, and through all our tomorrows until Victory is won, Canada's young manhood will answer the call. And when the last flak has pin-pointed the skies of Europe and the last cannon shell has been fired from a Spitfire's wings, you will return to a proud homeland, to carry into the world of peace the spirit of teamwork and partnership and brotherhood which is the cornerstone of the way of life of Canada's Fighting Comrades of the Sky.

ROYAL CANADIAN AIR FORCE
FIGHTING COMRADES OF THE SKIES

Canada's War in the Air

by

LESLIE ROBERTS

BOOK TWO

THE INDUSTRIAL MIRACLE

ALVAH M. BEATTY

MONTREAL

1943

TABLE OF CONTENTS

THE HONOURABLE C. D. HOWE, M.P.

Canada's Minister of Munitions and Supply, American-born and an outstanding engineer in pre-war and pre-political days. Mr. Howe first entered the Cabinet as Minister of Transport, where he was responsible for establishment of Canada's transcontinental airway. On formation of the Wartime Ministry of Munitions and Supply, he became its directing head and throughout the war period has been responsible for direction of Canada's great industrial effort.

4

FOREWORD BY:
THE HONOURABLE C. D. HOWE, M.P.,
MINISTER OF MUNITIONS AND SUPPLY

I am glad to have the privilege of writing a foreword for the new edition of "Canada's War in the Air", for it gives me an opportunity of extending my congratulations and thanks to the men and women of Canada's aircraft industry.

A few days ago I was able to tell Parliament that Canada had produced eight thousand (8,000) aircraft up to June, 1943. Aircraft are now coming from our factories at the rate of eighty a week, in nine types, four trainer and five combat. It is estimated that more than 100,000 men and women are employed in the industry. Every single plane we build today is the accepted leader in its class in the world, and the quality of workmanship and the methods employed in the manufacture of these planes are unexcelled anywhere. Those of you who have been associated with me in this great undertaking will know well the almost insurmountable obstacles we have had to overcome in reaching our production objectives. That we have been able to solve these problems is due to the combined ability and industry of Management and Labour in the aircraft industry.

We all take pride in the great accomplishments of the Royal Canadian Air Force and the unique contribution which Canada has made to the cause of the United Nations through the establishment and operation of the British Commonwealth Air Training Plan. It is fitting that the men who risk their lives in the defence of Canada should have first claim to recognition, but I know that the Canadian people will not stint a word of praise to the men and women on the industrial front who have had such a large part in making these heroic exploits possible.

C. D. Howe

OTTAWA, *July 26th, 1943.*

RALPH P. BELL, O.B.E.

Prominent Halifax, N.S., business man, is Canada's Director General of Aircraft Production. Mr. Bell first became associated with the industry in June, 1940, when he joined the Minister of Munitions and Supply's Executive Committee and, on the formation of Federal Aircraft Limited, became first president of that co-ordinating Crown Company which administers the Anson program. That Autumn he resigned as Federal's President to become the first Director General of the industry which he has guided dynamically through many vicissitudes to the point at which Canada has become the No. 1 producer of war aircraft on a per capita basis amongst the United Nations.

6

CANADA is the keystone of the arch of aerial transportation between the most important centres of the world. For our population, we probably have the greatest background of knowledge and experience in "Northern" flying of any country on the globe, with the possible exception of Russia. Relative to our population we probably will come out of this war with the largest proportion of trained airmen of any of the Allied Nations.

The part that Canada will play in the field of aerial world transportation and the position our Aircraft Industry maintains in the post-war economy will in a large measure determine the relative position we continue to maintain in world trade.

As to the former, there are two schools of thought: First, those who believe that under the spirit and broad general terms of the Atlantic Charter and subject only to adequate control and "policing" by the Allied Nations, the air oceans of the world and the great airports of the world must be as free to aerial traffic as the high seas and the world seaports have been and must always be; second, those who do not.

As to the latter, Canada has long since established itself as one of the four trading nations of the world.

The manufacture of aircraft has become one of the greatest industries in Canada in the sense of personnel employed—now over 100,000—dollar value of output, and extent, character, and geographic distribution of the capital facilities involved.

Since the middle of 1940 we have been engaged in a hectic scramble to procure orders, create facilities, and train personnel. Practically all major facilities are now completed or in process of completion. Every aircraft company in Canada has orders on its books until early in 1944 and many away beyond that date; and adequate personnel, in numbers at least, seems to be available.

We have come to a new fork in the road. We are entering that phase of our work where the emphasis will be on operating factors such as inventory control, scheduling and costs.

Commencing with January, 1943, operating results as expressed in terms of manhours, costs, overhead, etc., must be examined with a miscroscope, for apart altogether from the Industry's obligation to do a first-class operating job for the country, there is the question of what is going to happen to this Industry after the war.

No unit in the Canadian Aircraft Industry will have a chance in the post-war period unless it can produce aircraft as cheaply or more cheaply than our competitors in England or the United States.

In many other branches of war industry Canada is already producing at costs away below British or United States competitors.

Is the Canadian Aircraft Industry satisfied to take a position inferior to those other munition manufacturers?

We wouldn't think much of our Generals, our Admirals, or our Air Marshals if they were satisfied with soldiers, or sailors, or airmen who got licked every time they went up against the enemy, would we? We think the Canadian soldier, sailor, and airman are the best in the world. Is there any reason why we should not take the same pride in our war industry?

We have the facilities—than which there are none better in the world—and it is up to each of us individually, and all of us collectively, to devise ways and means to enable us to compete with all comers.

The post-war future of Canada's Aircraft Industry is a question that requires the broadest kind of imaginative thinking and planning coupled with capable executive direction.

What a challenge to the ingenuity and capacity of those who direct this giant infant industry!

—OTTAWA, July 14th, 1943.

The Biggest Air-freighting Job In The World: Carrying materials to the gigantic Ship[ ]power project stands as the biggest air-freighting job on record. It was done by Can[ ]Airways (now merged with Canadian Pacific Air Lines). The freighter at top left[ ]Junkers-52, with 3-tons payload. Horses, cattle, food and machinery were carried [ ]dam-site. Top right is the late James Richardson, pioneer of northern Canadian air-freigh[ ]

Canada's War in the Air

THE INDUSTRIAL MIRACLE

IN THE BEGINNING....

*P*icture a group of urgent looking gentlemen on a Nova Scotian hillside. Everybody wears a high neck-pinching collar and the lapels of every man's coat are narrow and short. Their pants are cut tightly. Some wear mustachios of the species known to today's irreverent youth as beer-strainers. The plug hat adorning one leonine head is something out of Currier and Ives. The time is 1907 and the gentlemen have foregathered to discuss the future of aviation, an industry without a past. The gentlemen call themselves the Aerial Experiment Association and the names of those subscribing to the general idea that it would be nice to fly are Doctor Alexander Graham Bell (inventor of the telephone), J. A. D. McCurdy (Supervisor of the Purchasing Division of the Aircraft Production Branch at Ottawa as this is written thirty-five years later), F. W. "Casey" Baldwin, Thomas Selfridge and Glenn Curtiss. Doctor Bell has just informed the gentlemen that his wife has agreed to put up $35,000 to finance the construction of their first flying machine. The gentlemen look as pleased as it was possible for anybody to look from inside the habilments worn by the man of affairs of the first decade of the new century.

Seventeen months pass. The day is February 23rd, 1909. On the ice of the lake at Baddeck, on Cape Breton Island, a strange looking contraption stands. In appearance it resembles an outsize kite, which is precisely what it is. Under the kite a pair of bicycle wheels have been attached. In its centre an engine sits precariously and in front of the engine is a seat, behind it a strange, oblong structure leading to a clumsy tail.

A young man walks bravely out onto the ice and climbs up into the seat. The local populace, gathered on the shore, are convinced he is about to kill himself and various worthy burghers have said he should be prevented from doing so. The cynics aver that he'll never get off the ice anyway, so why worry? An associate assists in getting the engine started. It sputters, roars and settles down to what passed for a purr in the engines of 1909. The young man in the chair waves to the people on the lake and the strange machine begins to move. At first it rolls slowly, then picks up speed. Skaters on the lake give chase, refusing to believe that the machine is about to enter an element in which a pair of ice-blades are of no use. The strange juggernaut takes a hop, skip and jump and is into the air! It flies straight ahead for a matter of moments, circles and comes back, glides to the surface of the frozen lake and lands without injury to plane or pilot! McCurdy steps down and walks

back to meet his partners. Baldwin, who had lifted this same power-driven kite off the ground at Hammondsport, N.Y., the previous fall, is the first to pump the hero's hand. The townsfolk stand in open-mouthed amazement. The strange contraption, which its owners called *Silver Dart,* had actually flown! Thus was the Canadian aircraft industry born on the frozen surface of a Nova Scotia lake! The first flight from British soil had happened near a remote Canadian village!

This same McCurdy was still running in front of Canadian thinking in the realm of aviation when war came to the western world in 1914. For its first two years he talked aircraft manufacture to and with anyone who would listen. Finally, in 1916, he succeeded in establishing at Toronto Canada's first factory to build aeroplanes on a commercial scale. The company, Curtiss Airplane and Motors, Limited, and its successor, Canadian Aeroplanes Limited, formed by the Imperial Munitions Board, contrived to turn out almost 3,000 stick-and-string aircraft during the last two years of World War I. a remarkable performance for the times. As soon as the war ended, a grateful nation, having no further use for machines which "obviously" had no place in a post-war economy, closed the place down. That was to be the record of aviation for long years to come. Somebody would always be trying to turn the key in the lock.

McCurdy and his friends were not the sole pioneers in the realm of aviation in Canada, however. As far back as 1902, Walter Rupert Turnbull of Saint John, New Brunswick, was conducting research in the realm of aerodynamics in the village of Rothesay, N.B. There he constructed the first wind-tunnel in Canada and invented an electrically controlled, variable pitch, constant speed propeller of the type since built in enormous quantity by Curtiss-Wright in the United States and Bristol Aeroplane in Britain. Turnbull's words, written about the time McCurdy was making his first flight in the *Silver Dart,* still called the shots for aviation midway through the century. Turnbull wrote:

"Just as soon as the mechanical engineer can command at his designing table full data concerning the lift, drag and centre of pressure of aeroplanes, the thrust and efficiency of different forms of aeroplane propellers, the strength and suitability of the aeroplane, just so soon and not before, can we reasonably expect the problem of aero navigation to be really solved."

It might almost be said that mankind is still working to the

9

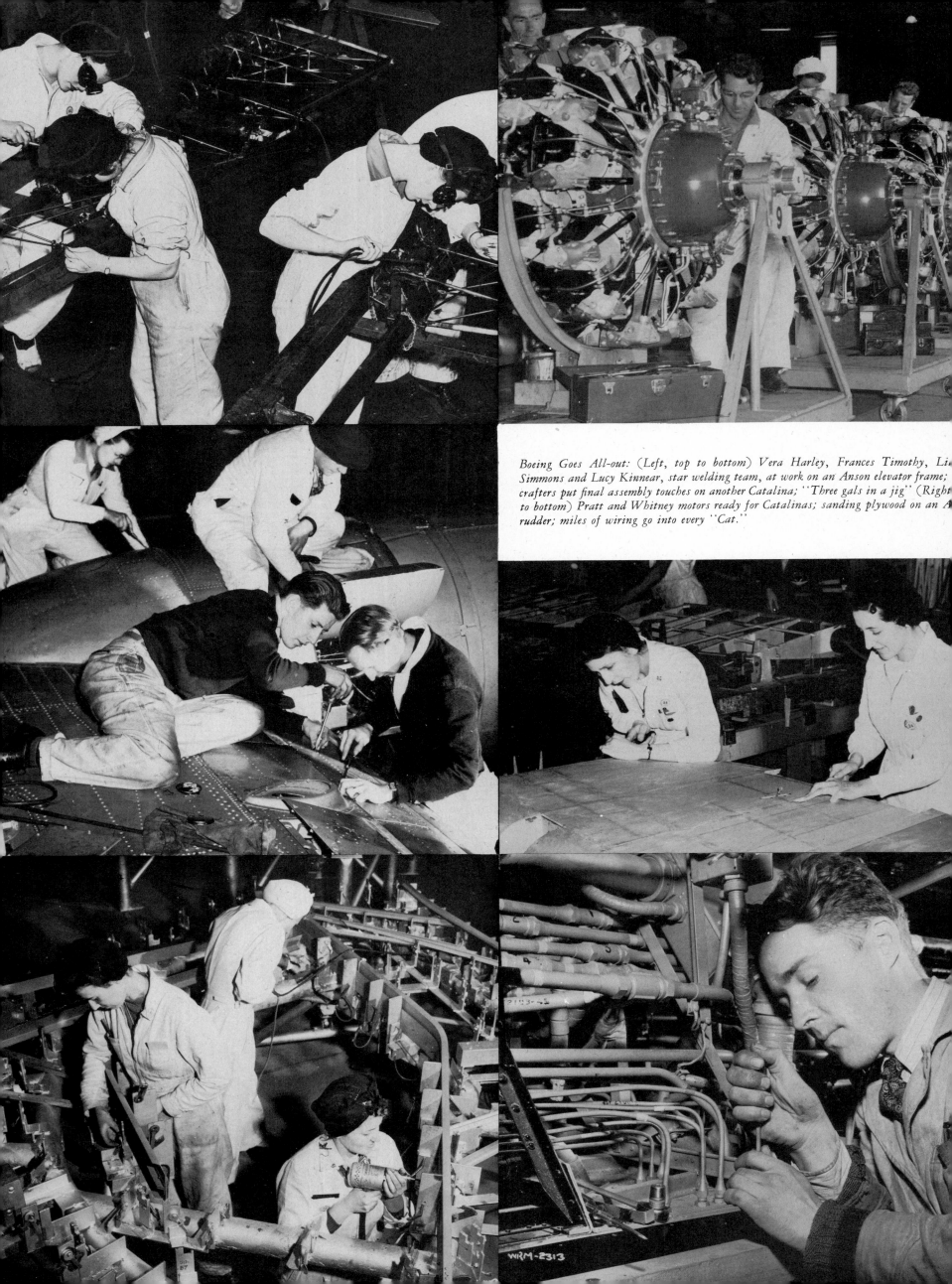

Boeing Goes All-out: (Left, top to bottom) Vera Harley, Frances Timothy, Li__ Simmons and Lucy Kinnear, star welding team, at work on an Anson elevator frame; crafters put final assembly touches on another Catalina; "Three gals in a jig" (Right __ to bottom) Pratt and Whitney motors ready for Catalinas; sanding plywood on an A__ rudder; miles of wiring go into every "Cat."

WRM-2313

Turnbull formula. The scientists of flight have travelled a long and arduous road, but they are still at the drafting board.

In order to bring into focus the early growing pains of Canada's aircraft industry during the years between wars, a review of the establishment of commercial flight in the Dominion during the early post-war years is necessary. Actually the first commercial flight in the Dominion took place prior to World War I, when on May 15, 1914, an inter-city passenger service was established between Toronto and the adjacent city of Hamilton. Four years later, on June 24th, 1918, Captain Bryan Peck flew 124 letters from Montreal to Toronto, the first air mail. On August 17th of that year an Air Force plane carried mail from the national capital, Ottawa, to Toronto. Such were the first faint stirrings of commercial flight in Canada.

After the war, as noted elsewhere in these pages, every possible discouragement was placed in the path of the returning aviator with a yen to keep flying. Some, however, would not be gainsaid, and to them goes the honour of keeping aviation alive (and therefore of being basically responsible for the establishment of an aircraft industry in the Dominion) and of developing in Canada what was in the 1920s and early 1930s perhaps the most useful work to which the airplane was then being adapted anywhere in the world, the transportation of men and materials into regions served by no other means of rapid transit.

Perhaps the first flight of great note in post-war days was that of Captain Ernest Hoy who, on August 7th, 1919, flew the Rockies from Lethbridge to Vancouver in 16 hours and 45 minutes, approximately the same number of hours which elapse in flying from Montreal to Vancouver by T.C.A. today. A year later the Canadian Air Force established experimental stations at Roberval, Quebec; Morley, Alberta; and Vancouver, B.C., from which photographic surveys were conducted.

In 1920 Imperial Oil, Limited, made the first venture into the field of natural-resources exploration, although the first flights were not successful. Two Junkers low-wing all-metal monoplanes were purchased in the United States and flown to Canada for the purpose of serving the Fort Norman oil wells on the Mackenzie River, just short of the Arctic Circle. The town of Peace River was chosen as a base, the route being laid out to follow the river north to a point just short of Fort Vermillion, whence it cut across country to reach the Hay River and the western end of Great Slave Lake. Thence the ships were to fly over the Mackenzie until the wells at Fort Norman were reached.

The two aircraft set out from the Peace on March 24th, 1921 and reached Fort Simpson, where engine trouble, ski and propeller breaks grounded them. By April 23rd, the machines were fit to fly again, but the far north's spring break-up impended and the two pilots, Elmer Fullerton and George Gorman, decided that discretion would be the better part of valour . . . and flew back to the Peace River base. A start had been made, however. Man's curiosity at least was piqued by the possibility of northern commercial flight.

What may justifiably be termed the first serious attempt to establish regular passenger, mail and freight services happened three years later, in 1924. That year Laurentide Air Services carried 1,004 passengers, 15,000 letters and telegrams and 78,000 pounds of freight into the newly staked Rouyn goldfields in Northwestern Quebec, first from the end of steel at Angliers, later from Haileybury.

The same year the same company contracted with the Federal Government to carry treaty-money to Indian settlements along the shores of James Bay and did so with success, covering a circuit of more than 1,000 miles circumference.

The next year Scott-Williams and Caldwell made their famed flight in a Vickers Viking amphibian up the coast of British Columbia from Prince Rupert, to which town their aircraft had been shipped by rail. Going north as far as Wrangell, this intrepid pair cut across the Coast Range and flew up the Stikine Valley 160 miles, into Telegraph Creek. There they sat and waited for the ice to go out of the rivers and lakes before moving ahead again on June 3rd to Dease Lake. At Dease, they dismounted the amphibian's wheels and carried on to Liard, using their ship as a flying boat, flying their prospecting syndicate's geologists up and down the mountainous northland on various metal-hunting missions. Early in July they moved on to Liard, which was used as a base until the end of August, when they returned to Prince Rupert by way of Wrangell, after three months absence on what was the first serious exploration venture ever undertaken by air.

These adventurous spirits and others had stirred the first faint interest in the possibility of establishing a home-grown aircraft industry with the result that, in 1923, the Canadian Air Board had given an order to Canadian Vickers, Limited, for the construction in Canada of eight amphibian craft. That was the beginning of today's vast industry. In it the same company, now producers of the famed PBY, remains a leader.

The first aircraft built in Canada after World War I were not commercial planes in the true sense of the term, however, nor (although built to the order of the Canadian Air Force) were they craft of military value. Primarily they were designed for survey work in the northern hinterland. Not for some time to come would other operators enter the field (To this day the Dominion possesses no engine industry, choosing rather to bring in its motive power from plants in the United States). The between-wars operators, therefore, relied almost entirely on aircraft of non-Canadian design and, in large measure, on aircraft of foreign manufacture.

Following Vickers, the first expansion of the baby industry came in 1926 when De Havilland established a Canadian branch at Toronto and Armstrong-Siddeley entered into arrangements with the Ottawa Car Company to assemble its engines in the Dominion. At the same time the Ottawa people established contact with Consolidated Aircraft of Buffalo for Canadian assembly work and Wright Aeronautical Corporation of Paterson, N. J., opened a shop in Montreal to assemble and service their engines. Sometime later Fairchild erected a small assembly and repair plant at Longueuil, across the St. Lawrence from Montreal. De Havilland began assembly of the first Moth in 1928 and for the next 10 years forged steadily forward until its plane became Canadian built, excepting motive power. The first Fleet plant was erected on a floor space of 60 feet by 125 feet in 1930. The beginnings, in fine, were exceeding small and slow. Canada was building aeroplanes in the woodshed.

Meanwhile, however, commercial aviation was forging ahead by leaps and bounds in the northland.

In 1926 one of the minor miracles of flight in Canada occurred when H. A. (Doc.) Oaks, pioneer bush flier, who had been trying to establish a commercial service from Hudson and Sioux Lookout, Ontario, into the Red Lake goldfields, went to Winnipeg and called on the late James A. Richardson, millionaire industrialist and grain man, and invited the latter to become an aviation magnate . . . in short, to put the first "responsible" Canadian money into commercial flying. Richardson, a far-seeing and adventurous man imbued with a deep love of Canada and a belief in its future, was attracted by the glamourous possibilities. He joined Oaks and the first solid corporate activity in the realm of commercial flight came into being under the name and style of Western Canada Airways. Richardson purchased two Fokker Universals in the United States, flew them to Winnipeg, and jumped into northern aviation with both feet by carrying fourteen

Here Come The Catalinas!: (Top to bottom, left) Boeing final assembly line, where wi[ng] and hull meet for the first time; hurrying wings to completion; "Hulls unlimited." (Rig[ht, top to bottom) Readying a monster patrol bomber for its maiden flight; hull assemb[ly]; making the last pre-flight adjustments.

men and eight tons of supplies to Churchill (now the northern terminus of the Hudson Bay Railroad) in a month.

The Churchill job opened the eyes of the mining world to the advantage of the aeroplane in northern Canada. Red Lake, then the centre of prospecting and exploration interest, was accessible only by dog team in winter, a seven days' pull from the nearest railroad. Richardson's Fokkers did the job in an hour and a half, and transported the passenger in comfort! It was into this country that the veteran prospector -promoter, Jack Hammell, ferried the first mining machinery by air to the Howey mine, taking in men and basic supplies in aircraft borrowed from the Ontario Provincial Air Service, the original northern fire-patrol, his heavy machinery following in Western Canada planes. Now Richardson's Western Canada undertook the establishment of a regular freight-and-passenger run, and made it stand up. Soon Western Canada had acquired more aircraft and crews and was flying freight into the great Flin Flon development on the northern borders of Saskatchewan and to the Sherritt Gordon mine, as well as into the Central Manitoba region. Bush flying was out of its swaddling clothes.

Western Canada Airways also developed other business, notably that of flying furs and fish out to market on return journeys from the Territories and had rendered great service in its first winter in the Far North to traders north of Great Bear Lake who were urgently in need of money but who could not have brought their furs out by the old methods of transportation for another year. They asked for help and got it. In a few days the furs were "outside", which resulted not only in traders getting their money quickly, but enabled them to sell on a fairly good market, whereas a year later they would have faced a collapsing market and a sharp loss.

The furs picked up off the MacKenzie River, actually had a direct bearing on the discovery of radium at Great Bear Lake. Gilbert LaBine who had been flying by Western Canada into a property in Central Manitoba, on which he had gone broke, went to Richardson and stated he would like to prospect the Great Bear area in the hope of recouping his Manitoba losses, but that it would cost too much money to get in. Richardson told him that he was just as interested in opening the country as LaBine. A plane would soon be going in on one of the trips for furs, or on other business. He could ride as far as "the end of the line" without cost and would simply pay for that part of the run that was off the direct regular route. On these terms, LaBine went in, discovered and staked the Eldorado radium and silver mines. As a result, great interest was created in this highly mineralized area, which comprises thousands of square miles of territory. And so the vast expanse of the Territories was opened.

By this time Western Canada Airways had been given government contracts to carry mail into Red Lake and Central Manitoba Mines. In eastern Canada several small air mail runs had been given out, one to Canadian Airways, operating between Montreal and Toronto, one to Canadian Transcontinental flying between Quebec and Seven Islands in the winter. Another service linked Moncton, N.B. and the Magdalen Islands, lying east of Prince Edward Island, in the winter. There was a ship-to-shore summer service based on Rimouski, Quebec. Small contracts were awarded in other isolated areas.

The Government of the day, realising at last that aviation had proved that it could be a great help to Canada, decided to give belated recognition to the service being performed by cutting down on Air Force expenditure to release funds to assist civil aviation! It was decided, therefore, to establish an Air Mail service between Moncton and Windsor and a service from Winnipeg covering the Prairies, leaving the Rockies and the barrens north of Superior as the only great gaps in a transcontinental system.

Looking forward to the days of a complete trans-Canada air mail it was felt that the Prairies were the natural section where the night mail should be flown. There were no night flyers in Canada then, and their training was undertaken over the flatlands of the Prairies. As a beginning the Post Office asked Western Canada to take on the Prairie air mail at 75c a mile. It was maintained by the Airways company that this was far below the price at which similar contracts had been given out in the United States, whereas Canadian operators, flying in a country virtually without a domestic aircraft industry, had to pay high duties on planes, engines, high prices for oil and gas, and operated under much more trying conditions than prevailed south of the border. 75c a mile, nevertheless was made a take-it-or-leave-it price and a contract was issued for 4 years to give the operators at least a chance to write off their equipment. Western Canada was to fly the mail from Winnipeg to Regina, Moose Jaw, Medicine Hat, Lethbridge, and Calgary and a branch line from Moose Jaw to Regina, Saskatoon, North Battleford and Edmonton. Later the main line was extended beyond Calgary to Edmonton and the line from Saskatoon to North Battleford and Edmonton was then abandoned.

The Prairie mail began on March 3rd, 1930. Some time prior to that, Western Canada had made test-runs over a 19-day period. Long before the service started Richardson had purchased his flying equipment. The planes were not entirely satisfactory, but more were bought by the faithful Richardson, who by this time was determined to make aviation in Canada fly on its own wings. His determination went further. It was to keep Canadian aviation in Canadian hands and not allow it to get under the domination of external manufacturers. He believed that the contract for carrying Canadian Government mails should not only be carried out by Canadian pilots, but by companies owned and operated by Canadians. Jim Richardson was a Canadian first, last and all the time.

The next stage of the development of airways came with the merging of Western Canada with smaller eastern operators. In January, 1927, Richardson met young Fairchild, whose father had invented the Fairchild camera and who had established a small company at Grand'Mere, Quebec, to do photographic work for the pulp and paper companies. Some time later, when the Prairie mail was running, he established contact with International Airways, organised by an influential group in Hamilton to operate the Montreal-Toronto contract. The company, however, had not met with success, and the only way the owners could see to get their money out was to sell to Americans, who were prepared to take it over on the basis of the cash the Hamilton group had put into it, the Americans feeling that they could ultimately reimburse themselves through the contracts. This matter was brought to Richardson's attention and he visited the International people in Hamilton, the leaders of whom were F. I. Ker, publisher of *The Hamilton Spectator;* H. B. Greening and A. V. Young, to whom he pointed out that the mail contracts had been given to Canadians and should not be turned over to an American company, that money could be found in Canada to carry on, that Canadians would take it over on the same basis as Americans were prepared to take over and could run it just as efficiently. The Hamilton group decided to forego the opportunity of taking their money out and left it in to stay with Canadian aviation. The money was forthcoming—from Jim Richardson's bank account.

The result was that a number of new interests agreed to put up additional money to help keep Canadian aviation in Canadian hands. Interprovincial Airways resulted. To get the business on a proper basis it was necessary to consolidate as many of the other mail runs as possible into one operation. For this reason Aviation

MAIN SHOP
NORTH AISLE
LOOKING WEST

C.C.&F.CO. LTD

AIR TABLE
AVION WORKS. BLADE DEPT.
PROP #20 C.C.&F. OCT. 1941

Canadians Produce Fighters for Active Service: Left, top to bottom: The tool-making at Point St. Charles (Montreal), sheet-metal workers in the Fort William plant and oleo-leg shop in Montreal. Right, top to bottom: Propellers in the making in Montreal, wing assembly jigs at Fort William. All pictures in Canadian Car and Foundry Company aircraft plants.

OLEO SHOP
LOOKING EAST

C.C.&F.CO. LTD. FORT WILLIAM WORKS. SEPT 18 1941. FINAL STAGE WING ASSEMBLY JIGS

TD. FORT WILLIAM WORKS. F.A.H-1. FIRST AIRCRAFT. VIEW SHOWING FUSELAGE AND FAIRING, CENTRE SECTION, ENGINE MOUN
LANDING GEAR INSTALLATION.

.26 C.C.& F.CO., LTD. FORT WILLIAM WORKS. F.A.H-1. FUSELAGE No.1 WITH COWLING IN POSITION 162

The Evolution of a Hurricane Fighter. Left, top to bottom: Fuselages, centre section, engine mounts, engines and landing gear come together as one. Right, top to bottom: Fuselage with cowling. The finished job on the testing field, a view of the Fort William assembly line. It will be noted that the first Canadian Hurricane was ready for test flight on January 9th, 1940.

D. FORT WILLIAM WORKS. F.A.H.I. SHIPS NOS. 1 AND 2 IN ASSEMBLY LINE. 154

C.C.& F.CO.LTD. FORT WILLIAM WORKS. JANUARY 9, 1940. F.A.H-1. AIRCRAFT No.1 READY FOR TEST FLIGHT. H.31.

TD. FORT WILLIAM WORKS. F.A.H-1. ENGINE INSTALLATION, LANDING GEAR, &c. COWLING AND FAIRING
FOREGROUND. AIRCRAFT No.1

216 C.C.& F.CO. LTD. FORT WILLIAM WORKS. SEPT. 18, 1941. ASSEMBLY LINE. LOOKING EAST. H.75

CO., LTD. FORT WILLIAM WORKS. SEPT. 18, 1941. ASSEMBLY LINE. PARTLY COMPLETED SEA HURRICANES. PRIMARY ASSEMBLY IN FOREGROUND. H.71 SEPT 13/41 ASSEMBLY IN BACKGROUND. 212

CAN. CAR & FOUNDRY CO. LTD. TURCOT WORKS - JAN. 1941 - ANSON WING CONSTR

Canadian Car and Foundry Co. Goes To War. Left, Top to Bottom: Assembly line o Hurricanes at Fort William, Hurricane fuselages awaiting shipment, the Assembl on Anson Wings at Turcot Works, Montreal. Right, top to bottom: Anson Wing a blies, Wings and Tail assemblies at Turcot. The beloved "flying greenhouse" on th at Amherst, N.S.

AIR CO. LTD. FORT WILLIAM PLANT. 1941. COMPLETED HURRICANE MARK I FUSELAGES IN STORAGE IN FOUNDRY BUILDING. H-83

224

AW. T.10. MAIN PLANE CONSTRUCTION. ANSON PLANE.

C.C. & F. CO, LTD. AMHERST PLANT. JANUARY 9, 1941. ENGLISH-BUILT ANSON AIRCRAFT

"D. AMHERST PLANT. JANUARY 9, 1941. AN.D-1. ASSEMBLY OF ENGLISH-BUILT ANSON AIRCRAFT. A.A.E-1.

P.P. 45 C.C.&F. Co. Ltd. AERONAUTICAL DIV. Pt. St. CHARLES PLANT.

INSPECTION DEPT. MAIN SHOP

Ansons and Hampdens at "Canadian Car": Top to bottom, left, Assembling English Ansons at Amherst, wing tips for the Hampden Bomber at Turcot, Hampden flaps and ailerons at Turcot. Right, top to bottom, Inspection of Bits and Pieces at Point St. Charles, the first Canadian Anson at Amherst, fitting Hampden wings at Turcot.

C.F. Co. Ltd., AIRCRAFT DIV. TURCOT - ASSY. OF HAMPDEN WING TIPS

AIRCRAFT DIV. TURCOT - FITTING FLAPS & AILERONS ON 1st. HAMPDEN WING

C.C.F. Co. Ltd. AIRCRAFT DIV. TURCOT - FINAL ASSY. & FITTING OF 1st. HAMPDEN WI

The Hell Diver In Action: Shots in flight of the great Curtiss dive bomber at Ca Car's Fort William plant and of girl workers on the job.

Corporation was formed as a holding company. It took over the control of International Airways, acquired the old Fairchild plant at Grand'Mere (not to be confused with the present Fairchild Aircraft at Longueuil) and purchased control of Transcontinental Airways, operating east of Montreal, the last named being acquired to prevent the company going into the hands of General Ryan of American Airways, who had in mind an ultimate outlet to the North Atlantic, if and when that route became a practical commercial possibility.

An effort was made to co-ordinate these different companies under the control of Aviation Corporation. Lines had to be extended to meet the policy of the Government to fly mail through from Moncton to Windsor.

There were, then, in Canada, two major operators, Western Canada Airways in the West and the International-Interprovincial-Aviation Corporation group in the East, both with approximately the same mail mileage. The Eastern company had little bush or mining work, however, but did have, through acquisition of the Fairchild company at Grand'Mere, a photographic unit comprised of men of long experience and an engineering department capable of doing as fine work as could be done anywhere in the world.

The whole structure rested, of course, on air mail contracts. Aviation was struggling, was still a transportation medium with virtually no production industry at its back.

In 1929 Sir Henry Thornton met Richardson in Winnipeg and discussed the possibility of Canadian National Railways taking an interest in aviation. The two men agreed that an interest in Richardson's operations might be acquired by Canadian National Railways and that, to avert suicidal competition, the Canadian Pacific, which already had a small investment in Aviation Corporation, should be consulted and asked to come in as well.

After further meetings it was agreed that Canadian Pacific and Canadian National should each invest $250,000 in a company to be known as Canadian Airways. Eastern and Western operations were merged. Richardson became President and the two railroad presidents the Vice-Presidents. In this way the two major transport companies took their first short steps into aviation. It was merely a token investment, however. Jim Richardson was still carrying the baby.

Then a change of Government occurred and the incoming regime, elected on an economy platform, sabotaged the Air Force and scrapped the air mail contracts.

The mail fliers were in a fine fix. To handle their job they had bought mail planes and radio-equipped them, bought fields, built hangars and made various commitments which they were compelled by law to fulfill. Office leases across Canada alone ran into $33,000 a year. Commitments made solely on the strength of air mail contracts could not be sloughed off just because the contracts had been broken.

What has been written in outline of the vicissitudes of those engaged in the attempt to establish aviation in Canada in the 1920s and early 1930s is put forward for a purpose . . . to bring home to the reader that it is in no degree surprising that no aircraft industry grew up in Canada during the pre-war years. True, from 1935 forward there was a great upsurging in air-mindedness in the Dominion. The Trans-Canada airway was undertaken by the Government, but when the time came it was necessary to go out of the country for flying equipment. The RCAF was expanded and the attempt made to lay a firm foundation for the future. But again Canada had no aircraft industry behind its military service. The reason for that is that neither Governments nor people had yet come to have a belief in flying, and, despite aviation's great contribution to opening the north, still regarded flight as no occupation for a serious, conservative people.

There were faint stirrings, however. In 1934 Bob Noorduyn had started work on the first plane of all-Canadian design, the Norseman, as stout a ship as ever flew the bush, and still used in war service by Canada and the U.S.A. In 1935 officers of the Canadian Car and Foundry Company came to the conclusion that the time was ripe for the construction of military aircraft in the Dominion, primarily as a reserve source for Britain, and that the day was not far off when planes would be built on this continent and flown to the British Isles. The plan was discussed with members of the Canadian cabinet and high officers of the RCAF who showed enthusiasm for the idea. When two directors proceeded to Britain in 1936, however, for the purpose of laying their plans before the British Government, they reported that Air Ministry officials in London had been "tolerantly amused" by the suggestion that first-line military aircraft could be built here. The door, in short, was closed. But the Company, notably in the persons of the late W. W. Butler, its then President, Victor Drury of Montreal, (Butler's successor), and L. A. Peto, the present Managing-Director, was determined to enter the field, primarily because of the conviction shared by these three men that a new clash of arms with Germany was not far off. Thus arrangements were made in the United States for production of the Grumman two-seater Fighter at Fort William and a "sample" was flown to Ottawa for Government inspection. At first the Grumman plan got nowhere, although production was undertaken later. Similar experience was had in subsequent plans to build Bristol Blenheims and other British ships in Canada.

At this juncture (1936) several intending aircraft manufacturers in Canada were advancing their claims, both on Ottawa and on London. In no case was much warmth manifested in the reception of ideas. It was obvious that the British had no intention of letting any part of their own aircraft production escape to "the colonies" and equally obvious that official Canada did not sense the impending catastrophe. Canadian Car, it should be noted, finally engaged in Grumman production and when war came had turned out a number, used later in patrol work. Before many months passed the Company was to establish an enviable record as a producer of Hurricane Fighters, but of this, more later.

As with Canadian Car, so with National Steel Car, which broke ground at Malton Airport, near Toronto, on April 11th, 1938, for the foundations of a huge aircraft plant. Its program called for production of 28 Westland Lysanders, an Army Co-operation aircraft now obsolete but used in such useful tasks as High Seas Rescue patrols. Negotiations leading to this contract had been begun in 1936, but not until February 1938 was an agreement signed. At first the Company planned a plant of 60,000 square feet floor space, but in November 1938 an order was received for Hampden Bombers and an additional 80,000 square feet of space were undertaken. On the outbreak of war another extension of 210,000 square feet was constructed to provide for "orders to be forthcoming immediately" from Britain. The orders didn't come. Instead a stopgap contract was received for 150 Lysanders and no further commitments were made by the British, even the Lysanders being changed over for delivery to the R.C.A.F. As war came our aircraft policy was still completely hit-and-miss. That is the starting point. And this was the picture:

Events in hand at the Canadian Car Fort William plant, and at National Steel Car at Malton, have already been noted. In Montreal, Canadian Vickers were working on a small order for the tailor-made Stranraer flying boat. Fairchild, which had built the 71 and 82 types of that name for the bush trade and the RCAF and had had no luck with its first two-engine job, the Sekani, had received an experimental order for Britain on the Bolingbroke bomber a few months prior to the invasion of Poland. Boeing were turning out a few Blackburn Sharks, a torpedo-plane, on the

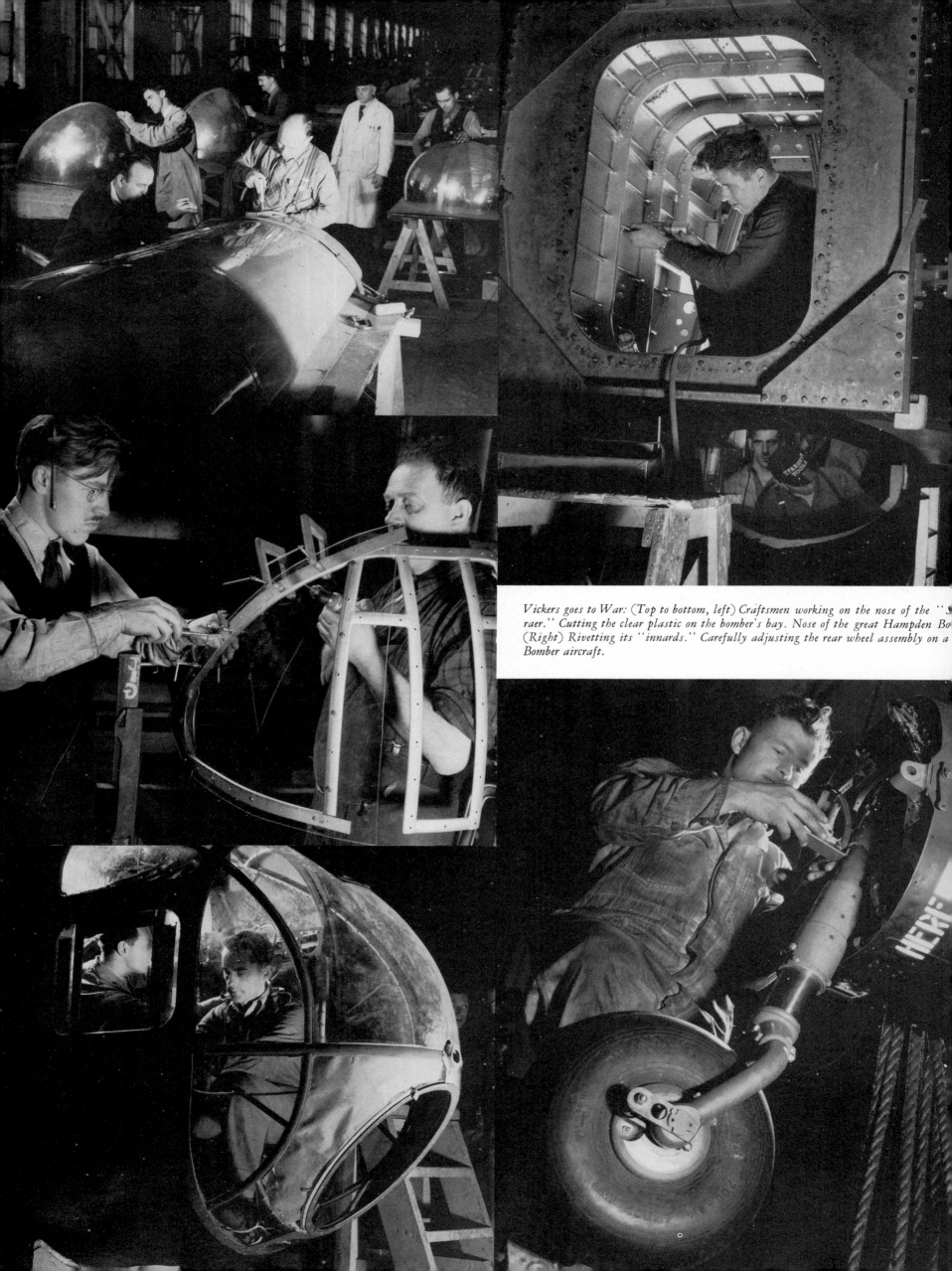

Vickers goes to War: (Top to bottom, left) Craftsmen working on the nose of the "S raer." Cutting the clear plastic on the bomber's bay. Nose of the great Hampden Bo (Right) Rivetting its "innards." Carefully adjusting the rear wheel assembly on a Bomber aircraft.

Vickers goes to War: (Top to bottom, left) Assembly line of fuselages on Hampden Bomber. Craftsmen speeding completion of the big bombers. Inspection and bomb rack assemblies. (Top to bottom, right) Completing framework of Pilot's "Office." Assembling the top gunner's sting. Rolling them out on the road to battle.

Princess Alice is launched: Vickers' first Catalina amphibian rolls out the hangar with suitable ceremonies, christened for H.R.H. Princess Alice, wife of Canada's Governor General. Pictures show the launching attended by military and civilian dignitaries. The Catalina plant is Canada's most completely streamlined aircraft production line.

west coast. Noorduyn was quietly making Norsemen in Montreal. Fleet had a small order for trainers for the RCAF and De Havilland had turned out its first Canadian Tiger Moths. In addition a six-company partnership had been formed of Vickers, National Steel Car, Canadian Car, Fairchild, Fleet and Ottawa Car during the summer of 1939 to assemble 160 Hampden bombers, but the first aircraft was still far from the hangar door when the guns began to thunder. Approximately 3,000 people working in less than 500,000 feet of manufacturing space, a production of 40 aircraft a year. That was Canada's aircraft industry when the war began. No wonder it was stunted in growth. Nobody had ever done anything for it. Nobody had ever taken it seriously, excepting a few determined men with faith in the future of aviation in a young country. Then war came . . . and the miracles began to happen, though not at first. First we had to get over a bad case of Maginot Mind.

The De Havilland Company's Plant and Aircraft: (Top to bottom, left) Assembly lin[e]
Tiger Moths. Anson Fuselage Assembly. Tiger Moth Trainers at an E.F.T.S. (To[p to]
bottom, right) Hoisting a Moth's engine into position. A "DeH." smart low wing mo[no]
plane two-seater. Pilots follow the leader over their Tarmac lined with Tiger Mo[ths]

The Stinging Mosquito—(Left and right, top) Loading the bomb-bay; a Mosquito above the clouds. (Centre) Mosquitos in flight. (Bottom) Bombs for Jerry, Skeeters in formation.

Scenes at Fairchild: (Top to bottom, left) Air Marshal W. A. Bishop, V.C., addres[s] workers' rally; looking down the assembly line; Bolingbroke assembly in progress. (R[ight] top to bottom) the menacing wing of a great bomber; H.R.H. the late Duke of Kent, the visitors' book as F. Bindoff, Mayor Pratt of Longueuil and Hubert Pasmore, child head, look on.

Where Bombers are Built: Scenes at the Fairchild Plant (Top to Bottom, left) His Excellency the Governor-General, the Earl of Athlone, marches up to the plant between rows of war-vet aircraft workers. (Right): H.R.H. the late Duke of Kent inspects Canadian built aircraft at Fairchild, then reviews aircraft workers. (Bottom right): Provincial Transport busses carry Fairchild workers from Montreal to their jobs across the river.

Bolingbrokes at Fairchild—(Left, top to bottom) a Bolingbroke in flight, approach to land, dusk on the landing strip. (Right, top to bottom) The R.C.A.F. accepts a Bolingbroke in flight and the servicing crew at work.

THE AGE OF MIRACLES

The single outstanding factor in the history of Canada's war aircraft production is the remarkable progress made in such a comparatively short space of time. As the reader will have gathered from the opening chapter, Canada started from scratch. During the period immediately prior to the war, small contracts for military aircraft had been awarded to a handful of companies only partially organized for serious aircraft production. None of these firms, judged by the size and scope of its operation, could be termed major. Without exception they faced tremendous difficulties in finding and training personnel, in constructing plant to meet their needs, in every phase of their new operations. At the start of the conflict, then, Canada had a handful of small aircraft plants (or what Canadians thought were aircraft plants in 1939). All these, in combined effort, produced about 40 aircraft a year. Of these, five were attempting to get into production with so-called educational orders; Canadian Car (Fort William) on the Hurricane, Fairchild on Bolingbrokes, National Steel Car on the Lysander, Boeing on the Shark and Vickers, far behind schedule, on the Stranraer for coastal patrols. De Havilland, Noorduyn and Fleet had small trainer orders. In addition six companies in combination were struggling with the Hampden program, already mentioned, but didn't fly their first ship until after the fall of France.

During the first nine months of war, the industry turned out about 200 units, most of which were elementary trainers while the country growled and said we were doing nothing and Britain, still committed to the idea that it would not be feasible, or commercially wise, to establish a major industry in Canada, played with the idea of feeding the requirements for the Commonwealth Air Training Plan out to Canada from the United Kingdom.

The determination of Canadian Car officials, more than any other factor, resulted in breaking-down British resistance through an educational order for forty Hurricanes to be completed by December 1940. Promptly the Company surprised its overseas clients by completing the job five months ahead of schedule. This brought a stepping up in production and orders to complete a total of 120 ships. This was subsequently increased to 400, then to 600, and from that point to four-figure quantities, plus spares, gun-wings, catapult machines, etc., until by April, 1941, an output of between 20 and 25 machines a week had been reached by the great aircraft plant at the Head of the Lakes. Whereupon Britain promptly cut production to 15 aircraft a week. The boys were going too fast! But that is another story, and part of the better-forgotten past.

The setting up of the British Commonwealth Air Training Plan entailed a complete recasting of the Canadian aircraft industry. To it the production of elementary trainers presented no insuperable problem—De Havilland and Fleet could attend to that! Plans were laid that first winter for the building of a single engine advanced trainer, the Harvard, and the job went to Noorduyn, where it remains. The need for a twin-engined advanced trainer was a poser, but Britain proposed a solution in the Avro Anson, which it was agreed she would ship in quantity for use on Canadian training fields. All well and good. Men did not then foresee Dunkirk and a British Commonwealth left standing alone against the enemies of freedom! This, as you shall see, entailed another complete recasting of the industry itself— actually its birth as a vital factor in Canada's war in the air.

Meanwhile all was not well that winter of Maginot. The Hampden program was sticking. In point of fact the aircraft industry was going to kindergarten on that job, although the invaluable lessons being learned at the time perhaps were not realised by aircrafters, Government, or a public longing for action. The

Bolingbrokes were not flowing from the line at Fairchild, either, and the Stranraer (even then an obsolete job) couldn't seem to get out of the door at Vickers. It was not a very happy winter in which to be an aircrafter.

Then Hitler struck at the Low Countries and, in rapid succession subjugated Holland, Denmark, Belgium, Norway, and finally, France. When that happened Canada was still struggling, trying to get its aircraft industry established as a going concern. It was on this scene that one of the great dynamic figures of the Canadian industrial war effort first appeared.

It is credibly reported that the first conversation Ralph P. Bell held with his future associates in Ottawa, was to inquire explosively when, if ever, Canada was going to do something about producing airplanes for its own defence—and by defence of Canada Bell has always meant the defence of any corner of a world involved in global war. Whether that conversation occurred, or not, the writer does not pretend to know. What he does know is that if the query is accurately reported, it was highly typical of the man. Ralph Bell probably has a lower explosion point than any highly placed Ottawa war executive, with the exception of his own chief, Hon. C. D. Howe, Minister of Munitions and Supply. In any event, by the time the Big Crumble began in Europe, Bell had accepted the presidency of a new Crown company, Federal Aircraft, and a post on the executive of Munitions and Supply. His committee man's post was "to interpret the then Director of Aircraft Supply to the Minister", a term which this writer will make no attempt to explain. What matters is that Bell appeared, completely cut himself off from his own business down on the Atlantic seaboard and rolled up his sleeves to do something about making planes in Canada. He has done plenty about it in the intervening years.

France fell. From Britain came a message not to expect the Ansons. Sorry, but we're in a spot! Either Canada must do something about it herself, find another advanced trainer, or forget the whole show. Canada decided to go ahead, full steam and throttle wide. The first job was to redesign the Anson and make it here. That is where Federal Aircraft really began to step into the picture. Production included the centralising of engineering and sub-contracting, the purchase of materials and moving these, and bits and pieces of the job, around from plant to plant. Actually Federal became primarily an administrative company. It still is in 1943. Associated in the plan were five major aircraft companies, Canadian Car; De Havilland; Ottawa Car & Aircraft; MacDonald Bros.; and National Steel Car's Malton plant (now Victory Aircraft Ltd.) In addition, smaller plants all over the country were included in the picture as suppliers of parts. During the various phases of Anson manufacture, the aircraft has been redesigned many times to fit the need of the day, but, in all, well over 1,800 of these trainers have been manufactured for Federal. It was a man-size job to get the first one into the air, however!

The original plan of operation could not be considered as ideal. It called for a system then in vogue in Great Britain known as the Shadow Factory Plan. By the same token, the methods adopted in the United States were totally unsuited to the Dominion, inasmuch as our then potential in the way of production was not of a character that called for giant assembly lines. The final scheme evolved, still in effect, called for the employment of almost innumerable sub-contractors, working in their own plants. Many of these smaller plants did not require much altering or retooling, and it was found that production for immediate use was more than a possibility. Nevertheless, the job seemed to remain at a standstill in the beginning. We hadn't got the hang of it yet. Similarly the assembly lines everywhere else seemed to be

*Fleet Aircraft "Fort" Trainer; early war-days Canadian design Elementary Trai
with assembly line shots. (Right, centre) a Hampden fuselage, manufactured by F
for Canadian Associated Aircraft.*

clogged. The aircraft simply were not coming through. That summer Bell took over as the first Director General of Aircraft Production, which post he still occupies, handing his duties at Federal to Ray Lawson, of London, Ontario, a prominent Canadian business man. Soon after the new set-up was created what may be termed the first miracle began to happen.

That was some months after Dunkirk. Prior to that time Canada was just beginning to go along nicely with the foundations of the British Commonwealth Air Training Plan, under the terms of which this country would create a coast-to-coast chain of elementary and service flying training schools and ground establishments, in which to train tens of thousands of young Canadians, Australians, New Zealanders and lads from Britain to be pilots, observers and wireless air gunners. Canada would have provided some of the training ships, but the twin-engine jobs, essential in the training of bomber pilots, observers and gunners, were all to have come from Britain. We had an outsize job on our hands! The Fall of France had put us into the aircraft business with both feet. The Maginot Mind was gone at last!

The news reaching Canada was bad enough without the inclusion of bulletins to the effect that no aircraft could be expected from England for many a month to come, if ever. But the tag-line, telling us that if we were hoping to manufacture aircrew the job of providing all the machines would be up to us was pure, unadulterated catastrophe. That was the point at which the first miracle went into high gear. The Honorable C. D. Howe, Supply Minister, and his then Director of Aircraft Supply, Jack Sanderson, scoured the United States and found the Jacobs engine. The Anson was redesigned to take the American power unit instead of the British Cheetah. The job of making Ansons in Canada was farmed out overnight to bits-and-pieces people all over the country, plus the main assembly shops. Canada had decided that if nobody else could equip her great university of the air she would do the job herself.

The story needs no elongated repetition here. It has been told time and again. Suffice to say that, somehow (and it is doubtful if anybody knows all of the how) the reconstructed Anson was brought into production and the Plan was saved, while the armchair critics, in and out of Parliament, proclaimed aloud that the production people had made a hopeless mess of the whole unhappy business. That they could not do. The mess was made for them by a perverted genius named Hitler. The production men simply disentangled the debris and rebuilt the plan. Thus did the first miracle happen. Its result was the coming into full production of the Air Plan five months ahead of schedule, a Plan of considerably greater scope than the one contemplated in the agreement signed between the British nations in December, 1939.

From that point the Dominion's aircraft producers went on to completely equip the schools with aircraft. Finally it began to dawn on the people of the country that, no matter what the critics might have said, we had put the Plan across under our own steam. Now we could sit back and keep it supplied with spares and replacements! That was the general expectation about the time Canadians realized that the first miracle had happened. But no. A second miracle was beginning to bear fruit.

It differs from the first in that it is the result of cold, calculated planning. But it is no less a miracle than the one which saved the Plan, for through it Canada has come to the point at which, in addition to supplying the Air Training Plan with its continuing aircraft needs, the Dominion is about to become, or has already become, an all-out producer of the highest types of combat aircraft currently on view in the skies of war. Examine the record. As this is written in 1943, we are going into production of the great Lancaster four-engined bomber.

Two plants will shortly be turning out in quantity the magnificent Hell Diver, the name of which pretty well explains its dive-bombing purpose.

We are into mass production of the highly fancy Mosquito, fastest bomber in the world.

The Catalina, in flying-boat and amphibian form, is in production in two huge plants.

All this is in addition to the standardization of production for the Air Plan itself. Thus Canada to-day is not merely one of the world's great producers of training aircraft, but is neck-deep into the job of turning out four of the war's outstanding combat machines, not merely for R.C.A.F. use, but for our Allies and partners as well. A country which, on the outbreak of war did not rate knee-high as an aircrafter producer, to-day ranks as the greatest producer of all, in terms of its population. It was done by miracles, at least two of which rank as major.

A full year has passed since Bell and his aides and the production men of the first-line aircraft factories decided that the time had come for a new era of expansion. They announced they could supply anything the Air Plan might require with one hand tied. "Give us something to do" they said. "New ships, new types, something to get our teeth into." Just about then the paper-and-pencil experts began to ask for particulars. How about the Moth program? What about the Ansons? How about Harvards? After all, it takes a lot of aircraft to keep the Plan going. Maybe we could help the neighbors with any extras we produce. But that wasn't what the aircraft industry wanted. From Bell at the top down through the nation's plants and the rank and file of its aircraft workers, the heat was on to get Canada into the ranks of the major producers of war aircraft. From all of which a program has emerged.

First of all, about trainers. Three types are required, the production experts said, no more—one basic trainer for the elementary schools, two for the service schools, to be used respectively for the fighter pilots of tomorrow and for the bomber crews. For the latter, let's keep the Anson and the Harvard; for the former let's replace the Moth with a new type and release the great De Havilland plant for a bigger job. So the British Commonwealth Air Training Plan's problems were settled by bringing in the sturdy little ship known as the Cornell and handing it over to the Fleet works for manufacture. Bob Noorduyn was given the duty of rolling out the Harvards, a job he was already doing to the Queen's taste, and the Anson program, after some streamlining, was left as was. That provided for the Training Plan. It also released a great deal of assembly-line space for the serious function of producing fighting and bombing planes.

De Havilland drew the Mosquito, the twin-engined marvel in plywood which is currently the rage of the R.A.F. and the despair of the *Luftwaffe*. For long months the De Havilland people were in what seemed to be an interminable huddle. No Moths slid out the hangar doors. A considerable air of hush-hush overhung the great plant. The Jeremiahs whispered that the place was full of confusion. Production, of course, ceased to exist. Then, out of the blue, the Skeeter came off the secret list and was exhibited before a notable gathering at Ottawa's Uplands Field. It did everything but go upstairs perpendicularly, backwards. This amazing aircraft had swung into full production in a Canadian plant while the pincenez-waggers maintained that the industry, De Havilland included, had gone to perdition.

Meanwhile urgent matters were afoot at the Head of the Lakes, where Hurricanes hitherto had come down the line like peas rolling from pods. The Hurricane problem had been tough from its beginnings. In the first place the manufacturers had trouble to get so much as an educational order to manufacture war machines in the heart of the great North American hinterland. Once they

Busy Days at Fleet Aircraft: (Left to right, top) A Fairey Battle on the field at Fort [...] and a Fleet "Finch". (Centre, left and right), "Finches" ready for fly-away and a ponto[...] equipped Fleet 50K. (At bottom), a girl-aircrafter takes welding instruction, as does ano[...] in the sheet-metal department.

Is Canada's Elementary Trainer Headquarters: (Top, left and right) a "Cornell" others in final assembly stage. (Centre) a P23 on the tarmac, the final assembly or the Cornell. (Bottom) machine shop and assembly line shots at Fort Erie.

Lockheed plays its part, in Canada as for Uncle Sam: (Left, top to bottom) a flig
Lightnings above the clouds; a Lodestar over the Rockies; the Ventura in the mounta
(Right, top to bottom) The Hudson Reconnaissance Bomber, one of the war's most w
used aircraft; the B-17 (Flying Fortress to you!) and another P-38.

had proved that they could do the job they had Joshua's own time keeping enough orders on hand to see two months ahead. Then by the time they had decided to switch to a new plane, Hurricane buyers cropped up on every hand. Hurries were wanted for the Dutch Indies, for Singapore, for every corner of the compass where the umbrella wouldn't open. Well, the Lakehead gentlemen kept on grinding out Hurricanes to fill the short orders, but meanwhile they were readying the Hell Diver. You will be hearing more about it—considerably more—before much time slips by.

The big four-engine Lancasters are something else again. Their new home is the sort of plant in which you can move a 20-car train complete with locomotive sideways down the assembly aisle with plenty of clearance on both sides. The luck in the Lancaster plant had not been very good until the big ships came along. Then, overnight, a *coup d'état* took place. The owners moved out for the duration and the Government moved in, formed the Crown company known as Victory Aircraft, topped by Toronto's J. P. Bickell and managed by the former plant boss, Dave Boyd, as hard-hitting a production man as may be found in the industry. Watch those Lancasters roll! And try to imagine what they will mean to Canada, sitting astride the cross-roads of a global war!

Of the fourth type, the Catalina, or PBY, of which more will be said later, suffice to say here that the great work horse of the coastal commands is rolling down the assembly lines of two vast plants, one west, one east, and that the sky is the production ceiling. The producers say they will hit that ceiling.

So a second aircraft production miracle has happened in Canada. A country with nothing to brag about as pre-war aircraft producer (a handful of bush planes per annum, plus the facilities for essential overhauls), has blossomed forth as one of the great aircraft makers of the world. Canadians solved the riddle of equipping the Air Training Plan when any man in his senses would have insisted that no solution could be found. Not satisfied with one miracle, the wonder workers promptly went about fabricating another—to make Canada a major producer of fighting machines of the types essential to our own defence, yet standard for our Allies, the best in each class. Now the second miracle has been wrought. There'll be a third, no doubt.

What is the secret? All very simple. The job has been done by men and women with no lessons to unlearn, no shibboleths to forget. The men who direct the aircraft industry were insurance salesmen, business executives, all manner of men, three years ago. The director-general was a maritime business man, deeply agitated by the need for aircraft and what he regarded as public and political lethargy. So they gave him the job, saying to him: "Okay, brother, let's see what *you* can do!"

Bell's right hand man was a young man who, three years ago, was only beginning to find his feet in the business world. But Fred Smye, now Director of the Production Program, was in every sense of the word a natural. The men and women of the industry—and they number more than 100,000—came from the farm, the bank, the loom, from every nook and cranny of Canadian life, to do this job. They and their leaders were the first people in North America to tackle the problems and ideas of employer-employee-government co-operation for victory. Nowhere in the land will you find *esprit de corps* to vie with their spirit. Everybody started from scratch. The result is miracles!

So while the Jeremiahs have been weeping along the Wailing Wall and while the magi of the club cars have been proclaiming the alleged discovery of new fissures in the war effort, the aircraft industry, which solved the riddle of the Air Plan, has done it again. Certainly production figures toppled. You don't just decide to build a new airplane type and start to roll 'em out the door in a week. It takes as long to turn out the first tailor-made machine as it does to produce the next 499. The figures fell because Canada had a long-term Plan. Now the Plan has come through. Another miracle has been wrought. Canada's wartime wonder-industry is on the march again! A few months hence, say by the end of 1943, it will have exceeded by far anything in the way of production figures contemplated in the past as a target for the present—and another miracle will have been performed!

Ansons on the Wing and in the Making: A series of pictures of MacDonald Brothers Aircraft, Winnipeg, showing wing manufacture, float construction and overhaul work in progress.

THE PEOPLE OF THE AIRCRAFT INDUSTRY

*W*ho are the people of this giant young industry which literally "came from nowhere" during the first three years of war? Were they aircrafters before the drums rolled again? Were they men and women used to the roar of airplane motors, who spoke the language of the machine shop, who knew the ways of the sky? They were not.

With few exceptions not even their employers were men knowledgeable in the production of machines to fly. True, there were men like Noorduyn, builder of the great bush-flying Norseman, like Hubert Pasmore of Fairchild, Vanderlipp, now of Vickers, Garratt of De Havilland, Burke of Boeing, a few others, schooled in the production of pre-war freighters and light airplanes. But in the main even the men destined to become the great executives and production-line genii were occupied with tasks far removed from the production of aircraft, when the war began. One, Vickers little ball-of-fire, Ben Franklin, was an insurance man. Others were building rolling-stock for Canadian railways; others again were engaged in lines of business ranging from banking to heavy industries. But without exception they were men of vision, men in whom the rivers of adventure ran deep. It was to such as these that the new industrial giant of Canada's war years called. Their answer to that call has been heard in the constantly increasing thunder of war-planes rolling out the hangar doors and taking to the skies. Like the industry itself, its people "came from nowhere," master as well as man. That has been the basic glory of the show.

But what of the men and women workers drawn to aircraft plants, as machines and more machines needed human hands on their levers? Whence did they come? What happened to them in the course of their transformation into aircrafters? What social upheavals have resulted? Turn aside now and look at Canada's number one aircraft centre, the Montreal area.

Employment application files for Canadian Car's Montreal plants, for Fairchild, Noorduyn and Vickers, are a lesson in Canadian geography from Red Bay on the Saguenay, to Lost River, St. Remi, Matane, Granby, Amqui. These people came from innumerable towns, villages, hamlets, hills and valleys over the hundreds of thousands of square miles that make up the sprawling province of Quebec and places even more distant. They came from secluded Prince Edward Island, from Maritime fishing villages, where more than a few had noted what havoc Hitler's subs can wreak on the ships of nations still free. These knew from first-hand knowledge how desperately-wanted were the planes they were about to make. They came from Ontario's towns and countryside, from the Prairies' wind-driven wheat fields, from British Columbia valleys and coastal towns. They came literally from everywhere along the ribbon-strip of territory where Canada's people once lived peaceful lives. They came from the United States, Newfoundland, St. Pierre and Miquelon. They were Blue Nosers, Herring Chokers, Habitants, every kind of Canuck, old and new, easterner and westerner. With them came Old Country British, Old Country French, Dutch, Negroes, Chinese. They came from sheet metal plants, from poring over office ledgers, from behind the plow. They had been engineers, doctors, dentists, newspapermen, farmers' daughters, domestics, waiters and waitresses. These were the people who lined up at aircraft employment offices, even to cow-hands, complete with two-gallon hats. The summons of the unmanned machines and tools set up to build aircraft to destroy the enemy of the free peoples went out. Canada's butcher, baker and candlestick maker responded. They came, these rank and file Canadians, to offer their thousands and thousands of hands, to play a great and vital role in the creation of a vast new war industry. These Canadians in their tens of thousands, were

revolutionising their ways of living, just as were their juniors at sea, in the army, in the air. Hitler made them aircrafters. The change has affected their lives deeply.

Look, for example, at the Montreal plants where more than half the workers are French Canadian. A sizeable proportion came from the "little places" of their province. Plucked from the quiet pools of rural life, they were dropped into the roaring whirlpool of giant plants amidst thousands of industrial workers. Crevices appeared in their sectional barriers, isolationist dams burst and merged with the surging currents of their war-angry country. The product of their new skills was destined to go to far lands to blast a liberty-stifling enemy. And there, before these men and women, opened the broad panorama of world war and their place in its historic struggle. Perhaps no more profound sociological upheaval has ever been visited upon the descendants of New France in Canada. World-minded Canadians by the thousand have been born amongst the French-speaking Quebeckers in the great aircraft plants of Montreal.

The particular meaning of the word "unity" in bi-lingual Canada came to be known, too, to the English-speaking workers in aircraft. With their French-speaking compatriots and foreign-born Canadians they joined to co-operate in erecting a huge industrial structure at break-neck pace. They did co-operate; so did the French; so, too, the new Canadians. The whole story of the building of the aircraft industry in the Montreal region, as in the Dominion's other centres, is a story of newly trained workers co-operating with supervising personnel to perform one of the biggest jobs in their country's economic history. Without the ready and patriotic co-operation of the shop-new aircrafter the job could not have been done at all.

How did so varied a lot of humans, male and female, with such varied skills—some long unemployed and without knowledge of craft or trade—create, together with managerial personnel, machines and capital, an aviation industry on an international scale? How were habits of coordination instilled into hands and eyes, enabling them to produce accurately wrought warplanes on mass output schedules?

Facing the Government, the employer, his supervisory staff and workers, was probably the stiffest problem in mass industrial training ever to confront any group of Canadians.

Bright spot in the picture of the upsurging aircraft industry was the immediate development of the co-operative spirit in industrial relations. If the biggest single job ever undertaken by the Canadian nation was the Air Training Plan, the most forward-looking attitude ever attained between Canadian employers and employees arose in plants feeding that Plan its machines. These employers and employees introduced ways of government-management-labor co-operation hitherto untried on the American continent, giving effect to methods later taken up by other Canadians and by leading American corporations, even by Uncle Sam's War Production Director, Donald Nelson. Hundreds of United States war factories have since introduced the joint union-management committees used before them by Canadian aircrafters. As has happened so often, Canadians once more showed the way to their rich neighbours! How?

As soon as leading Canadian aircraft companies and their workers came alive to the fearful urgency of getting the product out, they decided that something new in get-together methods must be attempted. Practices modelled on their British fellows' experience were suggested. Unfamiliar schemes were carefully examined and accepted. Then both employer and worker took a look at each other's problems at closer range than either had ever done before, cleared obstacles to step up assembly line pace. The

Edmonton's Big Repair Plant: (Top, left and right) U.S. Army Norseman with com[bina]tion ski-wheel arrangement installed; the engine shop at Aircraft Repair, Lim[ited]. (Centre, left and right) The main floor of No. 1 Plant at Aircraft Repair; an overha[ul] reaches the dope room. (Bottom, left and right) The machine shop and a shot of No. 2

result was one of the shining patches of co-operative patriotism in the North American industrial scene.

Throughout the story of the steeply graded rise of the industry designed to supply the Air Training Plan and later to send war-craft winging over Axis territory, the Canadian worker, with his traditional adaptability in picking up new skills, his spirit of ready co-operation, and his high patriotism, stands as one of the main bases of the industry's success.

Whether that support was collectively given through his, or her, union or offered individually by organized workers, it revealed the aircrafter's alertness to the overhanging menace of Hitlerism. Men and women applying tools to the fuselages and wings of 'planes went at their new jobs determined to build those weapons, the lack of which had left so many brave men facing the *Luftwaffe* terror inadequately protected.

Among men and women on the assembly lines an awareness of their responsibility grew as they observed extensions jutting out from their high-walled plants. They had heard that British co-workers were using the union not only as a bargaining instrument, but also as one to lift output to unscaled peaks. It led them to think of their own unions in similar terms. In plants in which the international unions were not represented, a similar urge was felt and followed. The Canadian aircrafter whether in or outside the unions, knew that more than ordinary peace-time organization ability had been required to create all the new machines and tools he was manning. He knew the engineering and supervisory people had been tackling a major earthquake. He also knew that, in a crisis like that confronting him, it was up to him and his sister worker to turn in a far better than ordinary performance.

After all, it was the aircrafter who had to see that the minute details of plane designs were followed to the last rivet. He was the on-the-spot person who must note when anything began to go wrong . . . as soon as it began to go. When production schedule lags occurred, he was there and it was his job to know the cause. It was up to him and the girl beside him to put fingers on bottle-necks for the foreman to break, and keep pushing the planes out to the airfields.

The first aircrafters to get together with company representatives and sign a collective agreement were those in Fort William's Canadian Car plant. But it was in Montreal and Vancouver where a high degree of organization were first achieved. In Montreal, perhaps because it is the country's largest aircraft production centre, the characteristic trend of the labor movement in the industry is most readily perceived.

Even before the war the International Association of Machinists, led by Robert Haddow, a fiery Scots-Canadian, anticipated a widespread demand for organization in the growing arms plants. During the 1914-1918 conflict, this union, which had established its first local in Canada in 1889, experienced a sharp rise in membership amongst munition workers. With the coming of war for a second time in a quarter-centry, the Association gave Haddow the assignment of organising the Montreal aircraft plants.

During the clouded months after the Nazi pincers closed Poland in their vise, the indefatigable Scot and his colleagues canvassed the aircraft workers. Not until the spring of 1940, six months after the start, however, did the International Association of Machinists issue a charter for a new local in Montreal aircraft plants. That was the beginning of what to-day is Canada's greatest single union local—Aircraft Lodge 712.

The ticklish diplomacy of opening negotiations, of employer and employee representatives sitting together and going into rates and conditions, was tackled. Both sides were sharply aware that their country was in for a fight for its life. Both knew that a basis

of understanding must be reached if those turning out weapons were to give their utmost. Both deemed friendly relations a prime factor in their country's productive effort.

They were not easy adjustments to make in a mushrooming mass production industry. War-sobered employer and employee sensed that heavy responsibilities rested upon each. With few exceptions that has been the story of internal relations in the industry through the war years. At times there have been acrid discussions over working conditions and wages. At times tempers have flared, strikes have threatened, one actually occurred, arising solely out of the question of rest-periods during shifts. But never has there been divergence between boss and worker on the prime issue—production for Victory.

The strained months after Dunkirk and the fall of France pointed the urgency of planes and more planes. Employer and employee saw clearly that survival itself was the stake. So they pulled together. If each sought the most favourable bargain he could get, each was prepared to make sacrifices for the cause. Thus, when the differences between Montreal aircrafters and their employers were heard before a conciliation board in '41, they renewed their pact.

During 1941, as news of Nazi enslavement of French employers and workers alike began to reach the free world, Canadian air-crafters and their employers entered into even more intimate relationships. Co-operate, they must. That was the watchword. Nothing so close in the way of co-operation as the situation demanded had ever been tried in North America. Canadian aircrafters, whether in or out the union movement, showed the way to the whole American continent.

Britain had been deeper in the battle than they, so they examined the things she had tried. What had she done to hang on when the Battle of Britain raged? One experiment, reported to have resulted in more 'planes in less time, was the production council. There Management could meet with the men and women with rivet guns in their hands and discuss how to get more done with each gun.

On October 12, 1941, Montreal aircraft workers and employers agreed by organization, co-operation and education, to work together to increase production. Union officials declared themselves ready and eager to organize conferences with management and government representatives to discuss, plan and carry out production plans and schedules.

The workers declared themselves ready "to sponsor campaigns to gather production suggestions, to eliminate waste, to do away with enforced loafing and idle time, to eliminate absenteeism, to organize interdepartmental competitions on production, to reduce the cost of production."

Finally it was proposed that "in each Montreal aircraft plant a joint committee of representatives of Labor and Management be immediately established, the sole function of such committee being to increase production. Such joint committees shall have the responsibility of receiving information from the Managements on production plans, of receiving proposals from the Union on measures proposed to increase production, and of organizing the most thorough educational work within each plant to acquaint the whole personnel with production plans and to organize them to carry it out, and to surpass it."

This was the real beginning. But such intimate teamwork was new, experimental. No similar attempt had ever been made in America by employer or employee. This was sheer innovation. Many on both sides doubted that the method would work. The notion of blitzkreiging production charts naturally conjured up a series of problems for management men with considerable experience in output feats behind them. Companies necessarily had to consider changes in schedules involved in any quick

The great Noorduyn Aircraft Plant: (Left, top to bottom) Router cutting alum[...]
patterns. The Tinsmith's Shop, a craftsman's paradise. A Chinese worker for Can[...]
War in the Air. (Top to bottom, right) 1,320 ton Hydraulic Stamping Press.[...]
assembly jig. A young Chinese working on the centre-section of a "Harvard" Train[...]

The great Noorduyn Aircraft Plant: (Top to bottom, left) Experts working on a "Norseman" Wing. "Harvard" assembly line in background, putting finishing touches on Wings in foreground. One of the many efficient aircraft women workers. (Top to bottom, right) One of the three or four "Harvard" assembly lines, "Norseman" assembly lines to right. View showing immense space of the assembly line. The famous "Norseman" transport, with "Harvard's" just off assembly line, in background.

Busy Days at Noorduyn — At top are Norsemen on the line for delivery to the U.S. Ar (Centre) a girl and her turret lathe; (at right) Norseman in flight. Bottom pictures s the pay parade and girl apprentices learning their new jobs in the school.

14-00-9

...rduyn Plant Hits The Target—Across the top are Harvard trainers for the R.C.A.F.
...tre, left and right) girls on the assembly line and pretty nearly a hundred Harvards
...u count 'em) lined up along the runway. At bottom, final assembly proceeds—and so
...the Harvard line.

06-102
5-42

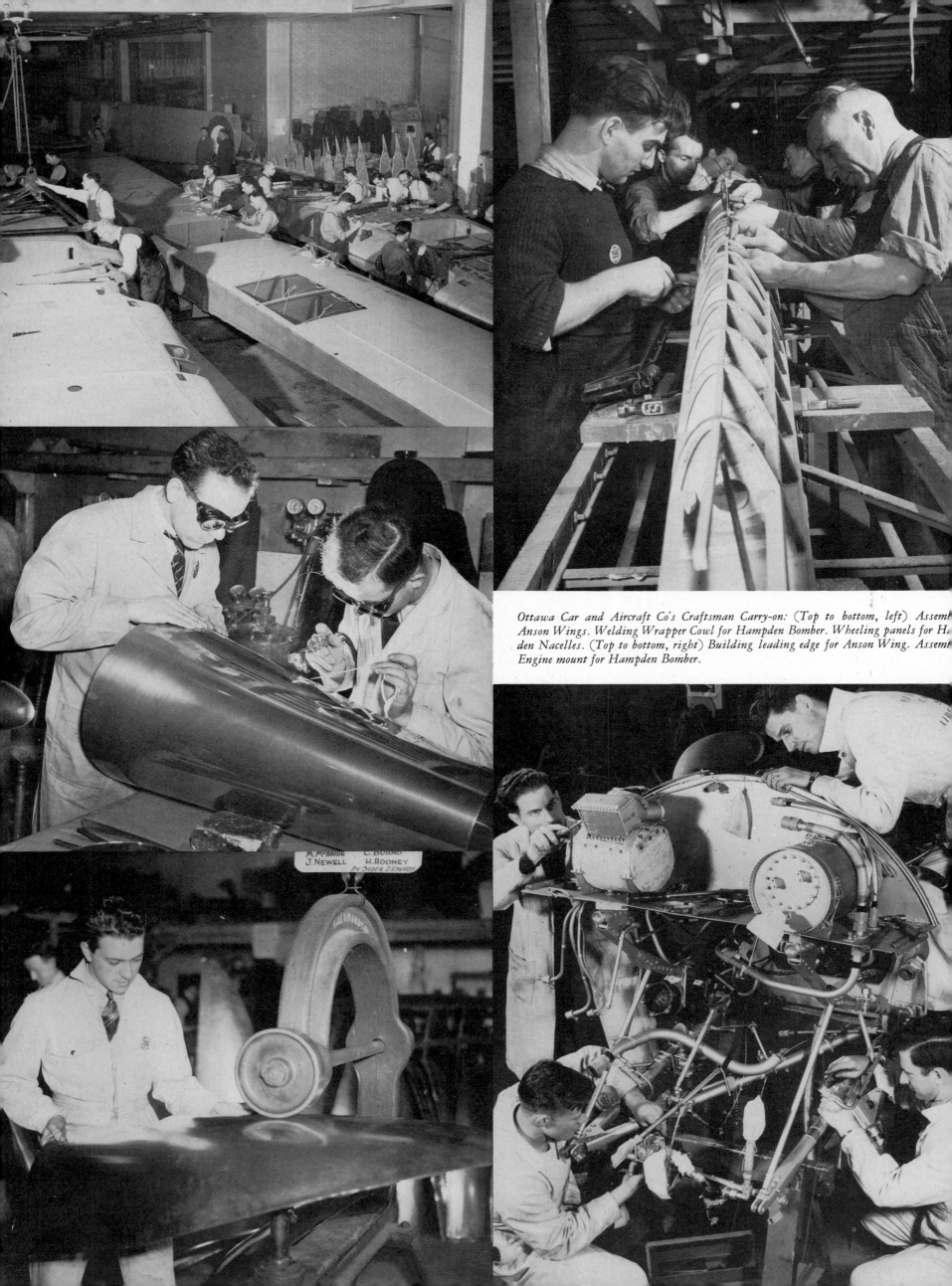

Ottawa Car and Aircraft Co's Craftsman Carry-on: (Top to bottom, left) Assemb[ling] Anson Wings. Welding Wrapper Cowl for Hampden Bomber. Wheeling panels for Ha[mp]den Nacelles. (Top to bottom, right) Building leading edge for Anson Wing. Assembl[ing] Engine mount for Hampden Bomber.

speed-up. Altered rates in the inflow of materials to their shops would call for adjustments in schedules elsewhere. Perhaps there were men in Management who deemed such suggestions an encroachment upon their special field. Some workers feared it would mean letting their own rights go by the board. It was no simple business.

But employer and employee had before them constantly their Prime Minister's then recent words: "Let us never forget the size and power of Germany's war machine, and that while German forces fight on distant fronts, Germany herself, and the countries controlled by Germany, continue to manufacture the equipment and munitions needed to effect the necessary repairs, and to keep her armed forces at the highest stage of efficiency."

A prodigious growth had already occurred and the forceful Ralph Bell, Canada's aircraft production director, declared that the program was pursuing a trend of "speedy and appreciable acceleration." But it was also true that the Axis raised every ante with each week of 1941's autumn, as the panzers probed deep into Russia and the roar of Hirohito's bombers over Pearl Harbour echoed around the world.

In this crisis the forward-looking Bob Noorduyn and Norman Bell, Noorduyn Aviation's vice-president and plant manager, decided to see what could be done to step up Harvard output. The newly set up, purely local, committee to boost production in the factory was called in. Before the meeting ended those present agreed to try out British labour-management co-operation ideas; a joint committee would be set up and at its meetings Management and Labour representatives would consider ways and means of feeding the Air Training Plan more Harvard trainers faster. Suggestions to this end would be studied from whatever quarter they came.

The dismal war news was having its effect on other plants as well. Across the St. Lawrence, at Fairchild, workers and supervising staff were smashing all records in getting out Bolingbrokes. Vickers sent eight new tailor-made Stranraers flying in 28 days! Out on the Pacific coast Boeing rushed to get its Catalinas into production. From De Havilland the Trainers poured in steady stream.

Prime Minister Churchill in one of his ringing speeches had just said "aircraft will be more than ever necessary now that the war has spread all over the world." Throughout the Dominion an extraordinary response was coming from company heads, supervising personnel and men and women workers, organized and unorganized alike. Wide-awake Government officials rose to the crisis too. Without delay, the Director General of Aircraft Production took up a suggestion of the Machinists' Union. "Your letter of December 23rd," he wrote, "is just about the most practical and appreciated message of season's greetings that one could ask, and I accept with pleasure and alacrity your suggestion that we get together at the earliest possible date to discuss closer co-operation for greater production."

Bell called on company men and workers' representatives to sit down and figure out how tighter teamwork might speed out warplanes. With the Government's senior aircraft official in the chair, Fairchild's Vanderlipp, Vickers' Franklin and Noorduyn's Noorduyn met with Robert Haddow and D. S. Lyons, the Machinists' Canadian vice-president, and other representatives of the workers in the board room of Canadian Vickers on January 8, 1942, to work out plans for greater warplane production. This was the real beginning of the movement in Canada.

The group explored every avenue, each realizing his need of the other. If pushing their differences aside would quicken the pace on the assembly lines, they'd push them clear into the ditch. So it went. At the close of deliberations Director General Bell announced that

"in each of the plants a Joint Committee of Employees and Management will be established which will meet monthly to consider any suggestions brought forward offering practical ways and means to increase output."

Bell further declared that "the manufacturers have now been given definite schedules of production required as far ahead as the end of 1943, and, in some cases, even further. This has made possible the long range planning of operation which is essential for the achievement of quantity production."

Such was the beginning of the cooperative movement throughout the industry.

More than one reason, of course, must be sought to explain the battering of production records in the succeeding months. There was a steadier stream of materials, the growing experience of supervisors and production workers was another. But manifestly a contributing factor of great importance was the high morale and spirit of co-operation between workers and company officials which has always marked Canada's war plane industry.

Noorduyn Aviation rang the bell during February, 1942, pushing 32 Harvard trainers past the apron of its big hangar. At Fairchild a campaign was started to check absenteeism. The spirit carried through to re-tooling and building Vickers' vast new plant for manufacture of the PBY. So it went, right across the country.

Before the year was out Management was loud in its praise of the aircrafters' spirit of co-operation. In the words of R. B. C. Noorduyn:—

"As I see it, these Councils are extremely valuable as a contact between management and labor. They let us see what is in the other fellow's mind, help us to understand why that thing or the other is done. When these misconceptions are removed, we are getting somewhere and this is a time for mutual confidence."

From N. F. Vanderlipp, then general manager of the Fairchild Plant (now with Canadian Vickers) came even more glowing encomiums.

Faced with an Ottawa demand to double the production of the Bolingbroke, he had called in the workers' members of the committee as a prelude to talk with the main body of the workers. That was on a Tuesday afternoon. On the Thursday they walked into Vanderlipp's office and their answer was "Yes, the boys and girls will do it." And they did it. They had done it by the time when the general manager took time out to sing his song of praise.

Mr. Vanderlipp told of another example of co-operation. The R.C.A.F. had a number of damaged 'plane wings on hand and no nearby repairer to whom to give them. The Air Force went to Fairchild, to save sending the wings to the Pacific coast, as they were needed in a hurry.

"I sent for the committee and asked them to tell every man in our wing department the story," Vanderlipp said, "to explain that the management was not trying to get more out of them for nothing. Faced with ten per cent more work, the wing men did not hesitate. They did the job in record time and kept up normal production of new wings."

The co-operation idea has paid dividends in countless places, according to another aircraft producer.

"Production may lag in some department. It may be a supervision fault that I do not know anything about. It is brought to my attention and the trouble removed. Or it may be that through no one's fault material is held up for a week. We go through the records with the committee. The production report shows that a department is 25 per cent below schedule for the week. Now the trouble, whatever it was, has been removed. Will the committee see if the department can catch up in the current week? You bet they will, and the department catches up, too. Why? Because they know that when their fellow-workers talk to them they are not

The Workers of Ottawa Car and Aircraft Co: (Top to bottom, left) Welding E[x]
Flame Damper and other details for Hampden Bomber. Assembly of Hurricane Ole[o]
Fairings. Hurricane Oleo Leg nearing completion. (Top to bottom, right) Asse[mbly]
part of Hampden Fuel System. Assembling Cheetah Engine after overhaul.

SMOKING REFUSE
IN THE CONTAINERS
PROVIDED

being taken for a ride. In the past, not always without reason, the workman has grown a bit suspicious, as you know, but we have given his own representatives full access to all our records. When management has fallen down, we admit the fault but we ask the workmen to help make up for our mistakes, and they never fail."
The record, then, is one of close cooperation. It is a record of which every Canadian aircrafter from Halifax to Vancouver may well be proud.
From what has been said it must not be inferred by the reader that the spirit of cooperative effort has been or is limited to those plants in which the International Unions hold contracts as the employees' bargaining instruments. In the first place there are no closed shops amongst Canada's primary aircraft producers. Hence even in the unionised plants many non-union aircrafters may be found. These have never been found wanting in matters of *esprit de corps*. Although the Labour movement, as such, has been widespread throughout the industry, and one after another most of the primary plants have moved into the union fold, a few remain in which local employees' associations are the contact point between employer and aircrafter. Here, too, the spirit of cooperation has ruled, for it has been the driving force of the entire industry. The union movement has been most active in Fairchild, Vickers, Noorduyn, Canadian Car (Fort William and Amherst) and Boeing. More recent to sign contracts with the unions have been Victory and De Havilland, the former with the Machinists (A. F. of L.), De Havilland with the C.I.O. MacDonald Brothers have signed contractual agreements with the Machinists (A.F.L.) and Fleet with the Canadian Congress of Labour, C.I.O. affiliate in Canada. In Ottawa Car, certain Canadian Car plants and smaller organizations, local committees, entirely independent of the international unions, function. These, too, feature close co-operative schemes.

* * *

As the months passed the movement towards still closer co-operation continued to increase. To accent it, Production Director Bell created a Personnel Relations Committee to co-ordinate and act as a clearing house for ideas. By Order-In-Council of May 29th, 1942, an official committee within the industry, known as the Aircraft Industry Relations Committee, was established by the government. Its functions are concerned with questions of *esprit de corps* and its birth stemmed from an aircraft convention, held in Ottawa a few days earlier, which sought "a well-planned effort to build up and maintain the morale of all workers in the industry."
A group of outstanding aircraft executives comprise the officers of the committee, headed by President J. E. Labelle of Canadian Vickers as chairman, the membership being composed of W. L. Bayer of Noorduyn, David Boyd of Victory Aircraft, P. C. Garratt of De Havilland and H. M. Pasmore of Fairchild. E. G. Hirst of Toronto, well-known Canadian publicist, who became connected with the industry in 1941, resigned as vice-president of Might Directories Limited, Toronto, early in 1942, to give all his time and effort to the committee, as Director of Personnel Relations. Hirst is the go-getter type with a flair for organisation.
Early in 1943, for example, his services were sought and secured from Ottawa and the directors of the aircraft committee to direct a monster parade to sponsor recruiting for the Reserve Army. In two weeks of high-powered organising Hirst produced a demonstration which the Toronto *Globe and Mail* editorially called "Toronto's most spectacular parade of the war."
Primary purpose of the Relations committee is to step up the workers' desire to constantly increase production levels. Under the terms of the order-in-council which created it, it must place its programs for final approval before the Director General of Aircraft Production.

Forty-nine of Canada's outstanding industrialists agreed to serve in a voluntary capacity, in committees created to cover various sections of the country. More than fifty specialists serve on voluntary working committees, to assist in various projects, on a Dominion-wide basis. Employees were selected from leading plants to participate in discussion and planning. In this way, the opinion of experienced business men, capable newspapermen, radio and other specialists and representatives of workers were gathered and considered. These opinions are then presented for the information of management and production committees in making decisions as to what plans should or should not be carried through.
By the Spring of 1942, most of the plants had appointed personnel directors and, under the co-ordination of the Aircraft Industry Relations Committee, these groups began to meet in various sections of the country to discuss material problems.
The committee was expanded. Mrs. Ethel Colwell, a recognized expert in the training of female workers, did particularly outstanding work. At the outset she conducted a survey of female working problems in Ontario and Quebec aircraft plants, prior to which she had established a joint employment bureau for National Steel Car Corporation and De Havilland Aircraft of Canada Limited, operating major plants in the Toronto area. Mrs. Colwell then, in addition to establishing close contact between the industry and National Selective Service and other government organizations, opened many new fields in the realm of personnel relations. Through visits to plants throughout the United States and Canada a great deal of important data was collected from many sources. On this she based a course for the training of personnel supervisors of female employees. These women were dubbed "House Mothers" by the press and it is their duty to look after the interests of female employees in the nation's aircraft plants.
The first class for House Mothers was held in Toronto in the fall of 1942 and was followed by classes in Winnipeg, Vancouver, and Montreal. The classes were so successful that by the Spring of 1943 requests for Mrs. Colwell's help were being received from companies not connected with the aircraft industry to institute similar classes for their supervisors of women. Mrs. Colwell helped many war plants select suitable women for these jobs. Her classes were so successful that requests were received from the Department of Labour and Selective Service to train instructors to carry on similar courses throughout the country.
The aircraft industry also led in another field which, though it may appear trivial to mere man, is of transcendent importance to the woman worker, the creating of worksuits which will not destroy milady's charm. In 1941 the only worksuits available for female employees had been the regulation coverall. Women workers simply did not like them. Meetings were held with designers, worksuit and sports goods manufacturers and more suitable types of work clothing, embodying many essentially feminine features, were designed. The matter of adequate protection for the hair was carefully studied and solved. All this "research" was conducted on the principle that the opinion expressed by one young woman "Unless we feel we look right, we don't want to work—we just want to go hide behind a post" was worthy of respectful attention, because appearance is the essence of feminine morale, at the workbench as at the opera.
Today's woman worker in aircraft, though dressed for the job, is nevertheless still a young woman easy on the eyes and, therefore, a contented worker.
The aircraft industry from the beginning pioneered plant rallies, visits by outstanding war heroes, plant receptions and other employee gatherings of an inspirational nature. Many of these

Aircraft Notables: That pleasant-looking gentleman at the desk is E. G. Hirst of the Aircraft Industry Relations Committee. The grinning trio, left to right, are Fred Smye, Director of Production Division, Aircraft Branch; W. J. McDonough, General Manager of Central Aircraft, and Ralph P. Bell, O.B.E., Director-General of Aircraft Production, snapped at a General Aircraft "open house" party. The lady at the desk is Ethel Colwell, Supervisor of Women for the Relations Committee, talking with "house mothers" and the much-admired gent is Jack Pritchard of De Havilland, top flight prize-winner for employee suggestions. Facsimile of Director-General's Award is also given.

The DIRECTOR-GENERAL of
the AIRCRAFT PRODUCTION BRANCH of the
DEPARTMENT of MUNITIONS and SUPPLY
Presents this

INDIVIDUAL MERIT
AWARD
to

Frederick Collins
of The Blank Aircraft Company

IN RECOGNITION OF INITIATIVE AND
PATRIOTISM WHILE ENGAGED IN THE
AIRCRAFT INDUSTRY

June 25th, 1943

nd Frolic In The Aircraft Industry: 6,000 people turned out to see the glider shown
ver left perform over the field at London, Ontario's, Central Aircraft plant. Other
es show Pilot Officer "Johnnie" Higham, Canadian bomber-pilot, shooting the breeze
De Havilland employees and members of the R.C.A.F. Silver Band on a visit to
eal aircraft plants. All the parties were sponsored by the Aircraft Industry Relations
ittee.

Early Days at Malton: (Top to bottom, left) The Lysander fitting shop. Buil[ ] Hurricane Wings. Hampden and Anson Wing assemblies. (Top to bottom, right) A[ ] assembly line. Yale Trainer assembly. Anson in foreground, Hampdens in distance[ ] assembly line.

have gained wide publicity through the press and have set the pace for other sections of the nation's war industry.

Soon the Committee was functioning so smoothly that half a dozen major requests for information were being received and handled daily, requests involving anything from simple queries to items which required the making of nation-wide surveys. Thus a clearing house was established throughout the Dominion, through which aircrafters were kept informed as to what was being done by others in the industry.

In the Spring of 1942, the committee undertook another task— to produce a magazine for employees throughout the industry. The magazine is of sixteen pages, of which eight are standard, and the other eight composed of local material prepared by editorial groups amongst the employees in individual plants. As a result, practically all major aircraft plants in Canada were publishing employee magazines by the end of 1942. Early in the committee's history, liaison was established with officials in Washington, and a great deal of helpful information and valuable data secured on personnel relations and plant efficiency. In return, at the request of U.S. officials, members of the Aircraft Industry Relations Committee made visits to Washington to explain details of efforts being pioneered in Canada. Various systems of training and educating employees were set up. Nineteen major plants were supplied with sound projection equipment and a sound film circuit was set up. Committees, personnel men and employees preview educational and other films to decide upon their suitability for being included in the circuit and select subjects. Stress is laid on educational films, which have always been enthusaistically received in the plants. Gatherings are arranged at which special inspirational films are shown to the families of workers. In many sections, unions use projectors and films at regular union meetings.

In some localities, the necessity for identification for the aircraft workers was apparent. Men and women engaged in vital war work are proud people and like their friends and neighbours to know they are playing their part, even though sex, age, physical fitness or specialised ability may forbid front line service. After consultation with employees' representatives, personnel directors and management, an attractive Aircraft Production badge was supplied.

Pioneering in its field, the Canadian Aircraft industry was bound to be criticised by older and more conservative sections of the industrial front. But time soon proved its people to be out in front of the parade in matters of personnel relations work. The faith and persistence of the many people from Management and Labour alike who believe in and fought for dynamic action, have paid off in production.

The keynote of Canada's aircraft industry from its inception has been co-operation. Its people, from the beginning, have recognized that their first job is to provide the aircraft to knock the enemy from the skies. To that end they have given their finest efforts since they came from the field and the counting house, from the kitchen and the beauty parlour, to enrol in the honourable army of the aircrafters. When the final score is set down, Canadians from coast to coast will recognize in the aircraft workers of the war years a body of men and women of high patriotic impulse who gave their best that those who fly should never want for the finest in equipment. No matter the problems of the day, the Canadian aircrafter has always done his job . . . and done it well. To him, belongs credit for the spirit of cooperation for victory which, sparked by Canada's aircrafters, soon was to become the keynote of North America's war-effort on the industrial front.

The Lancaster Comes To Town: *Most ambitious of all Canada's wartime aircraft-bu[ilding] projects is the four-engined Avro-Lancaster, a job alloted to Victory Aircraft, Limite[d.] this page a series of typical Lancaster shots gives a bird's eye view of this great [and] outstanding amongst the war's multi-engined aircraft.*

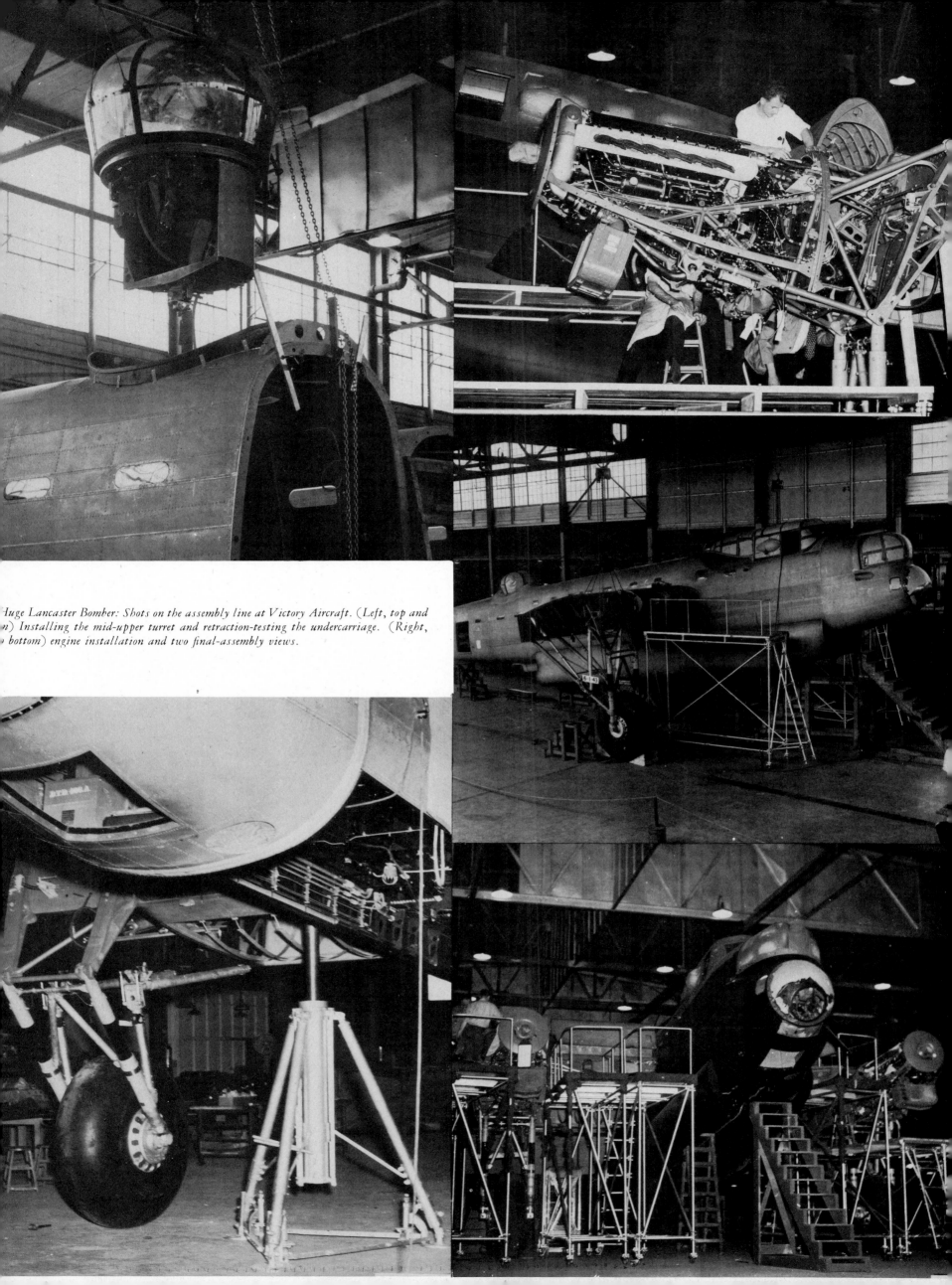

Huge Lancaster Bomber: Shots on the assembly line at Victory Aircraft. (Left, top and bottom) Installing the mid-upper turret and retraction-testing the undercarriage. (Right, top to bottom) engine installation and two final-assembly views.

Celebrating the Lancaster—(Left and right, top) Hon. C. D. Howe, Munitions Mini.
Ralph P. Bell, O.B.E., Director-General of Aircraft Production, and General Man.
David Boyd of Victory Aircraft. Extreme right is James Wark, president Aeronau.
Lodge 717. Mr. Howe disembarks. Centre and bottom show scenes on the field at Ma.

THE PRIMARY PRODUCERS

Since shortly before the commencement of hostilities Canada has produced or is now on the point of producing, aircraft to a total of 21 types; Fleet 16B, Tiger Moth and Menasco Moth, Fleet 60, Harvard, Anson, Cornell, Shark, Delta, Grumman, Norseman, Lysander, Stranraer, Hurricane, Bolingbroke, Blenheim, Catalina, Curtiss Dive Bomber, Lancaster, Mosquito, Hampden.

At this writing, May 1943, only 9 types remain on the production lines; Fairchild Cornell (elementary trainer), North American Harvard (advanced trainer), Canadian Anson (advanced trainer-bomber), Bristol Bolingbroke (bomber), Catalina (coastal reconnaissance), Hurricane (fighter), Lancaster (multi-engined bomber), De Havilland Mosquito (fighter-bomber), and the Curtiss dive bomber. These are produced, in the order shown, by Fleet, Noorduyn, Federal and Associated Companies, Fairchild, Vickers and Boeing, Canadian Car, Victory, De Havilland and Canadian Car. Of these Bolingbroke and Hurricane production were virtually at an end as this is written. The Noorduyn Norseman, last of the pre-war ships, is still being manufactured for the R.C.A.F. and the U.S. Army Air Corps as a transport and is admittedly the best in its field. Accurately it may be said that the key to the success of aircraft production in Canada from 1940 forward has been the streamlining of a compact program—the scrapping of obsolete types and concentration upon mass production of fewer types, each the best in its class. In this policy heads of the government's Aircraft Production Branch, with splendid cooperation from Management and Labour throughout the industry have achieved an enviable record.

Thus far Canada has produced more than 8,000 war aircraft. Of these more than 1,200 have gone forward to the fighting fronts . . . this from the standing-start of 1939 and the complete upset of every plan at the time of Dunkirk.

The only wholly-owned government aircraft companies in Canada are Federal Aircraft and Victory Aircraft. Federal, as previously noted, is almost solely an administrative company, distributing contracts throughout the aircraft industry, and responsible for the co-ordination and completion of the Anson program. With the exception of the work done in their Delormier Avenue plant in Montreal, the entire Anson output comes through to Federal from private contractors. Victory Aircraft is an operating company set up by the Government for the purpose of managing the Malton plant taken over from National Steel Car. There is not an aircraft plant for primary production in Canada today, however, in which Government financing has not occurred somewhere in the expansion necessitated by the war.

A large part of Canada's aircraft building involves the use of plants not entirely devoted to aviation, as parts manufacturers. Many others have been built to fill war needs. Thus the sub-contracting element assumes equal or larger proportions than the primary contractors themselves. For this reason the work of the sub-contractor in the building of aircraft forms the background for the whole industry's achievement. This will be discussed at length in a subsequent chapter. Substitute materials, as in the case of plywood in the De Havilland Mosquito, have effected tremendous savings in time, material and money, and other factors have arisen to contribute extensively to the sum-total of Canada's air effort. Vigorous government supervision, through the office of the Director General of the Aircraft Branch, has resulted in the creation of a closely coordinated young war industry.

As Canada entered upon its program of revamped 1943 production, the picture presented was vastly different from that in 1939. Today, the Canadian aircraft industry has come of age and is manufacturing types comparable to the best Britain and the United States can produce, concentrating on definite targets with the smallest risk of bottlenecks developing. By reducing the number of types on the assembly lines and going all-out on these, the Canadian aircraft industry has taken its place among the major producers of the world. That was the status as of June 1943.

Whether the industry will survive as a flourishing part of the Dominion's post-war economy is a subject which offers a definite challenge to all concerned. It will be discussed later. For the moment, however, the story concerns itself with the record of the primary producers for war. In order that none may appear to be placed in a position of higher importance to the industry than another, these are reviewed in alphabetical order.

* * *

First, Boeing.

Boeing Aircraft of Canada was formed in 1929 and entered the aircraft field with the Boeing 40-H-4 biplane for passenger and mail transport. This was followed by the manufacture of a number of Boeing flying boats, all single-engine, 5-passenger biplanes and by the Boeing Totem.

At the start of the war, Boeing was engaged in the manufacture of Blackburn Sharks, a British torpedo-firing aircraft. Its scope of operations was considerably widened with the formation of Federal Aircraft, the Vancouver firm contracting to produce Anson tail assemblies, spars, flaps, ailerons and fittings. More than 2,500 complete Anson tail assemblies had been produced by mid-1943, as had better than 1,000 wing spars—and the job was still proceeding in high gear.

In 1940, an entirely new plant was built by the Canadian Government for construction of the Consolidated Catalina amphibian on the Pacific coast and turned over to Boeing to operate. The first Catalina came in mid-1942. Getting a new aircraft type into production is no hurry-up job.

In December 1941, Boeing employed around 2,600 workers; by August 1942, the number had almost doubled. At the end of April, 1943, a figure of 7,733 people had been reached and more than 50 of the great Catalinas had come from the assembly line, with more than 300 more on order.

Three Boeing plants are engaged to-day in the production of Catalinas, an aircraft of intricate design and more than 100,000 parts. A fourth plant has been turned over to Canadian Pacific Air Lines as a repair and maintenance depot on Stranraers, Hudsons, Grummans and other aircraft used by the R.C.A.F. Coastal Command.

* * *

The record of Canadian Car and Foundry Company, on the Hurricane at Fort William, the Anson at Amherst, on propellers, oleo legs and bits-and-pieces in Montreal, has been a standout in an outstanding industry. The difficult beginnings of the company in aircraft have been covered in an earlier chapter, the dismal tale of months lost because the "right people" couldn't be convinced that first-line aircraft could be produced in the heart of the "Canadian wilderness". Well, they were . . . and at this writing they still are being produced; Hurricanes have been turned out in huge numbers. Hell Diver bombers for the U.S. Navy will fill the assembly lines of tomorrow.

When Hurricane production hit its peak, more than a year before this is written, approximately 5,500 men and women were on the payroll at Fort William. When the Hell Diver job really begins to roll a payroll of at least 7,000 is anticipated. They came from the country behind the town, from the mining towns of north-western Ontario (Sudbury, Geraldton and others), from distant

Trans-Canada at War: (Left, top to bottom) the engine assembly line at Winnip[...] corner of the big TCA hangar at Winnipeg; moving a Pratt and Whitney Twin Wasp[...] the shop for overhaul. (Right, top and bottom) removing repaired propellers from the [...] treat oven and an engine-assembly shot.

Kirkland Lake, from Toronto and Montreal and from peaceful farming villages in deep Quebec. Almost without exception they were without previous aircraft-construction experience when they appeared at the gate seeking work. Today's production lines abound in the neat smocks and bright faces of girl and women workers, for 60% of those employed on machines making minute parts, on wing assemblies, on the innumerable tasks which go into the job in hand at Fort William, are of the female of the species; highly efficient workers, perhaps because they had nothing to un-learn.

From one end of Canada to the other, from Edmonton in the west to the Maritime cities on the east, come the bits and pieces, which in assembled form become fighter aircraft. Plants by the score contribute. Yet a year before the outbreak of World War II, the buildings of this great plant were standing idle, aisles echoing in their emptiness, the bare bones of a skeleton staff of maintenance people employed. So this was where the Colonials planned to make Service aircraft, was it? The experts chuckled. It couldn't be done. And why carry work away out to the head of Lake Superior, when the job could be done somewhere adjacent to the Atlantic seaboard, if it had to be done in Canada at all? Perhaps, said the critics in the abiding places of red tape, the operators themselves could not be very efficient gentlemen, else why had their Fort William plant been empty since early in the 1920s, when the last railway car repair work had been done and the place closed down? Where would the experts come from? Where the common labour? Where the machinery? Finally to still the insistence of Drury, Peto and the others, what is called, for some inexplicable reason, an "educational order" was forthcoming. Now let them try to make a few Hurricanes and these Canadian business men would discover that you can't do such jobs in out of the way corners of the world. What apparently was not realized about these men was that behind them stood one of the great heavy industries of North America, staffed by people accustomed to performing the tasks which can't be done. It was impossible to obtain anything but hand-to-mouth orders. From the time when the plant was tooled (and many of its great tools were created on the premises) the Hurricane job was kept on that basis, so that the operators could seldom see more than a few weeks work ahead for their great assembly line. Rapidly and efficiently the huge empty halls filled with machines. Power was fed in. Men and women were trained. A machine-tool shop was established in a corner, primarily to create emergency tools, for the bulk of the tooling could be done in the company's great Point Saint Charles machine shop in Montreal, one of the finest, if not the finest, in Canada. Outside the gates newcomers sought boarding houses, homes. The shops of Fort William and Port Arthur thrived with the new trade, a trade which doubled and redoubled, grew beyond bounds. Ironically, as Canadian Car's aircraft division made ready for its new dive-bomber job (and this time there are no hand-to-mouth orders) requests to take time out and make more Hurricanes were still coming through. By the spring of 1943 the once-deserted railway-car plant which experts said couldn't be used had been remodelled for its second great war job, the murderous Hell Diver bomber. Somewhere the newcomers find homes. From somewhere comes transport to carry them to and from work. From somewhere come food and clothing for the shops. And from the great resurrected factory will soon pour another great stream of sudden death for Hitler and all enemies of civilisation—the finest dive-bomber in the sky.

Swinging over to the Hell Diver has not been accomplished without facing and licking major problems. At first it looked like plain sailing, a clean cut job where a man could step out and go to town, with the sky his only limit on production. But problem after problem cropped up; changes in design, developed in the parent-plant of the aircraft across the border, necessitated re-

blueprinting and more re-blueprinting; problems of tooling; problems of every shade and quality. Meanwhile, as has been happening in the industry ever since war began, the Jeremiahs revisited the Wailing Wall to moan the time taken in getting the new planes down the assembly lines. Jeremiahs never learn. Almost without exception the wails come from those who have never laid eyes on an assembly line, who know nothing of the problems of intricate, precision production or those of solving unceasing changes in design, for there is nothing static in the conduct of modern, streamlined warfare. The winner is he who is always a jump ahead of the enemy with improvements and refinements in the engines of war. So watch those Hell Divers roll! That will be the answer to the Jeremiahs at Fort William as elsewhere!

A summarizing of this one company's contribution to the production of aircraft is highly revealing. Over and above its activities at Fort William it has been turning out vast quantities of Hurricane parts, plus Anson parts on subcontract, in its Point St. Charles (Montreal) plant. A propeller division, also in Montreal, turns out constant speed and variable pitch prop hubs and a variety of alloy blades. At its Turcot Works more Hurricane parts have been produced and shipped to the Fort William assembly lines. Hampden centre-sections, outer wings, flaps and ailerons were built in the days of the six-company association. At Amherst, Nova Scotia, starting from scratch with a personnel inexperienced in aircraft production, English Ansons were assembled to the tune of one a day at a time when the Air Plan was literally starving for machines for its pupils to fly. Now Canadian Anson fuselages roll down the aisles at Amherst for Federal Aircraft and repair and overhaul work for Air Training schools in the seaboard area by this down-east shop. From a standing start, often against blockade tactics outside Canada, Canadian Car and Foundry Company has become one of North America's great aircraft producers, solely because those charged with direction of the company's affairs saw the war-clouds taking shape. Thus by sheer stick-at-it determination did one great Canadian corporation literally force its way into the field of aircraft production—and, once in, do a magnificent job.

* * *

Third in alphabetical order amongst the prime producers is De Havilland Aircraft of Canada, part of an organisation whose background is rooted deep in the history of British and world aviation. Situated at Toronto, De Havilland was one of the biggest and most efficient aircraft producers in Canada at the commencement of hostilities in 1939.

In 1937 the first Canadian-made Tiger Moth was delivered by De Havilland to the Royal Canadian Air Force, to be used as a trainer. From April 1940 for a period of about 2½ years, the company delivered more than 1,500 Tigers, the last one being completed about the middle of 1942.

Early in the war De Havilland was also entrusted with assembling Ansons, and when, after Dunkirk, Anson policy was altered by disastrous events, De Havilland was given a large portion of the Federal Aircraft program. 375 Ansons had passed through the big Toronto plant by the autumn of 1942.

On March 31st, 1928, three men working in a small 50 x 50 outbuilding on a farm in Mount Dennis, near Toronto, finished assembling an airplane from parts manufactured in England, the first DH 60 Cirrus Moth assembled by De Havilland of Canada. In October, 1941, a staff of over 2,400 men and women working ten-hour shifts in two huge plants, were beginning to produce great quantities of the Tiger Moth, then the standard basic trainer for the R.C.A.F. By the winter of 1942, an entirely new plant was full-out on Anson production. Then came the Mosquito, actually a lineal descendant of the famous De Havilland Comet

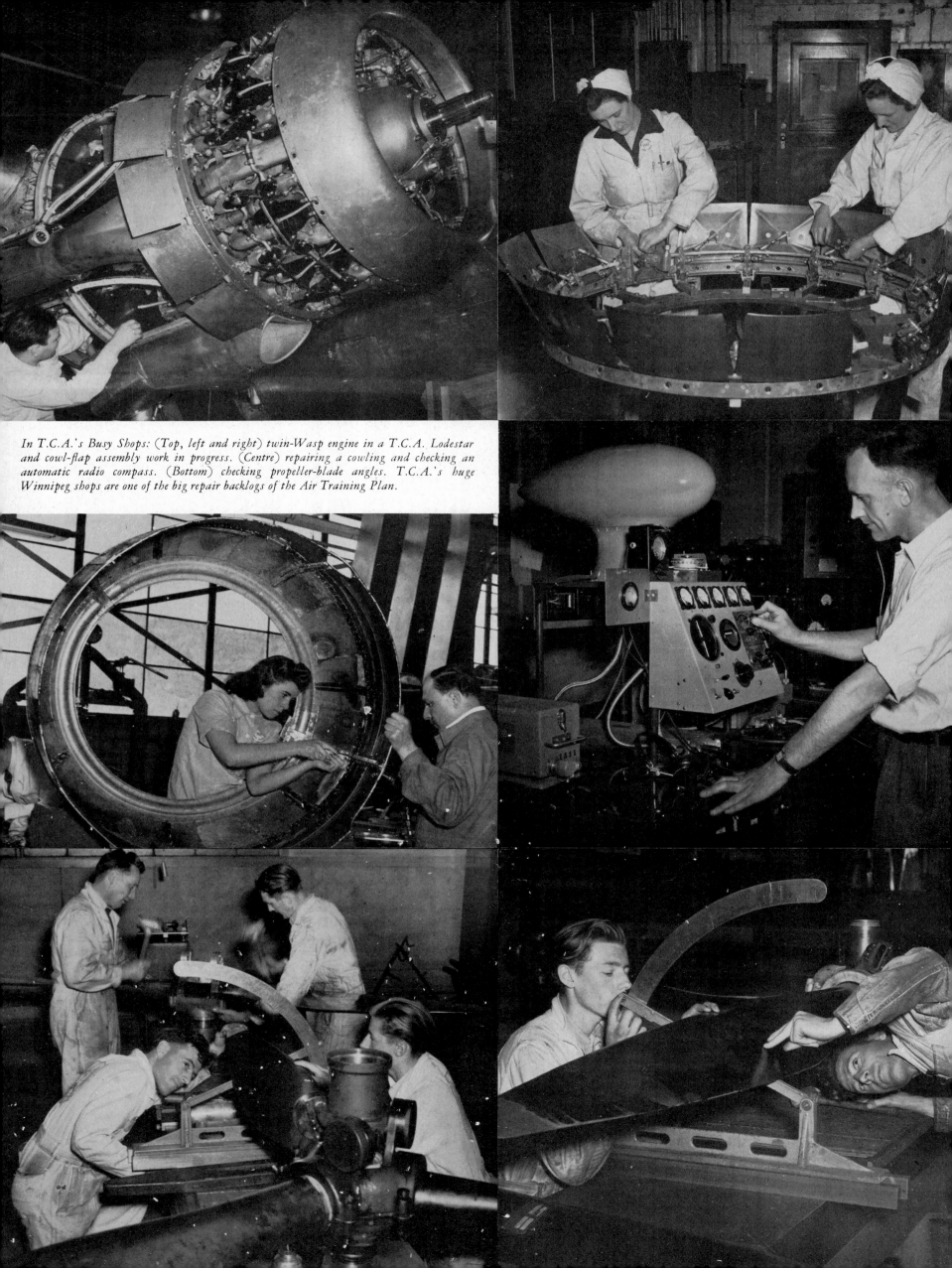

In T.C.A.'s Busy Shops: (Top, left and right) twin-Wasp engine in a T.C.A. Lodestar and cowl-flap assembly work in progress. (Centre) repairing a cowling and checking an automatic radio compass. (Bottom) checking propeller-blade angles. T.C.A.'s huge Winnipeg shops are one of the big repair backlogs of the Air Training Plan.

which won the air race from England to Australia in 1934, but nevertheless a newly-designed aircraft.

At first the idea of an all-plywood aircraft was ridiculed by the authorities in Britain and months passed before Captain Geoffrey De Havilland was able to prove by practical demonstration that he had a new answer to the problem of air power. The Mosquito soon went into mass production in Britain. The next step was Canada. De Havilland flew the first Canadian Mosquito early in 1943 and by summer they were beginning to roll for the R.A.F. as well as the R.C.A.F.

It has often been said that the Mosquito is primarily a development of the Comet, because of the pronounced taper common to both. In appearance the new job has been called "typically De Havilland."

It is powered by twin Packard-Rolls engines, each of 1,280 h.p., an American version of the Rolls Royce Merlin 21 with liquid cooled motors. Points of recognition are; the swept-forward shoulder wings with small, rounded tips; large, underslung motor nacelles with the fairing protruding beyond the trailing edge of the wing; short, transparent nose; small, raised cockpit enclosure and elliptically shaped tailplane with streamlined fuselage. The radiator intakes are set in the leading edge of the centre section. It carries four .303 machine guns and four 20 mm. cannon, and has an air speed well over 400 miles an hour.

The aircraft is almost entirely built of plywood although certain vital parts, such as engine cowlings, are of metal. Thus, it requires fewer man-hours to produce than any other twin-engined bomber made, and its construction is both rapid and economical. Unlike the ordinary production line, where the racket of riveter and the shrieks of beaten metal raise a bedlam of horror to the uninitiated, the quiet of the Mosquito line is broken only by the occasional tap of a hammer or the hum of sander or planer. The De Havilland woodshop is a hive of industry staffed by more than 250 men and girls since the Mosquito came along. Here the raw materials, timber and plywood sheets are glued and pressed. At the Dupont Street plant in Toronto, parts are bonded and glued and plywood is bent and shaped. In another part of the same plant fuselages are built in half-sections. Heavy wooden molds are spread over with plywood and balsa skin; grooves are interspersed at intervals. Wooden stays are placed in the grooves and covered with squares of plywood, steel-banded and held together by glue. The whole finally hardens into a solid mass.

An advantage of forming the fuselage in half sections is that interior fittings can be installed away from the cramped quarters of a narrow full-length fuselage. The halves are brought together and reinforced by an aluminum nailing strip. Heat is not used at any stage, the whole job being done by what is known as the cold-set process. No intricate rivet-driving is necessary. The plywood is weatherproofed before the outer fabric is applied. Construction is simple and rapid. Five reinforced sections act as braces to prevent warping and buckling and wing slots are not cut until the fuselage has been completed. Much of the manoeuvrability of the aircraft is directly attributed to wing design and construction. Wings, manufactured by Massey-Harris, are of plywood construction with reinforced stays. They need no waxing because of a fine smooth fabric which covers the wood. Gasoline tanks are housed under the fuselage and are self-sealing. The pilot has armor-plate protection at his back.

Plywood is better than metal in bullet resisting qualities. A tracer will pass through plywood without "mushrooming" as it does in the case of metal. Hence bullet holes are easily mended.

The aircraft carries a crew of two, the pilot-navigator and the co-pilot bomber. Either can take over the duties of the other. The Mosquito is the last word in modern war aircraft. In performance

it has no peer in all the world among aircraft of comparable character.

Large scale production of fuselages was undertaken by General Motors shortly before this is written and production will step up prodiguously as a result. No more Moths will come from the De Havilland plant. Mosquito and Anson, together with the making of spares for the Tiger Moth, will keep De Havillanders amply busy. The Tiger will soon be laid aside as the R.C.A.F. basic trainer.

* * *

And so to Fairchild.

The history of Fairchild Aircraft, of Longueuil, Quebec, goes back to 1928, when the original Fairchild came to Canada from the United States in the hope of supplying planes to operators in Northern Canada. Thenceforth, until shortly before war came in 1939, the company lived (at times precariously) on the bush trade. After tinkering with the Sekani, the first twin-engined aircraft ever built in Canada, Fairchilds turned to output for war. The first job was the Bristol Bolingbroke for the British market. That was in 1939. Fairchild designers and engineers were sent overseas to the Bristol plant to study details and, six months before the outbreak of the present war, the company was well on the way towards the production of Bolingbrokes.

At this juncture United States interests in the company were bought by Canadians and the firm became all-Canadian. At that time Fairchild had approximately 500 employees on the payroll. At the end of 1942, the number had been increased to 6,000, working two shifts. The total plant area in 1939 was 58,000 sq. ft.; it is now over 600,000 sq. ft. During the war period the company has shown a production increase of around 2,000 per cent. Bolingbrokes have been the only war output of the plant to the spring of 1943, but much repair work had also been done. At that time the company had been consistently ahead of production schedules for more than two years. An entirely new plant addition of 280,000 sq. ft. was well under way early in 1943 in preparation for the forthcoming change from Bolingbrokes to the Hell-Diver, scheduled to take place during the summer of 1943 when the Bolingbroke contract terminates. Tooling was then well under way for the Curtiss dive bomber, to handle which Fairchild was doubling previous manufacturing facilities. Inasmuch as Fairchilds have specialised in the building of a single bomber, the Bolingbroke, definite new trends in construction have been the outcome of specialisation. Manufacture was soon found to be of so intricate a nature that ordinary production line methods had to be discarded. The building of this type of aircraft requires 3,000 specifications, 14,000 blueprints, 600,000 rivets, 80,000 detailed parts and about 40,000 man hours of labor. In fine, it is precision built. Alteration in design and scores of modifications resulted in an aircraft far different from that demanded by the original specifications of 1938. Many man-hours per unit were soon saved as a result. Moreover, through precision requirements, a skilled organisation had been built up, the members of which could be relied upon to tackle the most intricate job and see it through to successful conclusion, an augury of high hope for the day when the company reaches its new goal of Hell-Diver production.

* * *

Bottleneck of all aircraft bottlenecks in Canada in the early days of the Training Plan was what is generally known as "the Anson program", production of the principal twin-engine trainer of the British Commonwealth Air Plan. As this is written, in June 1943, the problem is solved and more than 1,800 Ansons have rolled down Canadian assembly lines under Federal Aircraft aegis. Under tremendous difficulties Canada went into major production of the Jacobs-powered Avro Ansons in a period

Canadian Pacific Aloft—C.P. Airlines plays a great war role in transportation, repair
overhaul of service aircraft and the operation of R.C.A.F. schools. Here are typical
of each. The two officials are top right Captain C. H. (Punch) Dickens, General Man
and Captain W. B. (Wop) May, both famed pre-war bush pilots.

ings Over The North—Canadian Pacific Airlines transports over the Northwest Terri-
ies and the Rockies. (At top left) the course to be flown is plotted, (at centre right) the
atrol Tower says "Come in and land" and (at top right) the lovely hostess makes ready
welcome her passengers.

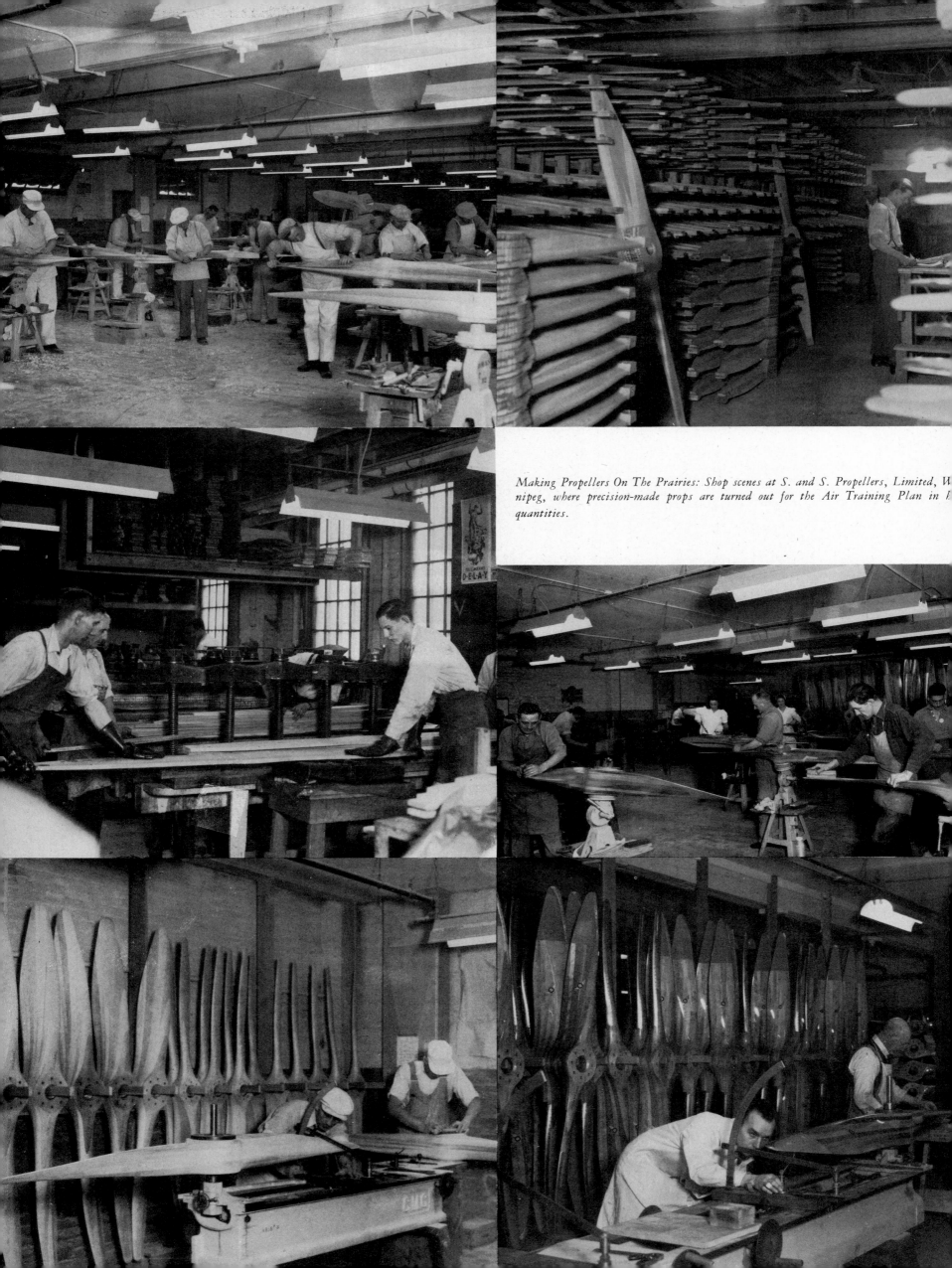

Making Propellers On The Prairies: Shop scenes at S. and S. Propellers, Limited, W nipeg, where precision-made props are turned out for the Air Training Plan in l quantities.

approximating 15 months. The target production rate was reached by the end of 1941, the first Federal-produced machine being flown at St. Hubert aerodrome in August of that year.

Federal Aircraft was established in June, 1940, as a completely government-owned organisation to solve a problem which, without a solution, meant the breakdown of Canada's whole Air Training Plan.

Under the original scheme British Ansons were to have been brought to Canada to equip the Air Plan schools. Dunkirk and the Fall of France changed all that. Somehow we must make them here. That, then, was the problem which brought Federal Aircraft into being. The result is an aircraft basically similar to its English counterpart—a twin-engined low wing monoplane, designed for reconnaissance and training—but readapted to the materials and power units available on this continent at the time of the 1940 crisis.

The Canadian Anson differs principally from the English type in that it uses the Jacobs L-6 Engine (Pratt and Whitneys on the new Mark V Navigation trainer) and, therefore, calls for a different cowling and nacelle. In addition, the Canadian aircraft has a hydraulically-operated retractable undercarriage instead of the hand-retracting British style. The Vidal moulded-plywood process used in fabrication of the fuselage is unique in aircraft production. Excepting these main changes the similarity of design between British and Canadian Ansons permits parts being approximately 75 per cent interchangeable.

When Federal went to work to solve the riddle, components and small parts were ordered from 183 factories in virtually every part of Canada, including plants formerly engaged in the production of agricultural implements, washing machines, and precision metals. Federal Aircraft administered all related contracts, coordinated and correlated the whole program. Through a centralized purchasing and engineering plan, Federal purchased raw materials, arranged for these to be fabricated into component parts, supervised manufacture and distribution of fuselages, tail units, undercarriages, nacelles, and wings.

The manufacture of the principal components is in the hands of 11 contractors, all in Canada. These components and materials are distributed to five main final assembly plants; Canadian Car and Foundry, at Amherst, N.S.; De Havilland Aircraft of Canada Limited, Toronto; MacDonald Brothers Aircraft Limited, Winnipeg; Ottawa Car and Aircraft Limited, Ottawa, and Victory Aircraft Limited at Malton, Ont. Federal's own plant for the manufacture of fuselages, located in Montreal, produced its first fuselage in June, 1941. This plant has a floor area of 45,000 square feet, and employs a personnel in excess of 500. At the Head Office, clerical, engineering, and inspection forces number about 180. One of Federal's biggest jobs is to keep track of the 45,000 parts which, joined together, comprise an Anson.

The Aircraft Production Branch of the Department of Munitions and Supply provides engines, instruments, and other special equipment, a total of 166 items and these are supplied direct to the contractors on Federal schedules for the Royal Canadian Air Force. Finally, in order to keep a strict accounting of a complicated production job, Federal Aircraft maintains tabulation of production in every plant and thus keeps its fingers on the program from day to day and hour to hour. The program faced severe criticism, in and out of the Canadian parliament, particularly during 1941 and until the production target was reached. That mistakes were made no one can question. But that the prime bottleneck of the Canadian aircraft problem was shattered when the Ansons began to fly is uncontrovertible fact, too, for without the Anson, Canada's training of bomber-crews and other urgently needed fliers could not have been carried out on the magnificent scale attained.

The Fleet Aircraft plant at Fort Erie, built in 1930, was a modest structure and gave little indication of the company's great future. Like others in the industry Fleet was "trying to build aircraft in the woodshed". Major R. H. Fleet, then president of Consolidated Aircraft Corporation of Buffalo, N.Y., headed the company, with W. J. Sanderson as manager and during its early days the firm assembled Fleet trainers, which were trucked across the Niagara River piecemeal from Buffalo. Later it became Canadian distributors for the Waco. In the beginning it was in every sense of the term a small operation.

During succeeding years the plant was twice extended and complete manufacture of aircraft frames undertaken! In 1936 Canadian interests acquired a majority of the company's stock from Consolidated Aircraft Corporation, and new money was provided by Canadian shareholders to finance the extension of the plant and the expansion of the business in general. Changes in executive personnel at that time resulted in W. J. Sanderson succeeding Major Fleet as President. During this period the Fleet 10 and the Fleet 16 were built.

The coming of war found the company engaged in business in a comparatively small way, but with an experienced organization which was ready to commence the production of aircraft for Canadian needs.

Prior to the war Fleet had been manufacturing for export and had opened markets in South America, Asia, Europe and New Zealand, in addition to supplying aircraft to Flying Clubs in Canada.

A small order was given to Fleet by the R.C.A.F. in the fall of 1939. It was followed in January, 1940 by a contract for 404 Finch Fleet trainers, to be built in two years. Final delivery was made in March, 1941, however, only 14 months after work on the job began.

Late in 1940 work was started on the Fleet Fort, an advanced trainer type, for the R.C.A.F. The original order was for 200, but owing to change of program in the Commonwealth Air Training Plan, only 100 were delivered. The company also undertook the making of parts and re-assembly of Fairey Battles, a number of which had been brought to Canada in conjunction with the Air Training Plan. Many of these had seen actual conflict in Europe. Fleet was also one of the partner-companies in the cooperative Hampden job mentioned in an earlier chapter. That was the beginning of what is now one of Canada's outstanding industrial operations.

In December, 1941, Fleet received a contract to manufacture an adaptation of the Fairchild PT-19, known in Canada as the Cornell, which it is now producing in quantity. Two variations of the Cornell design, the PT-23 for the United States Army Air Force and the PT-26 for the United Kingdom training program, are also in production at this writing.

The U.S. model has an open cockpit and is powered with a Continental radial engine. It is used solely as a primary trainer. The radial engine is replaced in the Canadian and United Kingdom models by a 200 H.P. Ranger in-line engine. The Canadian version, serving for both primary and intermediate training, in preparation for more advanced work on the Harvard, has a coupé top and carries instruments adequate for blind flying training. The rear cockpit is fitted with a hood which may be drawn for instrument flying. The wiring is so installed that the plane can be readily fitted for night flying.

The Canadian version is to be known as the Cornell MK. II, the British version (manufactured primarily for use in R.A.F. schools in Canada) the Cornell MK. III.

For the R.C.A.F. Cornells 470 revisions were made to the original design, for purposes of standardization and maintenance. Despite the added weight of more than 200 lbs. resulting from

Aluminum goes to War: (Top to bottom, left) Bauxite Mine in British Guiana. Loa[...]
Crane at Eastern Canadian Plant. Interior of an Aluminum Company of Canada [...]
"Somewhere in Canada." (Top to bottom, right) Ship loading Bauxite at a po[...]
British Guiana. Partial view of an immense Canadian plant. Aluminum in the m[...]
state.

these, an increase in engine power from 175 to 200 h.p. gives the Cornell an increased speed of 8 m.p.h.

Construction involves a wing centre section of wood, plywood covered, connected to the fuselage at four points. The fuselage is of tubular welded steel construction, and picks up the tail section by a two-point connection, the engine having a four-point suspension. The centre section receives the outer wings by three point-connections.

Much of Fleet success on the Cornell has resulted from well coordinated subcontracting and from co-operation between several manufacturers of the same plane. Four manufacturers—three in the United States—are building the machine, and orders of the four companies for components requiring large-scale tooling are pooled. The result is more efficient tooling and lower ultimate component cost.

Cornell construction follows the production-line plan—wing centre sections, outer wings, tail assemblies, fuselage welding, fuselage assembly and final assembly. As of May 1943, production was far ahead of schedule and reaching toward full equipment of the elementary training schools in which the Cornell will replace the Finch and Moth as the standard elementary trainer. Following a reorganisation prior to embarking on the Cornell program E. G. McMillan, K.C., became Chairman of the Board, E. G. Smith of Montreal, President, D. H. McDougall of Toronto, Vice-President, W. N. Deisher, Vice-President and General Manager, G. C. Chataway, Secretary-Treasurer and N. T. Berry Assistant Secretary.

* * *

MacDonald Brothers of Winnipeg, who come into the realm of primary producers through their final assembly on the Anson Mark V., (specially designed for the training of navigators), have been in Manitoba's industrial picture for thirty years, originally concentrating on the manufacture of sheet metal products. In 1930 MacDonald Brothers Aircraft, Limited, was formed to manufacture floats for aircraft, and to carry on a general supply business for aircraft operating companies. The founders were Grant MacDonald, now president and general manager; J. D. MacDonald, vice-president; and Edwin MacDonald, secretary-treasurer.

MacDonald Brothers still build most of the floats used in Canada, and have been major shippers in the export field notably to the United States, New Guinea, South America and Australia. A branch in Ottawa for several years has done an extensive business in general aircraft supplies.

When war broke out and the Commonwealth Air Training Plan developed, MacDonald Brothers became an important cog in the huge war machine. Increased facilities were required. In addition to expanding the company's original premises to some 65,000 sq. ft. of floor space, a huge modern industrial plant was built and put into operation six months after the first sod was turned, providing an additional 220,000 sq. ft. of floor space for the company's war operations.

Some 3600 employees were engaged in the MacDonald plants by 1943. A training school, manned by competent instructors, was set up early in the war and has achieved excellent results with boys under military age, men medically unfit for war service, and large numbers of women and girls. Skilled cabinet makers, many of them in the over-age group, form the backbone of the woodworking department. Greatly increased use has been made of women and girls, as the man power problem has grown, these being employed in the woodworking welding, fabric, painting, sheet metal, assembly, overhaul and stores departments.

The manufacture of floats and parts and the business of aviation supplies are carried on at the original MacDonald plant, now greatly expanded. The new plant adjoining the airport at St.

James is engaged in assembling and overhauling aircraft used in the Commonwealth Air Training Plan. Its chief production is in wings for Anson trainers. Other component parts made elsewhere in Canada are brought in and the complete aircraft is now assembled by MacDonald.

The design of the new Anson V, assembled at MacDonald Brothers, has entailed a complete revision of the fuselage, which is now constructed of moulded plywood veneer, excepting tubular structure at the cockpit, and complete revision of the engine installations due to the fittings of larger and more powerful Pratt & Whitney engines in place of British Cheetahs or American Jacobs.

The use of plastic bonded veneers eliminates a great deal of strategic material previously used in the Anson II. It also sharply reduces the number of skilled welders required, a class of craftsmen extremely difficult to obtain under wartime production conditions. This also makes possible the use of many skilled tradesmen from woodworking factories, hitherto not fully absorbed by war industry.

One of the new features of the Anson V is the elimination of the old gun turret and the installation of an astral dome for sextant shots. The glassed-in, draughty cabin of the earlier Ansons is a thing of the past. The moulded plywood veneer fuselage keeps out the winter wind, gives roomier accommodation, and results in a streamlined job, where navigators can learn their art in comfort. The twin motors of the new model have stepped up its top speed from 180 to 200 m.p.h. The cruising speed has been increased from 140 to 165 m.p.h. and the rate of climb from 1000 feet to 1600 feet a minute. The first test flights of the new plane, carried out by the company's test pilot, showed highly satisfactory operational performance.

* * *

Immediately before the outbreak of war a small aviation plant in Montreal was producing annually a handful of bush freighting Norsemen 'planes. That plant immediately proved to be a valuable asset to Canada's war-production. From a pygmy plant covering 36,000 square feet of floor space, employing 140 men at the start of the war, the Noorduyn establishment has grown until it occupies over three-quarters of a million square feet of floor space, employs 9,000 men and women, and is producing Harvard advanced trainers and a special type of Norseman, the UC-64, for the American Army.

To-day Nooduyn is turning out more than ten times as many aircraft per month as were produced in a whole year before the war; the output of Harvards in 1942 was 4.39 times that of the previous year; in the last six months of 1942 production was 3.2 times that of the first half of the same year, while in the last two months of 1942, alone, production exceeded the whole output of the plant for 1941 by six per cent.

Behind these figures lies a story of planning and foresight, of visualizing problems in advance, and providing solutions as they arose. Above all the story rests on the foundation of the knowledge of design and production and on the organizing ability of Bob Noorduyn.

R.B.C. Noorduyn was born in Holland of Dutch and English parentage. In his youth his hobby was building flying models, and after acquiring a sound engineering knowledge at college he graduated into the aviation industry with the Sopwith company in Britain, a year prior to the outbreak of the first world war. Thereafter he was associated with Sir W. G. Armstrong, Whitworth & Company as design engineer and chief inspector and, in 1917 joined the British Aerial Transport Company as chief assistant to the managing director and chief engineer.

Three years later Bob Noorduyn was in the United States working with the famous Dutch designer and producer, Anthony Fokker,

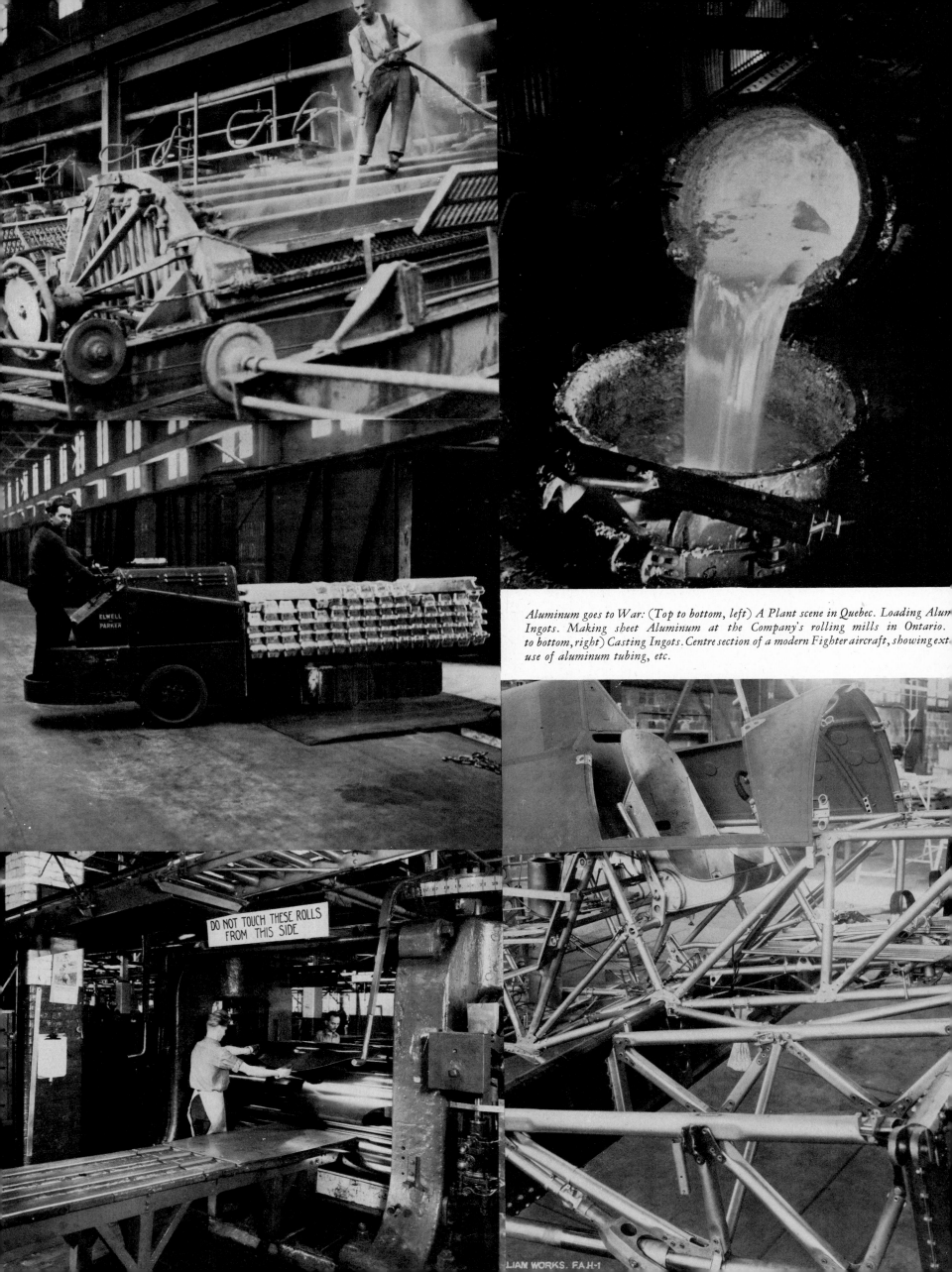

Aluminum goes to War: (Top to bottom, left) *A Plant scene in Quebec. Loading Alum Ingots. Making sheet Aluminum at the Company's rolling mills in Ontario. to bottom, right) Casting Ingots. Centre section of a modern Fighter aircraft, showing ext use of aluminum tubing, etc.*

DO NOT TOUCH THESE ROLLS FROM THIS SIDE

devoting his spare time to perfecting himself as a pilot. During his association with Fokker, which lasted until 1929, Noorduyn managed the rapidly expanding factories of the famous designer's company, and played a major role in equipping the spectacular trans-ocean and polar flights of Byrd, Wilkins and Kingsford-Smith, aviation pioneers of the late 20's.

From 1929 to 1932 he was with Bellanca Aircraft at Newcastle, Delaware, as assistant to the president and vice-president. Two years passed, during which he designed a series of cabin-type autogyros for the Pitcairn Company before he came to Canada, and drew his first design of the Norseman, as an aircraft especially suited to the Canadian scene.

Noorduyn's company started modestly with 30 employees in 1934 in a plant covering only 12,000 square feet of manufacturing space. Bush operators quickly became enthusiastic about these Norsemen freighters of the skies, however. During the later 1930's Norsemen began to appear on virtually all the down-north routes—through the Northwest Territories, northwestern Ontario, wherever pioneers were breaking open the frontier by air. It soon proved itself to be the air-freighter *par excellence*—a ship of Canadian design for an essentially Canadian job. Since the war began it has proved itself equally adaptable to the transport purposes of a world under arms. When Hitler started out to change the map of the world, the licence to build the Harvard advanced trainer, developed by North American Aviation in California, was acquired by Noorduyn. From that time forward the plant began to expand. The rapid expansion is attested by a few statistics. In December, 1939, it employed 140 men. The payroll, in that month, was $17,000. Employees in December, 1940, totalled 1,465. A year later, 3,642 were on the pay-roll. In December, 1942, Noorduyn was paying nearly 9,000 men and women. Monthly payrolls dollarwise increased from the modest $17,000 of December 1939, to $1,440,000 within the space of three years. But as the Harvards rolled out in steady stream, Bob Noorduyn's first love, his own Norseman, was not forgotten.

During 1942 a modernized version was accepted by the U.S. Army for utility transport purposes, on wheels, skis or floats, and is the only aircraft of Canadian design in production for the United States today. It has that key job primarily because Canadians, more than any airminded people in the world, knew the problems of the tough transport jobs. Canadian experience in breaking open the north provided that knowledge. Bob Noorduyn's Norseman is the answer—and an effective answer it has proved itself to be.

While this current history has been in the making, the Noorduyn management has been constantly on the alert for improvements in production methods and in the aircraft itself. In both types of plane, Norseman and Harvard, many refinements have resulted.

* * *

Ottawa Car & Aircraft Ltd. was active in aircraft overhaul in Canada for many years prior to World War II and for the past 15 years, has represented Armstrong Siddeley Motors in Canada. During this period, it has engaged continuously in the overhaul of aircraft engines of the British firm's manufacture.

Shortly before the present war, the company became one of a group of Canadian corporations which combined to produce the Hampden bomber. Hence at the outbreak of war, Ottawa Car was already occupied in producing such items as engine mounts, nacelles, fairings, fuel tanks and oil tanks. This program was extensively enlarged in 1940 when a contract was placed with Ottawa Car & Aircraft for the manufacture of a quantity of Anson wings and the final assembly of a corresponding number of aircraft, thus placing the company in the ranks of primary producers. During the same period sub-contracts were also under-

taken from Canadian Car and Foundry Company for machine parts and sheet metal components for the Hurricane fighter.

As of 1943, the main work of the plant is production of components for the Lancaster . . . ailerons, flaps, elevators, wing tips, bomb doors, flare chutes and other miscellaneous parts, the manufacture of which requires the complete facilities of the company.

An engine overhaul division is also maintained at Ottawa. In addition to overhauling Armstrong-Siddeley motors, this plant has undertaken the overhaul of British Cheetah engines, the type used in the first Ansons assembled in Canada as well as in Airspeed Oxfords.

* * *

Two decades ago, Canadian Vickers Ltd., Montreal, formally laid the cornerstone of what has since become one of Canada's main aircraft producing units.

The aircraft division, managed today by a pre-war insurance man and human ball of fire, Ben Franklin, first came into being with the manufacture of the Vickers Viking, in 1923, the aircraft having its initial flight on July 25th of that year.

In those early years of commercial flight Vickers were constantly engaged in experimenting with new types of aircraft. As soon as the success of the Viking had been established, work was started on the Avro 504, a biplane of British design. Even while this was being built, the engineering staff was designing the Vedette, and the prototype was completed in December, 1924. During the following five years, sixty of these aircraft were completed in the Vickers plant. They were intended for, and used by, the R.C.A.F., the Forestry Patrol, and the Chilean Government.

During the latter period, one each of four new types of aircraft were also built; the Varuna, Vanessa, Vista and Vigil. The next step occurred with the building, under licence from the American company of the Fairchild FC-2. Preliminary work was also started on the Vancouver. Then came the completion of a contract from the Fokker company, as well as an overhaul job on Bellana Pacemakers. By then Canada's baby aircraft industry had fallen upon lean years of depression and Vickers, in common with the rest of the nation's aircrafters, barely kept going. For one brief period the management was reduced to making brewing vats to keep its aircraft people busy!

In 1934, however, the company started work on a contract to adapt the Northrop Delta, used extensively in the United States, to floats and skis for Canadian use, primarily for the R.C.A.F., as a reconnaissance and photography aeroplane. That brought Vickers back alive.

In 1936, the Company was awarded a contract for the Vickers Supermarine Stranraer flying boat, the largest aircraft built in Canada up to that time, with a wing span of 85 feet, and an overall length of 54 feet, 6 inches, and gross weight of 18,950 pounds. The Stranraers were powered by two Bristol Pegasus engines, rated at 840 horsepower. While obsolete today, it was then considered a rugged high-performance aircraft. It was capable of maintaining flight on one engine, with full military load. It has done excellent service with the R.C.A.F. during the war on convoy escort and coastal patrols.

During the last year of production on this tailor-made aircraft, eight completed ships were delivered to the R.C.A.F. in 23 days, no mean achievement under the working conditions of the early war months.

During 1940 and 1941, eighty main fuselage sections for the Hampden bomber were manufactured and turned over to Canadian Associated Aircraft for final assembly. An English-designed reconnaissance bomber, now obsolete, the Hampden could carry a load of 6,976 pounds, with a ceiling of 22,700 feet and a top speed of 265 m.p.h. Then came the Catalinas—a story which

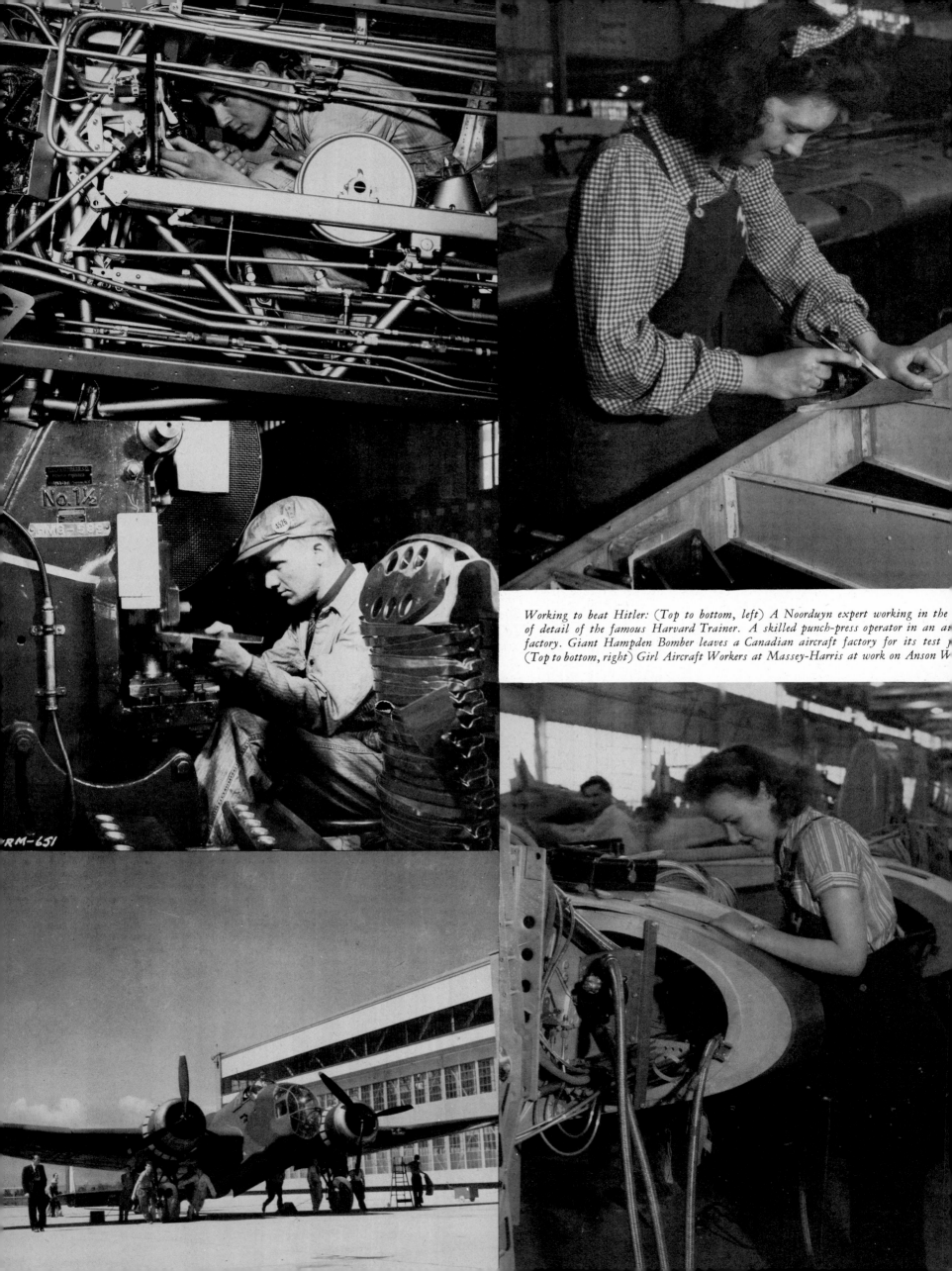

Working to beat Hitler: (Top to bottom, left) A Noorduyn expert working in the
of detail of the famous Harvard Trainer. A skilled punch-press operator in an a
factory. Giant Hampden Bomber leaves a Canadian aircraft factory for its test
(Top to bottom, right) Girl Aircraft Workers at Massey-Harris at work on Anson W

rates a place in any attempt to assess the achievement of Canada's aircraft industry. The story of how these Catalinas happened is one of the epic tales of this great young industry.

Picture a scene, far removed from the icy spume of the north Atlantic, but closely related to the hunt for Hun marauders and, therefore, to the defence of Canada's shores.

Around an outsize table in an air-conditioned office in Washington, a group of earnest-looking people are seated. Some are Americans, some are Englishmen, some Canadians. Some are in uniform, some in mufti. Some write notes on scratch pads, while others talk. Some engage their neighbours in whispered conversations. An air of tension fills the room.

Leader of the discussion is a pleasant-faced man in a double-breasted pin-stripe suit, a man just shy of middle-age and obviously one who is ready to argue at the drop of an adjective. His name is Ralph Bell. His rank is Director-General of Aircraft Production for the Dominion of Canada and he has something on his mind. You have heard of him before, if you have come this far with the story.

Up to now Canada had been buying Catalinas from Uncle Sam, but now Bell wanted to build them in Canada in two mammoth plants, one east, one west. Moreover, he wanted to build just as many Catalinas as could be yanked off the production lines, which means to build them for everybody around these United Nations who can use the toughest over-water aircraft ever made, which means for just about everybody who is mad at Hitler, plus Hirohito. By the time the meeting ended everybody present agreed that Mr. Bell should get his wish.

That was along in January, 1942. As this is written the Canadian-built Catalinas are rolling off the Boeing assembly line in the west and Vickers mammoth plant is turning out amphibians in Montreal. Up to the coming of the Catalinas, events had forced Canada to concentrate largely on trainer types, bar the Hurricane. The big flying boats and amphibians constitute another leg towards fulfillment of a full-out ambition to mass produce the best fighting ships as well—a dream which has come true.

What makes this Catalina so important that Canada has doubled and redoubled the floor space of one existing aircraft plant and turned loose with priorities to erect a brand new industrial behemoth now in production as well? On the strength of the record it is the ace of all aircraft for the offensive defence of a country with huge coastal areas to protect. It is a job built for the rough and tumble of war work over the oceans, highly powered, long of range and with a hide like a rhinoceros to withstand the buffetings of rough water landings and take-offs. Time and again the big boats have been towed in safety to port after forced landings at sea under conditions which would have battered ordinary craft to pulp. It can lug great loads. It can match anything our enemies have produced, or seem likely to produce, for long-range over-ocean work. It will not be obsolete, the experts say, until long after *fuehrers* are. Let us look at the record.

It was a Catalina which spotted the *Bismarck* and sent the Royal Navy in for the kill.

In the Battle of Midway the bold night attack on the Japs, which stands as one of the great aerial successes of the war, was delivered by four of these great flying boats. Since the invention of the torpedo, night has been recognized as the ideal time for attack upon surface ships, but the use of aircraft had long been avoided, due to the difficulties of boring in at low altitudes in the darkness, involving the risk of striking water, or of being unable to zoom out of harm's way after the attack has been driven home. The coming of the Catalina solved the problem. She can run in at high speeds for great distances before reaching the target, at altitudes below the visibility range of searchlights. She did so at Midway, with devastating results.

Or consider the action off the Aleutians late in June 1942. This time Catalinas located an enemy carrier and its attendant ships off Unalaska and stalked them for 48 hours before finally leading U.S. Army bombers to the attack on two Jap carriers, by then riding 250 miles south of Umnak Island. Fighters rose from the carriers' decks. The Catalinas fought back. One went down in flames. An ack-ack shell tore through the hull of another, but failed to explode. The big boat returned in safety to its base. Others came home literally riddled with shell fragments and bullets. But the next day the Catalinas were out again, armed with torpedoes, and over Kiska they rained down six tons of high explosives to destroy Jap vessels in its roadstead.

The secret is toughness, range and power, the ability to trail the enemy all day and bore in with darkness for the attack.

Bell and his aides knew all this when first they put on their drive for major production on Canadian soil. That was long before Midway and the Aleutians proved their point. The first ships had been purchased before the end of the first year of war from the American manufacturer to replace land-based machines and the Stranraer boat on the coasts, and had been turning in magnificent performances. For some whimsey of its own the R.C.A.F. promptly began to call them Cansos. Nobody else does. With that purchase Canada had secured the right to manufacture, but what the technicians call the guts of the job were to come from the States. Then Bell and Ben Franklin, pint-sized dynamo of the big eastern plant, put their heads together and the next thing you knew the two-plant idea was on the way. The R.C.A.F. came through with a sizeable order, but Bell wanted something more . . . top-speed production to the limit of plant capacity. That meant something much bigger than production in Canada for Canuck fliers. No ceiling. Simply shoot the works. There was more to it than that, but that was the working basis. It has all the earmarks of the sort of idea which will have much to do with licking Herr Hitler.

As this is written the job is well into stride. The original Boeing plant which employed a total of 443 people in 1938 and concerned itself primarily with comparatively minor tasks had more than 7,500 men and women on its payroll in the spring of 1943 and more than 50 Catalinas had left the hangar door. The second Canadian plant followed close behind. Its bosses vow they will lick their friendly competitors in the west despite the latter's head start and Munitions Minister Howe and Aircraft Production Director Bell are egging both gangs on. The race is likely to develop into something worth watching.

Back of it all, of course, as with all the great tasks on the production front, stand men. Number one among those in the west ranks P. C. Johnson, top man of Uncle Sam's great Boeing Aircraft. Johnson has had ups and downs in the aircraft field, but up or down, has always enjoyed the repute amongst his own kind of being one of the best men in the business. When Canada set out to build its own great transcontinental airway and the Transport Minister wanted the best man in the Americas to put it together, it was Johnson he brought from the States to do the job.

Then he went home and set about the business of pouring aircraft from his own production lines. There are hosts of others. I. M. Laddon, graduate of McGill, and world-renowed aircraft designer is one. No tale would be complete which failed to mention designer Stan Burke, president of Canadian Boeing. The result is an extremely hard-hitting team. Back east is Benjamin Franklin, Benny to everybody in the Canadian aircraft industry from Director-General to tyro apprentice, a supercharged gentleman who in 1939 was selling insurance and who walked into a great, but badly tangled aircraft plant and made it say uncle. With him is N. F. Vanderlipp, formerly of Fairchild, but now part of Vickers' triple-threat two-man attack. And back of these stand thousands of skilled aircraft workers possessed of an *esprit de*

The "Art of Casting" at Robert Mitchell's: (Left to right) Melting temperature co[...] Making the mould. Pouring the metal. Shaking out the Castings. Removing pouring [...] and rises. Filing and cleaning Castings.

corps the like of which you will not find nowadays in Karlsruhe, Bremen, Cologne, or Essen. All of which is likely to be very damaging to the enemies of the common man!

This then, in rough outline, is the tale of how the Catalinas came to Canada.

Not all the story is here. Some of it will not be told until after the shooting finishes, but enough of the tale is in these lines to bring home the fact that we have reached out into a field in which we are serving not merely ourselves but our Allies in the places where the blows are driven home. Not all the tale of how and why Ralph Bell cinched the deal for all-out Canadian production is written. The details don't matter and most of them are pretty private anyway, but you can bet Bell did some fancy persuading, first in Ottawa, then in Washington. What matters is that the job is big, and that it is on the move, with no limits on the people who have been given the green light to produce a great ship, with full-out production to mid-1944 already approved in firm orders for Canada and our partners.

Aircraft Production Director Bell called the tune at the first launching ceremonies when he turned to the wife of the Lieutenant-Governor of British Columbia and said: "Mrs. Woodward, will you christen the plane and let us all get back to our jobs?"

Mrs. Woodward did and the workers did. And here come the Catalinas from Vickers in the East, Boeing out west.

*   *   *

Last, but not least, no matter how you measure such things, the Canadian aircraft industry owes a deep debt of gratitude to the National Steel Car Corporation, its Malton plant now Government-operated and known as Victory Aircraft. Back in 1938, without any volume orders in sight and in the midst of an actual slump in the industry, its top men, and, in particular, the late R. J. Magor, had the courage to erect the largest aircraft plant in the Dominion. In short they had vision to look ahead to the time when the aircraft industry would become one of Canada's greatest national assets, and, as well, felt in their bones that war was not far away.

Originally planning to manufacture the Lysander used in the early part of the war as a basic trainer and operational aircraft, the company later acquired part of the six-way contract for Hampden bombers.

Then, with formation of Federal Aircraft Ltd., National Steel Car commenced to build Ansons as well. Such were the preoccupations at Malton until the fall of 1942 when the arrival of the first Lancaster bomber from Britain heralded a new era of manufacture in Canada.

By then National Steel Car had begun re-tooling for this famous first-line bomber, with 4,500 employees on the job. Then Death struck an unexpected blow at the big factory and suddenly its human spark plug, Bob Magor, was no more. Overwork, the carrying of the load of a dozen men, had struck him down in his prime, as Death has struck down so many of his breed in these years. Quickly a crisis developed at Malton and work slowed down to a walk, so much so that the seriousness of the situation was brought to government attention. Action on the part of the Minister of Munitions and Supply and of the Director-General of Aircraft Production was precipitated with the sudden resignation of General Manager Boyd. Without warning the Federal Government decided on a step until then without precedent in aircraft, and took over the Malton plant, lock, stock and barrel. Changing the name to Victory Aircraft, it employed Boyd as General Manager and invited J. P. Bickell, prominent Toronto mining man, to become President. Bickell accepted. The job went on at top speed again. Today the Malton plant is a hive of industry. As the summer of 1943 arrived, giant Lancasters were beginning to roll off the assembly lines.

No accident led to the selection of the Malton plant for the Lancaster job. With a wing spread of 102 ft. the four-engined bomber requires vast assembly space. At Malton, it will be possible to send the Lancasters down the assembly lines in three huge bays. By the end of the summer of 1943 Victory Aircraft will have taken its rightful place again among the top producers of aircraft in Canada.

The Lancaster can fly from England to the farthest point in Germany with a heavy bomb load, and has a maximum speed just short of 300 miles per hour, when light. It has 10 guns in four power-operated turrets. It is said to be remarkably easy to produce considering its size and complexity.

The official R.A.F. report says: "Even with two motors stopped on the one side, the performance is exceptional. Baulked landings present no difficulty even with 60,000 lb. loaded weight. Take-off and night landings are straight forward. Manoeuvrability is good, and evasive and jinkings tactics easy."

The Lancaster is a four motor mid-wing monoplane of all-metal stressed skin construction, twin fins and rudders and a fully retractable undercarriage. Two versions have come into service, the Lancaster I with four 1,280 horsepower Rolls-Royce Merlin XX motors and the Lancaster II with four 1,600 horsepower Bristol Hercules radials.

*   *   *

These, then, are the primary producers of Canada's giant aircraft industry—making Catalinas, Lancasters, Mosquitoes and Hell-Divers for the attacking fronts, for the defence of Canada, for our allies; supplying, too, every need and requirement of the Air Training Plan—the Cornells, the Harvards, the Ansons and the Norsemen. This was their war record, as of June 1st., 1943:—

ELEMENTARY TRAINERS

Tiger Moth	1,384	
Menasco Moth	10	
Wireless Moth	126	
Cornell	409	
Fleet 16	431	
		2,360

ADVANCED TRAINERS

Harvard	1,059	
Norsemen	51	
Fleet 60	101	
Bolingbroke	367	
Anson	1,850	
Lysander	150	
		3,578

SERVICE AIRCRAFT

Shark	15	
Grumman	15	
Stranraer	32	
Delta	8	
Lysander	75	
Norsemen	69	
Bolingbroke	169	
P.B.Y.	63	
Hurricane	1,451	
Hampden	160	
D.H. 98	19	
		2,076
		8,014

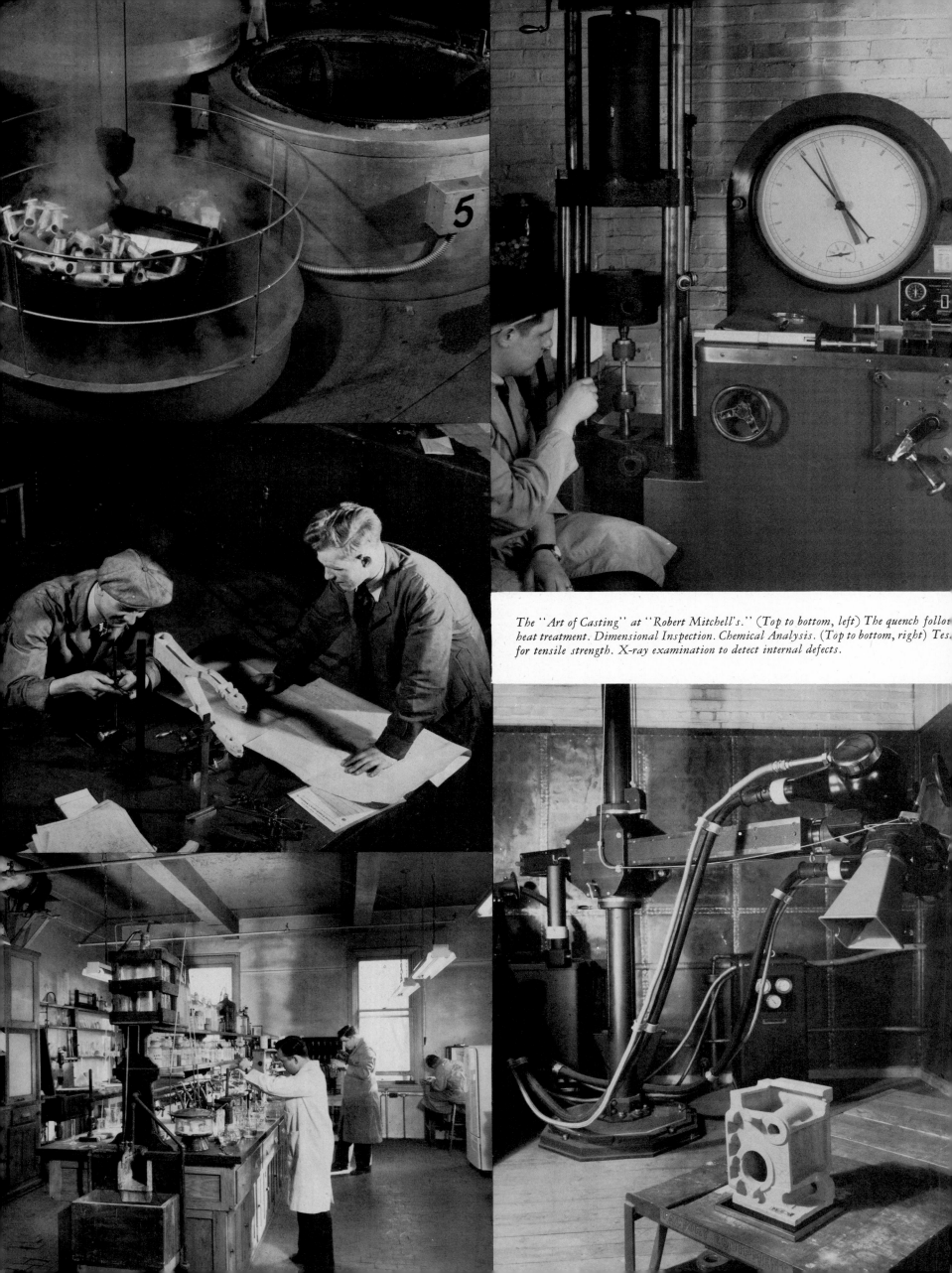

The "Art of Casting" at "Robert Mitchell's." (Top to bottom, left) The quench follow[ing] heat treatment. Dimensional Inspection. Chemical Analysis. (Top to bottom, right) Tes[ting] for tensile strength. X-ray examination to detect internal defects.

THE INDUSTRIAL FRONT

So much has been said and written of mass production, of the tremendous volume of material which flows from the assembly lines of the United Nations, that it is only natural that the conclusion of the public should be that the only problem facing those who operate the arsenals of democracy is quantity. While such an estimate holds true of ammunition and many other war products, it is by no means so in the case of aircraft components and parts. Although Canada's job is to get as many airplanes as possible off the assembly lines of the nation, the fact remains that the making of major parts and what are generally known as bits-and-pieces is not invariably a mass production job. On the contrary.

Actually the only aircraft parts which may be produced in tremendous volume are rivets, bolts and suchlike odds and ends. Otherwise the number of identical pieces which go into the fabrication of a plane do not average more than two. The stream-lined contours of wing and fuselage construction produce constantly changing shapes which do not permit duplication of structural members. In short each individual aircraft is primarily a custom-made job.

The widespread concept of mass production in its relation to war arose in the first instance from the automotive industry and has become what may be called the great North American fetish. But the manufacture of an automobile and of an aeroplane are as far apart as the Poles. In the case of the motor car, for example, there are plants in the United States capable of launching a completed vehicle every two minutes. On the basis of an eight hour day and a twenty-five day month, that is 6,000 cars a month. If the factory price is $600. per car that is a turnover of $3,600,000. monthly, a figure for which no more than 36 medium-range twin-engined aircraft can be made. To carry on the analogy, inasmuch as there are usually no more than two duplicate parts in one such machine, the result would be that in an output of 36 two-motored aeroplanes no more than 72 copies of any one piece (other than bolts and rivets) would be required. How, then, could you attain mass production? That is what is meant when it is said that aircraft-building is a tailoring job, whereas the automotive industry can be compared to that of the large-scale pants-maker.

This circumstance creates many and varied problems for the manufacturer and for the Aircraft Production Branch of the Department of Munitions and Supply, the government's coordinating medium in the industry. Long runs to create stock piles of any individual part are out of the question, partly because they would tie-up urgently required strategic materials, partly because such stockpiles would call for the creation of huge storage space, partly because of the possibility of day by day changes in the design of the aircraft itself.

The problem of aircraft parts manufacture in Canada, therefore, resolves into the production of a sufficiency of bits and pieces to keep the assembly lines supplied and to maintain a comfortable backlog of spares. The job, in short, is to produce a small number of a tremendous variety of individual parts, an infinitely more troublesome job than to turn out a great number of a small variety, as is the case in the automotive field. All of which is said at the outset to bring the picture into focus.

A second impression of erroneous concept is that what the public calls "the aircraft factories" are plants in which virtually everything which goes into the making of an aeroplane is fabricated on the spot. Actually the plants of the prime producers are assembly points to which are brought main components, items of equipment and innumerable bits and pieces to be fastened together and rolled out the door in the form of completed aircraft. Each such plant draws its main components from a dozen sources (though it

may manufacture some of these itself). Consider, for example, the Mosquito.

From a factory in southwestern Ontario come various jacks, valves and valve parts, pumps. Fuel tanks are turned out in Toronto. Boeing makes the tailplanes in Vancouver and ships them across the continent. Fuselages and other major pieces come from Canadian Power Boat in Montreal. Cockshutt Plow of Brantford, Ontario, contributes rudders, elevators, the pilot's seats and half a dozen other items. General Engineering of Toronto makes the spring struts. General Motors produce fuselages, engine mounts, other outsize pieces. Gutta Percha and Rubber Company of Toronto make three kinds of tank coverings. Tail Wheels and Wheel Assemblies come from Kelsey of Toronto. Massey-Harris produce wings. Certain types of tank come from Moffats, peace-time makers of kitchen ranges. Otaco, Limited, of Orillia, Ontario, turn out other major components, as do George W. Reed Company of Montreal. Remington Rand of Toronto and Universal Cooler of Brantford round out the list. These are makers of major components. Behind them range hundreds of other plants making innumerable parts, great and small, plus the entire equipment industry of the Dominion and the engine industry outside Canada.

The picture is similar throughout the industry. Major components producers will be found on the lists of several final assembly contractors. Cockshutt, to quote an outstanding example, appears as sub-contractor to Boeing and Vickers on the Catalina, De Havilland on the Mosquito, Federal on the Anson, Fleet on the Cornell, Noorduyn on the Harvard and on the Lancaster for Victory Aircraft.

Thus to an aircraft industry with growing pains, centred in plants from Amherst in the east to Vancouver on the Pacific, with its always swelling production of elementary trainers, advanced trainers, fighters and bombers, land machines, amphibians and water-borne aircraft, the whole great structure of Canadian commerce contributes raw materials, component parts, equipment and bits and pieces. But this is not the sum of the record of lathe and bench. Canadian industry and Canadian workers have united, behind them the men of science and the men of management, to bring forth from an industrial structure in no wise created for such tasks the innumerable thousands of parts which, when added together, become fighter, bomber or trainer. They have made the tools. They have equipped the aerodromes. They have supplied fighting airmen with virtually their every need . . . and they have done it from a standing start.

To etch in the complete panorama within the confines of such a work as this is impossible. To set down, name by name and place by place, the points of origin of the infinitesimal rivets, the little bits of rubber, the component parts of hubs, the dashboard instruments, the "dope", the innumerable thisses and thats, would necessitate a work of encyclopedic proportions. All that can be attempted here, with occasional reference to case-examples, is a broad and general outline of a great job, the primary result of which has been the equipping of the Air Training Plan.

Hundreds of new industries have come into being throughout the Dominion under the driving impetus of war and the greatest aerial effort per capita of population in the world's history. Great companies and small alike have flung themselves into the tasks of Make 'Em And Keep 'Em Flying. From munitions plants each so vast that the visitor cannot see the complete operation in a week's march, pour millions of rounds of ammunition which Canadian airmen overseas are pumping into the enemies of civilisation, which anti-aircraft gunners from London to the shores of Sicily have sent flying aloft to destroy marauding Hun aircraft. From

The Job Always Goes On: (Left, top to centre) Scenes in the Montreal plant of Aviation Electric, specializing in the servicing and repair of all manner of electrical equipment for war aircraft. (Lower left) That hose is made of "Flexatex" and is better for carrying gas to an aircraft's tanks than is rubber. (Right, top to bottom) Major-General Lafleche, Minister of National War Services, visits the R.C.A. Victor plant. H.R.H. the Earl of Athlone, Governor-General of Canada, visits the R.C.A. Victor plant. Air crew students study technical apparatus at R.C.A. Victor.

huge new plants for the production of explosives come forth tremendous tonnages of the raw material of sudden death. From a pre-war elevator factory in Hamilton, Ontario, the Bofors gun emerges, a death-dealing ack-ack weapon. Near Toronto is situated one of the greatest plants in the world for the production of automatic-firing weapons. In a little Ontario village expert Czech toolmen carry out intricate gun-mount production in the employ of Bata, expatriate shoe-producers of that democratic land, for lack of the will to defend which (or the lack of will in their leaders) the free peoples came within an inch of marching over the precipice to destruction. So goes the tale of industrial warfare. Go where you will, the story is the same. Canada has gone to Total War on the industrial front through the development of great industries based mainly on her own storehouses of raw materials. Nor is this great effort undertaken for Canada alone but for wherever the front lines of these United Nations may be.

Finely wrought propellers from Canadian factories are fitted to the ships which flow down the assembly lines of Canadian aircraft plants. Yet, looking back to 1939, there was scarcely a prop in the country to affix to the first aircraft acquired by the Dominion. By 1942, however, a major industry had been established. In Montreal Canadian Car were making the Hoover propeller for the Anson and Singer Sewing Machine of St. Johns, Quebec, were making wooden blades to fit the Hoover hub. Canadian Propellers of Montreal were making the Hamilton Standard propeller for the Harvard trainer and for other types of craft. S. and S. of Winnipeg were producing blades of laminated wood for Ansons, Fleets and De Havillands. Vickers were making wooden props. Canadian Car were making metal blades for Curtiss and Aluminum of Canada were turning out rough castings of blades in quantity. Another new Canadian industry had been born under the necessity of war!

From south of the border still come some of the delicate scientific instruments essential to precision flying. But here again Canadian industry has done a magnificent job. Prior to the war we had no aviation instrument production. By 1942, however, the Dominion had become virtually self-sustaining in instruments, as in so many other urgently needed things. Bombsights, astrographs, astro-compasses, aircraft compasses of all types, drift recorders, navigation computers, air speed indicators, altimeters of all types, manifold pressure gauges, rate-of-climb indicators, turn and bank indicators, tachometers, a wide range of engine instruments, oil temperature and pressure gauges and fuel pressure gauges. Pioneers in this field have been Canadian Westinghouse, Canadian General Electric, Canadian Aviation Instruments and Accessories, Limited, Sutton-Horsley, Limited, Stanley Precision Instrument and Stanley Tool Company, Dominion Electric Protection Company, Ontario Hughes-Owens, Limited and Instruments, Limited. They comprise an honour roll of achievement. Virtually everything which goes aloft when the battleship of the skies leaves the ground, from armament and tires to the parachute and goggles the pilot wears and the flare pistol his navigator carries, comes today from the war plants of the Dominion.

Consider goggles, for example. Prior to the war the R.A.F. had virtually standardised on the Livingston type, a large goggle with flat laminated lenses. The United States, on the other hand, used a cylindrical lens, perfectly flat on the vertical meridian, but curved in a horizontal meridian and hardened. From tests made, however, the R.C.A.F. decided that any glass in front of a man's face should be laminated, as the hardened lenses provide an unnecessary hazard. They also decided that flat lenses are desirable, as there is no distortion when looking through a flat lens at an angle. The difficulty prompted the medical division to undertake solution of the goggle problem and, with the help of Safety Supply Manufacturing Company, a new type was developed.

Such examples as this are true across the whole structure of Canada's air effort, for Canadian industry quickly established itself as the great backlog of the Commonwealth Air Training Plan, of the R.A.F. schools in Canada and of the Dominion's fighting forces of the air beyond the seven seas. The architects of the Air Plan, the men who put it on paper, may have viewed it as a composite arrangement in which a small population country would provide aerodromes and the mills of Britain the materials. No doubt such a Plan would have been eminently satisfactory if the enemy had permitted us to fight a war of attrition and blockade. But Hitler decreed otherwise. And when the storm broke loose Canadian industry and Canadian workers, each with little experience in the tasks to be undertaken, buckled down to the task of saving the Plan. That is what was meant in an earlier chapter by the remark that what began as Britain's Plan, after Dunkirk became Canada's. This aspect of Canada's War In The Air cannot be overemphasized. It cannot be repeated too often.

Canada's success on the war-industry front must be credited primarily to the North American flair for innovation and our disregard for tradition. Faced by tasks never before attempted in the Dominion, the approach of the production man has almost invariably been "just another job". If the man on the job did not measure up to that standard another man was found. No time could be lost in worrying about the tender feelings of individuals. Canada, for example, had never produced guns of major size, but during the war years has become an important maker of ordnance, ranging from huge naval guns and mounts to 25-pounders, anti-tank weapons and down through the whole gamut of aircraft armament and guns for anti-aircraft defence. In the realm of aerial warfare the principal Canadian weapon is the Browning gun for aircraft, while the outstanding Bofors ack-ack gun, with carriage and equipment, as well as 3.7 anti-aircraft guns are mass-produced in Canadian plants. For this armament Canada also turns out an endless stream of projectiles and propellents, a range which takes in thirty types of shells, eight of small arms ammunition and twelve types of cartridge cases. Bombs up to 500-pound weight are made and filled in Canadian plants. Tens of millions of rounds of rifle and machine-gun ammunition are made in one plant alone, operated by Defence Industries, a war-subsidiary of the great C.I.L. Tracer is produced in a small Canadian town in a plant which, after turning out millions upon millions of rounds of .303 and other types changed its whole production line to the ammunition which keys the flier's machine-gun bursts. Canadian tracer is a combination of the similar British and American products and has proved highly successful in the field. Approximately 3,000 people are employed in this one plant alone, a division of the great D.I.L.

In the realm of raw materials Canada was singularly fortunately placed to meet the challenge of war. The Dominion produces and refines great quantities of copper. In the rocks of Northwestern Ontario lies 90% of the world supply of nickel. The greatest plant in the world for the production of raw aluminum abuts on one of Quebec's northern rivers, adjacent to one of the world's greatest sources of electric power, the Shipshaw development. Canada has huge steel furnaces, though we are not as well situated as our neighbour to the south in output of the product of the great iron ranges. Nevertheless the Dominion can be said to look to its war-production tasks with the knowledge that on the home front, and in the reservoirs from which it can draw, are raw materials which make possible a huge output of the machines of modern war. Perhaps the supply of raw materials, more than any other single factor, is responsible for our sudden development into the world's fourth-greatest manufacturing country, its greatest on a population basis.

From the point of view of aircraft such a statement is doubly true,

Making Propellers For the Commonwealth's Flying Men: (Top to bottom, left) Checking the vertical balance of an aluminum blade, milling the profile of the blade shank, grinding an aluminum blade. (Right): Magnetic inspection of components, machining component parts and inspection of components of a variable pitch propeller. All pictures from Canadian Propellers Limited.

for the basic structural substance of the modern aeroplane is aluminum. Thus, if we examine the part played by aluminum in the creation of Canada's aircraft industry, we shall perhaps be able to obtain a point of approach to the importance of our raw materials. On the outbreak of war in September, 1939, Canada, already the third ranking nation in aluminum production, was called upon to expand existing facilities to the greatest possible extent in the shortest possible time. To understand the task imposed, it is necessary to realize that the production of aluminum can be divided broadly into two aspects. First, the reduction of bauxite to pure aluminum in ingot form (known as pig, or raw, aluminum) and, second, the fabrication of this raw aluminum into finished aircraft parts.

Before the war the major part of Canada's aluminum production was devoted to raw aluminum which was then exported throughout the world to be fabricated. Manufacture in Canada was largely limited to the making of household utensils, foil and cable. Our consumption seldom exceeded 10% of our production. The two broad problems, then, were first, to increase the facilities for producing raw aluminum and, second, to create new, expanded facilities so that complicated aluminum forgings, castings and other necessary aircraft parts could be turned out. While plant expansion was in hand the existing works of the Aluminum Company of Canada at Arvida and Shawinigan Falls in Quebec and Toronto, Ontario, were producing at top speed . . . raw and fabricated aluminum at Shawinigan, raw aluminum at Arvida (even then the world's largest aluminum works), fabricated aluminum in Toronto. The great expansion program took part at Arvida in the Saguenay district. As fast as new rows of pots could be installed gangs of skilled workmen moved in to tend them, often before the walls to close-in the pots had been finished. To maintain a high, even flow of water for electric power two great storage dams were undertaken on the Manouan River and at Passe Dangereuse on the Peribonka. Men, materials and animals were taken by air to the Manouan job, the largest air-freighting contract ever given in Canada being awarded to Canadian Airways, now a part of Canadian Pacific Airlines. A townsite was cut out of the virgin forest at the dam site. Trucks, bulldozers, cranes and tractors were flown in. The dams were built in record time. This development has since become the core of controversy in the realm of politics, opponents of the government maintaining that the people's birthright has been bartered away to the company. To outline this argument is not the function of this work. Here we may record only the achievement, take no sides in debating the methods used. Whatever else may be said, the building of the dams and the great increase in plant made possible by added power, gave Canada and her allies the aluminum they needed so urgently.

Across the Americas, in tropical British Guiana, the production of bauxite was hurriedly stepped up. To show how the people involved were swinging into their jobs, one engineer within a few days settled major problems in two tropical countries, problems arising from the production and transportation of bauxite, raced north to the Manouan job to smash construction bottlenecks. Expansion of raw aluminum production rapidly doubled, redoubled and doubled again.

In the realm of fabricated aluminum it was necessary not merely to work existing facilities to the utmost, but to create new facilities as well, involving processes and production methods never before attempted in Canada. Thus, at Kingston, Ontario, 1,300 men were soon busily engaged in turning out the complicated tubings, castings and forgings required for aircraft and other intricate machines of war. At Kingston, too, an industrial research laboratory was set up to improve and perfect materials. By such devices did aluminum go to war. With the installation of ma-

chinery to stamp-out propellers, all structural parts of Canada's fighting and training aircraft could be made in the Dominion.

From this basic ingredient of the aeroplane come the light alloys which go into the precision castings vital in war planes. While aluminum and its alloys, in the forms of sheet, rod and tubing, are evident to the observer on any aircraft line, many less noticeable but equally essential structural pieces are called for in the specifications for any type of aircraft in production. These are used, to offer examples, for instrument fittings, gun mounts, bomb-release mechanisms, rudder and steering equipment, landing gear and in many other parts of the finished plane. Few Canadian factories were equipped to undertake such delicate work when war came. One, Robert Mitchell Company, had been producing high grade aluminum alloy castings in Montreal under laboratory-controlled conditions. Others were making industrial grade aluminum alloy castings, but these must not be confused with the precision work required in the making of aircraft. As other plants began to produce castings of these types, X-ray radiography inspection was instituted by the National Research Council and the Department of National Defence, which quickly bares any inadequacies. The Mitchell foundry was approved from the outset for such precision work and, after a probationary period, during which every casting was sent to Ottawa for X-ray, was authorised to instal its own inspection equipment and was the first Canadian plant to be so approved. Soon Aluminum Company of Canada was to become engaged in producing its own castings under identical controls. Many other companies are working in steel, zinc and other metals. Canada's metal-working industry has expanded by leaps and bounds under the impact of war.

Aluminum, nickel, copper, steel . . . all these pour into the factories where the parts and components of Canadian aircraft are made. From British Columbia come the world's finest aircraft woods, widely used today in substitution for metal. Brakes for wheels tired by Canadian rubber plants . . . instruments . . . a hundred and one rivets, gadgets, nuts, screws . . . a great outpouring of work from a thousand mills and more, and no end to the job. All modern aircraft, for example, depend in large degree upon plastics in the construction of important parts . . . windshields, gun bays, bomb windows, etc., etc. In these complete clarity of vision for pilot or gunner is essential. Lucite, produced in Canada by Canadian Industries, Limited, provides the answer to that problem. Plexiglas, a similar material, is used in the United States. All plastics in this group are completely free from distortion, more optically perfect than glass. Bullet-proof windshields are manufactured in Canada from alternate layers of clear plastic and glass.

In the field of aircraft lacquers Canada has developed an industry which fills all requirements of the primary and components plants, the repair and overhaul shops. At the outset Canadian paint manufacturers prepared and submitted formulas to fit British specifications. These called for a non-fading pigment, glossless and with a minimum of air resistance or drag. The acceptable lacquer must also have a sympathetic adherence to aluminum. Tests were run for almost a year. What emerged was perhaps the best line of aircraft lacquers the world knows, now being manufactured with success by such people as International Paints, Berry Brothers, C-I-L, Sherwin-Williams and Thorp-Hambrock. Look wherever you like in Canada. You'll find something going on which has the war in the air as its destination. Even the identification marks on our aircraft have been developed here, in the plant of Canada Decalcomania.

In a little town in southern Quebec a metal-working plant stood beside a C.P.R. branch-line siding before the war. From it came oil-burners, household gadgets of one kind and another. Today that metal plant acts as the main feeder for a factory of strange

Signs of the Times: Those red, white and blue circles you see on Canadian aircraft decalcomania transfer roundels by Canadian Decalcomania Company, Limited, just the ones you used to put on the back of your hand as a child. Pictures show the m of transferring them to aircraft fuselages. On the other side of the page are scenes i busy Montreal shop of Pratt and Whitney, showing engine overhaul and manufa and propeller repair.

appearance which stands in a clearing not far from this same village of Waterloo. The second plant is a veritable town on stilts, its buildings separated by block-length open spaces, across which boardwalks run, high above the snow-line. Why this strange community? It is a plant in which the pyrotechnics of modern war are made and the construction plan was dictated purely by the safety-factor question. Should something unexpectedly explode in one of these isolated hutments any resulting fire can be brought quickly into control and prevented from spreading to cause what might easily, under other conditions, become a catastrophe of major proportions. So the townsfolk of Waterloo, Quebec, who, not long ago, guided the plow, milked the cows, fed the chickens and garnered their crops, today are expert in the manufacture of flares, sea-markers and all manner of pyrotechnic equipment. Because of events happening in a quiet Quebec backwater, in the plants of International Flare Signal and Macdonald Metal Products, other strange events result over land and ocean, half way across the world.

In Montreal the writer visited a new textile plant in a teeming industrial area. Here another kind of tale unfolded, another phase of the war-life of a people who, in their quiet, assiduous way, have gone into total action. A long room thrummed with the racket of hundreds of sewing machines, each operated or tended by a young or middle-age woman. Into this room huge quantities of superfine silk were being delivered, to be cut into precise panel shapes which, after assembly on the sewing machines, and rigged with a strange yet ordered assortment of cords, would become the giant parachutes which bring ill-fortuned fliers down to safe landings and carry our infiltrating troops behind enemy lines. A parachute consists of eighty separate pieces, each of which must be perfect if the wearer is to get down alive. Switlik Canadian Parachutes, Limited, this brand-new war industry, has specifically trained each individual employee in her or his all-important task. Many today are R.C.A.F.-certified parachute packers. The job is so big that five machine shops are kept busy, full time, making the metal parts for this one plant. Another big-time show, carried out in efficient manner. But back to the aircraft line . . .

In the realm of landing gear Canada has become a major producer under war conditions, primarily through development of this highly technical equipment by Dowty Equipment, Limited, specialising in the manufacture of retractable undercarriages and complete hydraulic systems which operate various services in the modern aeroplane, such as the retraction of undercarriages, operation of flaps, bomb doors, radiator shutters, fuel jettison valves, power-operated gun turrets, control trimming tabs . . . in short, the actuation of any moveable part of an aircraft which can be done by hydraulic means. The Canadian company was established in the early months of the war with a view to producing undercarriages and hydraulic equipment for British aircraft to be made in Canada. It has gone far beyond that point today. The Canadian Anson, for example, incorporates a power-operated Dowty hydraulic system for the retraction of undercarriage and operation of flaps. On the Bolingbroke, long manufactured at Fairchild, Dowty supplied a tail wheel made entirely in Canada and followed by producing a set of main undercarriage legs and tail strut for use with ski-undercarriage. The same company supplied all tail wheels and hydraulic equipment for the Canadian Hurricane, now turns out undercarriages, tail wheels and the complete hydraulic system for the giant Lancasters.

Consider the role played by communications in Canada's war in the air . . .

One day in the spring of 1940 men carrying instruments and tripods journeyed into the deep back country of Ontario and set up their gear. They worked steadily for days, made scientific calculations, packed up their equipment and left. A day or so later another crew arrived. These men spoke in the jargon of the construction fraternity as they studiously examined blueprints and looked over the scene. Finally all but one of them packed and made ready to leave. "The job's up to you now," the Boss of the departing crew remarked to the one man who would remain behind.

"The first thing I need around here," the stay-behind remarked aloud, "is a 'phone." In a matter of days a shack had been put up, a telephone line had been slung through the bush to the nearest exchange and *voilà!* . . . the wilderness was the wilderness no more. Sounds like the story of Aladdin's magic lamp!

That phone in the forest was an extremely handy instrument. Over it materials and supplies were ordered, workers were hired and the thousand and one urgencies of a major contracting job looked after. As a result an amazing transformation took place in what had been yesterday's forest. In a great clearing a vast modern airport appeared, an air-training centre for the Royal Canadian Air Force. Instead of serried ranks of tall trees, trim administrative buildings fringed the scene. Clean runways crisscrossed the clearing. Hangars, repair depot, barracks, recreation huts, a direction-finding station and control tower, all manner of buildings appeared. And what happened in the Ontario bush was taking place all over the Dominion. Without adequate communications the job wouldn't have been finished by 1950.

Before the airport took shape consideration was given to the phone requirements, necessary to maintain and operate a major station. Switchboard connections were installed. The field was put into immediate touch with the rest of the nation. Telephone-typewriter systems were added to make rapid communication possible throughout the Training Command and to headquarters in Ottawa. But that is not an end of the matter . . .

From the nation's telephone laboratories came a two-way radio telephone system, by means of which the pilot in the air keeps touch with his home field, or talks on the intercommunication system to other members of his bomber-crew. Communications systems—RT to the fliers—permit the stacking of aircraft at varying altitudes and keep the air clear of dangerous congestion. Another strange device, a product of telephone research, guides planes when rain or fog makes safe landings difficult. Other intricate equipment translates sound signals into light signals. In the administration building a tiny speck of green light moving across a screen of frosted glass gives the exact position of the plane, so that ground officers may correct any error the pilot may make while coming in to land when fog or mist blots out the field. The throat-microphone, which picks up the pilot's voice distinctly through the roar of motors, was brought to perfection in the telephone laboratories. In the plants of such corporations as Northern Electric, RCA-Victor, Canadian Marconi, Canadian General Electric and others, scientists have developed and produced all manner of secret devices which increase the safety factor of flight. The achievements of Canadian industry and its people are without number or limit.

The railroads hauled in the supplies which made this great network of aerodromes possible. They carry the bits and pieces of aircraft production from manufacturer to components-plants. From the huge aisles of factories in which wings, fuselages, centre sections and tail assemblies come together they transport finished components to the final assembly lines of the nation. Railways, tramway companies and bus operators carry several hundred thousand Canadian war-workers to and from their jobs every day.

Most aircraft plants in Canada were built many miles from the transportation facilities existing in the early days of the war. Before aeroplanes fly, aircraft workers must be provided with the means of reaching their daily tasks. The majority of aircraft

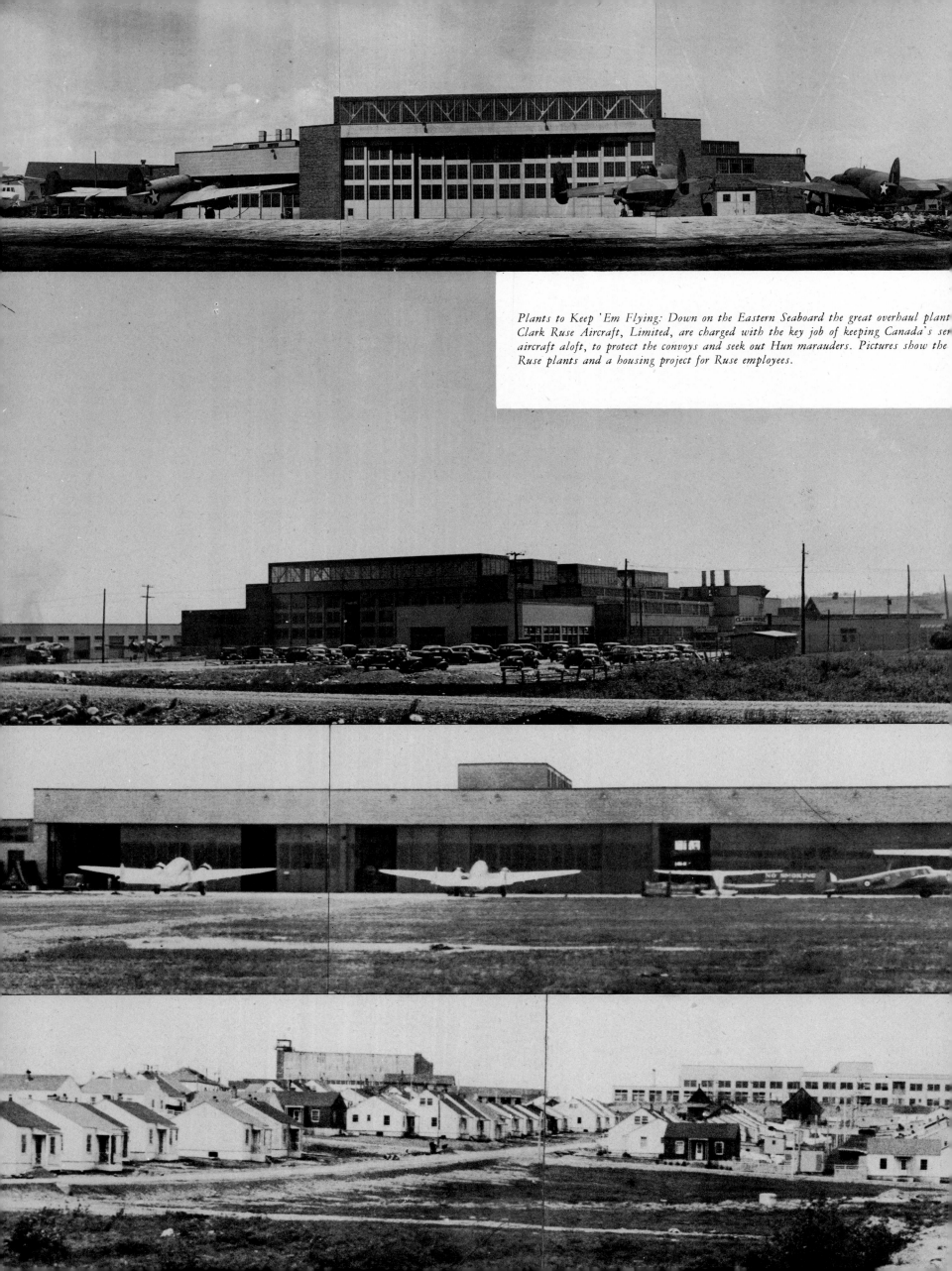

Plants to Keep 'Em Flying: Down on the Eastern Seaboard the great overhaul plants [of] Clark Ruse Aircraft, Limited, are charged with the key job of keeping Canada's ser[vice] aircraft aloft, to protect the convoys and seek out Hun marauders. Pictures show the [Clark] Ruse plants and a housing project for Ruse employees.

workers travelled to and from the plants by private motor car until gasoline and tire rationing took serious toll of this form of transportation. The organised inter-city bus operators of Canada were requested to provide transportation to fill the vacuum created by the rationing of motor fuel.

The Provincial Transport Company of Montreal is an example of what has been done to provide transportation for war industry. New motor coach equipment was not only costly but difficult to obtain and in many cases it was only supplied by curtailing services over important but less essential routes. In the Montreal area, for example, the busses of Provincial Transport carry 300,000 people a month to war plants, of which Fairchild, Noorduyn and Vickers are in the final aircraft assembly field.

Services have also been provided for the Royal Air Force Ferry Command located at Dorval Airport and the Canadian Car Aircraft Maintenance centre, located at St. Johns.

A flexible form of transportation, the motor coach has assisted aircraft industries in solving a major labour problem. Motor coaches can and are being routed to and through residential areas in which aircraft workers are domiciled, transporting them direct to the main gate at their place of employment. This reduces to a minimum the elapsed time that the worker spends in transit. In some cases, the aircraft companies pay the total cost of the employees' transportation. In other instances, the employee pays part of the cost, the employer making up the difference.

The motor coach has enabled many of the aircraft companies to employ split shifts or small groups of workers at hours most convenient to the plant. Frequently, when overtime work is necessary, the departure of one or more coaches is delayed for the use of those who remain at the plant.

Aircraft industries have been called upon to augment or reduce staff on very short notice. Shortage of materials sometimes necessitates a temporary curtailment; the use of the coach has enabled the aircraft plant to increase or decrease at will the number of employees. A survey of various types of transportation reveals the fact that bus transportation is an important factor in reducing absenteeism to a minimum.

In the same city the tramway service picks up hundreds of thousands more, in addition to caring for the added demands of wartime public movement.

Automotive manufacturers provide the almost innumerable things-on-wheels which every airport must have. Specialists have designed the ambulances and crash-wagons which stand beside every hangar in the land, ready for service on an instant's notice. Manufacturers of pleasure-craft have turned to the production of crash-boats. By these and ten thousand other devices has the great Air Training Plan been rolled into high gear as the greatest Canadian industrial achievement of all time.

But it is not enough simply to build aircraft and turn them over to the gentlemen in uniform. That is only the first part of the job. Somebody has to keep them flying . . . and keeping 'em flying has become a job as important as that of rolling new ships off the assembly lines. As time goes on that importance increases, for every aircraft saved to fly tomorrow is an aircraft which does not need to be replaced by a new one. The answer is a nation-wide Overhaul and Repair industry of great efficiency, the people in which are as proud as any aircrafter in the prime assembly plants —and rightly so. These are the men and women who Keep 'Em Flying.

The floor space devoted to overhaul and repair in 1941 totalled 900,000 square feet. During the next year the area increased by more than 50%. As this is written in 1943 it was still growing. Many thousands of people were engaged in the highly expert tasks of keeping 10,000 aircraft in the air, day in and out.

Overhaul and repair function under the watchful eye of the Aircraft Production Branch, working in close cooperation with the R.C.A.F., which keeps exacting record of every machine in the country and attends to day-to-day maintenance and minor repair jobs. The overhaul plants, then, may be said to be complementary to the run-of-mill maintenance work of the Air Force itself. Apart from routine inspections every aircraft and every engine must go into shops for complete everhaul after a given number of hours aloft, the number of hours varying according to type. Engines must be dismantled to the smallest components, each part thoroughly examined and tested and, if necessary, renewed. Re-assembly is a job calling for even greater care than was the first putting-together of the power unit, for it is a matter of extreme urgency that no slightly worn bit or piece shall go back into service.

In the case of the aircraft itself, all fabric must be stripped off and every section of the frame submitted to rigid tests, leading to replacements where required by the wear and tear of time. The overhauled and reassembled ship must then be tested with a care as great as if it had just come brand-new from the assembly line. That is the story of overhaul.

Behind this comes the job of salvaging, reconditioning and rebuilding planes which have been seriously damaged . . . the trickiest job of all, involving as it does the saving of every part of possible future use, without lessening the overall strength or safety of the rebuilt plane. The provision of adequate stockpiles of spare parts in each repair plant, without over-production of pieces which may soon be obsolescent, presents another problem. There is one training plane, for example, which, in looping, tends to strain or damage the left wing in much greater degree than the right. Hence the spares list for this type involves having seven spare left wings ready for use as against one right.

The number of plants designed for special overhaul tasks which were in service by the time the Commonwealth Plan was in full stride was as follows: Airframe overhaul, 22; Engine overhaul, 14; Airframe and engine overhaul combined, 5; Airscrew overhaul, 5; Instruments, 8; Electrical spares, 6; Batteries, 10; Tires and tubes, 4. These plants are not all under civilian management. One of the largest engine overhaul plants in the country, for example, is Number 6 R.C.A.F. Aircraft Repair Depot, where the principal job is to do complete overhauls on the Rolls Royce Merlin. Some plants are operated by private corporations. Others have been built by the government and turned over to knowledgeable aircraft executives for operation. In times of stress such things must be undertaken in whatever manner seems most likely to get the individual job done most efficiently and quickly.

Canada's two great railway systems have played major roles in creating and operating these great overhaul plants. The Canadian Pacific, in addition to running flying schools under the Training Plan and its own network of strategic air lines, is deep into the overhaul and repair industry through its wholly-owned St. Maurice Aircraft Repair plant at Cap de la Madeleine, Quebec; the two plants of Mid-West Aircraft in the Winnipeg area and an engine overhaul plant in the same city; Prairie Airways at Moose Jaw, Saskatchewan and another plant recently taken over from Boeing in New Westminster, B.C. In these plants approximately 2,500 people are employed, of whom 25% are women. Overhaul is done on ten aircraft types and on five engines . . . Pratt and Whitneys, Cheetahs, Gypsies, Menascos and Rangers. Trans Canada Airlines, subsidiary of the Canadian National railway system, carries out work of great importance in its huge Winnipeg shops, where work of a scientific nature is done on instruments and other delicate equipment, as well as general aircraft repair.

In the west the great plants of Aircraft Repair, Limited, at Edmonton have been built up under the experienced direction of Leigh Brintnell, bush-flying ace of pre-war days. In the Maritimes

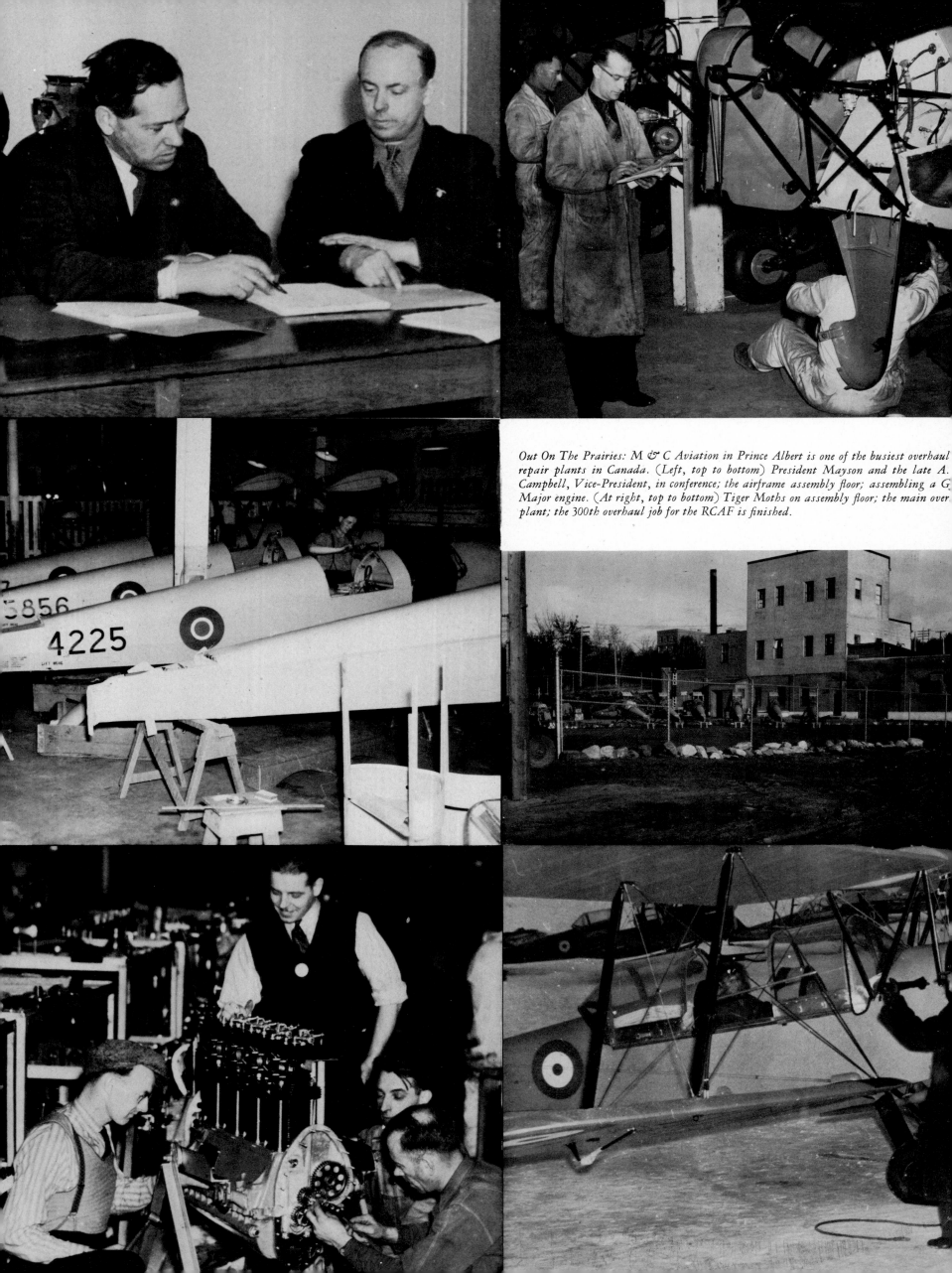

Out On The Prairies: M & C Aviation in Prince Albert is one of the busiest overhaul repair plants in Canada. (Left, top to bottom) President Mayson and the late A. Campbell, Vice-President, in conference; the airframe assembly floor; assembling a G Major engine. (At right, top to bottom) Tiger Moths on assembly floor; the main over plant; the 300th overhaul job for the RCAF is finished.

another outstanding northern flier, Clark Ruse, directs the operation of two great overhaul and repair plants, built by the government but operated by Clark Ruse Aircraft, Limited. They say that John McDonough of Central Aircraft has never said "it can't be done" to any job thrown in the direction of his plant in London, Ontario. M. and C. Aviation in Prince Albert, Saskatchewan, has become the industrial hub of that thriving, war-conscious northwestern city. Coates of Vancouver and Leavens Brothers in the southern Ontario area are other busy repair and overhaul people. In addition many prime producers—Boeing, Canadian Car, Canadian Vickers, De Havilland, MacDonald Brothers and Noorduyn—play important roles in keeping flying the aircraft which once rolled down their own assembly lines.

In the performance of these myriad tasks the government itself must play an important role, primarily in the field of coordination. A Production Control Unit, functioning within the Aircraft Branch of the Department of Munitions and Supply, divides the aircraft industry into four groups—prime contractors; suppliers of materials, forgings and castings; manufacturers of airframe components and suppliers of equipment and miscellaneous parts. The unit functions under the chairmanship of F. T. Smye, Director of the Production Program. Its task is to assure an even flow of materials and equipment to the places where they are needed, in short to hold a watching brief over the industry as a whole to prevent the forming of bottlenecks and to crack those which form.

Today Canada's aircraft industry, from prime producers to overhaul plants, from major components factories to the places where bits and pieces are made, has become a smooth functioning unit, a credit to those who have done the job and a credit to the nation itself.

No pretext is advanced that what has been written in these pages constitutes the complete story of Canadian industry's contribution to the fashioning and maintenance of the British Commonwealth Air Training Plan. All it has been possible to do is to etch in the broad outlines, to get a panoramic view of the immense responsibilities which Canada has taken on in this one field alone. Here are 11,000,000 people, occupying half a continent, a people whose habitations often are mere dots on the map of a land greater in size than the United States. These people, with virtually no preparation for war, have accepted and discharged its full responsibilities. They have sent overseas two army corps and ancillary troops. They have doubled, redoubled and continued to redouble the size of their small-ship Navy, making it one of the great factors in the sea-movement of these United Nations. They have created a vast industrial structure out of next-to-nothing, yet have maintained their great agricultural industry to feed their friends, partners and allies. Superimposed on all this they have devised and then taken over the greatest university of flight in man's history . . . and have made it the pattern for the comparable schemes of their partner-nations. The visible externals of this great Plan are the young men to be seen on the streets of every city and town in Air Force blue and the aircraft they fly. But underlying the visible picture is the canvas on which it has been painted. That canvas is the huge framework of Canadian industry, from the aircraft plants to the laboratories of the radio scientists and the factories where millions of rivets are spewed out by automatic machines, within which mills unsung men and women in tens upon tens of thousands toil, that freedom shall not perish from the earth. It is an amazingly diversified effort and it appears in strange places . . . in the machine shops of great paper mills, in the repair plants of railways and commercial airlines, in every nook and cranny of the nation's life into which the eye can peer. That is the crux of this story. Canada's War In The Air is a national job. And in some manner, no matter how minor, every man, woman and child in Canada is joined to it. Canadians have just reason to be proud not merely of the brave lads who fly, but of the unsung heroes of lathe and bench who are the cornerstone on which this amazing edifice rests.

Making the Pyrotechnics of Aerial Warfare: (Top to bottom, left) Packing the Para in the Parachute Flare. Finishing off a Sea-Marker Bomb. Véry Pistol cartridge in tion. (Top to bottom, right) Packing and shipping Parachute Flares. Assembling Markers. Lacquering identification markings on Signal Cartridges.

...AND TOMORROW

Wherever Lancasters, Bostons, Spitfires, Mosquitoes or Catalinas take to the air young Canadian airmen are wondering if there'll be air jobs for the bomber or fighter pilots back home after the war. On aerodromes in Canada and Britain, on Malta and in North Africa, the ground crews are thinking about the servicing and repair jobs of the future. In tremendous numbers the flying and ground personnel of the RCAF hope to spend their working years somewhere near aircraft.

In huge plants throughout the Dominion tens of thousands of men and women discuss what the fate of their bread and butter, the aircraft industry, will be in a world at peace. In quiet offices in these same plants, as in Ottawa, highly placed executives, Government officials, engineers and all manner of specialists are moving pawns on the chessboard of Canada's aerial future. Elsewhere air line operators, on Government and private payrolls, are trying to visualise the future of internal and intercontinental transportation. Will the Government stick to the Prime Minister's declaration that its own air transport agency, Trans-Canada Air Lines, is going to be the sole operator in the international field? Or will Mr. King relax his pronouncement and permit private enterprise to share in Canada's intercontinental air trade of the future? Such questions as these are debated hotly wherever men of the air get together. In the realm of transport the debate brings out all the old arguments concerning Public versus Private Enterprise. In the realm of manufacturing it exhumes the age-old dispute; Economic Nationalism against International Cooperation. War has taken Canada clear up over its ears into flying and the production of machines to fly, and everybody associated with aviation apparently wants to spend the rest of his life maintaining the association. The fact remains that the whole question is in a state of flux. The answers will not be available until a number of major points can be settled. Over one or two of these Canada may exert sole control. Others, of immense future importance to all men, will depend upon international post-war agreements.

First, about people. Set down that when peace comes at least 200,000 young men who will be in the Royal Canadian Air Force and the RAF will need jobs. Many of them will either want to fly or to service aircraft. While it is reasonable to believe that Canada will maintain an aerial striking force of considerable power for many years to come, not even Air Minister Power or Mr. King can tell today what its strength or its function, national or international, will be. The Air Minister is frankly worried about what is to become of his boys, so much so that shortly before this was written he invited every Member of Parliament to go hide in a corner and come back with suggestions. One point is sure: The future of the R.C.A.F. will be decided by the deals in which we engage with our Allies and partners at the Peace Conference. From this basic guide post, it is fairly safe to assume that nothing approaching war-strength will be maintained. The great majority of present service personnel, therefore, will not find their future livelihood in military aviation.

As to the people engaged in the production of aircraft, what about them? At the present time almost 100,000 men and women are turning out planes in primary plants, and producing bits and pieces in factories great and small throughout the Dominion. Their future as aircrafters rests entirely upon factors over which they have no control and on policies still unborn. The markets available to the Canadian aircraft industry after the war will depend upon

(1) How large an Air Force we maintain,

(2) What production can be absorbed in medium and long-range aircraft for the internal domestic trade,

(3) what aircraft will be required for Canadian intercontinental traffic,

(4) the number of individuals who will want to own their own small planes and

(5) the export trade we can secure in any or all of these brackets, our operation in each field being conditioned by our ability to produce machines in price-competition with the aircrafters of other countries.

The crystal-gazer who can supply the answers to any or all of these would be well advised to drop whatever he is doing and ask for an appointment with Boeing, Vickers, Fleet, De Havilland, Fairchild or Noorduyn, or with Munitions Minister Howe and his Director General of Aircraft Production, Ralph Bell. There should be an easy million dollars to be picked up.

In the aircraft industry, as in the Service, only one factor appears certain; Canada cannot support in peace an aircraft production comparable to its wartime output unless we can develop great external markets. Canada's post-war aircraft production will be further conditioned by the nation's international commitments in the economic sphere, as in the military. And the answers haven't been tabled yet.

So much for what may be called the negative approach. What have we in hand with which to move into the age of air transportation? We have plants capable of producing multi-engined ships, medium range planes and small aircraft, plus our service requirements of the future. Such plants will have to be adapted to new needs as time goes on, but so will other peoples'. We have a superabundance of skilled people in every field associated with flight, production and aviation science. Our aerodrome, repair and overhaul facilities are unexcelled. In the realm of global aviation geography favours us, situated as we are at the crossroads of the two Great Circle routes connecting the Americas with Europe and Asia, but the favours are not as extravagantly bestowed as some enthusiasts would have us believe.

The global aviation discussion actually had its inception in the United States and was launched by what may be called air-nationalists or air-imperialists. The views voiced have run a strange gamut, from the demand that the U.S. acquire all-time ownership of the air lines and air bases it now controls and operates for war purposes all over the world, to the equally irrational presumption that prior rights in the field of global flight should be grabbed as the pay-off for Lend-Lease. The opinions expressed, though largely those of irresponsible (if prominent) people, who know little about aviation and its problems, at least served to toss the bone of contention to every nation's dog, albeit prematurely. Members of the British House of Commons promptly began to ask what Britain is doing to protect its own far-flung transport lines. The U. K. Government set up a committee to explore and report. The British Chambers of Commerce named another to go fact-finding. In Canada Prime Minister King made a policy-speech in which he informed anybody who cared to listen that the future of global aviation is something for the United Nations, acting in concert, to determine, that Canada is prepared to cooperate with all friendly Powers to that end, but that she will stoutly defend her own rights as a nation occupying an important strategic position. All agreements into which we have entered with our allies for the use of bases on Canadian soil will terminate with the end of the war, or immediately thereafter, the Prime Minister added.

It was from this statement of policy that a great misconception arose, through no fault of Mr. King's. People jumped to the conclusion that nobody will be able to fly the Great Circle routes east

Making a Parachute: (Left to right) Hanks of Pure Silk being examined. Spin[?] Silk Yarn at British American Silk Mills. Weaving Silk. Making Web Elasti[c?] Granby Elastic Web Co. Sewing the canopy and cording the shroud lines in the canop[y?] Switlik Canadian Parachutes Limited.

and west without first doing business with Canada. That is largely nonsense. Through the medium of 99-year leases in Labrador and Newfoundland, which were part and parcel of the 1940 destroyers-for-bases deal, and the construction of airfields in its own Alaska, the United States is assured of all the major landing facilities required by long-range aircraft for the intercontinental runs. Canadian aerodromes will be useful primarily for forced landings caused by weather (provided weather is still a flight-factor in the aviation of the future) or engine-trouble. Our meteorological and radio services will be handy but not indispensable to the neighbours. The right to fly through Canadian air is necessary, of course. But if we deny the right to fly over Canadian soil to the aircraft of friendly nations on peaceable missions, whose air, excepting our own, is Canada going to be allowed to use? Carry such modes of reasoning to a logical conclusion and global aviation dies for lack of air to fly in. So put aside the thought that the best routes can't be flown by outsiders other than with Canadian permission. Canada holds strong cards, given to us by geography and made better by the facilities for flight we have developed. But we do not control the disposition of world air-travel and anyone who says that we do is going out on a limb just as long as any occupied by Uncle Sam's aero-imperialists.

The point, then, is what part Canada plans to play in world aviation on its own account. Are we simply going to provide facilities for other nations to use? or are we going into the carrying trade on our own? If so, from Where to Where?

The first two questions have already been answered by the Prime Minister's announcement that intercontinental air transport will be carried out by the Government agency, T.C.A., (because it takes our entry into the world-air for granted), a statement which promptly threw the Private Enterprise element into a state of high, low and medium dither, of which more later. The question From-Where-To-Where? is not as easily answered, for the simple reason that nobody knows what world, or United Nations, or even British Commonwealth policy is going to be. Thus if Canada were to attempt to write its own ticket today, it is extremely likely that we might have to do considerable humble revamping in the not distant future. Here, for example, are questions pointing up the problem:

Is every nation currently engaged in the war going to attempt to establish its own air lines, as in other days it established ship routes, to every other corner of the globe?

Are we going to have Freedom of the Air, as once we had Freedom of the Seas, and allow half a dozen air lines, flying under as many national registries, to compete for traffic on, say, the London to Montreal run?

Or are the United Nations in concert likely to allot specific zones of operation to each other?

All manner of arrangements are possible. When the time comes no doubt they will be explored. But at this writing it is impossible to say who will fly where, and on what terms, because nobody knows. So far as Canada is concerned, all we know is that it is Government intention to draw cards in the game, and that Mr. King says that whatever our job turns out to be it will be done by Trans-Canada, currently engaged in extending its own service eastward to Britain.

Many leaders in Canadian aviation stoutly maintain that the P. M.'s statement in respect of T.C.A. was untimely, that if we do not know the size and extent of the job ahead it is wrong-headed to restrict the performance in advance to any single agency. Staunch defenders of Private Enterprise assert that the C.P.R., which recently jumped into aviation with both feet, has just as much right to enter the world air-carrying trade as T.C.A., an estimate which, it may be said without fear of over-statement, is shared by the Canadian Pacific, which wants to occupy the same

role in world flying which its ships established on the seven seas in other days. In other words the C.P.R. wants to fly from anywhere to anywhere in competition with anybody. Whether they, or any other private Canadian operator who turns up, will be able to do so depends upon the Canadian Government in part, but also on what the international air rules of the future are going to be. Meanwhile the argument is not far removed from the well-worn Public versus Private ownership debate. As these paragraphs are written in June, 1943, the Private Enterprisers are sitting in the game with a four-flush to fill, whereas the Public Ownershippers had three-of-a-kind going in.

In fairness to Mr. King, it must be admitted that he has solid ground under his feet, so far as the record is concerned. Trans-Canada has not cost the public a dime. It operates a highly satisfactory internal service, ample to fill the needs of peacetime cross-continent or inter-city travel, and capable of being stepped up to look after any added call for service. In short, Canada has withheld its internal aviation from the ruinous possibilities of unbridled competition and the policy has worked satisfactorily. In assigning external aviation as well to T.C.A. the Prime Minister is trying to make sure that the scramble for business, with everybody cutting everybody else's throat—and maybe everybody losing his shirt—doesn't happen over the oceans either. He is also keeping Canada free in the field of international negotiation and agreement, which might not be possible if we were committed in advance to a policy of free-for-all. From all of which it becomes crystal clear that the problems of global aviation haven't jelled yet.

There is nothing wrong with our facilities. On our two coasts we have constructed some of the finest airports in the world. We possess great inland termini. Due to the intensity of its air training program the country is pocked with excellent flying fields. The Alaska airway is an outstanding war-miracle. Every scientific device is available to our airmen. Our repair and overhaul facilities are top-notch. Our people at last appear to be air-minded. The primary job, then, is to keep abreast of the game. In the realm of aircraft production a similar statement holds true. Recently the Government, with its eye on post-war global aviation, appropriated monies for the production of designs for new multi-engined ships, the work to be carried out in its own plant at Malton, Ontario, currently engaged in the manufacture of the four-engined Lancaster bomber. Here again a degree of misconception has existed in the public mind. Critics of the new policy tend to laugh it off as dreamy-eyed experimentation. The Director General of Aircraft Production sweeps all such talk aside. "Does this look like experimentation?" Bell asks, pointing to the instructions to the gentlemen at Malton which are to come out with designs for a plane to compete with the best anybody in the world can turn out; a sizeable order. But the program is important if only as it keynotes the outlook of the entire industry, its determination to stay in business on a major scale after the war. To this end a committee has been appointed, on the instructions of the Minister of Munitions and Supply, comprising the following: The Director-General of the Aircraft Production Branch, the Deputy Minister of Transport, the Air Member for Aeronautical Engineering, the Director of the Division of Mechanical Engineering of the National Research Council, the Vice-President of Trans-Canada Air Lines, the President of Canadian Pacific Air Lines, and Mr. Walter Thorn, representing the eight prime aircraft contractors, for the following purposes:

(a) To consider and recommend as to the types of planes most useful in the postwar period, on which design effort should be concentrated;

(b) To recommend what arrangements in the nature of subsidy

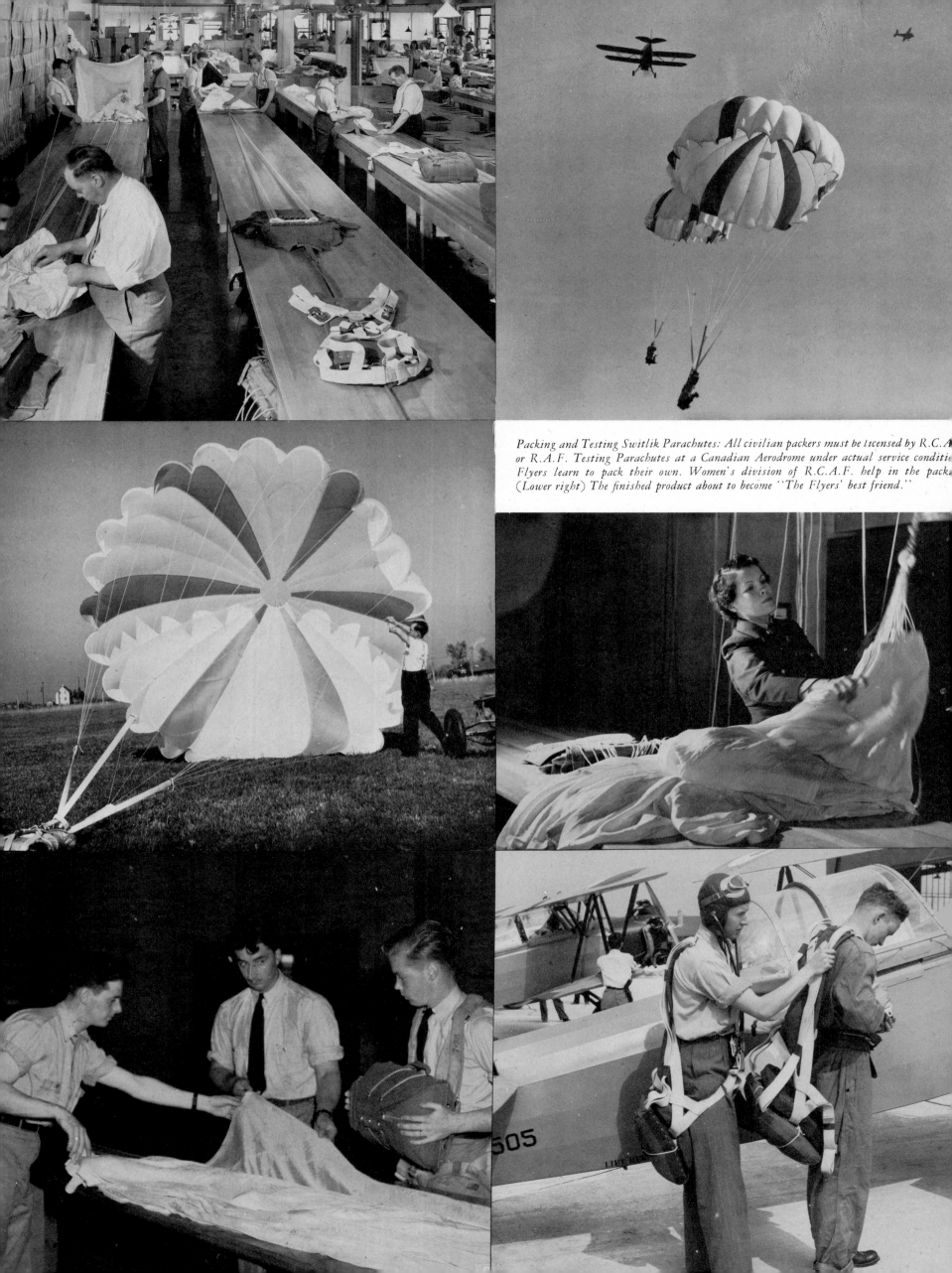

Packing and Testing Switlik Parachutes: All civilian packers must be licensed by R.C.A.F. or R.A.F. Testing Parachutes at a Canadian Aerodrome under actual service conditions. Flyers learn to pack their own. Women's division of R.C.A.F. help in the packing. (Lower right) The finished product about to become "The Flyers' best friend."

or otherwise should be made to enable the Industry to carry out such design work;

(c) To suggest for what period of time such contracts should be made; and

(d) To advise in what manner this work could be most fairly and advantageously distributed throughout the Industry.

It will not be as simple to enter the realm of postwar production particularly in the field of outsize ships, as it is to state the desire and intent, however. Can Canada compete with the manufacturers of the United States for possession even of our own large-ship market? Is the home market sufficient in itself, even with the benefits of a tariff wall (if economic nationalism is to be the order of the post-war era), to support such an industry? At this writing T.C.A. is providing a fast-moving transcontinental service from Newfoundland to B. C. with less than thirty aircraft. Presuming that the first peace job will be to completely replace current flying stock and adding perhaps another thirty aircraft for the Government line's use on external routes, and to fill the needs of private operators (if we are going to have any), what does the big ship plant do to earn its keep thereafter? Certainly overhauls and replacements for the domestic market will not keep it going. Can we capture a place in the export field in competition with our neighbours, with the Old Country and the nations-at-large? Your guess is probably as good as anybody's. For the moment all that can be said is that everybody in the business is laying plans and doing a great deal of thinking, some of it wishful.

Here again the views of the Director General of Aircraft Production, contained in a memorandum to leaders of Canada's aircraft industry which the writer has been privileged to see, are of interest, particularly as the question of costs enters into the discussion, said Mr. Bell:—

"No unit in the Canadian Aircraft Industry will have a Chinaman's chance in the post-war period unless it can produce aircraft as cheaply as, or more cheaply than, our competitors in England or the United States. I don't know of any reason why we shouldn't be able to beat both these countries; in fact, there are many reasons why we should. We have the facilities—than which, there are none better in the world—and it is up to each of us individually and all of us collectively, to devise ways and means which will enable us to compete with all comers . . . Don't immediately start to think up reasons why Canadian costs in aircraft production must be high. If nobody can solve the problem of putting them on a competitive basis with the rest of the world, then, having regard to the post-war period at any rate, you can kiss this industry goodbye, and I am sure none of us want to envisage that prospect, so let us get our thinking caps on; roll up our sleeves; and make up our minds that we are going to produce the craft that we are now building cheaper than they are produced anywhere else in the world—cheaper and better."

As with other aspects of the complex aviation problem, it is impossible to look too far ahead, however, for the good reason that the shape of post-war economy is not yet on view. If we are going back to economic nationalism, presumably we can give the Canadian manufacturer a restricted but protected home market and be similarly restricted ourselves in other peoples' markets. The Canadian market alone will not be sufficient to provide for capacity production, once the replacement job is finished. If the attempt is seriously made to establish a planned world economy to replace the constant struggle for markets and its attendant international jealousies, however, that will be something else again. In point of fact Canada might find itself favourably situated under such conditions, because of the abundance of the raw materials which enter into the production of airplanes available in this country and the existing facilities for the production of instruments, trick undercarriages, and, in fact, every major aircraft component and accessory, bar engines.

The lack of an engine industry is brushed aside by most aircraft leaders as unimportant, due to the expected revolution in what are unctuously termed aircraft propulsion units. With the war behind us, engineers insist that motive power units of completely new design and capability will drive our aircraft through the skies and render obsolescent virtually every engine now in use. Canada, for its part, is keeping abreast of developments and will have access to engines recently developed in Britain, which conceivably may be manufactured here when Peace comes. Hence, say those in the know, we are losing nothing by our lack of an engine industry to equip war-planes of Canadian manufacture, because the engines we might build now will be obsolete on the day of Unconditional Surrender. So once again the answers lie in the future.

Probably of all those engaged in aircraft production today the manufacturer of light aircraft faces fewer problems than any. If signs can be read rightly, the future beyond peace will open a great market in every country for light, low priced, high safety factor aircraft which can be flown cheaply. As the President of one Canadian corporation said to this observer on the day this is written: "The country is a maze of aerodromes. You can fly from anywhere to anywhere. Of the thousands of pilots who will come home from the war, great numbers who can't spend their lives in commercial aviation are going to want to fly their own planes. The kids who came home from the last war all wanted automobiles. Those who come home this time will want to fly. Add them to all the other people who will want to go places as soon as the shooting stops and a wonderful market is in sight!" Maybe this is an over-enthusiastic approach. But these are strange days. Who would have dreamed in 1939 that the twin miracles of the Air Plan and the Aircraft Industry could happen? If everybody wants his own airplane after the war, if all first class mail is to be whisked across the country and overseas by air (as it may), if all the tourists choose the world's airlines in preference to the sea lanes the Canadian aircrafter has nothing to worry about.

Meanwhile the future of world aviation, and therefore, that of Canadian aviation is in a state of flux. Most of the problems must await the coming of peace for settlement, if only because they do not come entirely within our own control, and because we must share the responsibility of shaping the world of tomorrow. Having changed overnight from an agricultural and natural resources nation into one of the world's great industrial producers our problems will be many and varied. Because aviation is a young industry, run by young men in a young country, however, our chances ought to be good . . . provided we do not lag behind the parade. The lag seems unlikely, to judge by all the planning and arguing to be seen and heard as this book is finished.

INDEX TO BOOK TWO — THE INDUSTRIAL MIRACLE (*Continued*)

INDEX TO AIRCRAFT AND ENGINE TYPES

INDEX TO AIRCRAFT AND ENGINE TYPES

GLOSSARY OF ABBREVIATIONS

R.F.C.
Royal Flying Corps

R.C.A.F.
Royal Canadian Air Force

R.A.F.
Royal Air Force

C.A.F.
Canadian Air Force, predecessor to Royal Canadian Air Force

A.O.C.
Air Officer Commanding

G.O.C.
General Officer Commanding

AC/2:
Aircraftman, Second Class

L/AC:
Leading Aircraftman

W.A.G.
Wireless-Air Gunner

I.T.S.
Initial Training School

E.F.T.S.
Elementary Flying Training School

S.F.T.S.
Service Flying Training School

A.O.S.
Air Observers School

A.N.S.
Air Navigation School

B. & G.S.
Bombing and Gunnery School

C.F.S.
Central Flying School

C.W.A.A.F.
Canadian Women's Auxiliary Air Force (Now R.C.A.F.-Women's Division).

C.O.T.C.
Canadian Officers' Training Corps

V.C.
Victoria Cross

D.S.O.
Distinguished Service Order

D.S.C.
Distinguished Service Cross

M.C.
Military Cross

D.F.C.
Distinguished Flying Cross

A.F.C.
Air Force Cross

D.C.M.
Distinguished Conduct Medal

INDEX TO
ANNOUNCEMENTS OF INDUSTRIES REPRESENTED IN
"CANADA'S WAR IN THE AIR"

INDUSTRY'S ROLE
IN
CANADA'S WAR IN THE AIR

DIGNIFIED and informative display advertising is, in itself, an important factor in Canada's war effort. This view finds confirmation in the volume of institutional publicity undertaken by leading Canadian and American corporations, engaged wholly, or almost so, in the production of essential war materials, and the value of whose contribution to final victory is beyond assessment.

The executives of these corporations have had vision extending beyond the moment, and they have seen clearly that national unity is helped by the dissemination of authentic information as to what they are now doing.

A better understanding is created throughout the country by the fact that from corporations down to the humblest citizen a common effort is being made in the hour of peril, and that in the years to come the public will realize and appreciate that the experiences of war production and the lessons learned in efficiency and economy will enable these corporations to be of better and greater service.

Such an outlook is particularly necessary in Canada, where industrialization has increased by leaps and bounds during the war years, to the point that our economic future has been cast in a completely new mould, for to-day Canada, whose pre-war economy rested on the cornerstones of agriculture and natural resource industries, has become the fourth greatest manufacturing nation of the world.

The world, as well as Canadians themselves, needs to be told what has been done.

The story of the contribution of Canadian Industry to the building of the aircraft flown by the young men of the Royal Canadian Air Force is one of glowing achievement and permanent interest.

In the pages which follow there will be found the announcements of many of the industries serving the Allied Cause, without whose cooperation this book could not have been produced.

In almost every instance they gave their support sight unseen, out of nothing but the belief that the story of "Canada's War in the Air" should be told.

A bow then, to each and all of them.

Publisher.

Aug. 20, 1943.

Sacrifice ?

The name "Dieppe" resounds today ;
  A stirring battle call
Of men who counted not the cost,
  Of men who gave their all !

The outmatched crew of the "Raccoon"
  Fought till their ship went down:
So did our sons and brothers on
  The corvette "Charlottetown" !

The grim destroyer "Ottawa"
  Gave all she had to give;
Her gallant skipper, half her crew,
  They died that we might live!

Each day adds to the mounting roll
  Of flying heroes, who
Have met their rendezvous with death
  That freedom shall win through !

Oh, how can we, in safety here
  Count pennies or upbraid:
What is our sacrifice compared
  With that these men have made ?

G. R. Allerton

For Distinguished Service

IN AIRCRAFT PRODUCTION

To COMPANIES, as well as individuals, engaged in this struggle for the triumph of freedom, awards of distinction for meritorious service rendered are fitting tributes of courage, and no organization is more richly deserving of such honour than Canadian Car and Foundry Company, Limited.

Truly, it can be said that Canadian Car and Foundry Company, Limited, through its self sustained group of plants throughout Canada offers greater facilities for the complete manufacture of aircraft and all of the many components, and accessories related thereto, than any other industrialist on this Continent.

Long before the present war was forced on a righteous people, Canadian Car had foreseen the threatening future, and quietly, efficiently, had commenced the transition in its idle plants, from builders of railroad equipment to constructors of aircraft.

As thoroughly as they had through the years developed the manufacture of rolling stock of all descriptions, they now applied their knowledge of production to the design, fabrication and assembly of aircraft for National Defence — Commercial Operation — All Out War!

Not content alone with the making of the aircraft itself, they embarked upon a program of supplying the nation with squadrons of ready-for-flight military planes, undertaking within their own factories, the design and manufacture of aircraft engines, propellers, and the complementary machined parts, castings and forgings.

The skies of harassed London were darkened with the surge of Hawker Hurricanes from the Company's plants; roaring, diving machines of destiny, bearing so valiantly the burden of repelling a vicious attacker.

These planes are still issuing forth from the assembly lines of the Company in an unbroken chain of the tools Churchill demanded.

For the shaping of the future guiders of such sky armament, Canadian Car build the training craft in which the fledgling pilot is groomed for combat through the British Commonwealth Air Training Plan. Twin-engine Ansons, in vast array, emerge from assembly lines fed from the associated plants of the Company to join wings with the flight upon flight of these mobile schoolrooms.

All of this co-ordinated, smoothly running, competent effort is dedicated to an achievement of deadly and grim purpose — the total destruction of a barbarous and unholy force, but when this task has been successfully accomplished, Canadian Car will convert all its resources and practical experience to peace time pursuits of manufacture; once again supply the needs of a progressive nation whose citizens travel the Airlanes.

CANADIAN CAR & FOUNDRY COMPANY LIMITED

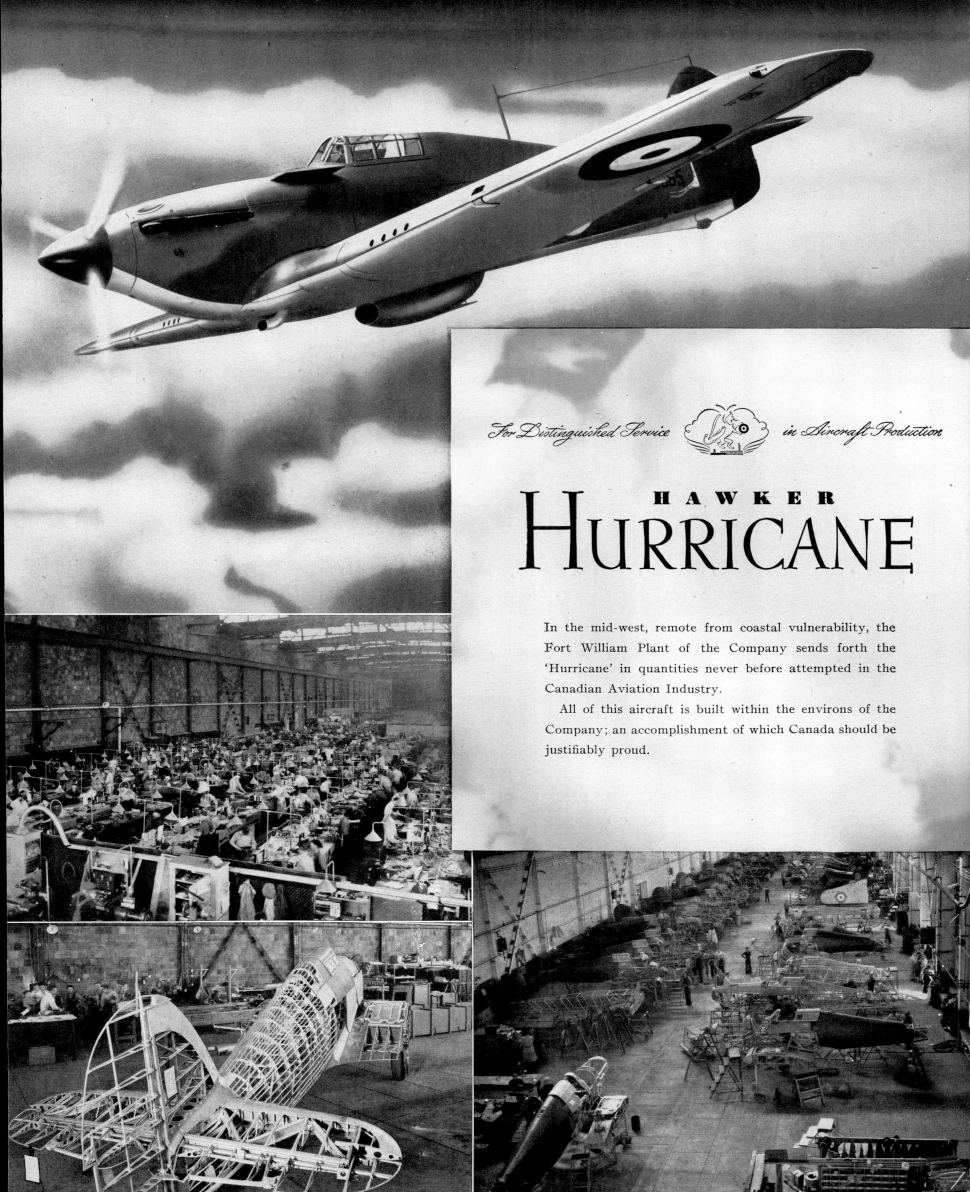

For Distinguished Service *in Aircraft Production*

HAWKER
HURRICANE

In the mid-west, remote from coastal vulnerability, the Fort William Plant of the Company sends forth the 'Hurricane' in quantities never before attempted in the Canadian Aviation Industry.

All of this aircraft is built within the environs of the Company; an accomplishment of which Canada should be justifiably proud.

CANADIAN CAR & FOUNDRY COMPANY LIMITED

For Distinguished Service in Aircraft Production

AVRO ANSON

In the Amherst plant of the Company the Avro Anson Twin-engine Training Aircraft is produced. Sub-assemblies come from the Montreal Plants and in addition to the building of the Canadian Anson, the Amherst Plant assembles and services the English Anson and other training aircraft used in the Maritimes.

For Distinguished Service in Aircraft Production

SBW-1

CURTISS
DIVE BOMBER

The outstanding facilities of this Company for the production of Aircraft is further evidenced in its recent choice as builders of Curtiss Dive Bombers.

For Distinguished Service in *Aircraft Production*

ENGINES

The Company through its own engineering division, designed and completed an aircraft radial engine in the 180 H.P. class for use in the lighter training planes of the British Commonwealth Air Training Plan.

The Company has under development a 3000 H.P. fuel oil injection engine capable of powering the mammoth Bombers of the immediate future.

For Distinguished Service — in Aircraft Production

PROPELLERS

In a separate plant in the vicinity of Montreal the Company produces complete aircraft propellers. Both blade and hub is of an original design from within the Company itself and is for use with engines within the 300-1100 H.P. range.

The propeller is a hydraulically controllable unit, with constant speed and full feathering features optional on all models. The blades are of solid aluminum alloy, and as an adjunct to hub and blade, this division supplies hydraulic governors and booster control valve pumps.

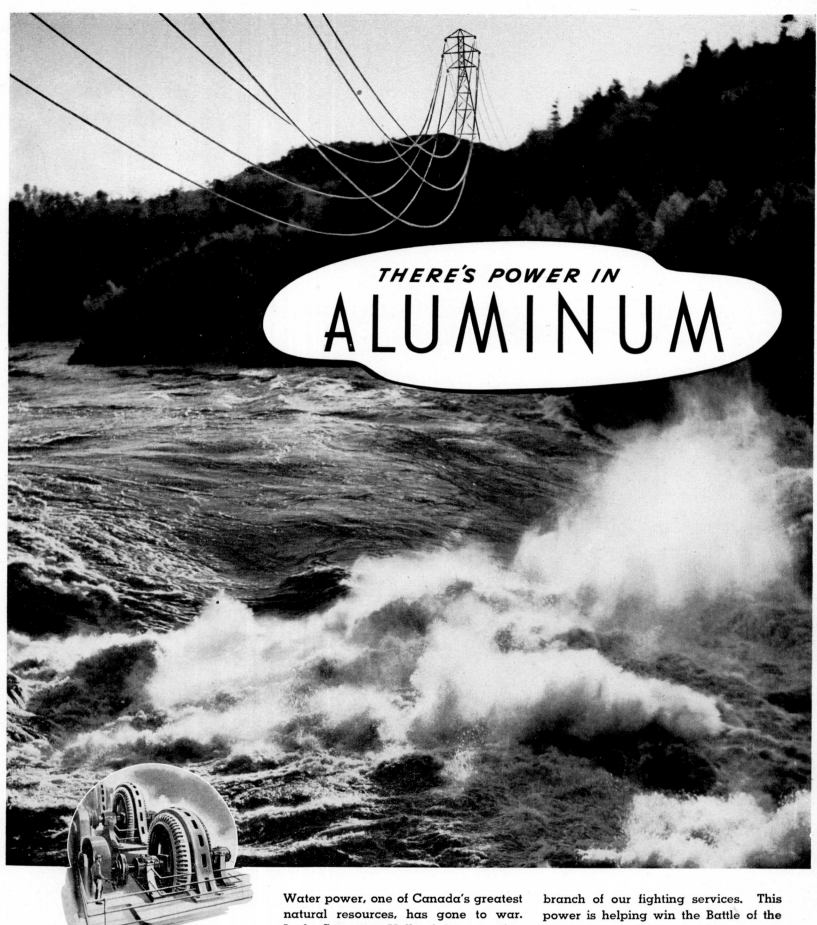

THERE'S POWER IN
ALUMINUM

Water power, one of Canada's greatest natural resources, has gone to war. In the Saguenay Valley it is generating energy in tremendous volume to transform British Guiana bauxite into strong, light aluminum, the metal of air mastery and victory.

Aluminum production depends on power. Aluminum *is* power in every branch of our fighting services. This power is helping win the Battle of the Atlantic; played a part in throwing back the Germans in Russia; helped defeat the vaunted Luftwaffe over England and is aiding in carrying aerial warfare to the enemy with ever-mounting fury. It is power that means final victory.

ALUMINUM COMPANY OF CANADA, LIMITED

ALUMINUM GIVES WINGS TO *Victory*

From Canada comes raw
and fabricated Aluminum
to Give Wings to Victory.

Men of the Empire are aloft
on Wings of Aluminum.

ALUMINUM COMPANY OF CANADA, LIMITED

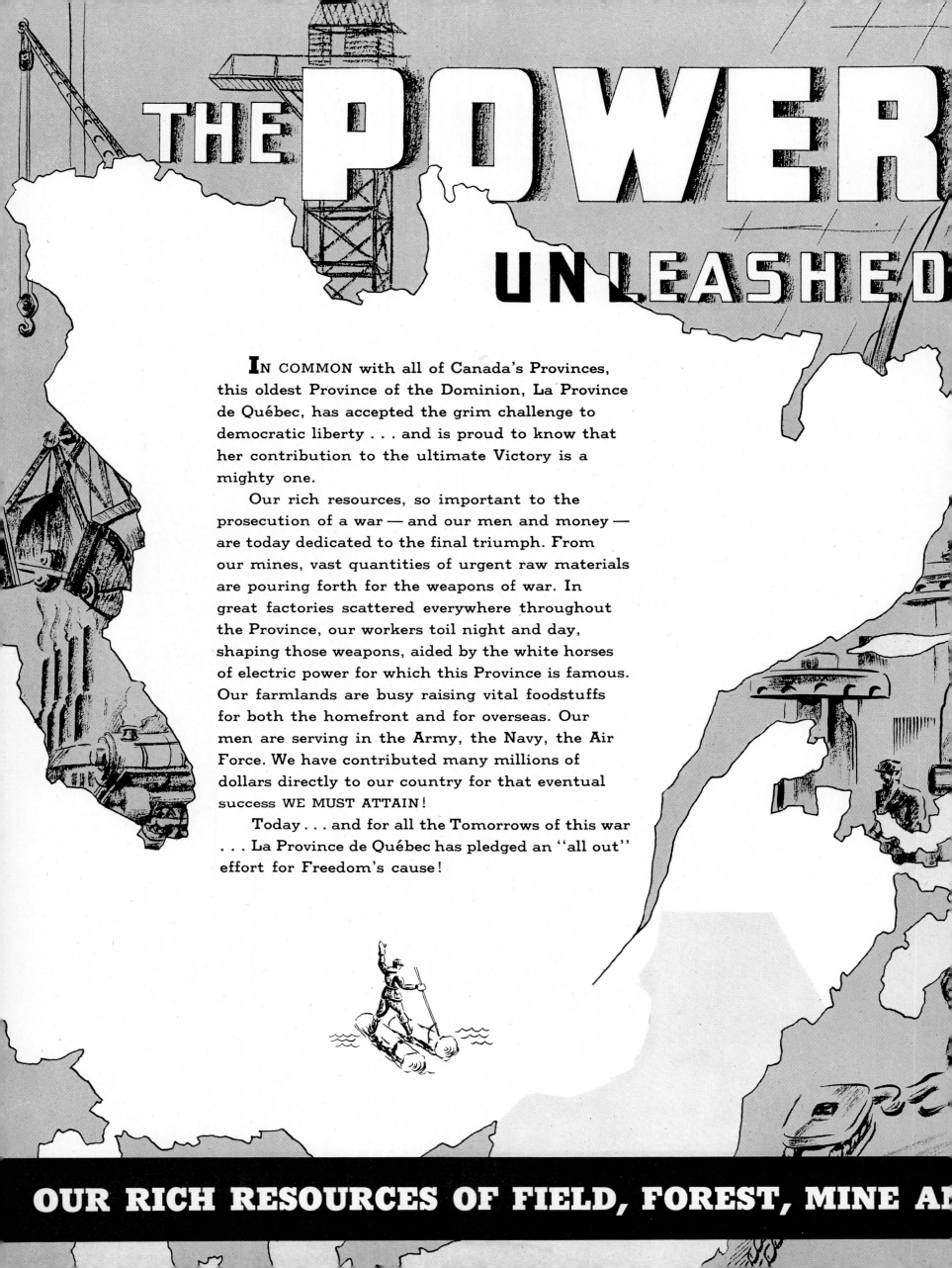

THE **POWER** UNLEASHED

IN COMMON with all of Canada's Provinces, this oldest Province of the Dominion, La Province de Québec, has accepted the grim challenge to democratic liberty . . . and is proud to know that her contribution to the ultimate Victory is a mighty one.

Our rich resources, so important to the prosecution of a war — and our men and money — are today dedicated to the final triumph. From our mines, vast quantities of urgent raw materials are pouring forth for the weapons of war. In great factories scattered everywhere throughout the Province, our workers toil night and day, shaping those weapons, aided by the white horses of electric power for which this Province is famous. Our farmlands are busy raising vital foodstuffs for both the homefront and for overseas. Our men are serving in the Army, the Navy, the Air Force. We have contributed many millions of dollars directly to our country for that eventual success WE MUST ATTAIN!

Today . . . and for all the Tomorrows of this war . . . La Province de Québec has pledged an "all out" effort for Freedom's cause!

OUR RICH RESOURCES OF FIELD, FOREST, MINE A

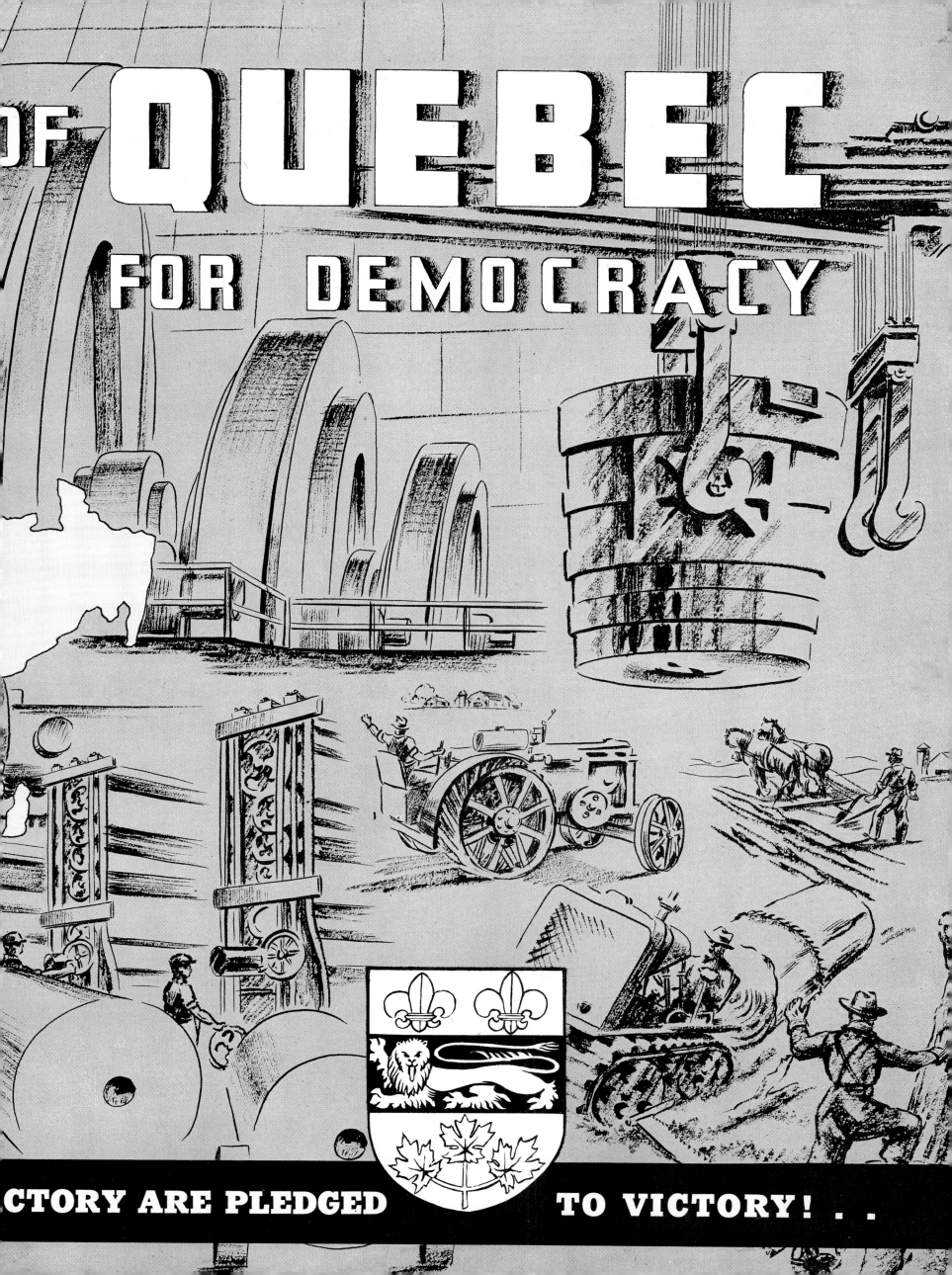

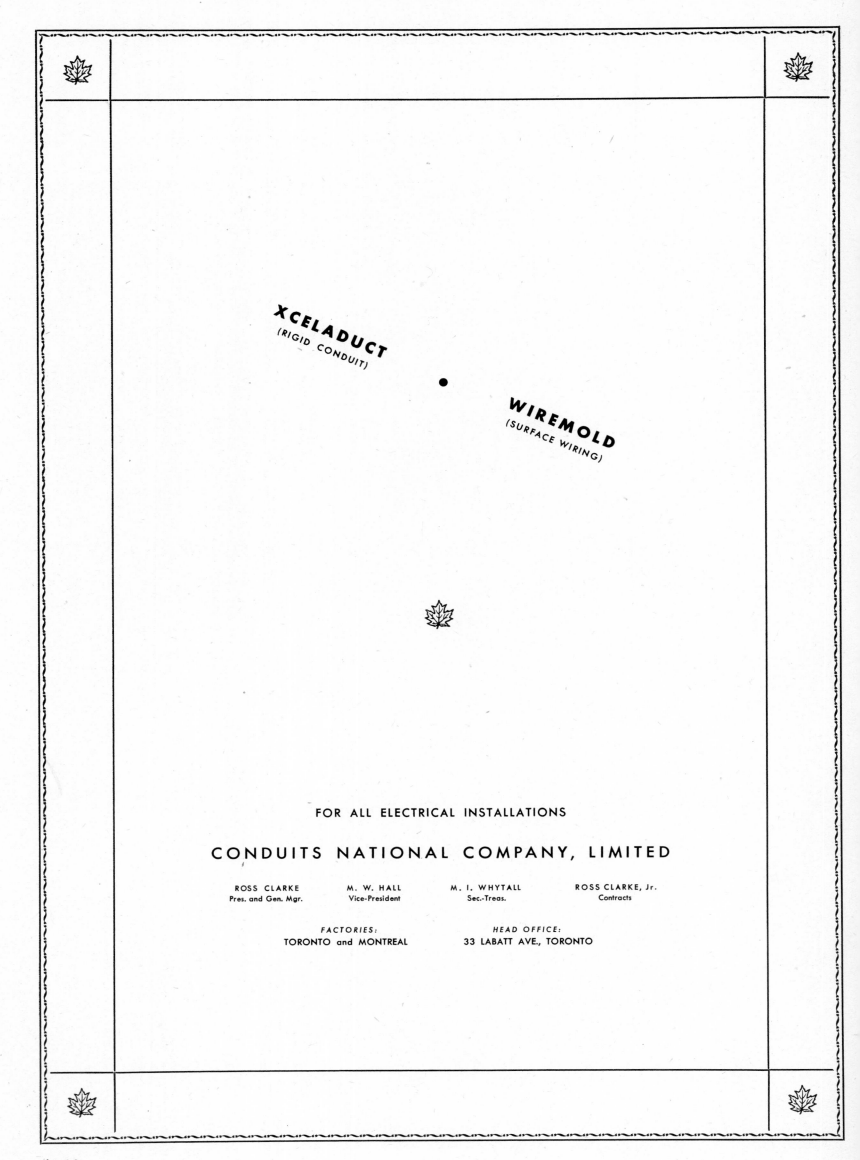

XCELADUCT
(RIGID CONDUIT)

WIREMOLD
(SURFACE WIRING)

FOR ALL ELECTRICAL INSTALLATIONS

CONDUITS NATIONAL COMPANY, LIMITED

ROSS CLARKE
Pres. and Gen. Mgr.

M. W. HALL
Vice-President

M. I. WHYTALL
Sec.-Treas.

ROSS CLARKE, Jr.
Contracts

FACTORIES:
TORONTO and MONTREAL

HEAD OFFICE:
33 LABATT AVE., TORONTO

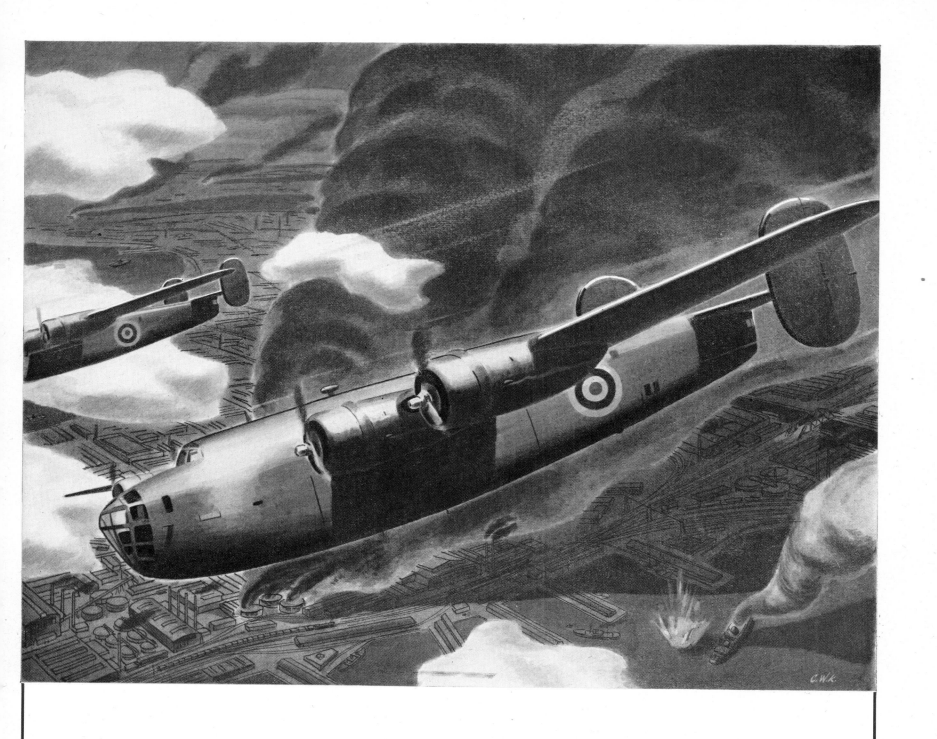

PER ARDUA
AD ASTRA

HULL STEEL FOUNDRIES LIMITED · HULL · QUEBEC

CONTROL OF THE AIR . . . A COMBINED ACHIEVEMENT

VITAL to victory, control of the air will be attained through the bravery of our airmen, the skill of our ground crews, the diligence of our workmen, the capacity of our industry, the aggressiveness of our management, the persistence of our engineers.

No single group, no single industry, can claim more than a share of the credit. Working together each has an indispensable part to play in helping to obtain and maintain supremacy in the air.

We at Trane are only *one* link in this chain. In supplying heating equipment for hangars, workshops, offices, sleeping quarters, hospitals and mess halls in the air training schools across Canada, Trane met the need for economical, efficient,

quick-action heat distributing units in the quantities demanded. Trane engineers, working to Government specifications, developed air conditioning equipment for Link Trainer rooms to protect delicate parts and to contribute to the efficiency of the operators. Trane equipment is being used to cool the oil when overhauled airplane engines are being tested. Similar cooling equipment, supplied by Trane, is essential in the successful operation of the practice gun turrets so important to the training of airmen.

These are a few of the ways Trane executives, engineers and employees are working with the Government, helping to meet the numerous new problems as they arise in the field of *heating*, *cooling* and *air conditioning*.

TRANE COMPANY OF CANADA LIMITED

Heating—Cooling      *Air Conditioning*

HEAD OFFICE AND FACTORY, TORONTO   **ENGINEERING OFFICES, ACROSS CANADA**

A Salute to the Corvettes of the Air

... from Canada's sea-going corvettes!

These are the fast-moving, hard-striking wasps of modern war . . . the Spits, the Defiants and the Hurricanes, flying over the roof of the world . . . the sleek, manoeuverable corvettes in the mountainous rollers of the Seven Seas. One strikes at the Hun air-raider, escorts the huge bombers over Berlin, Hamburg, Cologne and Mannheim. The other seeks out the sub and the surface raider, convoys the food and munitions of war to the fronts of the United Nations, brings the gallant young grads of the Air Training Plan safely into port "over there". They are a team, one afloat and the other aloft; corvettes of the sea and the air. This, then is our salute, the salute of the seaman to the airman. Good luck and a safe return to each of us!

Published in fraternal greeting to the men of the corvettes and the men of the skies, and in admiration of the builders of Canada's great Air Training Plan, from men who are proud to have played a part in Canada's great Navy building program . . .

MARINE INDUSTRIES LIMITED

BUILDERS OF CORVETTES, MINESWEEPERS, FREIGHTERS, ETC. FOR THE UNITED NATIONS

"THAT FREEDOM SHALL NOT PERISH"

When Dependability Counts Most . . .

More than thirty years ago, when aeroplanes were fledglings, Goodyear was actively pioneering in the field of aeroplane tires. Today, when thousands of speedy fighters and high-flying bombers are rolling off the production lines, Goodyear still leads the field in tire, wheel and brake assemblies. As aeroplanes progressed to finer and finer performance, so did Goodyear tires . . . until . . . today, in the aviation field as in others, Goodyear is "The Greatest Name in Rubber".

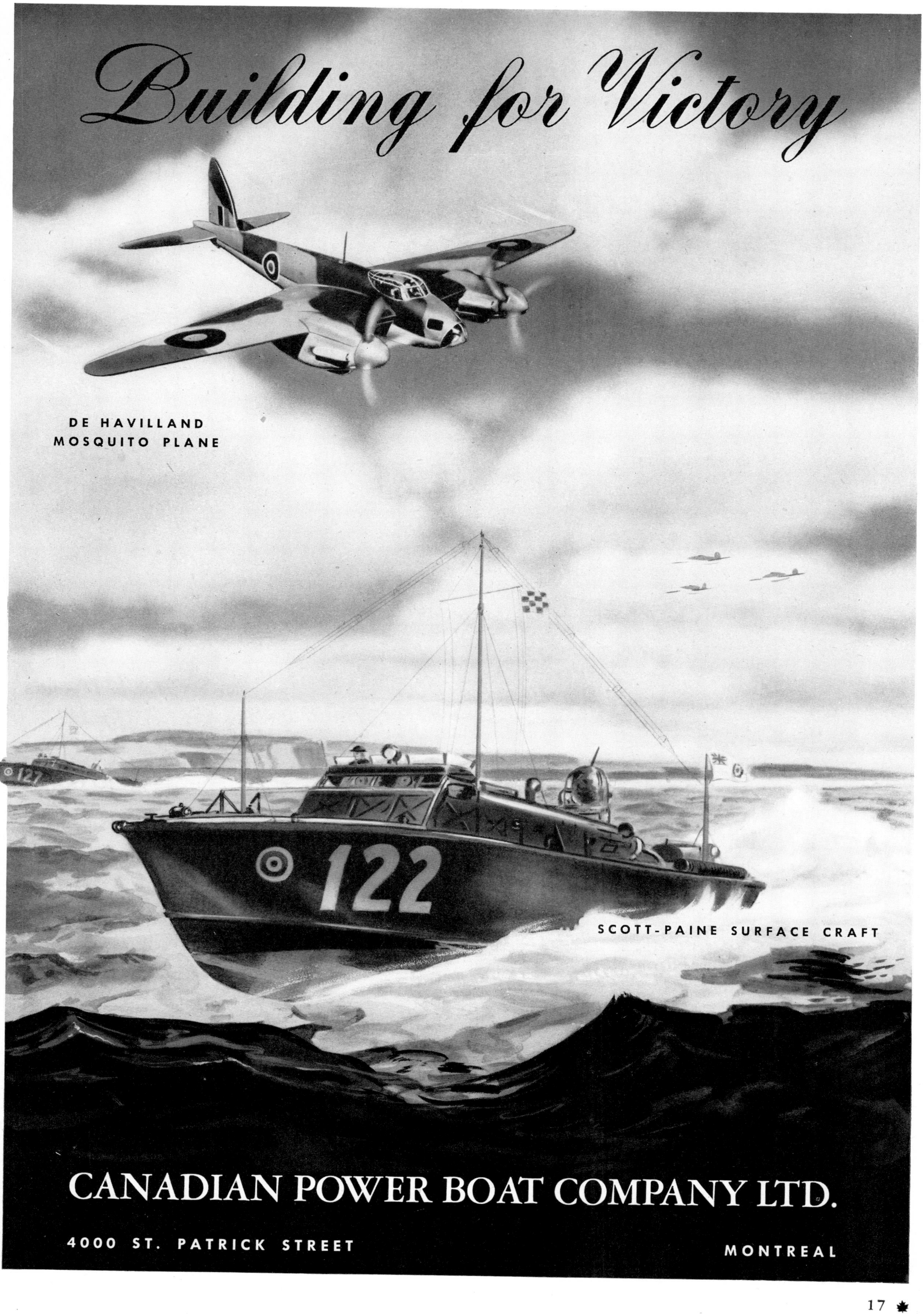

Building for Victory
DE HAVILLAND
MOSQUITO PLANE
122
SCOTT-PAINE SURFACE CRAFT
CANADIAN POWER BOAT COMPANY LTD.
4000 ST. PATRICK STREET
MONTREAL

PARTS THAT PLAY THEIR PART...

WE ARE PROUD that it has been possible for us to play an important part in Canada's War in the air by supplying to the aircraft industry many of the vital parts and equipment units required for the production of Trainer, Fighter, and Bomber aeroplanes.

The co-operation of these companies for whom we are exclusive representatives in Canada has made this service possible.

AIR ASSOCIATES INCORPORATED . . . . . . BENDIX, NEW JERSEY
HOMER D. BRONSON COMPANY . . . . . . BEACON FALLS, CONN.
CHAMPION AVIATION PRODUCTS COMPANY . . LOS ANGELES, CAL.
CRUCIBLE STEEL COMPANY OF AMERICA . . . . NEW YORK, N.Y.
DZUS FASTENER COMPANY . . . . BABYLON, N.Y.
LORD MANUFACTURING COMPANY . . . . . . ERIE, PENNSYLVANIA
PARKER APPLIANCE COMPANY . . . . CLEVELAND, OHIO
RUSSELL MANUFACTURING COMPANY . . . . MIDDLETOWN, CONN.
SUNCOOK MILLS . . . . NEW YORK, N.Y.
JUBILEE MANUFACTURING COMPANY . . . . . OMAHA, NEBRASKA

RAILWAY & POWER ENGINEERING
CORPORATION LIMITED
MONTREAL . . HAMILTON . . NORTH BAY . . **TORONTO** . . . . WINNIPEG . . . . VANCOUVER

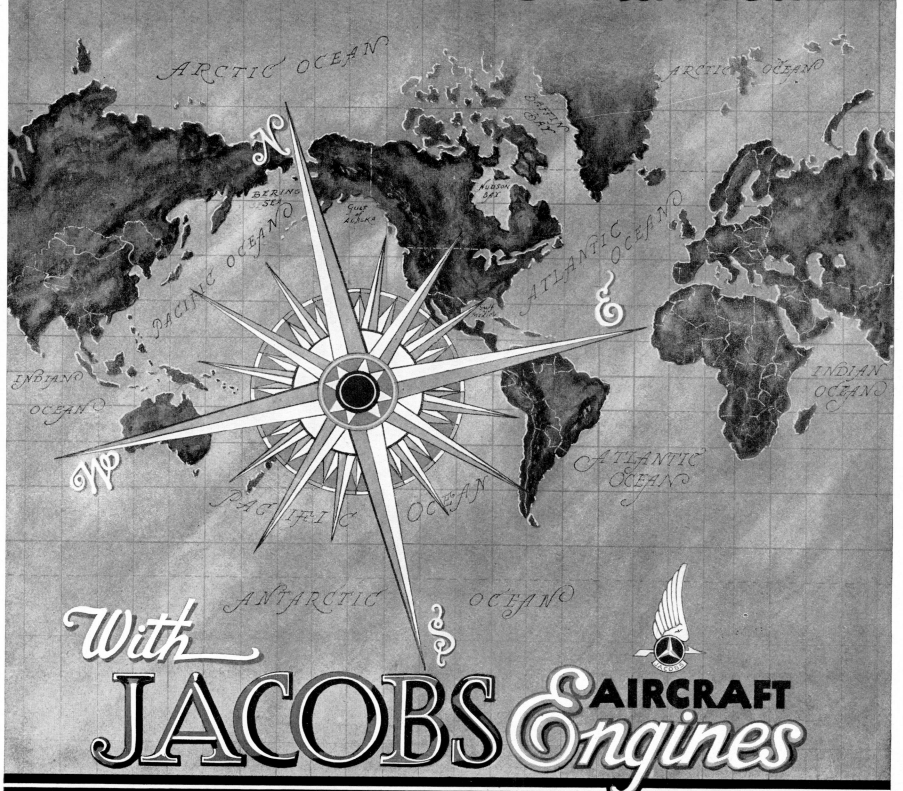

IN ALL BATTLE AREAS ARE FOUND
BOMBER PILOTS *trained*

With JACOBS AIRCRAFT Engines

"...with melting wax
and loosened strings
sunk hapless Icarus
on unfaithful wings"

REMEMBER ICARUS—the pathetic figure in Greek mythology who flew with wings held together by wax and string?

Poor navigator, Icarus. He flew too near the sun. Wax melted. Icarus fell into the sea.

Refrigeration would have helped Icarus. Just as it is helping the wartime wings of Canada.

Link Trainers, for instance, are being air-conditioned by Frigidaire.

Modern methods call for chilling of airframe rivets and other metal parts by Frigidaire.

Frigidaire equipment protects the emergency food supplies in R.C.A.F. rescue boats.

In nearly half a hundred Air Training Schools and Depots across Canada Frigidaire protects the wholesomeness of food, cools drinking water, etc.

Yes, Frigidaire too, is playing its part, albeit a small one, in "Canada's War in the Air".

FRIGIDAIRE PRODUCTS OF CANADA, LIMITED
Leaside, Ontario

20

Alert!!

On all R.C.A.F. and R.A.F. Aerodromes, our "Crash Tenders" await the warning order from the Signal Tower . . . "Pilot expects landing trouble on Aircraft . . . ."

Under all weather conditions our all-wheel-drive **Marmon-Herrington Ford V-8** equipment is always ready to go, straight to the point of landing.

Mud, sand, snow, or other hazards are no obstacle in getting to the spot in the shortest possible time and with the most efficient life-saving apparatus.

In the theatre of War, we serve in other ways too. We read, with personal pride; "The enemies' patrols have been contacted and destroyed." The same engineering achievement, the all-wheel-drive **Marmon-Herrington Ford V-8** chassis, drives many thousands of armoured cars, gun tractors and other vehicles of the United Nations in the Battle of Freedom.

Canadian Traction Limited

WINDSOR   MONTREAL   OTTAWA

TOP PRODUCTION FOR VICTORY

All "IN"

for "All Out"

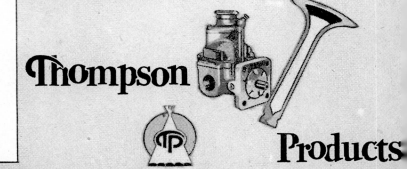

_For what avail the Plough or Sail,
or Land or Life, if Freedom fail ?

EMERSON

BECAUSE without freedom, the fruits of labour —the fullness of civilized living are as dust, we Canadians, free people in a free land, are pledged to all-out effort for all-out victory. Knowing that Freedom itself is at stake in this titanic struggle it is for us to afford all aid and strength to Great Britain in her time of greatest need.

This Company is proud of its place in the vanguard of Canada's great industrial army, an army which is helping to produce the tremendous flood of supplies now steadily streaming into the theatres of war. Proud, too, of its close association with the growth and achievements of the British Commonwealth Air Training Plan.

RENFREW ELECTRIC
AND REFRIGERATOR
CO. LIMITED
Renfrew *Ontario*

ight

"A wrong label on a cartridge can cause a wrong signal. A wrong signal can destroy a plane and its crew, perhaps a squadron. A defective flare can be more costly in lives and money than a defective bomb or shell. By the colour of a flare a squadron of flyers can live or die. Such is the importance of pyrotechnic signals in modern war."

On parachute flares the bomber aircrew depend for lighting brilliantly, "Target for Tonight" — or for forced landings by night — or for lighting the enemy's terrain ready to photograph.

We are proud that our task is to provide the brave flying lads of the United Nations with a complete range of Flares, Pyrotechnics and Sea Markers, and other equipment in this highly important part of the Road to Victory.

INTERNATIONAL FLARE SIGNAL CO. LIMITED
MACDONALD METAL PRODUCTS CO., LIMITED
MACDONALD CHEMICALS LIMITED

WATERLOO, P. Q.

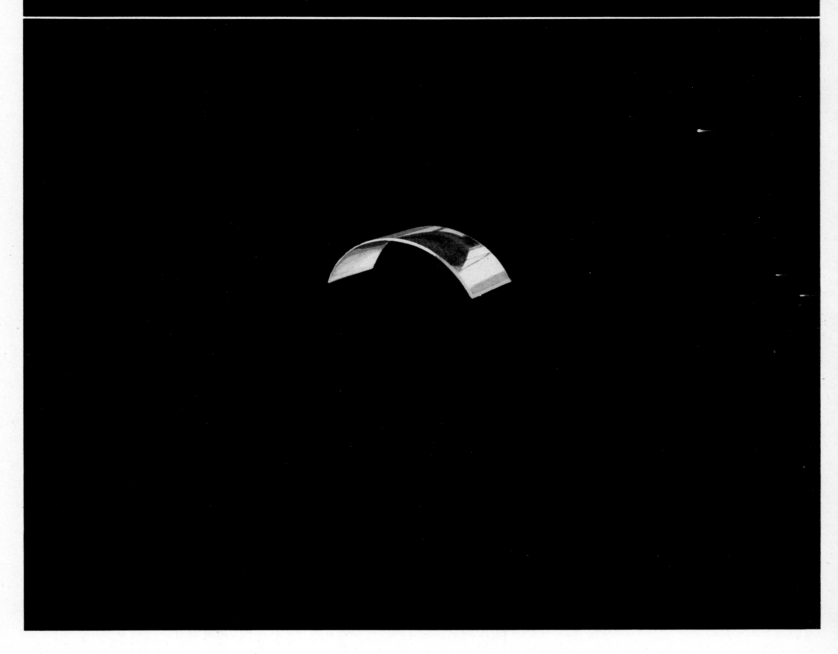

Between Humanity and the Dark . . .

POISED between human lives and the hostile night rides a thin curved plate, smooth and transparent as glass.

It is one of the thousands of parts that comprise a modern warplane, yet perhaps none has a more essential role. Set in the cowl above the pilot's head, it shields him from wind and weather and gives him clear vision overhead.

This panel is of Lucite, a transparent plastic. It came from the plant of Duplate Canada Limited at Oshawa, Ontario, where this and other plastic parts for Canada's fighting planes are made.

Foreseeing the urgent need that would arise for plastic parts in a Canada at war, Duplate installed extensive equipment for molding and fabricating these versatile materials. Today it is making plastic parts for airplanes, motor vehicles, electrical apparatus and other wartime and domestic equipment, the demand for which is increasing by leaps and bounds.

In addition, Duplate has added to its specialized equipment for making glass—laminated safety glass, specially hardened glass to withstand terrific shock and strain, glass for naval and merchant vessels, for

searchlights, for army vehicles and motor cars, for new and revolutionizing uses.

Thus, in the service of war-girded Canada, Canadian enterprise has developed at Oshawa an undertaking of wide scope and mounting capacity, dedicated to the furtherance of our war effort.

———

DUPLATE
CANADA, LIMITED
OSHAWA, ONTARIO

OFFICE OF THE PRIME MINISTER

CANADA

Ottawa,
November 19, 1941

F. G. Robinson, Esq.,
    President,
        Canadian Pulp and Paper Association,
            3420 University Street,
                Montreal, Quebec.

Dear Mr. Robinson:

I thank you for your letter of the 17th of November, enclosing a copy of the report on the operations of the Wartime Machine Shop Board.

The programme which has been carried out under the direction of this Board is assisting materially in speeding up war production. To the Executive Committee of the Canadian Pulp and Paper Association, through whose interest and initiative the Board was organized, and to the workers in the mills, whose loyal co-operation has made possible the success of the programme, I wish to extend, for myself and for my colleagues in the Government, an expression of warm thanks and appreciation.

Yours very sincerely,

W. L. Mackenzie King.

THE PULP AND PAPER
INDUSTRY OF CANADA
972 SUN LIFE BUILDING MONTREAL

Forward to Freedom!

Canada's Soldiers, Sailors and Airmen wear our products — for we specialize in web equipment and accessories.

It is in this way that we have been honoured with the privilege of contributing our services in the Canadian War effort and today, our factory and our employees are working night and day for the Armed Forces.

Ours may not be a great share in deciding the eventual Victory, but, we are glad to be playing our part in the scheme of things — and take this opportunity of expressing our admiration of the superb work of the gallant R.C.A.F. and all the armed forces. CARRY ON, CANADA!

MONTREAL SUSPENDER & UMBRELLAS LIMITED

M O N T R E A L

DOW

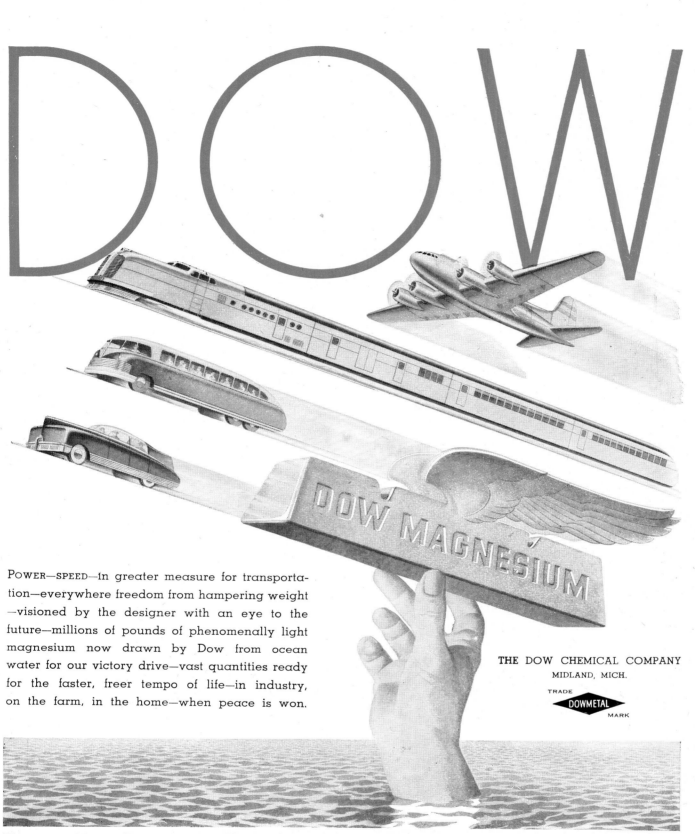

POWER—SPEED—in greater measure for transportation—everywhere freedom from hampering weight—visioned by the designer with an eye to the future—millions of pounds of phenomenally light magnesium now drawn by Dow from ocean water for our victory drive—vast quantities ready for the faster, freer tempo of life—in industry, on the farm, in the home—when peace is won.

THE DOW CHEMICAL COMPANY
MIDLAND, MICH.

TRADE ◆ DOWMETAL ◆ MARK

MAGNESIUM

The Lightest Structural Metal . . . One-third Lighter Than Any Other in Common Use

Providing the Tools to Finish the Job

MONTREAL OFFICE
SHOWROOM AND STORE

AS in 1914, Williams & Wilson Limited is again throwing every ounce of energy . . . every resource . . . into the task of aiding Canada's ever-growing war effort. Throughout the nation, the company's engineers are on the job—helping in the giant task of setting up new production lines, providing the machine tools and machinery supplies so vital to the sinews of modern war.

Fortunately, the first thunders of war found Williams & Wilson Limited well-prepared for its job. The greatest mechanical and production developments in the world's history had come about during the fifty years of the company's business life. Year by year, as Canada's industry grew, Williams & Wilson Limited had been privileged to grow with it—to supply the type of machine tools and mill supplies needed to meet production demands which become constantly more exacting.

Vast as are the manufacturing exigencies of today, this half-century's experience has provided the solid bed-rock of expert knowledge, the trained personnel and the facilities to meet the emergency. Hence, it is not surprising that among the largest plants in the country are those equipped almost entirely by Williams & Wilson Limited.

TORONTO OFFICE
SHOWROOM AND STORE

1891 **WILLIAMS & WILSON LIMITED** **1941**
TORONTO   MONTREAL   QUEBEC

1891 - FIFTY YEARS - 1941

Frederick C. Wilson
Founder

Frederick W. Wilson
President

THE MEN - THE ORGANIZATION
THE SERVICE

Fifty years ago, Frederick C. Wilson assembled a group of engineers and began operations in a modest way under the firm name of Williams & Wilson. Fifty years have passed and the organization founded in 1891 has earned a leading position in the world of engineers, manufacturers of engineering equipment and suppliers of machine tools and machinery supplies. The secret of its success is found in the happy faculty of its founder in attaching to himself men of ability and integrity and the unusual loyalty of his staff.

The firm of Williams & Wilson Limited is proud that its innumerable facilities, covering 80,000 square feet of floor space, are actively engaged every minute of the day in supplying the tools that will finish the job!

WILLIAMS & WILSON
LIMITED

ESTABLISHED 1891

TORONTO • **MONTREAL** • **QUEBEC**

Serves the Nation in War and Peace

TRANS-CANADA AIR LINES are an indispensable arm of transport to a nation at war. In peace they accelerated the tempo of Canadian life. Now they operate over a 4,850-mile route from the Atlantic to the Pacific, from Newfoundland to British Columbia, to speed men, materials and mails essential to Victory.

They fly 8,250,000 miles a year. In 1942, they carried 2,260,000 pounds of air mail, 106,000 passengers and 396,000 pounds of air express.

In addition to a great transportation task, T.C.A. repairs and overhauls military aircraft including engines, propellers and instruments. T.C.A. crews are making flights across the Atlantic as part of the war effort and T.C.A. ground crews overhaul and maintain the trans-oceanic transports from Canada. In peace and war alike Trans-Canada Air Lines have one constant unvarying objective — to serve the Nation.

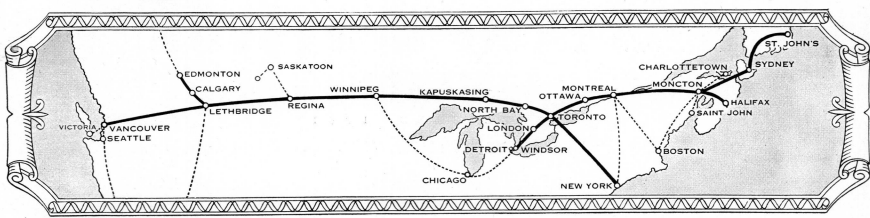

Cafeteria — — No. 1 Plant — — No. 2 Plant — — No. 4 Plant —

AIRCRAFT REPAIR LTD. —1943— 276,000 SQ. FT. Floor Space.

The above photograph shows our plant as it appears to-day

Below: Photograph of our 98th Street Shop, taken in 1940.

AIRCRAFT REPAIR LTD. 98 ST. —1940— 12,000 SQ. FT. Floor Space.

• Contractors to the Department of Munitions and Supply for the overhaul, repair and assembly of Aircraft, Engines, Propellers and Accessories under the British Commonwealth Air Training Plan.

• Contractors to the United States Army Air Corps.

• Manufacturers of Aircraft Skiis and Ski-wheel Landing Gear and of Aircraft and Engine Parts.

AIRCRAFT REPAIR LIMITED

P. O. BOX 517

EDMONTON   CANADA

A VITAL FORCE
IN A VITAL INDUSTRY!

SINCE its incorporation in 1930, Fleet Aircraft, Limited, has played a progressively important part in the development of Canadian aviation. Starting with a small factory at Fort Erie, Ontario, facilities have been steadily expanded until today the Fleet Aircraft plant constitutes one of the most modern and efficient units in Canada's aircraft industry.

During its lifetime the Company has, we believe, produced more aircraft than any other single firm in the Dominion. Before the war, Fleet supplied hundreds of trainers to the R.C.A.F., Canadian light aeroplane clubs and numerous foreign countries; since the beginning of the present war the Company has produced many hundreds more for the British Commonwealth Air Training Plan. All its facilities are now devoted to manufacturing standard primary trainers for the Combined Training Organization of the United Nations.

Through its long association with the aircraft industry, Fleet Aircraft has acquired a background of invaluable practical experience. This experience is built into every product of Fleet Aircraft, Limited today—and will be ready to serve aviation in the post-war era.

FLEET Aircraft
LIMITED, FORT ERIE, ONTARIO

FLEET BUILDS PLANES TO-DAY.

"Cornells" on the assembly line in the Fort Erie plant of Fleet Aircraft, Limited.

WITH its entire manufacturing facilities now devoted to production of the Fleet "Cornell" and the PT-26, Fleet Aircraft, Limited, is now operating on an advanced production schedule which calls for heavy output of these new planes which have been adopted as standard primary trainers for the Combined Training Organization of the United Nations.

Assembling centre section ribs and stringers in the centre section for a Fleet "Cornell".

AN ADAPTATION of the primary trainer originally engineered and designed by Fairchild Engine and Airplane Corporation of Hagerstown, Maryland, U.S.A., the Fleet "Cornell" marks an important forward step in elementary air training.

Scene at Station 3 on the final assembly line.

MAKING planes today for pilots of tomorrow is a job in which every employee of Fleet Aircraft takes sincere pride. In the Fleet "Cornell" and the PT-26 they are making planes in which instructors and students have that prime requirement of air training—confidence in a good aircraft.

FORT

FOR THE PILOTS OF TO-MORROW!

THE Fleet "Cornell", illustrated above, marks an important forward step in elementary air training. The performance and design of this machine permit students to move from elementary to advanced trainers with considerably increased ease and speed—gives confidence and skill to today's students who are the fighting pilots of tomorrow.

FLEET Aircraft LIMITED

ERIE ONTARIO

IN making wings for bombers, shells for field and anti-aircraft guns, and equipment for mechanized transport, the management and workers are proud of the part being played by Massey-Harris in the war-time program of Canadian industry. In addition to these products for the battlefield, Massey-Harris, in the providing of modern equipment for the sowing and reaping of the crops, is helping farmers faced with an acute shortage of manpower to produce the prodigious quantities of foodstuffs required by an Empire at war.

MASSEY-HARRIS COMPANY, LIMITED

HEAD OFFICE - TORONTO   ESTABLISHED 1847

THE LARGEST MAKERS OF FARM IMPLEMENTS IN THE BRITISH EMPIRE

Plans and Planes
begin on
PAPER

WARTIME ROLE OF CANADA'S GREATEST INDUSTRY EMBRACES ALL FRONTS

The British Commonwealth Air Training Plan itself began on paper and its financing has been aided in no small measure by the foreign exchange acquired from exports of newsprint and other pulp and paper products; these are Canada's great single source of dollar balances; they are currently running at the rate of a quarter billion dollars a year.

Each day the war makes new and greater demands on the resources of the industry. Paper goes into the construction of every plane; into the gaskets of engines; into radio equipment. It is used for the fusing and wrapping of shells; for depth charges; for naval and land mines. Pulps are needed for explosives; wallboard for housing the armed forces, for war plants and workers' housing; container board and wrappings for munitions and food, newsprint to sustain a free press.

Pulp and Paper is Canada's greatest industry. To meet the essential needs on the battlefront and on the home front, it is daily establishing new production records. The Industry is proud of the job its workers are doing . . . proud that they are doing their bit in the fight for freedom.

THE PULP AND PAPER
INDUSTRY OF CANADA
972 SUN LIFE BUILDING MONTREAL

DOWTY
LIVE-LINE
hydraulic pump

Star Performer

IN

HYDRAULICS
WITHOUT TEARS

DOWTY EQUIPMENT (CANADA) LIMITED, Dominion Square Building, **MONTREAL**
Parent Company: DOWTY EQUIPMENT LIMITED, Cheltenham, ENGLAND
Associated Company: DOWTY EQUIPMENT CORPORATION, 41-28 37th Street, LONG ISLAND CITY, N.Y.

World Famous AIRCRAFT INSTRUMENTS

The Gyro-Horizon shows pilot whether plane is banking, climbing, gliding or flying level.

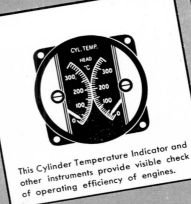

Sensitive Altimeter indicates the height plane is above sea-level.

This Cylinder Temperature Indicator and other instruments provide visible check of operating efficiency of engines.

The position of Wheels, Flaps and Tail are automatically shown to provide flying and landing safeguards.

...to guard and guide our Airmen when flying ... fighting ... landing !..

Precious lives . . . our fighting edge in the air . . . depend very greatly on accurate aircraft instruments. So in Ontario Hughes Owens' modern factory, all the skill of master instrument makers . . . all the accuracy of the finest precision machinery . . . all the enthusiasm of loyal workers is concentrated on producing Aircraft Instruments that are thoroughly reliable.

Accurate and dependable service is being rendered by the instruments we have supplied to the R.C.A.F., British Admiralty, Wartime Merchant Shipping and the Canadian Naval Service on all fighting fronts. Painstaking research, based on millions of miles of actual flying experience is back of the outstanding record of these world famous instruments.

In addition to the manufacture of instruments, our facilities enable us to render a valuable maintenance service to flying stations in Canada. We calibrate, overhaul and repair* all types of aircraft and marine instruments.

CANADIAN REPRESENTATIVES FOR

SPERRY · PIONEER · LEWIS · SMITH'S

*As an indication of our accuracy and reliability, we are authorized by the R.C.A.F., Civil Aviation Branch and British Air Commission, to issue our own "Release Notes" certifying repaired or corrected instruments are in good working order.

AIRSPEED INDICATORS
SERVICE ALTIMETERS
SENSITIVE ALTIMETERS
(with temperature compensation)
CLIMB INDICATORS
(Altitude and Temperature Compensated, Self Contained)
COMPASSES
LANDING FLARES
MANIFOLD PRESSURE GAUGES
OXYGEN REGULATORS
PITOT STATIC TUBES
(Electrically Heated)
TURN & BANK INDICATORS
TACHOMETERS, CENTRIFUGAL
TACHOMETERS, SENSITIVE, ELECTRICAL
GENERATORS
CYLINDER TEMPERATURE INDICATORS
CARBURETOR AIR TEMPERATURE INDICATORS
DIRECTIONAL GYRO
GYRO HORIZONS
AUTOMATIC PILOTS
PRESSURE GAUGES
SUCTION GAUGES
THERMOMETERS
WARNING UNITS
CLOCKS
SEXTANTS
CHRONOMETERS
NAVIGATION PLOTTING INSTRUMENTS
TESTING INSTRUMENTS

Above is shown our "Non-Magnetic" Hut . . . the only one in Canada . . . where compasses are checked and adjusted. *Right*—a section of our instrument assembly department working on P8 compasses for Aircraft.

The "P8" Compass for Aircraft

THE ONTARIO HUGHES OWENS CO. LIMITED
Manufacturers and Importers of
Aircraft and Marine Instruments

Head Office: 527 SUSSEX STREET   OTTAWA   Production Division: 3 HAMILTON AVE.

ENGINEERING ability with years of experience . . . Modern factory and precision equipment . . . Skilled Canadian craftsmen . . . all these made possible our quick response to Canada's War-Demand for Precision Parts and Products.

Our personnel is happy to have been in a position to render and continue to render utmost assistance to "Canada's War in the Air".

OUTBOARD, MARINE & MANUFACTURING CO.
OF CANADA, LTD.

PETERBORO - CANADA

Manufacturers, also, of

The World-Famous Johnson Sea-Horse Outboard Motors
Evinrude and Elto Outboard Motors
The Johnson-Tremblay Centrifugal Fire-Fighting Pumps
The Johnson Chore-Horse and the Johnson
Iron-Horse Electric Light and Power Plants

OUTBOARD, MARINE & MANUFACTURING CO.
OF CANADA, LTD. • • • PETERBORO, CANADA

Builders of Precision Products, Parts and Equipment

Look at a Bomber~

deHavilland Mosquito.

you see Northern Electric at WAR

No, we don't build bombers . . . *our* job is to give speech, sight and hearing to those argosies of victory — those D-for-Donalds, C-for-Charlies and their gallant crews who are making aerial history. And into this work go sensational developments in electronic equipment fashioned and perfected to guide our airmen (many of them our fellow workers) to *any* target . . . through *any* weather . . . and to bring them safely home again. The men and women of Northern Electric . . . the hands that man the machines . . . are working at high speed, accurately, in a full-time effort to produce the world's best equipment for the world's best fliers. Only when peace comes will the hands of Northern Electric return to their regular activity of manufacturing wires and cables, telephones, radio receivers for civilian use . . . all the products of a national electrical service.

INFORMATION

"Our war production job is by no means confined to bombers alone. Vital equipment for all the Services —Navy, Army, Air Force— is our full-time schedule".

40-31-SS

Northern Electric
AND ITS EMPLOYEES

IN WAR AND IN PEACE—A NATIONAL ELECTRICAL SERVICE

Believed to be the only Minot de blé in existence, this dry bushel measure was used in Canada during the French regime (before 1759) and is now in the possession of the Château de Ramezay, Montreal.

A Bushel of Trouble for Hitler

CANADIAN and American grain fields, Herr Hitler, have caused you a lot of trouble . . . and they are going to cause you a lot more. Because, from these grain fields of ours comes an all-important weapon of war — high-proof alcohol.

As you well know, Herr Hitler, high-proof alcohol is an essential ingredient in the manufacture of smokeless powder for our shells, bombs, mines, torpedoes. You know too, that high-test alcohol is used to make synthetic rubber for our jeep, truck and aeroplane tires . . . pharmaceuticals to keep our boys well . . . shatterproof glass for our aeroplane windshields . . . and a host of other products our Army, Navy and Air Force are using to cause your destruction.

Over here, Herr Hitler, we have plenty of grain and ample facilities to make almost unlimited quantities of alcohol for war—so don't think there is any shortage when some night our Lancasters with their 8,000-pound "block-busters" fail to appear over Essen, Cologne or Berlin — the only reason will be "impossible flying conditions." And, when your "Tirpitz" gets a mighty broadside from the 14″ guns of our battleships, you can credit the alcohol which makes possible the manufacture of our death-dealing shells.

Yes, Herr Hitler, you are really in trouble.

All our distilleries in Canada and the United States are pouring out an endless stream of high-proof alcohol for war. And you can be sure, Herr Hitler, that this stream will never stop until your last gun has been silenced.

THE HOUSE OF SEAGRAM

Every Seagram plant in Canada and the United States is engaged 100% in the production of ALCOHOL FOR WAR

WINGS
OVER THE NORTH
...and Beyond!

HISTORY repeats as Canadian Pacific extends another of Canada's frontiers . . . this time northward . . . *this time by air!*

More than half a century ago Canadian Pacific drove its steel across Canada, linking ocean to ocean by rail. There followed great ships plying the broad Pacific . . . then the Atlantic. Now, opening wide the door to Canada's New North, Canadian Pacific Air Lines reaches out to tap new and fabulous resources . . . to give access to the short, roof-of-the-world air routes to Europe and Asia.

Today these northern air routes form a vital link in global war strategy. Tomorrow they will help to reshape the commercial map of the world . . . for the shortest distance from Toronto or Detroit to China and India is via the Yukon and Alaska! Dedicated now to bringing victory nearer (90% of its total traffic is connected with the war effort), Canadian Pacific Air Lines will be ready to build and serve a greater Canada when peace returns.

Canadian Pacific
AIR LINES

THE WINGS OF THE WORLD'S GREATEST TRAVEL SYSTEM

FOR THE NAVY and merchant marine, Canadian General Electric is producing equipment for service on the seven seas: massive marine engines, stern gear, rudders, circulating pumps, electric motors and generators, wire and cable.

All for One Purpose ....—*Victory*

FOR THE ARMY, hard-hitting anti-tank guns, anti-aircraft guns, powerful anti-aircraft and coastal defence searchlights, and other vital military equipment are built by C.G.E. These weapons are on "active service" on many Empire battlefronts.

The men and women of Canadian General Electric day and night are producing Vital Equipment for the United Nations

Forging vital weapons of war for service on the battlefronts of the world are the thousands of production soldiers of Canadian General Electric. They know, these resolute, resourceful men and women, that it takes determined, unremitting effort to win through to Victory.

Night and day they are putting every ounce of their energy and skill into the grim task of building guns, searchlights, marine engines, vital parts for planes, tanks and ships—and into the making of essential electrical equipment for other war plants.

The Navy's orders...the Army's orders...the orders of the Air Force—are *their* orders now. They are sparing neither time nor talent in delivering the tools of war to the men who fight with them. Conscious of the obligation which has been laid upon them, they are pledged to one purpose—to all-out war production for Victory!

FOR THE AIR FORCE—To help fight the war in the air, C.G.E. is producing precision instruments for fighter and bomber aircraft, gun turrets for mighty bombing planes, plastic control panels, lighting equipment and wiring installations.

FOR INDUSTRY—C.G.E. is supplying Canada's war industry and mines with important equipment for the generation and distribution of electrical power, with sturdy motors, electric furnaces, welding equipment and with an impressive volume of other machinery and materials.

CANADIAN GENERAL ELECTRIC CO.

Aircraft INSTRUMENTS *and* ACCESSORIES

—A¢A—

Air Speed Indicators
Manifold Pressure Gauges
Standard Altimeters
Oil Pressure Gauges
Fuel Pressure Gauges
Rate of Climb Indicators
Oxygen Demand Valves
Electrical Heated Pressure Heads
High Pressure Couplings
Electrical De-Icing Pumps
Electrical Fuel Pressure Pumps, Type E P-1
Electrical Fuel Transfer Pumps
Hand Emergency Pumps
Hand Priming Pumps
Hand De-Icing Pumps
Regulating Valves
Valves and Cocks
Fuel Filters

ELECTRICAL FUEL PRESSURE PUMP TYPE EP-1

CANADIAN AIRCRAFT INSTRUMENTS & ACCESSORIES LTD.
LEASIDE - ONTARIO - CANADA

Associated with:
SELF-PRIMING PUMP & ENGINEERING CO. LTD. SLOUGH, BUCKS., ENG.

Associated with:
K. D. G. INSTRUMENTS LTD. CROYDON, SURREY, ENG.

Agents for:
AVIMO LIMITED TAUNTON, SOMERSET, ENG.

ON THE APPROVED LISTS OF THE R.C.A.F. AND BRITISH AIR COMMISSION

METAL MEN
TO A
NATION
AT WAR!

Since 1883 through the second Riel Rebellion, the South African War and the

Factories at:

**TORONTO - MONTREAL
WINNIPEG - VANCOUVER**

First Great War, we have been suppliers of metal to Canadian Industry.

We are proud to be again serving the industry during these strenuous days of the Second Great War and contributing, however humbly, to the arming of Canada's Fighting Forces.

THE CANADA METAL COMPANY, LIMITED

Aerial Combat
BROWNING MACHINE GUNS BY INGLIS

Ground Defense
BREN MACHINE GUNS BY INGLIS

JOHN INGLIS CO.
LIMITED
TORONTO

52

A Glorious Tradition Inspires
Canada's War in the Air

CANADA'S *Air* **HERITAGE**

Per Ardua ad Astra

"Today another generation of Canadians . . . is writing its deeds in the skies over England and Europe. Some may have opportunities for spectacular flying, some may ride with a kindlier fate than others. There will be the unsung heroes; the regular duty men flying from dawn to dawn; the thousands of loyal men whose work is on the ground, who give untiring and ungrudging service in order to make possible the achievements that are being written into the imperishable records of our Service."

Excerpt from booklet issued under authority of the Minister of National Defence for Air and distributed to graduates of the British Commonwealth Air Training Plan about to be confirmed to their rank in the Royal Canadian Air Force.

Power for Victory

● From the roaring rivers of the Province of Quebec come millions of harnessed white horses, the driving power of electricity to turn the wheels of a thousand war industries.

Because of Quebec's immense water powers the raw material of giants of the skies pours out from the world's greatest aluminum plants.

On the assembly lines of Quebec's huge new aircraft factories Bombers, Fighters and Trainers first feel their wings, roll out to the runways and take to the air.

On flying fields throughout the land thousands of young Canadians, and their cousins from Britain, Australia, New Zealand, have earned their coveted wings. Today the graduates of Canada's great University of the Air are locked in combat with the Hun in every theatre of war.

We of Shawinigan salute them and are proud to have contributed our part to Quebec's magnificent air effort . . . prouder than we know how to say of the lads who are the front-line troops of Canada's War in the Air.

The
Shawinigan Water & Power
Company

FROM THE GROUND UP

IN AIRPORT construction and in the manufacture and servicing of the aircraft which soar over these flying fields, products of Canadian Ingersoll-Rand Company play an important part.

Canadian Ingersoll-Rand air compressors and rock drills have broken ground for many a runway, while air-operated tools have facilitated construction of buildings on airports from coast to coast. In the aircraft factory, compressed air speeds up many important operations through the use of pneumatic tools, air hoists, spray guns and other labour saving equipment.

In the repair depot compressed air increases the "availability" of aircraft for service through reducing overhaul time, while on the airport Canadian Ingersoll-Rand pumps supply water for many services, including heating and fire protection.

* * *

We are pleased to have this opportunity of paying tribute not only to the Air Service, but also to those men who, through engineering genius and constructional ability, have contributed to the success of the British Commonwealth Air Training Plan.

42 P2

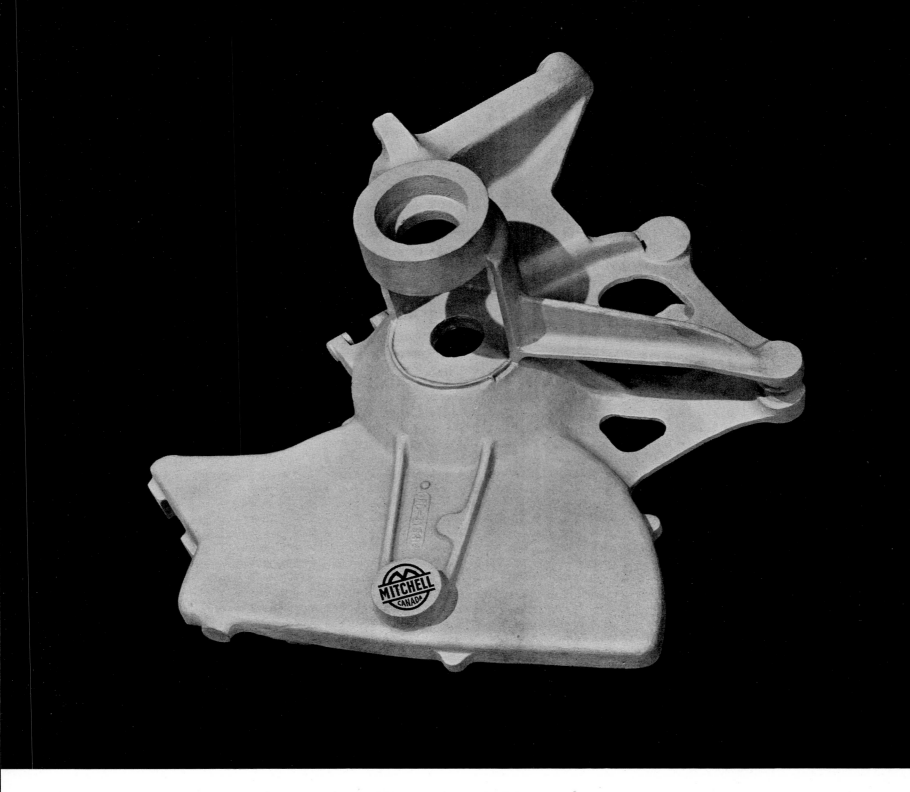

Light Weight Champion

THE "ELEKTRON" Magnesium Casting illustrated above is a typical example of the quality and intricacy of our sand casting production in this new and rapidly expanding field.

"ELEKTRON" Magnesium alloys are lighter than aluminum and possess a higher strength-weight ratio. They play the part of a champion in today's demand for a "fighting" product, and are destined to become one of the major metals of industry and commerce after Victory has been won.

Up until this year, 1942, however, it has been Aluminum Alloy Castings, that have borne the main brunt of battle and our Aluminum alloy aircraft castings have fully proven themselves in the strains and hazards of air fighting.

Careful workmanship and strict laboratory control follow all light alloy aircraft castings through every stage of manufacture.

Production in quantity is never allowed to obscure the fact that on each individual casting will depend the lives of men and the fortunes of war.

THE ROBERT MITCHELL COMPANY LIMITED

"Specialists in the Casting and Fabrication of Modern Alloys"

Foundries: ST. LAURENT, P.Q.   1851 — 1942   Factories: MONTREAL, P.Q.

Power
KEEPS 'EM FLYING

From the landing lights and beacons on the innumerable aerodromes of Canada's great university of the air . . . The British Commonwealth Air Training Plan . . . to the great day-lighted assembly lines of the aircraft plant night shifts, the rushing flow of Canadian rivers is the power-unit without which we could not work or fly for Victory.

Electricity is the beating heart of the great Canadian war effort, as for years it has been the core of our peaceful national life.

We salute those who defend that way of life by seeking out the enemy in the skies, those gallant youngsters of the Air Training Plan who know that the best form of defence is attack.

To you who carry Canada's torch on high goes the undying gratitude of every Canadian . . . We shall never let them down, we who remain behind in factory, on the farm, or in the great power plants beside Canada's mighty rivers.

MONTREAL LIGHT HEAT & POWER CONSOLIDATED

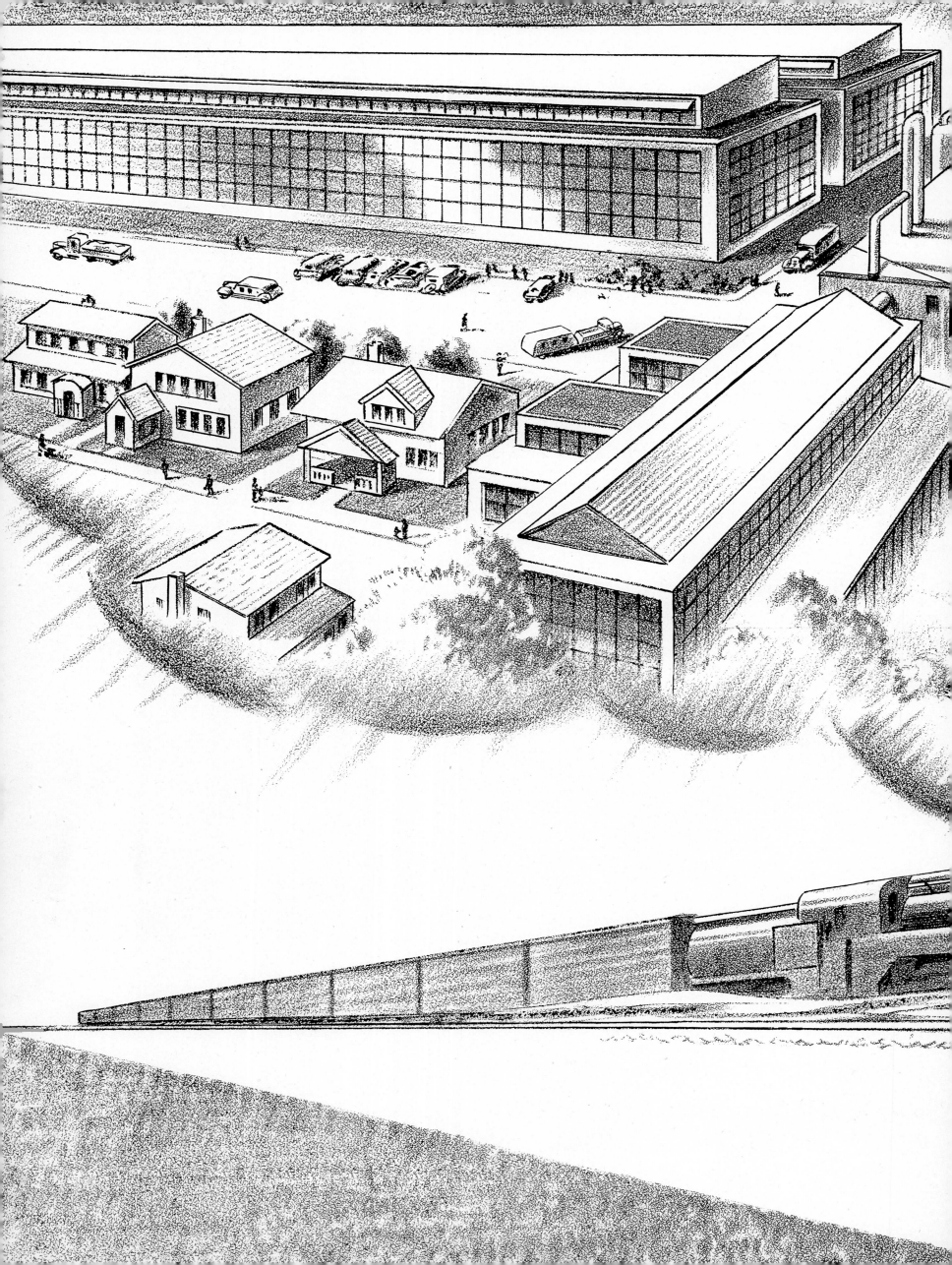

Organized for VICTORY

We are proud to play a part in Canada's great War Effort in the Fight for Freedom. H. F. McLean, Limited have built Munition Plants and have assisted in the Canadian Government's War Housing Plan. Affiliated Companies are building Naval Bases for the Canadian and United States Governments, while other associates efficiently maintain the Right of Way for the great trains which haul with speed the Troops, Tanks, Aircraft and Guns and the supplies of War.

H. F. McLEAN, LIMITED · MONTREAL

· AFFILIATED COMPANIES ·

Grenville Crushed Rock Co., Limited, Montreal • Dominion Construction Co., Limited, Toronto

H. F. McLean Inc., White Plains, N.Y., U.S.A.

"The pick of them all,!"

● With their uniformly high standard of quality and performance, White Rose Petroleum Products are proving their dependability and efficiency in all branches of the Services.

Canadian Oil Companies, Limited is proud of the fact that it has the facilities to produce . . . and is producing . . . large quantities of petroleum products for use in the Army, the Navy and the Air Force.

Today, reliability is of vital importance . . . White Rose Products, with a 33 year record of proven service, are standing up to every test imposed on them by modern machines of war.

WHITE ROSE
PETROLEUM PRODUCTS

CANADIAN OIL COMPANIES, LIMITED
THE ALL-CANADIAN COMPANY

A Full-Time, Full-Out War Effort...

We are proud to say that every man-hour in our plant, every job turned out is for Canada's War Effort. Until Victory is won the normal pursuits of trade must wait—else we shall know no Victory and no longer enjoy the free commerce which is the core of Democracy — Intricate precision castings for all manner of armament and ammunition for Army as well as Air Force is our job. To the lads who fly, we pledge ourselves always to work at top speed and efficiency to provide them with the Tools to Finish the Job.

•

PRESSURE CASTINGS OF CANADA LIMITED

ALUMINUM AND ZINC BASE ALLOY • DIE CASTINGS

WESTON   **ONTARIO**

"To Them!"

CYCLONE-POWERED *"Flying Fortresses"*

STRENGTHEN HEMISPHERE DEFENSE

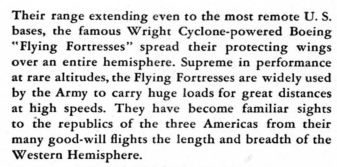

Their range extending even to the most remote U. S. bases, the famous Wright Cyclone-powered Boeing "Flying Fortresses" spread their protecting wings over an entire hemisphere. Supreme in performance at rare altitudes, the Flying Fortresses are widely used by the Army to carry huge loads for great distances at high speeds. They have become familiar sights to the republics of the three Americas from their many good-will flights the length and breadth of the Western Hemisphere.

"Fly with Wright the World Over"

CANADIAN WRIGHT LIMITED
MONTREAL   **CANADA**

WRIGHT
Aircraft ENGINES

Noorduyn's "Marks on the Door"

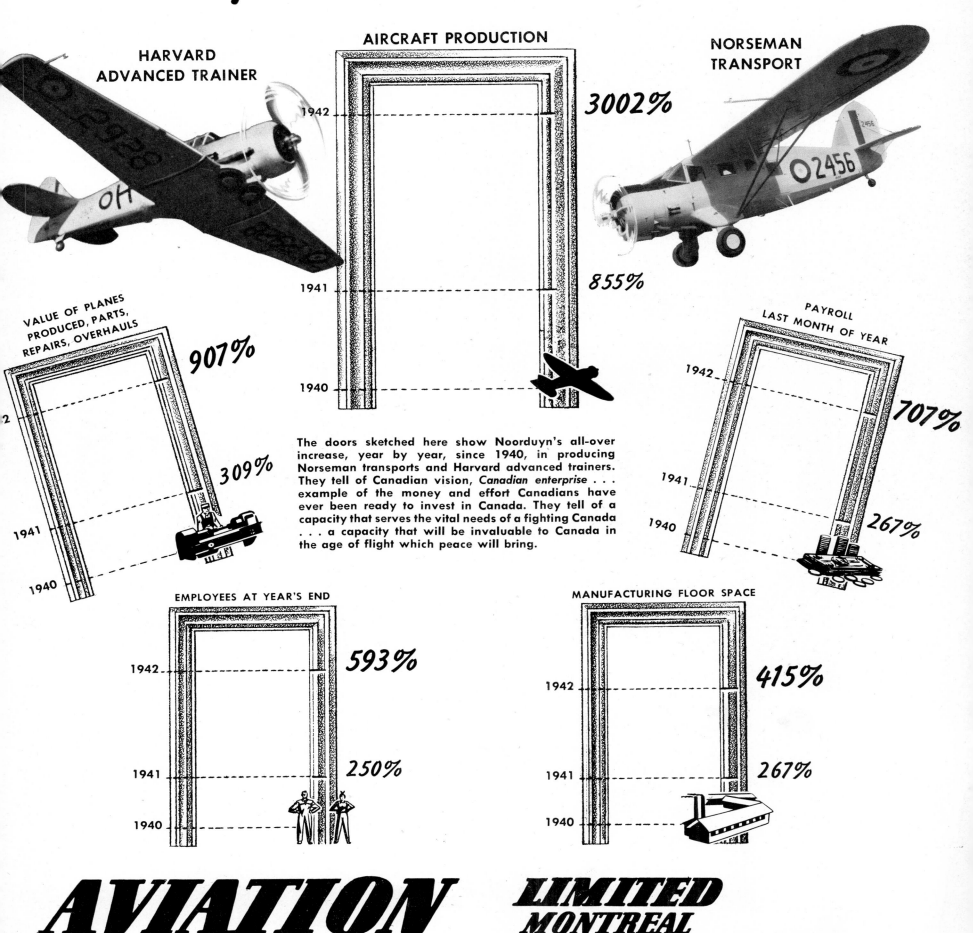

HARVARD ADVANCED TRAINER

AIRCRAFT PRODUCTION

1942 — 3002%

1941 — 855%

1940

NORSEMAN TRANSPORT

VALUE OF PLANES PRODUCED, PARTS, REPAIRS, OVERHAULS

907%

1942

309%

1941

1940

PAYROLL LAST MONTH OF YEAR

1942

707%

1941

267%

1940

The doors sketched here show Noorduyn's all-over increase, year by year, since 1940, in producing Norseman transports and Harvard advanced trainers. They tell of Canadian vision, *Canadian enterprise* . . . example of the money and effort Canadians have ever been ready to invest in Canada. They tell of a capacity that serves the vital needs of a fighting Canada . . . a capacity that will be invaluable to Canada in the age of flight which peace will bring.

EMPLOYEES AT YEAR'S END

1942 — 593%

1941 — 250%

1940

MANUFACTURING FLOOR SPACE

1942 — 415%

1941 — 267%

1940

AVIATION LIMITED MONTREAL

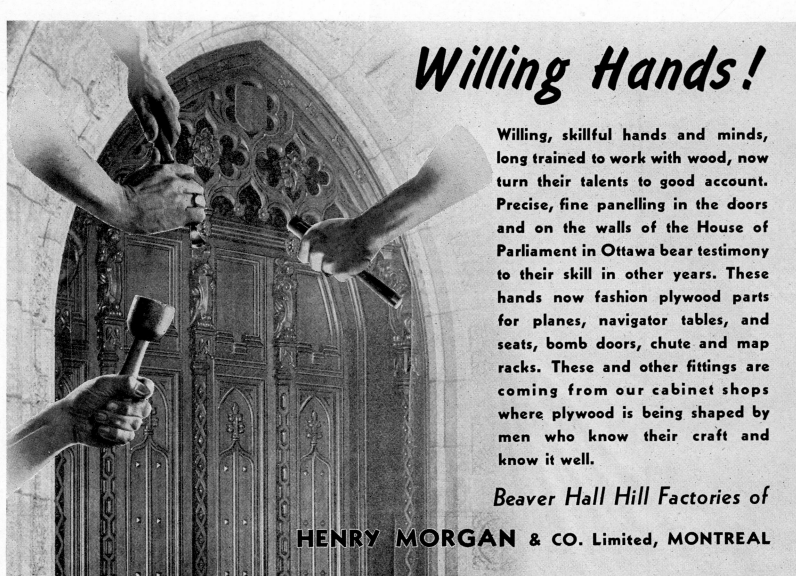

Willing Hands!

Willing, skillful hands and minds, long trained to work with wood, now turn their talents to good account. Precise, fine panelling in the doors and on the walls of the House of Parliament in Ottawa bear testimony to their skill in other years. These hands now fashion plywood parts for planes, navigator tables, and seats, bomb doors, chute and map racks. These and other fittings are coming from our cabinet shops where plywood is being shaped by men who know their craft and know it well.

Beaver Hall Hill Factories of

HENRY MORGAN & CO. Limited, MONTREAL

1929 · · · 14 YEARS · · · 1943
From years of peace to years of war.

To the paths of war Fairchild brought
10 years of experience in the manufacture of commercial planes — all
of which, in these 4 years of strife,
has proven an invaluable asset in
establishing it as one of the leading
builders of military aircraft in Canada.

FAIRCHILD AIRCRAFT LIMITED
LONGUEUIL   (Montreal), QUE.

Bolingbroke Bombers . . . . Curtiss Hell-Diver

NOW YOU SEE IT

NOW YOU DONT...

..the Disappearing Wall!

This immense door, 200 feet long, 30 feet high, at the Dorval Airport, is one of the largest automatic doors in the world. Counterweighted to eliminate strain on operating mechanism, it is fully automatic, and in sixty-five seconds opens or closes to the entire width of the building. In case of electric failure each of the seven individual doors comprising the whole can be operated by hand.

ROLL FORMING of dural stock is speedily and accurately performed at the Cresswell-Pomeroy plants.

STEPPED UP plane production—beyond the most optimistic forecasting of experienced production men—this is what Cresswell-Pomeroy have helped to make possible.

We are equipped to manufacture in millions of lineal feet metal sections of almost every conceivable shape, and to do all of the engineering, designing and toolmaking required.

Engaged at this moment 100% on war production, we shall still welcome your enquiry as to HOW, WHY and WHEN we may serve you.

CUTTING to micrometrically precise lengths—an important part of the Cresswell-Pomeroy service.

CRESSWELL-POMEROY *Limited*

604 DE COURCELLE ST., MONTREAL
ALSO 989 BAY STREET, TORONTO

BOLT FROM THE BLUE!

NOT ONE
BUT THOUSANDS!

An aircraft dives at its objective . . . deadly—
powerful—delicate—accurate . . . product of man's
ingenuity . . . built of every refined metal and
substance known to modern research, science and
engineering. And yet, its power . . . its effectiveness . . .
its stability . . . hangs by a million threads — threads
of a thousand bolts, and nuts, and screws. Tiny
parts locking and welding each intricate shape
into a magnificent weapon of modern warfare.

Our large stocks of A G S and A N
parts are continually available to
Canada's Aircraft Industry.

JOHN MILLEN & SON LIMITED

MONTREAL   ESTABLISHED 1869   CANADA

Our Squadrons of the Air

THEIR SUCCESS AND SAFETY... OFTEN DEPENDS ON **RADIO!**

TONIGHT — from carefully hidden airdromes in England — Canadian flying men will ascend swiftly into the midnight sky and turn the snouts of their bombers directly for their Nazi targets.

And as they go forward, gallant and confident — and return, gallant and victorious — they keep in touch with one another and with their homes bases by means of radio — modern radio! Day and night, the engineers and the workers at Rogers Majestic toil willingly so that they may do their share in seeing to it that every plane may have its radio — and so that every radio may be scientifically abreast of — and ahead of — the apparatus of the enemy.

And when peace comes, this day-by-day research will be reflected in the radically new Rogers, Majestic and De Forest sets — once again assuming their leadership in domestic radio.

ROGERS MAJESTIC LIMITED
A N D   A F F I L I A T E D   C O M P A N I E S

Manufacturers of Rogers, Majestic and De Forest Radios and Rogers Long-Life Fully Guaranteed Radio Tubes. A Tube for Every Purpose.

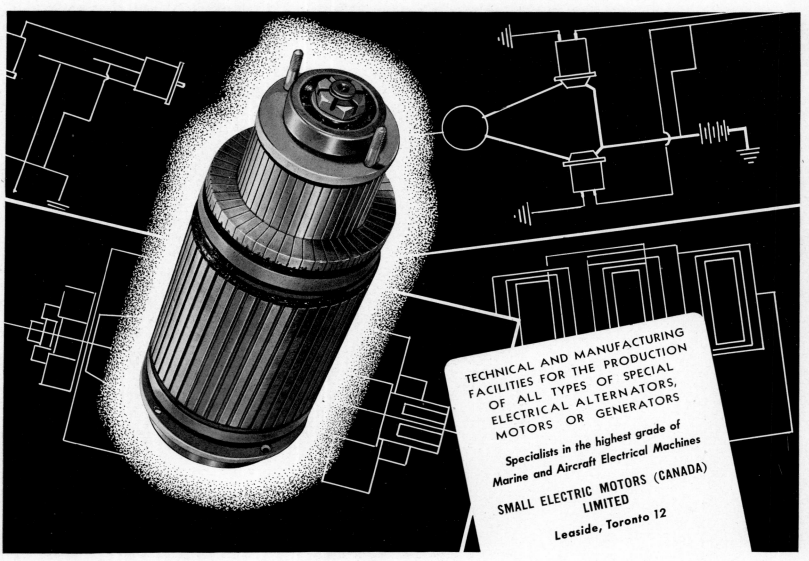

TECHNICAL AND MANUFACTURING FACILITIES FOR THE PRODUCTION OF ALL TYPES OF SPECIAL ELECTRICAL ALTERNATORS, MOTORS OR GENERATORS

Specialists in the highest grade of Marine and Aircraft Electrical Machines

SMALL ELECTRIC MOTORS (CANADA) LIMITED

Leaside, Toronto 12

LET us therefore brace
Ourselves to do our Duty
and bear Ourselves
That if the
British Commonwealth
and Empire
Last for a Thousand Years
Men will say - -
"This was their Finest Hour."

—*Rt. Hon. Winston Churchill*

CANADIAN WESTINGHOUSE COMPANY, LIMITED, HAMILTON, CANADA

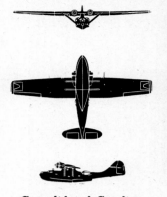

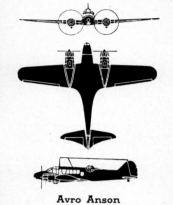

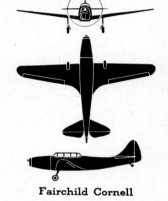
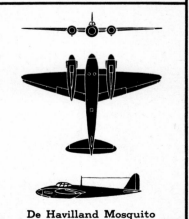

WHEN
Jupiter Pluvius
GETS THE RANGE...

WHEN he grows hostile, he rains showers of "water bombs" that can harm the human as well as the earth. It's not always he drops blessings on the land.

When the jockeys of the clouds are afoot they must have full protection against that "water bombing." Physical fitness, freedom from colds and chills are a "must" at all times.

So, CROYDON GABARDINES of English fabric, completely rainproof due to the waterproof interlining, put up a stout defence against watery blasts from the sky . . . the AIR FORCE appreciates their worth.

In winter, reinforcement in form of a detachable polo lining keeps the forces warm, and secure from any "attack".

Croydon MANUFACTURING CO., LTD. MONTREAL

"Give Us The Tools—" *said* WINSTON CHURCHILL

WITH the right equipment he knew the United Nations could finish the job. In those few words he sent out a call to industry to speed up production, to CLEAR THE WAY for an all out job. That's where we stepped in with LAURENTIDE EQUIPMENT service.

When ground had to be broken for airport and factory construction, when hauling had to be done inside the finished buildings, we provided the necessities.

And when there'll be peace in the world there'll be the same hearty service for those, whose needs call for any of these leaders:—

INTERNATIONAL TRACTORS, BUCYRUS-ERIE BULLGRADERS AND SCRAPERS
LORAIN AIRPORT MOTO CRANES
LORAIN DIESEL AND GAS SHOVELS, DRAGLINES, etc.
HEBARD AIRPORT TRACTORS
NIAGARA SNOWBLOWERS, SNOW SLEIGHS and PLOWS
MURPHY DIESEL ENGINES
BROOKVILLE LOCOMOTIVES
ELECTRIC LIGHT PLANTS
EUCLID SELF-POWERED HAULING EQUIPMENT
REX MOTO MIXERS, CONCRETE MIXERS and PUMPS
PAVERS, CRUSHERS, CONVEYORS.

LAURENTIDE EQUIPMENT
COMPANY LIMITED
SALES · SERVICE · PARTS
440 BEAUMONT AVENUE   MONTREAL

International TracTracTor and Bucyrus-Erie Scrapers Dig in to make chance of Axis Victory quite hollow.

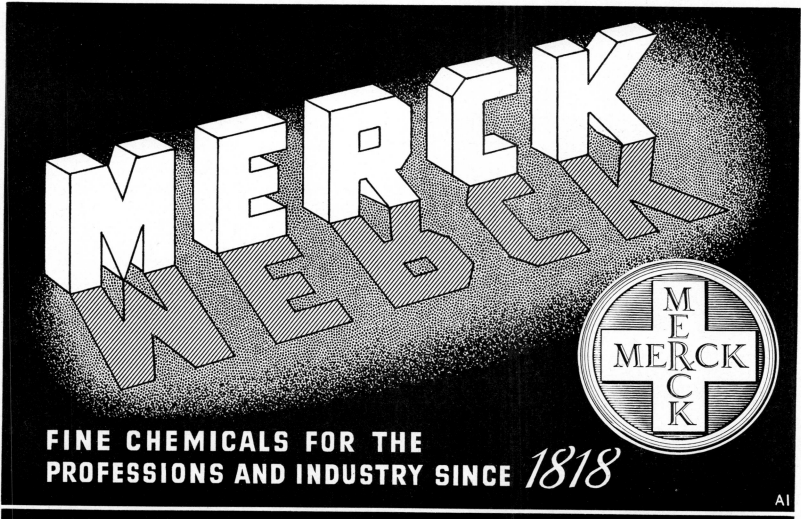

Helping to KEEP 'EM FLYING!

Installing engines in Cessna plane used by R.C.A.F. for training.

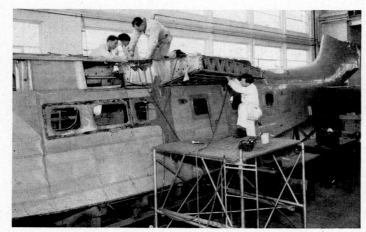

Extensive repairs to a Stranraer flying boat being made for R.C.A.F.

Carrying out repairs to the wings of a Stranraer at a C.P.A. repair plant.

Overhauling and installing electrical accessories and instruments.

Women workers in fabric and dope shop of a repair plant operated by C.P.A.

WHEN the last word in the story of Canada's war in the air has been written and the page has been finally turned there will be many unsung heroes whose names will not appear in the record. There will be the thousands whose work upon the ground—given untiringly and ungrudgingly—made possible the brilliant exploits of the men who fly, the men whose achievements are making the name of Canada great among the nations.

CANADIAN Pacific Air Lines is privileged to play a part in this air war effort. Under contract to the Department of Munitions and Supply, C.P.A. operates six plants for the overhaul and repair of aircraft and engines used in the training schools and on R.C.A.F. operations. Here planes are made fit and engines are tuned to watch-like precision by approximately 2,200 civilian workers to the end that gallant fledglings may become monarchs of the air, flying the way to victory.

●

ST. MAURICE AIR-CRAFT PLANT,
Cap de la Madeleine, Que.

CANADIAN AIRWAYS LIMITED,
Overhaul Dept., Winnipeg, Man.

MID-WEST AIR CRAFT LIMITED,
Air Craft Division, Winnipeg, Man.

PRAIRIE AIRWAYS LIMITED,
Repair Plant, Moose Jaw, Sask.

MID-WEST AIR CRAFT LIMITED,
Engine Division, Winnipeg, Man.

CANADIAN PACIFIC AIR LINES,
Repair Plant, New Westminster, B.C.

Operated by

Canadian Pacific AIR LINES

THE WINGS OF THE WORLD'S GREATEST TRAVEL SYSTEM

✹ 80

WE, of Clark Ruse Aircraft

Limited, having been denied the oppor-

tunity of participating with the gallant

men of the Royal Canadian Air Force

in their air operations, are proud to be

identified with the equipment they fly.

We regard it as "our job" to deliver air-

craft worthy of the men who fly them.

CLARK RUSE AIRCRAFT LIMITED

DARTMOUTH, N.S. AND MONCTON, N.B.

1923 • To Conquer Northern Frontiers

PIONEERING Canadian-built aircraft, the Vickers-made Vedette flying boat placed the untold wealth of Canada's Northland at the service of mankind in the early 20's.

Sturdy, safe, the best of its kind in those early aviation days, the famous Vedette shrank months to hours, reduced hazards and hardships to a minimum, in prospecting and surveying the great resources of our country.

Continuing aircraft manufacture since those early days Vickers aircraft is still serving Canada and the Empire with quality and craftsmanship unsurpassed.

• • •

When war shook the earth, the long experience and vast facilities of Canadian Vickers stood the Empire in good stead. Overnight the building of war weapons commenced and in the Aircraft Division every

I F   I T   F L I E S   O R   F L O A T S

1943 • To Conquer the Skulking U-Boat

resource was turned to the creation of fighting planes. Now, the "CANSOS", famous PBY Catalina amphibian bombers are in full production. It was a PBY that marked the doom of the Bismarck . . . it is these great machines that ceaselessly course the sea-lanes protecting precious cargo ships and the valiant men who sail them from enemy undersea marauders.

Twenty busy years of plane-building experience goes into the making of every Vickers-built "CANSO" . . . experience that assures the standards of our war-planes of today . . . of our peace-planes of tomorrow.

CANADIAN VICKERS LIMITED

HEAD OFFICE—MONTREAL

AIRCRAFT DIVISION

CARTIERVILLE, QUE.

V I C K E R S   C A N   B U I L D   I T

"SWITLIK" *for the Safety of our Air Forces*

Testing Parachutes at a Canadian Aerodrome.

"Canopies for Victory"

The SWITLIK parachute, life-saving unit of the Air Forces and offensive equipment of the Commando and Paratrooper, is made in its entirety by an all-Canadian Company. British American Silk Mills Limited, Granby Elastic Web Company, Belding-Corticelli Limited, National Electric Refrigerator Co. Limited, and Bruck Silk Mills Limited, co-operate with us in this aspect of Canada's great Air War. Good luck to the Armies of the Sky as they swoop down to destroy the enemies of Civilization.

SWITLIK CANADIAN PARACHUTES LIMITED

MONTREAL

"Safety Assured"

Contributors to The Success of The Commonwealth Air Training Plan

They Are In It!

Enthusiastically employees of firms below work to keep the Switlik factories supplied with the materials that enter into the continuous flow of Free Jump Chutes, Paratroopers' Chutes, Flare Chutes, Cargo Chutes, Towed Targets and Fighting Belts that mean so much to the brave lads fighting for world freedom.

BRITISH AMERICAN SILK MILLS LIMITED

Flawless as have been the fabrics produced at these leading mills, still more than ever is the expert eye of the examiners fixed on the material that flows to the SWITLIK factory to become the CANOPIES OF SAFETY.

NATIONAL ELECTRIC REFRIGERATOR CO. LIMITED

In peace time National Electric Refrigerators provided security for the nation's food. Now it's safety harness for parachutes, sturdy metallic fittings that make things safe for the men who fight that all can eat in peace and quiet.

BELDING CORTICELLI LIMITED

That same CORTICELLI precision and fineness of work that has characterised their silken hose and dainties for women is once more evident in the nylon cords they supply for the SWITLIK parachute.

GRANBY ELASTIC WEB LIMITED

There was no lack of elasticity when they got the signal to produce more and more of webbing and duck that make for much of the stoutness of the SWITLIK parachute.

BRUCK SILK MILLS LIMITED

Now that name stands out in service to and co-operation with the manufacturers of SWITLIK through the maintenance of supplies of fabric of worth. Their mills are doing much to help in the fight.

A batch of SWITLIKS awaiting test.

SWITLIKS as they're packed for drop-testing.

Fearless test jumpers know the sturdiness of the SWITLIK.

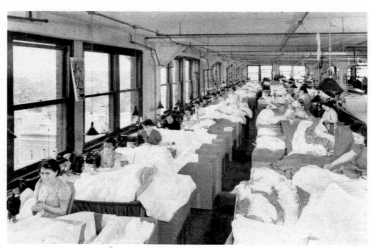

SWITLIK employees stitch and stitch carefully fashioning chutes.

SWITLIK fighting belts in the making.

R. TAMPIER BLOCTUBE CONTROLS

The de Havilland Mosquito Bomber—another British success. It has two Rolls-Royce engines and is of simple wooden construction. Both the undercarriage and tail wheel units are retractable. It has the de Havilland three-blade Hydromatic type propeller. Offensive armament may consist of four 20 mm cannon and four .303 machine guns. Made in Canada.

The de Havilland Aircraft
OF CANADA LIMITED
TORONTO

Powered to Win

High in the skies many decisive battles are being fought—battles where superior power means Victory. Playing an increasingly effective role are planes powered to win by Pratt & Whitney engines and Hamilton Standard propellers.

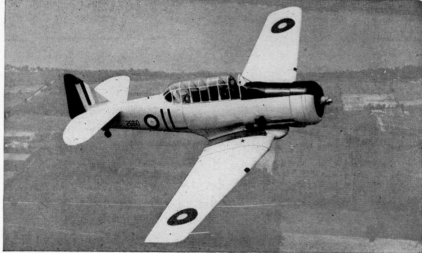

IN TRAINING—Students in the Harvard Advanced Trainer gain quick confidence in the superior qualities of Pratt & Whitney engines and Hamilton Standard propellers.

IN THE FIGHTER COMMAND—Scourge of the skies is the heavily armoured Douglas Havoc night fighter, powered by two Pratt & Whitney twin wasp engines.

IN THE BOMBER COMMAND—carried into the stratosphere by four Pratt & Whitney twin wasp engines, the Consolidated Liberators are hurling tons of destruction on Axis centres.

"These engines are due for an overhaul"

AT REGULAR intervals all Pratt & Whitney engines are returned for complete overhaul and they are stripped down to their smallest part, each part being cleaned, inspected, tested and replaced, if necessary.

A full record is kept of every engine—a record as complete as the case history of a patient in hospital.

In this way we ensure the dependability of Pratt & Whitney engines—a dependability which guarantees the utmost in performance and gives the greatest measure of safety to our intrepid airmen.

Canadian Pratt & Whitney
AIRCRAFT COMPANY LIMITED · LONGUEUIL, P. Q.

PRATT & WHITNEY ENGINES — HAMILTON STANDARD PROPELLERS — De HAVILLAND PROPELLERS — PESCO ACCESSORIES

THE *Little Things*
ARE THE BIG THINGS OF WAR

The tiny seeds from which is grown the food of the nation . . . the micrometrically accurate bomb sight that puts a bomb in a flour barrel . . . Radar, Britain's marvellous secret weapon that finds the enemy's ships in the dark . . . these are all the little things that are the big things in war.

The little things and big things in the aircraft industry . . . STARTERS, GENERATORS, CONTROL BOXES, DYNAMOTORS, DE-ICERS, ANTI-ICERS, AIR PUMPS, HYDRAULIC PUMPS, MAGNETOS, SPARK PLUGS, SWITCHES, CARBURETORS . . . are our particular business. A highly specialised business and a very important one.

AVIATION ELECTRIC
LIMITED
3483 PARK AVENUE, MONTREAL

"BLOCK"-BUSTERS ON WHEELS

Every day of every week in the year, Provincial Transport coaches carry more than 10,000 war workers to and from their jobs.

Some thousands of these are engaged in the manufacture, operation or maintenance of aircraft, and the Provincial Transport Company is proud to serve them.

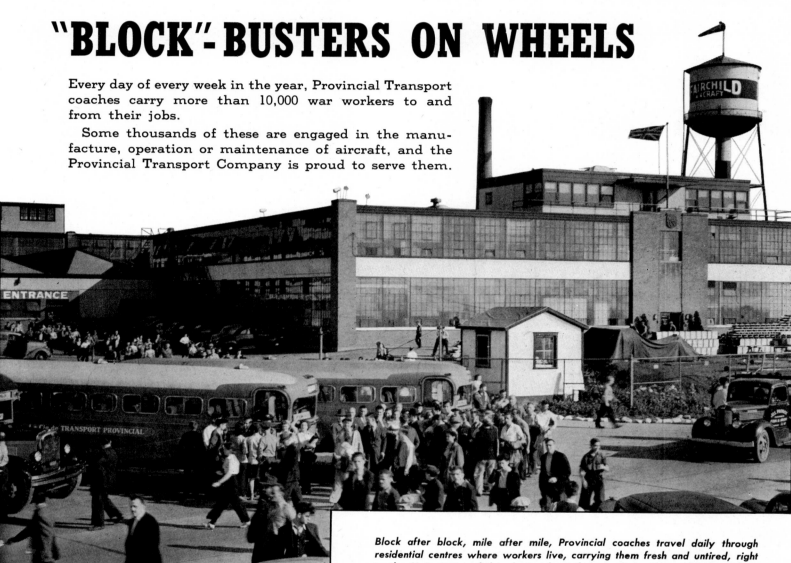

Block after block, mile after mile, Provincial coaches travel daily through residential centres where workers live, carrying them fresh and untired, right to the Main Gates of the plants where they do their all-important work, delivering their loads with precision regularity at each change of shift.

THE flexibility of Provincial Transport service made it an instant and valuable asset to the war industries of Canada, for most of them — including large aircraft plants — were established some distance from existing means of transportation. Only motorcoach service could provide facilities of the size required, at short notice.

Employment problems have been lessened by Provincial motorcoach transportation; fatigue reduced; time consumed in travel shortened; and emergencies swiftly met. Split shifts can be run, and overtime workers transported readily, with the aid of Provincial coaches. It is a privilege to be associated with so much of Canada's war work.

PROVINCIAL TRANSPORT COMPANY

1188 DORCHESTER STREET WEST (AT DRUMMOND), MONTREAL

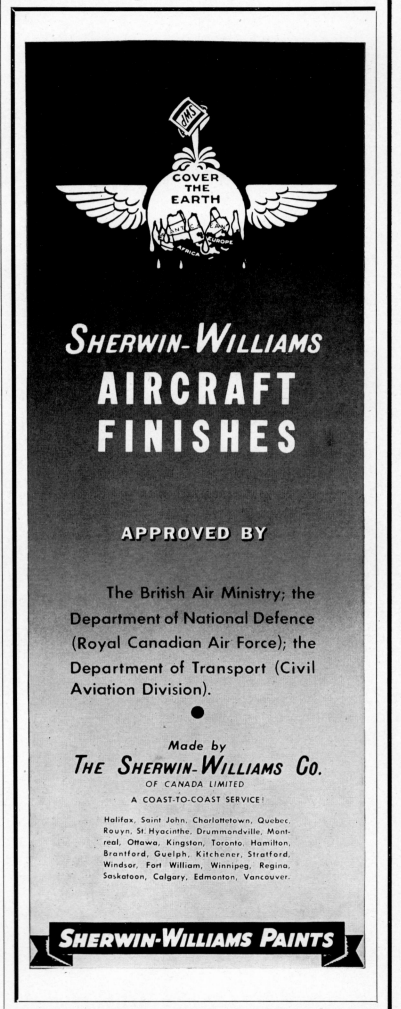

Tuning the singing
Blades of Wrath

Behind the singing silvery aluminum blades of Hamilton Standard Propellers the dauntless airmen of the Allied Nations stretch their wings and learn the arts of flying.

From a vacant lot to full production within a year is the record of Canadian Propellers, Limited, who are concentrating on the manufacture of Hamilton Standard Propellers for the advanced Trainers used in the air training programmes of Canada and the United States.

Illustrated below at left: The New and thoroughly modern plant of Canadian Propellers Limited. The ground was broken on June 8th, 1941, the plant was erected, machinery and equipment installed and first propeller finished on February 22nd, 1942.

At right: A propeller blade being given its final hand polishing. Before this operation, which is No. 28, it had been turned, drilled, reamed, twisted, and profile-milled—these being just a few of the 48 operations necessary before the propeller is ready for use.

CANADIAN PROPELLERS LIMITED MONTREAL
SUBSIDIARY OF *Canadian Pratt & Whitney* AIRCRAFT CO. LTD.

24 BUS TICKETS $2.00 **32 TRAM TICKETS $2.00** **24 BILLETS D'AUTOBUS $2.00** **32 BILLETS DE TRAMWAYS $2.00**

TICKETS IN BOOKS
save your time

WHEN you board a tram or bus with your ticket ready you pass the conductor at once.

When you buy your TICKETS IN BOOKS you adopt the most convenient way to have your ticket ready. You make one purchase for 32 trips. You avoid the frequent nuisance and delay of getting change, while others pass ahead of you into the tram or bus.

When you get the TICKETS IN BOOKS habit, you save your time as you are helping to " speed up " service. The books are so convenient to carry, you find it easy to have your fare ready. If our passengers help, by having their fares and transfers ready, our operators are able to start their vehicles more quickly after each stop.

TICKETS IN BOOKS can be obtained regularly, according to your needs, from one of our Agencies, probably near your home or office, from Department Stores and from Tramways Company Street Vendors at many crowded intersections and safety zones.

MONTREAL TRAMWAYS COMPANY

LES CARNETS DE BILLETS
vous épargnent du temps

Quand vous montez à bord d'un tramway ou d'un autobus avec votre billet à la main, vous ne vous attardez pas devant le percepteur.

Acheter des CARNETS DE BILLETS, c'est la meilleure façon d'avoir son billet prêt. Vous faites un seul achat pour 32 voyages. Vous vous évitez l'ennui d'attendre de la monnaie, tandis que les autres voyageurs passent avant vous dans le tram ou l'autobus.

L'habitude d'acheter des CARNETS DE BILLETS vous épargnera du temps et vous contribuerez aussi à " accélérer le service ". Il est si facile de garder les carnets sur soi que vous aurez toujours aisément votre billet prêt. Si nos clients nous aident en ayant leurs billets et leurs correspondances prêts, nos gardes-moteurs pourront démarrer plus tôt après chaque arrêt.

Vous pouvez obtenir des CARNETS DE BILLETS régulièrement, selon vos besoins, à l'une de nos agences, située probablement tout près de votre demeure ou de votre bureau, aux magasins à rayons et des vendeurs de la Compagnie des Tramways postés à plusieurs intersections et îlots de sécurité très achalandés.

LA COMPAGNIE DES TRAMWAYS DE MONTRÉAL

®

THE ROBERTSON
TRADE-MARK SINCE 1857
HAS BEEN CLOSELY ASSOCIATED WITH THE
R.C.A.F.
IN ITS FLIGHT TO
VICTORY

True, we haven't built the planes they fly—but solid buildings are essential if the men of the air are to be solid. Solidity and sanitation are mates of construction.

Many ROBERTSON products have become part of the great construction mosaic of the R.C.A.F. We're proud to have been part of the "ground" crew in our own way.

THE JAMES ROBERTSON CO.
LIMITED
TORONTO   MONTREAL   SAINT JOHN, N.B.

Manufacturers and Wholesale Distributors of:
QUALITY PLUMBING
—AND—
HEATING PRODUCTS

What the Ventura Does...

This is the Vega Ventura! It can bomb accurately from high-level flight—swoop down on its target for low, fast attack—strafe troop concentrations — blast tanks — tow gliders loaded with men and supplies, and tow targets for fighter practice — a combination of tasks no other medium bomber can do.

The Ventura patrols thousands of miles of cold gray ocean to drop depth charges when it finds a sub—carries torpedoes to attack enemy ships and plants mines to trap them.

The Ventura has the same basic qualities of all Lockheed and Vega planes, *extra* strength, *extra* dependability. That's why the R.C.A.F. is using them—lots of them!

A SUBSIDIARY OF LOCKHEED

Vega
AIRCRAFT CORPORATION

Lockheed Aircraft Corporation · Vega Aircraft Corporation, Burbank, California, U.S.A.

IT'S COLD UP THERE!

So, we're doing everything humanly possible to provide woolly warm protection for the aces aloft, as they battle against those bent on the elimination of that warmth of international friendship, which Democracy has generated and is determined to maintain.

Every operation in the production of GROVER or KNIT-TO-FIT woollens registers the honest prayer of management and employee alike that the United Nations' plans already knit will prove the combination that will weave the web of Axis defeat.

*We're proud of the boys
in the "cold up there".
God bless them.*

GROVER MILLS LIMITED
KNIT-TO-FIT MFG. CO. LTD.

MONTREAL

A Job
FOR THE PRINTED WORD

WITHOUT in any way detracting from the war effort, we should now be shaping our lives and businesses for the reconstruction period. Definitely, the war comes first. Beyond those limits, however, our every action should be aimed at establishing a sound foundation on which to build the future.

In re-establishing contacts during the change-over from war to peace, the printed word will be called upon to shoulder a mighty burden. That burden will not be too great if contact—it momentum—is maintained in the interim.

It is our suggestion that, in keeping with availability of supplies and with due regard for good taste, you give careful consideration to the printed word . . . NOW . . . as a safeguard for the future.

Call us and we'll call on you—without expecting your signature on the dotted line.

METCALFE ROBINSON
PRESS LIMITED

PRINTING SERVICE
LIMITED

PLateau 8991   -   CLairval 4019
395 Dowd Street   —   Montreal

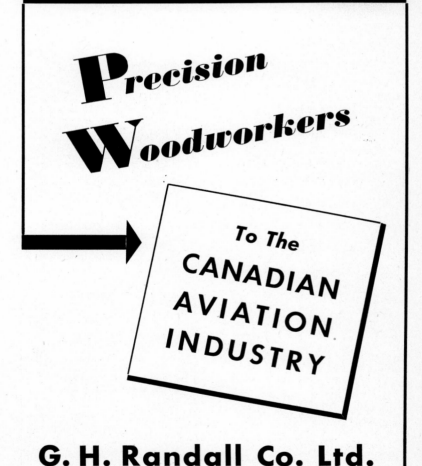

I.C.S.
Specialized Training in
AERONAUTICS

Aviation needs skilled men . . . aircraft builders need skilled workers. But training in aeronautics is not obtainable in a few weeks or months.

In striving to answer the question "What is Aeronautical Education?" the Daniel Guggenheim Foundation reached the conclusion that one phase or another of aeronautics is directly connected with some eighteen different subjects.

I.C.S. training in aeronautics is complete and thorough and approved by unquestionable acceptance. In the last three years, I.C.S. has paid to specialists $34,740 for the data only from which training for aircraft mechanics and aviators is provided. This training is available in the following specialties:

Ground Engineering
Airplane Maintenance
Air Pilotage
Radio Engineering
Navigation and Seamanship
Aircraft Mechanics
Airplane Engine Mechanics
Aircraft Inspection and Overhaul
Airplane Drafting
Aeronautical Engineering
Machine Shop Practice
Gas and Electric Welding
Heat Treatment of Metals
Tool Making.

If you have a definite aeronautical objective, we will be glad to send you an interesting booklet "A Career in Aviation." A letter or postcard will bring it to you by return mail.

INTERNATIONAL CORRESPONDENCE SCHOOLS CANADIAN, LIMITED

MONTREAL   CANADA

OUR PART
IN THE AIR

Right from the beginning of the war BEAUPRE engineering skill has more than kept pace with the pressure on aircraft builders for more and more parts. Recognized by industry for skilled craftsmanship

BEAUPRE

management and employees heartily bent to the task, and when there'll be peace in the world manufacturers will still be sure of dependable service from

BEAUPRE ENGINEERING
WORKS REG'D.
2101 Bennett Ave., MAISONNEUVE, P.Q.

OUR PARTS
IN THE AIR

Morale!

The printed word has been the medium of Morale in all times of stress. It is morale that cheers and inspires the people - - that bucks up the Gunner, the Airman, the Sailor and the men and women behind the lathes of Industry. We have been greatly honoured in the important war work that has been entrusted to our care - - Posters, Booklets and Pamphlets - - all part of Canada's War Effort towards Victory.

WOODWARD PRESS INC.
MONTREAL

Some Chicken!
Some NECK!!
...some joint!!!

Thirteen years ago, the first sheet of a new English product on the Canadian market left our premises to find a better home in a transformer. The manufacturers said it would resist oil and spirits and we took their word for it.

Since then, many a troublesome joint has disappeared and LANGITE, the patented oil-resisting cork sheet with the specially shrunk, cotton lamination to provide extra tensile strength, replaced gasket after gasket and oil leakage, one of the vital problems confronting engineers generally, in Canada, literally died a natural death.

And speaking of death and destruction . . . Britain was rated as unprepared in 1939, but, a year or so before that, British engineers had produced a special grade of LANGITE AERO, to Spec. 219A and this aero grade proved itself in the Battle of Britain. The designers of Spitfires, Lancasters, Mosquitoes, Avro Anson, Hawker Hurricanes, Bolingbrokes, Hampdens and other British planes know Langite as standard equipment, specified on their respective blueprints.

Regardless of where future planes may be designed or built, in view of these facts, the engineer specifying Langite or substituting Langite upholds a worthy tradition and protects himself against doubts and worries with one stroke of the pen.

Talking about manufacturing! The school of hard knocks has produced a dynamic organization unafraid and ambitious. Consequently, our production of many items previously imported into Canada have been made on the spot, in record time, without interference . . . *and we love it!*

▼

F. ROY HEDGES
& CO. REG'D
318 CASTLE BLDG. · MONTREAL

LANGITE · HALLITE · REDEX
Cork   Asbestos   Oil Activator

Sheets, Strips, Gaskets and Washers

Canada's War in the Air ✦

MEMORANDUM OF AGREEMENT BETWEEN THE GOVERNMENTS OF THE UNITED KINGDOM, CANADA, AUSTRALIA AND NEW ZEALAND RELATING TO TRAINING OF PILOTS AND AIRCRAFT CREWS IN CANADA AND THEIR SUBSEQUENT SERVICE.

---

1. It is agreed between the Governments of the United Kingdom, Canada, Australia and New Zealand that there shall be set up in Canada a co-operative air training scheme as set out in this agreement, and that the personnel so trained shall be allocated in accordance with Articles 14 and 15.

2. This Agreement shall become operative at once and shall remain in force until 31st March, 1943; unless, by agreement between the Governments concerned, it be extended or terminated at an earlier date.

GOVERNMENT OF CANADA THE ADMINISTRATOR

3. The Government of Canada will act as administrator of the scheme for itself and the other Governments concerned, as hereinafter provided, and it is understood that the undertakings given herein by the Government of Canada to the other Governments concerned are respectively subject to the due performance on the part of such Governments of their several undertakings given herein in support of the scheme.

4. The Government of Canada, acting as administrator, will endeavour to complete, as quickly as possible, the organisation it considers necessary to give outputs of pupils in the numbers and at the rates agreed upon.

AGREEMENT AS TO PUPILS AND INSTRUCTION

5. (a) The Governments of the United Kingdom, Australia and New Zealand will endeavour to send from time to time enough pupils for training to Canada to keep filled the agreed proportions of places in the various training schools in Canada. The numbers sent by the United Kingdom may include pupils from Newfoundland. The Government of the United Kingdom will also endeavour to send and the Government of Canada, as administrator of the scheme, undertakes to receive pupils for training in Canada in sufficient numbers to keep filled any deficiency in the supply of such pupils from Australia, New Zealand and Canada.

(b) The numbers, and the categories of pupils sent, may be varied from time to time by agreement between the Governments concerned.

(c) It is agreed that if the Governments of Canada, Australia and New Zealand fail to keep filled the training places allotted to them respectively they will nevertheless bear their full respective shares of the costs and expenses.

6. Pupils sent for training in Canada under the provisions of Article 5 will receive pay, allowances and other emoluments in accordance with the provisions set out in Appendix II to this Agreement.

7. The training to be given shall be in accordance with the syllabus of instruction laid down for each similar course of training in the United Kingdom.

8. To assist in the carrying out of the training scheme, the Governments of the United Kingdom, Canada, Australia and New Zealand will lend personnel in such ranks and in such numbers as may be agreed upon with the Government of Canada as administrator of the scheme.

AGREEMENT AS TO COSTS AND EXPENSES

9. The share of the cost of the scheme to be borne by the Government of the United Kingdom will take the form of contributions in kind, to be delivered at such times and in such numbers as may be required for the efficient carrying out of the scheme. In addition, the Government of the United Kingdom will bear the cost of packing, loading and transporting to Canada the supplies she contributes in kind. The cost of unloading and of transportation in Canada will be borne by the Government of Canada, as administrator of the scheme.

The supplies to be provided by the United Kingdom Government under the foregoing arrangements may be varied from time to time by agreement between the Governments concerned.

10. The Governments of Canada, Australia and New Zealand agree that costs and expenses paid or incurred by the Government of Canada as administrator of the scheme (exclusive of the contribution in kind and expenses to be made and borne by the Government of the United Kingdom as provided for in Article 9) shall be apportioned between them as follows:—

(a) The Government of Canada will bear the whole costs and expenses of the Initial Training and Elementary Flying Training.

(b) The costs and expenses remaining will be shared between the Governments of Canada, Australia and New Zealand, in agreed percentages based on the numbers and categories of pupils

I ✦

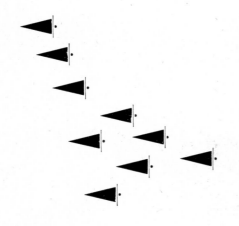

they are entitled to have trained in Canada; and it is agreed that if any substantial changes in the allocations of training places are made by mutual agreement between the Governments concerned, the percentages will be reviewed.

11. (*a*) Except for any advances made by the other Governments concerned, as provided for in clause (*b*) of this Article the Government of Canada, as administrator of the scheme, will in the first instance advance all the costs and expenses incurred as such administrator under the provisions of this Agreement, and the Governments of Australia and New Zealand will repay to the Government of Canada, as herein provided for, in Canadian dollars, their share of the amounts so advanced, in the agreed proportions.

(*b*) The Governments of the United Kingdom, Australia, and New Zealand will make advance payments necessary for pay and allowances, transportation charges, and other expenses during the journey to Canada in respect of pupils sent to Canada by such Governments for training, and for such other costs and expenses as may be agreed to from time to time; and the Governments of the United Kingdom, Australia, and New Zealand will, immediately after the end of each month, notify the Government of Canada, as administrator of the scheme, of the amounts of any advance payments made by them during such month and will, as soon as possible thereafter, send to the Government of Canada a detailed statement in respect of such advance payments.

(*c*) In connection with the repayments to be made by the Governments of Australia and New Zealand, as provided for in clause (*a*), due allowance will be made for any advance payments made and notified by the Governments of Australia and New Zealand under the provisions of clause (*b*).

(*d*) The Government of Canada, as administrator of the scheme, will refund to the Government of the United Kingdom any advance payments made by that Government under the provisions of clause (*b*), and the amount of such refunds shall be included in the costs and expenses of the scheme to be apportioned between the Governments of Canada, Australia, and New Zealand, as provided for in clause (*a*) and in Article 10.

(*e*) In this Agreement the term "costs and expenses" shall mean all expenditures, costs, charges and liabilities made or incurred by the Government of Canada, as administrator of the scheme, and without restricting the generality of the foregoing shall include:—

(i) Pay, allowances, and other expenses of the personnel lent under the provisions of Article 8 and a cash contribution (computed in accordance with recognized practice as between Governments in such cases) towards the future non-effective benefits of such personnel.

(ii) Pay, allowances, transportation charges, and other expenses connected with the training of Canadian pupils in Canada from the date of their enlistment to the dates of their embarkation in Canada under the provisions of Article 16; or, in the case of Canadian pupils taken to fill vacancies in the Home Defence Squadrons of the Royal Canadian Air Force as provided for in Article 14, to the dates of their being so taken.

(iii) Pay, allowances, transportation charges, and other expenses connected with the training of pupils in Canada from the dates of their leaving the United Kingdom, Australia, New Zealand or Newfoundland for the purpose of taking up training in Canada to the dates of their embarkation in Canada under the provisions of Article 16

But the term "costs and expenses" shall not include:—

(iv) The contribution in kind and expenses to be made and borne by the Government of the United Kingdom as provided for in Article 9.

(v) Costs and expenses of clothing and personal equipment of pupils other than such replacements as may be necessary during the period of training and other than flying clothing and equipment.

(vi) Pensions or allowances to personnel lent under the provisions of Article 8 and to pupils or their dependents in respect of disability or death.

The costs and expenses mentioned in (*b*) and (vi) above will be borne by the Governments lending the personnel and sending the pupils in respect of whom such costs, expenses, pensions or allowances are incurred.

METHOD OF PAYMENT AND ACCOUNTING

12. The Governments of Australia and New Zealand will from time to time, within one month after a summarized statement of accounts has been presented to them (showing the payments made during the

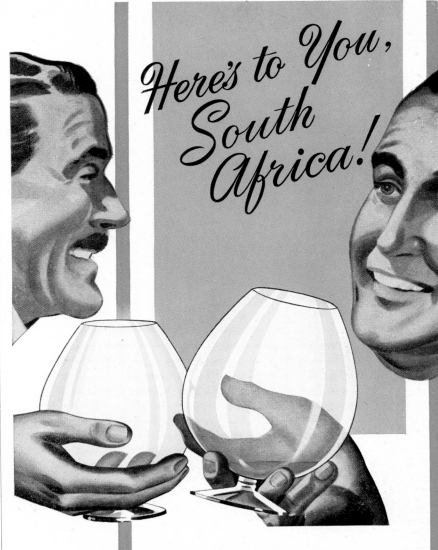

Here's to You, South Africa!

● A toast to the land of golden sunshine, of broad, fertile valleys, where world-famed vineyards produce the luscious grapes from which South African Brandy and Wines are made—vintages with the character, the flavour and the bouquet developed through nearly 300 years of wine-making tradition.

In 1654 the first grape vine was planted by the first Governor of the Cape of Good Hope. Later came the French Huguenots to perfect the art of brandy and wine making in the best tradition of their fathers . . . laying the foundation for the inimitable flavour and character of South African Brandy and Wines.

And so today — thanks to inter-Empire tariff agreements — Canadians can enjoy these superb vintages at surprisingly low prices.

BRANDY
78% proof spirit
(5 Years Old and
Pure Vintage Liqueur)

●
PAARL TAWNY
(Port)
34% proof spirit
PAARL SHERRY
(Old Oloroso or Pale Dry)
35% proof spirit
●
*Other Superb
South African Vintages
sold in Canada:*

PAARL VERMOUTHS
(Sweet or Dry)
PAARL DRY WHITE
PAARL WITZENBERG
PAARL SAUTERNES
PAARL DRY RED
(Burgundy Type)
PAARL
SPARKLING BURGUNDY
PAARL
SPARKLING WINTERHOEK
(Champagne Type)
PAARL MUSCATEL

*Groot
Constantia
(South Africa's
most famous
Wine farm)*

SOUTH AFRICAN
Wines AND *Brandies*
GUARANTEED FOR AGE AND PURITY BY THE SOUTH AFRICAN GOVERNMENT

MONTREAL —
Hub of Canada's War-Wheel

By air, water, bus or rail, a modern network of transportation facilities connects Montreal with points near and far, to the markets of the Dominion and of the world. Every route leads to the Great Metropolis of Canada. Over 50% of all commodities shipped by water into this Dominion — and out of it — are handled yearly in the Port of Montreal. East- and west-bound merchandise meets at this crossroads of inland distribution . . . via the mighty St. Lawrence River, gateway to and from the sea from which, in every direction, north, south, east, west, flow the products of a great nation at war. Thanks to this great background of industry and transportation, Montreal plays a worthy role in Canada's war-effort and is making a tremendous contribution to the industrial phase of Canada's War In The Air.

**MONTREAL
INDUSTRIAL
AND
ECONOMIC
BUREAU**

•

**VALMORE GRATTON
GEORGE S. MOONEY**
Co-Directors.

preceding month by the Government of Canada, as administrator of the scheme, and taking account of any receipts, and of any advance payments made and notified, as provided for in Article 11 (*b*), by the Governments of Australia and New Zealand, and also of any adjustments in respect of previous months) pay or cause to be paid to the Government of Canada their due proportion as agreed upon in Article 10 of the costs and expenses of the scheme as shown by such statement.

These monthly payments will be regarded as advances on account, and the costs and expenses of the scheme as at the end of each financial year will be finally adjusted and paid when the accounts for such year have been audited.

13. (*a*) The Government of Canada will, in consultation with the other Governments concerned, appoint an officer to act as its Financial Adviser in carrying out its functions as administrator of the scheme. Such proposals for expenditure as the said Financial Adviser may require shall be referred to him for approval and no expenditure on such proposals shall be incurred until his approval has been given. Any proposal disapproved by the Financial Adviser may, at the instance of the officers responsible therefor, be referred to the Minister of National Defence for final decision. Any reports made by the Financial Adviser shall be made available by the Government of Canada to all the other Governments concerned, and these latter shall be entitled to obtain from the Financial Adviser information on all matters affecting the cost of the scheme and their participation in it.

(*b*) Monthly financial statements shall be furnished by the Government of Canada to the Governments of Australia and New Zealand.

(*c*) A record of all expenditure and all sums received in connection with the training of pupils in Canada under this scheme will be maintained by the Comptroller of the Treasury of the Government of Canada, and will be audited by the Auditor General of Canada. This record will be made available after audit for examination by representatives of the Governments concerned.

(*d*) The Government of Canada shall make available to the Governments of Australia and New Zealand, as early as possible after the close of each financial year ending the 31st March, a statement, accompanied by a certificate of the Auditor General, of the receipts and payments in connection with the scheme showing the expenditure under appropriate heads.

TRAINING FOR R.C.A.F. MERGED WITH JOINT TRAINING

14. It is agreed that the Government of Canada may, out of the Canadian pupils who complete their training under this scheme, fill vacancies which occur in the Home Defence Squadrons of the Royal Canadian Air Force. All the other pupils, on completion of their training, will be placed at the disposal of the Government of the United Kingdom, subject to that Government's making the arrangements indicated in Article 15, and bearing liability as provided for in Articles 16 and 17 of this Agreement.

MAINTENANCE OF IDENTITY AND CONDITIONS OF SERVICE

15. The United Kingdom Government undertakes that pupils of Canada, Australia and New Zealand shall, after training is completed, be identified with their respective Dominions, either by the method of organizing Dominion units and formations or in some other way, such methods to be agreed upon with the respective Dominion Governments concerned. The United Kingdom Government will initiate intergovernmental discussions to this end.

16. The Government of the United Kingdom will, subject to the provisions of Article 17, provide the pay, allowances, pensions and other non-effective benefits, maintenance and other expenses of the pilots and aircraft crews who are trained in Canada (other than those made available for service with the Royal Canadian Air Force in accordance with the provisions of Article 14) with effect from the dates of their embarkation in Canada for service with, or in conjunction with, the Royal Air Force. The Government of the United Kingdom also undertakes to arrange for those pupils who are made available for service with, or in conjunction with, the Royal Air Force, to be embarked as speedily as possible after the completion of their training, and to defray the cost of their passages to the stations to which they are appointed on leaving Canada.

17. The pay, allowances, pensions and other non-effective benefits, maintenance and other expenses, for which the Government of the United Kingdom undertakes liability under the provisions of Article 16 will be as laid down in Royal Air Force regulations. If it should be decided by the Government of Canada, the Government of Australia, or the Government of New Zealand to supplement the amounts so issued, any such supplement will be borne by the Government concerned.

Note the throat microphone, developed by Bell Telephone Laboratories. It picks up vibrations from the flyer's vocal chords. Motor roar and machine-gun chatter don't get in to drown out his radio message.

Your telephone in war-time!

When there's a job to be done—and quickly—we reach for the telephone!

The six and a half million local, and 86,000 long distance telephone calls now being made in the average day, in Ontario and Quebec alone, are an index of the great part the telephone is playing in Canada's vast war job.

The scientists of the Bell Telephone Laboratories, engineers, linemen, operators—all appreciate the need for their utmost in devotion to the task of speeding the war effort.

Your co-operation is important!

Here's how you can help to protect the country's vital telephone service—

BE SURE you have the right number . . . consult the directory.

SPEAK distinctly, directly into the mouthpiece.

ANSWER promptly when the bell rings.

BE BRIEF. Clear your line for the next call.

USE OFF-PEAK hours for your Long Distance Calls.

On Active Service   THE BELL TELEPHONE COMPANY OF CANADA   LOCAL LONG DISTANCE TELEPHONE   *Giving Wings to Words*

DISTRIBUTION OF ASSETS UPON TERMINATION OF AGREEMENT

18. The Government of Canada as administrator of the scheme will have charge of the assets acquired for the purposes of the scheme. On the termination of this Agreement such of the said assets as have been acquired and paid for as part of the cost of the scheme will be disposed of as follows:—

(*a*) Any land, but not buildings, structures or fixtures thereon, acquired or improved for the purpose of the scheme will become the property of the Government of Canada.

(*b*) The assets acquired for the purposes of the Initial Training Schools and the Elementary Flying Training Schools will become the property of the Government of Canada.

(*c*) All other assets, except those contributed in kind by the Government of the United Kingdom, will be shared between the Governments of Canada, Australia and New Zealand in the same proportions as are laid down in Article 10 for the apportionment of the costs.

(*d*) Any of the assets contributed by the Government of the United Kingdom which remain will revert to that Government.

The distribution of the assets under the above arrangements may be made in kind or otherwise, as may be agreed upon.

COMMUNICATIONS BETWEEN GOVERNMENTS

19. Arrangements will be made between the Governments concerned to facilitate communications between them under this Agreement or otherwise in connection with the Scheme either by means of cable or through representatives in Canada to be named by them.

SUMMARY OF SCHOOLS REQUIRED

Programme of development of the training scheme in Canada

1. To produce the necessary output of pupils, the following schools will be necessary in Canada:—

Initial Training Schools........................	3
Elementary Flying Training Schools............	13
Service Flying Training Schools................	16
Air Observer Schools..........................	10
Bombing and Gunnery Schools.................	10
Air Navigation Schools........................	2
Wireless Schools..............................	4

2. The Flying Training and Air Observer Schools will be developed at rates which will provide for their peak capacity for training pupils being reached by the following number of weeks after the date of opening:—

Elementary Flying Training Schools.......	4 weeks
Service Flying Training Schools..........	12 "
Air Observer Schools....................	6 "

The remaining schools will open at full capacity.

3. It will be necessary to establish:—

(i) Schools for the training of the staff of the schools given in paragraph 1, and for the organization at (ii) below.

(ii) An appropriate command, recruiting and maintenance organization.

These will include:—

(iii) Air Armament School...........	1
(iv) School of Aeronautical Engineering	1
(v) School of Administration.........	1
(vi) Equipment and Accountant School	1
(vii) Flying Instructors' School........	1
(viii) Recruit Depots...................	2
(ix) Technical Training Schools......	2
(x) Repair Depots...................	3
(xi) Equipment Depots...............	3
(xii) Record Office....................	1 (or enlargement of existing organization).

The dates of formation and rate of development of these units will be governed by the dates of opening of the pilot and air training schools. (iii) to (ix) will cease to function, or will be reduced to the size necessary to meet wastage, as the scheme develops.

4. Table A shows the requirements in personnel when the scheme is in operation.

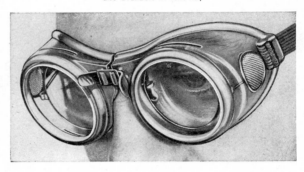
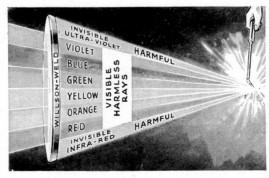

3000 Victory Torches

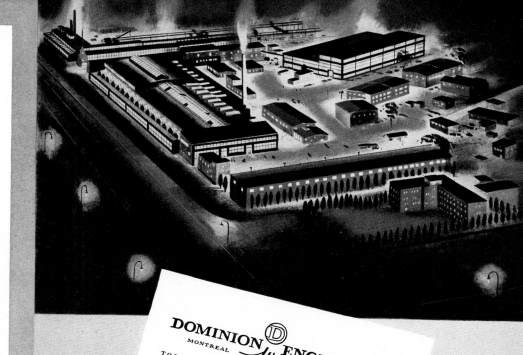

These are the lights of Dominion Engineering Works Limited, which will burn unceasingly UNTIL VICTORY.

"What is Dominion making?" is a question frequently asked by nocturnal passers-by, who sense unrelenting activity going on beneath the lights. "Shells?" "Tanks?" "Aeroplanes?"

No! Dominion is not building shells, nor tanks, nor aeroplanes but we are building the machinery and equipment which is enabling hundreds of manufacturers in all parts of the Dominion, to build, at an ever-increasing rate of production, these and other vital war supplies.

These are the "tools" produced by DOMINION'S skill and experience, towards an intensified War Effort and . . . VICTORY.

TURBINES PUMPS VALVES and other hydraulic machinery and equipment for the generation and harnessing of increased quantities of power needed for Canada's War Industries. STATIONARY DIESEL ENGINES for power generation and for stand-by purposes and MARINE DIESEL ENGINES for powering naval craft—SPEED REDUCING and INCREASING GEAR UNITS, GEAR MOTORS, GEARS, ANTI-FRICTION BEARINGS and other transmission machinery for putting this additional power to work. ROLLING MILL MACHINERY and ROLLS for the increased production of steel and other metals needed by War Industries. Special production machinery for the manufacture of war supplies, SHELL FORGING PRESSES, SHELL LATHES, SHELL CARTRIDGE CASE PRESSES STEAM ENGINES for Naval Service and Cargo Carrying. ANTI-TANK GUNS. NEWSPRINT MACHINERY to produce more foreign exchange.

DOMINION ENGINEERING Works Limited
MONTREAL
TORONTO
WINNIPEG
CANADA
VANCOUVER

GECO

DESIGNS, BUILDS and OPERATES TO AID THE WAR EFFORT

SCARBORO

This fuse filling plant for the Allied War Supply Corporation designed, constructed and operated by GECO occupies over 300 acres and was in production seven months after the starting date.

LONDON

22 Ordnance Storage buildings for the Department of Munitions and Supply were built complete and GECO was consulted on design for these structures. Project was completed in 5 months and the floor area covers 443,520 square feet of space.

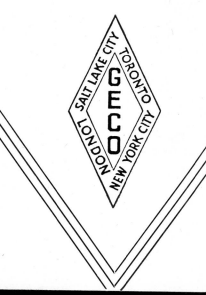

MALTON

No. 1 Elementary Flying Training School including hangars, bunk houses, kitchens, etc, were constructed completely by GECO in five months.

FINGAL

No. 4 Bombing and Gunnery training school. Constructed by GECO. Will accommodate approximately 1,500 officers and men and the buildings were erected in the short space of six months.

GENERAL ENGINEERING COMPANY (CANADA) LIMITED

WA. 8605   Cable GECORING

100 ADELAIDE ST. W. TORONTO

R. M. P. Hamilton   P. D. P. Hamilton

CONCRETE
AT WAR

Concrete runways, involving the placing of 623,000 square yards of 6″ concrete, laid at a rate as high as 13,000 square yards per 12 hour shift, are a vital feature of America's greatest northeastern air base. Starting from scratch in virgin territory hundreds of miles from anywhere, this great air base was completed and in full operation in less than a year. Write us for full information on concrete and the part it plays in air base construction.

CANADA CEMENT COMPANY LIMITED

Canada Cement Company Building, Phillips Square, Montreal

Sales Offices at : QUEBEC MONTREAL TORONTO WINNIPEG CALGARY

Lighting the path to FREEDOM

Ours has been a fairly simple task, designing and producing modern Fluorescent lighting for the plants that make the Tools and Weapons for Victory. We are grateful to have played this part in Canada's War Effort — and at this great moment in our history to salute the Boys of the R.C.A.F. and their brothers in Arms.

Superior Fixtures
1096 CLARKE STREET
MONTREAL

"Forgings for Victory"

HEAVY - FORGINGS - DROP
FROM ¼ POUND TO 40,000 POUNDS
CANADA FOUNDRIES & FORGINGS LIMITED
MONTREAL BROCKVILLE WELLAND, ONT. TORONTO WINNIPEG

TABLE 'A'

PERSONNEL REQUIREMENTS

THE PERSONNEL REQUIRED TO MAN THE SCHOOLS, ETC., IN CANADA
WHEN THE SCHEME IS IN FULL OPERATION IS AS UNDER

———	Officers	Airmen	Civilians	Works Maintenance personnel
Commands and Groups, and Extra Headquarters Organization..............	288	603	134	....
Initial Training Schools.....	39	393	....	36
Service Flying Training Schools..................	752	11,376	64	320
Air Observer Schools	250	2,470	....	100
Bombing and Gunnery Schools..................	450	6,920	....	150
Elementary Flying Training Schools..................	351	4,134	....	130
Wireless Schools............	96	1,284	....	80
Air Navigation Schools......	126	1,278	....	40
Repair Depots..............	51	141	1,308	36
Equipment Depots..........	66	228	3,318	60
Technical Training Schools .	41	627	....	30
Records Office..............	14	277	....	....
Recruit Depots..............	28	424	....	40
Recruiting Organization.....	134	211	105	....
	2,686	30,366	4,929	1,022

(*a*) Civilians may replace a proportion of the airmen in certain units.

(*b*) The above table does not include schools, etc., which close as the scheme approaches completion; the personnel from these schools will be absorbed into other units.

(*c*) Some, or all, of the Elementary Flying Training Schools and Air Observer Schools may be organized on a civilian basis.

CONDITIONS OF SERVICE OF PILOTS AND AIRCRAFT CREWS

(*a*) PUPILS FROM CANADA.

Pupils will be enlisted in the Royal Canadian Air Force as Aircraftmen, Class II (standard group).

Rank during Training in Canada.

Course	Rank
Initial ground training..	Aircraftman, Class II (standard group)
Pilot...................	Leading Aircraftman " "
Observer.............	" " " "
Wireless operator (air crew)............	Aircraftman, Class II " "
Air gunner............	" " " " " "

Rank on completion of Training.

Duty	Rank
Pilot..............	*Sergeant (group B)
Observer..........	*{ Acting Sergeant (group C) / Sergeant (group B) }
Wireless operator (air crew).....	L.A.C., A.C. I or A.C. II (group B), according to percentage of marks obtained on passing out of training.
Air gunner	L.A.C., A.C. I or A.C. II (standard group), according to percentage of marks obtained on passing out of training.

Pay and additional pay will be at the rates and subject to the conditions laid down from time to time in Financial Regulations and Instructions for the Royal Canadian Air Force on Active Service.

During service in Canada, allowances, etc., will be admissible under the conditions laid down in Financial Regulations and Instructions for the Royal Canadian Air Force on Active Service.

Pay, allowances, etc., during service with, or in conjunction with, the Royal Air Force.

On embarkation for service with, or in conjunction with, the Royal Air Force, officers and airmen will, subject to the conditions laid down in King's Regulations and Air Council Instructions, receive from the appropriate Royal Air Force paying authority the pay, allowances, etc., of the rank and branch (or group) in the Royal Air Force corresponding to that held in the Royal Canadian Air Force, except that the following special arrangements will be made in regard to the issue of allowances to dependents in Canada.

---

* A number of pilots and observers will be selected, on passing out of training, for commissioned rank in the Royal Canadian Air Force (General List). Observers will be on probation as acting observer for a period (normally six months) after passing out of training.

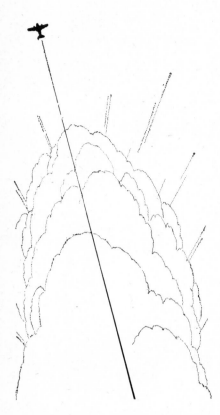

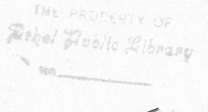
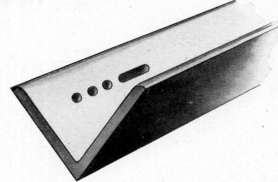

The allowances and compulsory allotment from pay in respect of family or other dependents which may be payable under Royal Air Force regulations will, if the family or other dependents reside in Canada, be credited to the Government of Canada, as administrator of the scheme, who will issue to the family or other dependents the allowance and assigned pay which may be payable under Royal Canadian Air Force regulations.

If the pay and allowances under Royal Canadian Air Force regulations should exceed those admissible under Royal Air Force regulations, the difference (after taking into account the payment made under the preceding paragraph) will be issued by the Government of Canada as deferred pay, either on termination of service or otherwise in special circumstances.

Personnel will not be insured under United Kingdom insurance schemes, and any insurance contributions (employers' and employees' shares) necessary to ensure benefits under Canadian schemes will be paid by the Government of Canada, as administrator of the scheme, who will arrange with the Government of the United Kingdom to recover from pay any employees' shares of such contributions so recoverable.

(b) PUPILS OTHER THAN THOSE ENLISTED IN THE ROYAL CANADIAN AIR FORCE, THE ROYAL AUSTRALIAN AIR FORCE AND THE ROYAL NEW ZEALAND AIR FORCE.

Pupils other than those enlisted in the Royal Canadian Air Force, the Royal Australian Air Force and the Royal New Zealand Air Force will be enlisted in the Royal Air Force.

For the period of the journey to Canada, airmen of the Royal Air Force will receive pay, allowances, etc., at the rates and subject to the conditions laid down from time to time in King's Regulations and Air Council Instructions for the Royal Air Force.

During service in Canada, airmen of the Royal Air Force will be attached to the Royal Canadian Air Force, and, subject to the conditions laid down in Financial Regulations and Instructions for the Royal Canadian Air Force on Active Service, they will receive from the appropriate Royal Canadian Air Force paying officer the pay, allowances, etc., of the rank and group in the Royal Canadian Air Force, as appropriate under (a) above, except that the following special arrangements will be made in regard to the issue of allowances to family or other dependents outside Canada.

The allowances and compulsory allotment from pay in respect of family or other dependents which would be appropriate under Royal Air Force regulations will, if the family or other dependent reside outside Canada, be issued by the Government of the United Kingdom, who will reclaim from the Government of Canada, as administrator of the scheme, the amount so issued. The Royal Canadian Air Force officer paying the airman will deduct from the airman's pay the amount of the assigned pay under Royal Canadian Air Force regulations.

Airmen will not be insured under Canadian insurance schemes and any insurance contributions (employers' and employees' shares) necessary to ensure benefits for United Kingdom airmen under United Kingdom schemes will be paid by the Government of the United Kingdom, who will arrange with the Government of Canada, as administrator of the scheme, for the recovery from pay of any employees' shares of such contributions so recoverable.

(c) PUPILS SENT BY AUSTRALIA AND NEW ZEALAND.

Pupils sent by Australia and New Zealand will be enlisted in the Royal Australian Air Force and in the Royal New Zealand Air Force, respectively.
Pay, allowances, etc., for the period of journey to Canada.

For the period of the journey to Canada, airmen of the Royal Australian Air Force and of the Royal New Zealand Air Force will receive pay, allowances, etc., at the rates and subject to the conditions laid down from time to time in the Regulations for the Royal Australian Air Force and the Royal New Zealand Air Force, respectively.
Pay, allowances, etc., during service in Canada.

During service in Canada, airmen of the Royal Australian Air Force and of the Royal New Zealand Air Force will be attached to the Royal Canadian Air Force, and, subject to the conditions laid down in Financial Regulations and Instructions for the Royal Canadian Air Force on Active Service, they will receive from the appropriate Royal Canadian Air Force paying officer the pay, allowances, etc., of the rank and group in the Royal Canadian Air Force, as appropriate under (a) above, except that the following special arrangements will be made in regard to the issue of allowances to family or other dependents outside Canada.

The allowances and compulsory allotment from pay in respect of family or other dependents which would be appropriate under Royal Australian Air Force or Royal New Zealand Air Force regulations will, if the family or other dependents reside outside Canada, be issued by the Government of Australia or the Government of New Zealand, who will reclaim from the Government of Canada, as administrator of the scheme, the amount so issued. The Royal Canadian Air Force officer paying the airman will deduct from the airman's pay the amount of the assigned pay chargeable under Royal Canadian Air Force regulations.

Airmen will not be insured under Canadian insurance schemes, and any insurance contributions (employers' and employees' shares) necessary to ensure benefits for Australian or New Zealand airmen from Australian or New Zealand schemes will be paid by the Government of Australia or the Government of New Zealand, who will arrange with the Government of Canada, as administrator of the scheme, for the recovery from pay of any employees' shares of such contributions so recoverable.
Pay, allowances, etc., during service with the Royal Air Force.

On embarkation for service with the Royal Air Force, officers and airmen will be attached to that force, and, subject to the conditions laid down in King's Regulations and Air Council Instructions, they will receive from the appropriate Royal Air Force paying authority the pay, allowances, etc., of the rank and branch (or group) in the Royal Air Force corresponding to that held in the Royal Australian Air Force or in the Royal New Zealand Air Force, except that the following special arrangements will be made in regard to the issue of allowances to family or other dependents in Australia or New Zealand.

The allowances and compulsory allotment from pay in respect of family or other dependents which may be payable under Royal Air Force regulations will, if the family or other dependents reside in Australia or New Zealand, be credited to the Government of Australia or to the Government of New Zealand, who will issue to the family or other dependent the allowance and compulsory allotment from pay which may be payable under Royal Australian Air Force or Royal New Zealand Air Force regulations.

If the pay and allowances admissible under Royal Australian Air Force or Royal New Zealand Air Force regulations exceed those admissible under Royal Air Force regulations, and the Government of Australia or the Government of New Zealand decide that this difference is to be credited to the officer or airman, the difference (after taking into account the payment made under the preceding paragraph) will be issued by the Government of Australia or the Government of New Zealand as deferred pay, either on termination of service or otherwise in special circumstances.

Personnel will not be insured under United Kingdon insurance schemes, and any insurance contributions (employers' and employees' shares) necessary to ensure benefits under Australian or New Zealand schemes will be paid by the Government of Australia or the Government of New Zealand, who will arrange with the Government of the United Kingdom to recover from pay any employees' shares of such contributions so recoverable.

END OF ADDENDA

TYPE SET BY FRED. F. ESLER LIMITED
MONTREAL

❧

OFFSET BY WOODWARD PRESS INC.
MONTREAL

❧

PRINTING BY PRINTING SERVICE LIMITED
MONTREAL

PRINTED AT MONTREAL, CANADA